T0281044

# Lecture Notes in Computer Science 14707

Founding Editors

Gerhard Goos

Juris Hartmanis

The series Lecture Notes in Computer Science (LNCS), including its subseries Lecture Notes in Artificial Intelligence (LNAI) and Lecture Notes in Bioinformatics (LNBI), has established itself as a medium for the publication of new developments in computer science and information technology research, teaching, and education.

LNCS enjoys close cooperation with the computer science R & D community, the series counts many renowned academics among its volume editors and paper authors, and collaborates with prestigious societies. Its mission is to serve this international community by providing an invaluable service, mainly focused on the publication of conference and workshop proceedings and postproceedings. LNCS commenced publication in 1973.

Jessie Y. C. Chen · Gino Fragomeni
Editors

# Virtual, Augmented and Mixed Reality

16th International Conference, VAMR 2024
Held as Part of the 26th HCI International Conference, HCII 2024
Washington, DC, USA, June 29 – July 4, 2024
Proceedings, Part II

Springer

*Editors*
Jessie Y. C. Chen
U.S. Army Research Laboratory
Adelphi, MD, USA

Gino Fragomeni
U.S. Army Combat Capabilities
Development Command Soldier Center
Orlando, FL, USA

ISSN 0302-9743         ISSN 1611-3349 (electronic)
Lecture Notes in Computer Science
ISBN 978-3-031-61043-1         ISBN 978-3-031-61044-8 (eBook)
https://doi.org/10.1007/978-3-031-61044-8

This Springer imprint is published by the registered company Springer Nature Switzerland AG
The registered company address is: Gewerbestrasse 11, 6330 Cham, Switzerland

If disposing of this product, please recycle the paper.

# Foreword

This year we celebrate 40 years since the establishment of the HCI International (HCII) Conference, which has been a hub for presenting groundbreaking research and novel ideas and collaboration for people from all over the world.

The HCII conference was founded in 1984 by Prof. Gavriel Salvendy (Purdue University, USA, Tsinghua University, P.R. China, and University of Central Florida, USA) and the first event of the series, "1st USA-Japan Conference on Human-Computer Interaction", was held in Honolulu, Hawaii, USA, 18–20 August. Since then, HCI International is held jointly with several Thematic Areas and Affiliated Conferences, with each one under the auspices of a distinguished international Program Board and under one management and one registration. Twenty-six HCI International Conferences have been organized so far (every two years until 2013, and annually thereafter).

Over the years, this conference has served as a platform for scholars, researchers, industry experts and students to exchange ideas, connect, and address challenges in the ever-evolving HCI field. Throughout these 40 years, the conference has evolved itself, adapting to new technologies and emerging trends, while staying committed to its core mission of advancing knowledge and driving change.

As we celebrate this milestone anniversary, we reflect on the contributions of its founding members and appreciate the commitment of its current and past Affiliated Conference Program Board Chairs and members. We are also thankful to all past conference attendees who have shaped this community into what it is today.

The 26th International Conference on Human-Computer Interaction, HCI International 2024 (HCII 2024), was held as a 'hybrid' event at the Washington Hilton Hotel, Washington, DC, USA, during 29 June – 4 July 2024. It incorporated the 21 thematic areas and affiliated conferences listed below.

A total of 5108 individuals from academia, research institutes, industry, and government agencies from 85 countries submitted contributions, and 1271 papers and 309 posters were included in the volumes of the proceedings that were published just before the start of the conference, these are listed below. The contributions thoroughly cover the entire field of human-computer interaction, addressing major advances in knowledge and effective use of computers in a variety of application areas. These papers provide academics, researchers, engineers, scientists, practitioners and students with state-of-the-art information on the most recent advances in HCI.

The HCI International (HCII) conference also offers the option of presenting 'Late Breaking Work', and this applies both for papers and posters, with corresponding volumes of proceedings that will be published after the conference. Full papers will be included in the 'HCII 2024 - Late Breaking Papers' volumes of the proceedings to be published in the Springer LNCS series, while 'Poster Extended Abstracts' will be included as short research papers in the 'HCII 2024 - Late Breaking Posters' volumes to be published in the Springer CCIS series.

I would like to thank the Program Board Chairs and the members of the Program Boards of all thematic areas and affiliated conferences for their contribution towards the high scientific quality and overall success of the HCI International 2024 conference. Their manifold support in terms of paper reviewing (single-blind review process, with a minimum of two reviews per submission), session organization and their willingness to act as goodwill ambassadors for the conference is most highly appreciated.

This conference would not have been possible without the continuous and unwavering support and advice of Gavriel Salvendy, founder, General Chair Emeritus, and Scientific Advisor. For his outstanding efforts, I would like to express my sincere appreciation to Abbas Moallem, Communications Chair and Editor of HCI International News.

July 2024                                                Constantine Stephanidis

# HCI International 2024 Thematic Areas and Affiliated Conferences

- HCI: Human-Computer Interaction Thematic Area
- HIMI: Human Interface and the Management of Information Thematic Area
- EPCE: 21st International Conference on Engineering Psychology and Cognitive Ergonomics
- AC: 18th International Conference on Augmented Cognition
- UAHCI: 18th International Conference on Universal Access in Human-Computer Interaction
- CCD: 16th International Conference on Cross-Cultural Design
- SCSM: 16th International Conference on Social Computing and Social Media
- VAMR: 16th International Conference on Virtual, Augmented and Mixed Reality
- DHM: 15th International Conference on Digital Human Modeling & Applications in Health, Safety, Ergonomics & Risk Management
- DUXU: 13th International Conference on Design, User Experience and Usability
- C&C: 12th International Conference on Culture and Computing
- DAPI: 12th International Conference on Distributed, Ambient and Pervasive Interactions
- HCIBGO: 11th International Conference on HCI in Business, Government and Organizations
- LCT: 11th International Conference on Learning and Collaboration Technologies
- ITAP: 10th International Conference on Human Aspects of IT for the Aged Population
- AIS: 6th International Conference on Adaptive Instructional Systems
- HCI-CPT: 6th International Conference on HCI for Cybersecurity, Privacy and Trust
- HCI-Games: 6th International Conference on HCI in Games
- MobiTAS: 6th International Conference on HCI in Mobility, Transport and Automotive Systems
- AI-HCI: 5th International Conference on Artificial Intelligence in HCI
- MOBILE: 5th International Conference on Human-Centered Design, Operation and Evaluation of Mobile Communications

# List of Conference Proceedings Volumes Appearing Before the Conference

1. LNCS 14684, Human-Computer Interaction: Part I, edited by Masaaki Kurosu and Ayako Hashizume
2. LNCS 14685, Human-Computer Interaction: Part II, edited by Masaaki Kurosu and Ayako Hashizume
3. LNCS 14686, Human-Computer Interaction: Part III, edited by Masaaki Kurosu and Ayako Hashizume
4. LNCS 14687, Human-Computer Interaction: Part IV, edited by Masaaki Kurosu and Ayako Hashizume
5. LNCS 14688, Human-Computer Interaction: Part V, edited by Masaaki Kurosu and Ayako Hashizume
6. LNCS 14689, Human Interface and the Management of Information: Part I, edited by Hirohiko Mori and Yumi Asahi
7. LNCS 14690, Human Interface and the Management of Information: Part II, edited by Hirohiko Mori and Yumi Asahi
8. LNCS 14691, Human Interface and the Management of Information: Part III, edited by Hirohiko Mori and Yumi Asahi
9. LNAI 14692, Engineering Psychology and Cognitive Ergonomics: Part I, edited by Don Harris and Wen-Chin Li
10. LNAI 14693, Engineering Psychology and Cognitive Ergonomics: Part II, edited by Don Harris and Wen-Chin Li
11. LNAI 14694, Augmented Cognition, Part I, edited by Dylan D. Schmorrow and Cali M. Fidopiastis
12. LNAI 14695, Augmented Cognition, Part II, edited by Dylan D. Schmorrow and Cali M. Fidopiastis
13. LNCS 14696, Universal Access in Human-Computer Interaction: Part I, edited by Margherita Antona and Constantine Stephanidis
14. LNCS 14697, Universal Access in Human-Computer Interaction: Part II, edited by Margherita Antona and Constantine Stephanidis
15. LNCS 14698, Universal Access in Human-Computer Interaction: Part III, edited by Margherita Antona and Constantine Stephanidis
16. LNCS 14699, Cross-Cultural Design: Part I, edited by Pei-Luen Patrick Rau
17. LNCS 14700, Cross-Cultural Design: Part II, edited by Pei-Luen Patrick Rau
18. LNCS 14701, Cross-Cultural Design: Part III, edited by Pei-Luen Patrick Rau
19. LNCS 14702, Cross-Cultural Design: Part IV, edited by Pei-Luen Patrick Rau
20. LNCS 14703, Social Computing and Social Media: Part I, edited by Adela Coman and Simona Vasilache
21. LNCS 14704, Social Computing and Social Media: Part II, edited by Adela Coman and Simona Vasilache
22. LNCS 14705, Social Computing and Social Media: Part III, edited by Adela Coman and Simona Vasilache

23. LNCS 14706, Virtual, Augmented and Mixed Reality: Part I, edited by Jessie Y. C. Chen and Gino Fragomeni
24. LNCS 14707, Virtual, Augmented and Mixed Reality: Part II, edited by Jessie Y. C. Chen and Gino Fragomeni
25. LNCS 14708, Virtual, Augmented and Mixed Reality: Part III, edited by Jessie Y. C. Chen and Gino Fragomeni
26. LNCS 14709, Digital Human Modeling and Applications in Health, Safety, Ergonomics and Risk Management: Part I, edited by Vincent G. Duffy
27. LNCS 14710, Digital Human Modeling and Applications in Health, Safety, Ergonomics and Risk Management: Part II, edited by Vincent G. Duffy
28. LNCS 14711, Digital Human Modeling and Applications in Health, Safety, Ergonomics and Risk Management: Part III, edited by Vincent G. Duffy
29. LNCS 14712, Design, User Experience, and Usability: Part I, edited by Aaron Marcus, Elizabeth Rosenzweig and Marcelo M. Soares
30. LNCS 14713, Design, User Experience, and Usability: Part II, edited by Aaron Marcus, Elizabeth Rosenzweig and Marcelo M. Soares
31. LNCS 14714, Design, User Experience, and Usability: Part III, edited by Aaron Marcus, Elizabeth Rosenzweig and Marcelo M. Soares
32. LNCS 14715, Design, User Experience, and Usability: Part IV, edited by Aaron Marcus, Elizabeth Rosenzweig and Marcelo M. Soares
33. LNCS 14716, Design, User Experience, and Usability: Part V, edited by Aaron Marcus, Elizabeth Rosenzweig and Marcelo M. Soares
34. LNCS 14717, Culture and Computing, edited by Matthias Rauterberg
35. LNCS 14718, Distributed, Ambient and Pervasive Interactions: Part I, edited by Norbert A. Streitz and Shin'ichi Konomi
36. LNCS 14719, Distributed, Ambient and Pervasive Interactions: Part II, edited by Norbert A. Streitz and Shin'ichi Konomi
37. LNCS 14720, HCI in Business, Government and Organizations: Part I, edited by Fiona Fui-Hoon Nah and Keng Leng Siau
38. LNCS 14721, HCI in Business, Government and Organizations: Part II, edited by Fiona Fui-Hoon Nah and Keng Leng Siau
39. LNCS 14722, Learning and Collaboration Technologies: Part I, edited by Panayiotis Zaphiris and Andri Ioannou
40. LNCS 14723, Learning and Collaboration Technologies: Part II, edited by Panayiotis Zaphiris and Andri Ioannou
41. LNCS 14724, Learning and Collaboration Technologies: Part III, edited by Panayiotis Zaphiris and Andri Ioannou
42. LNCS 14725, Human Aspects of IT for the Aged Population: Part I, edited by Qin Gao and Jia Zhou
43. LNCS 14726, Human Aspects of IT for the Aged Population: Part II, edited by Qin Gao and Jia Zhou
44. LNCS 14727, Adaptive Instructional System, edited by Robert A. Sottilare and Jessica Schwarz
45. LNCS 14728, HCI for Cybersecurity, Privacy and Trust: Part I, edited by Abbas Moallem
46. LNCS 14729, HCI for Cybersecurity, Privacy and Trust: Part II, edited by Abbas Moallem

47. LNCS 14730, HCI in Games: Part I, edited by Xiaowen Fang
48. LNCS 14731, HCI in Games: Part II, edited by Xiaowen Fang
49. LNCS 14732, HCI in Mobility, Transport and Automotive Systems: Part I, edited by Heidi Krömker
50. LNCS 14733, HCI in Mobility, Transport and Automotive Systems: Part II, edited by Heidi Krömker
51. LNAI 14734, Artificial Intelligence in HCI: Part I, edited by Helmut Degen and Stavroula Ntoa
52. LNAI 14735, Artificial Intelligence in HCI: Part II, edited by Helmut Degen and Stavroula Ntoa
53. LNAI 14736, Artificial Intelligence in HCI: Part III, edited by Helmut Degen and Stavroula Ntoa
54. LNCS 14737, Design, Operation and Evaluation of Mobile Communications: Part I, edited by June Wei and George Margetis
55. LNCS 14738, Design, Operation and Evaluation of Mobile Communications: Part II, edited by June Wei and George Margetis
56. CCIS 2114, HCI International 2024 Posters - Part I, edited by Constantine Stephanidis, Margherita Antona, Stavroula Ntoa and Gavriel Salvendy
57. CCIS 2115, HCI International 2024 Posters - Part II, edited by Constantine Stephanidis, Margherita Antona, Stavroula Ntoa and Gavriel Salvendy
58. CCIS 2116, HCI International 2024 Posters - Part III, edited by Constantine Stephanidis, Margherita Antona, Stavroula Ntoa and Gavriel Salvendy
59. CCIS 2117, HCI International 2024 Posters - Part IV, edited by Constantine Stephanidis, Margherita Antona, Stavroula Ntoa and Gavriel Salvendy
60. CCIS 2118, HCI International 2024 Posters - Part V, edited by Constantine Stephanidis, Margherita Antona, Stavroula Ntoa and Gavriel Salvendy
61. CCIS 2119, HCI International 2024 Posters - Part VI, edited by Constantine Stephanidis, Margherita Antona, Stavroula Ntoa and Gavriel Salvendy
62. CCIS 2120, HCI International 2024 Posters - Part VII, edited by Constantine Stephanidis, Margherita Antona, Stavroula Ntoa and Gavriel Salvendy

**https://2024.hci.international/proceedings**

# Preface

With the recent emergence of a new generation of displays, smart devices, and wearables, the field of virtual, augmented, and mixed reality (VAMR) is rapidly expanding, transforming, and moving towards the mainstream market. At the same time, VAMR applications in a variety of domains are also reaching maturity and practical usage. From the point of view of the user experience, VAMR promises possibilities to reduce interaction efforts and cognitive load, while also offering contextualized information, by combining different sources and reducing attention shifts, and opening the 3D space. Such scenarios offer exciting challenges associated with underlying and supporting technologies, interaction, and navigation in virtual and augmented environments, and design and development. VAMR themes encompass a wide range of areas such as education, aviation, social, emotional, psychological, and persuasive applications.

The 16th International Conference on Virtual, Augmented, and Mixed Reality (VAMR 2024), an affiliated conference of the HCI International Conference, provided a forum for researchers and practitioners to disseminate and exchange scientific and technical information on VAMR-related topics in various applications. A considerable number of papers have explored user experience topics including avatar design, walking and moving in VR environments, scene design and complexity, 360o immersive environments and the design of 3D elements, cybersickness, and multisensory feedback. Moreover, submissions offered a comprehensive examination of perception aspects, including our understanding of body image, self-presentation, visual realism, and awareness. A key topic that emerged was interaction in immersive environments such as haptic interaction, tangible VR, and gestures. Furthermore, emphasis was given to the application domains of VAMR including collaboration, cultural heritage, education and learning, health and well-being, but also software programming, crime data analysis, terrain exploration, and astronomical visualization. We are thrilled to present this compilation of VAMR submissions encompassing a wide range of topics and exploring the current state of the art, while also highlighting future avenues in the design and development of immersive experiences.

Three volumes of the HCII 2024 proceedings are dedicated to this year's edition of the VAMR conference. The first focuses on topics related to Perception, Interaction and Design, and User Experience and Evaluation. The second focuses on topics related to Immersive Collaboration and Environment Design, and Sensory, Tangible, and Embodied Interaction in VAMR, while the third focuses on topics related to Immersive Education and Learning, and VAMR Applications and Development.

The papers in these volumes were accepted for publication after a minimum of two single-blind reviews from the members of the VAMR Program Board or, in some cases, from members of the Program Boards of other affiliated conferences. We would like to thank all of them for their invaluable contribution, support, and efforts.

July 2024

Jessie Y. C. Chen
Gino Fragomeni

# 16th International Conference on Virtual, Augmented and Mixed Reality (VAMR 2024)

Program Board Chairs: **Jessie Y. C. Chen,** *U.S. Army Research Laboratory, USA,* and **Gino Fragomeni,** *U.S. Army Combat Capabilities Development Command Soldier Center, USA*

- J. Cecil, *Oklahoma State University, USA*
- Shih-Yi Chien, *National Chengchi University, Taiwan*
- Avinash Gupta, *University of Illinois Urbana-Champaign, USA*
- Sue Kase, *U.S. Army Research Laboratory, USA*
- Daniela Kratchounova, *Federal Aviation Administration (FAA), USA*
- Fotis Liarokapis, *CYENS - Centre of Excellence, Cyprus*
- Jaehyun Park, *Incheon National University (INU), Korea*
- Chao Peng, *Rochester Institute of Technology, USA*
- Jose San Martin, *Universidad Rey Juan Carlos, Spain*
- Andreas Schreiber, *German Aerospace Center (DLR), Germany*
- Sharad Sharma, *University of North Texas, USA*
- Simon Su, *National Institute of Standards and Technology (NIST), USA*
- Denny Yu, *Purdue University, USA*

The full list with the Program Board Chairs and the members of the Program Boards of all thematic areas and affiliated conferences of HCII 2024 is available online at:

**http://www.hci.international/board-members-2024.php**

# HCI International 2025 Conference

The 27th International Conference on Human-Computer Interaction, HCI International 2025, will be held jointly with the affiliated conferences at the Swedish Exhibition & Congress Centre and Gothia Towers Hotel, Gothenburg, Sweden, June 22–27, 2025. It will cover a broad spectrum of themes related to Human-Computer Interaction, including theoretical issues, methods, tools, processes, and case studies in HCI design, as well as novel interaction techniques, interfaces, and applications. The proceedings will be published by Springer. More information will become available on the conference website: https://2025.hci.international/.

General Chair
Prof. Constantine Stephanidis
University of Crete and ICS-FORTH
Heraklion, Crete, Greece
Email: general_chair@2025.hci.international

**https://2025.hci.international/**

# Contents – Part II

**Immersive Collaboration and Environment Design**

Navigating Real-To-Virtual Onboarding: A Holistic Exploration
and Framework for Immersive Transitions ............................ 3
  *Priyanka Bharti, Sanika Bhide, and Chirag Savaliya*

Research on the Benefits of Biophilia Effects in Virtual Environments ......... 16
  *HsinChiao Chan and Yinghsiu Huang*

LimberUI: A Model-Based Design Tool for 3D UI Layouts
Accommodating Uncertainty in Context of Use and User Attributes ........... 29
  *Jamie W. Lee and Kwang Lee*

XR Smart Environments Design and Fruition: Personalizing Shared Spaces .... 41
  *Meng Li, Flora Gaetani, Lorenzo Ceccon, Federica Caruso,*
  *Yu Zhang, Armagan Albayrak, and Daan van Eijk*

Exploring VR Wizardry: A Generic Control Tool for Wizard of Oz
Experiments ......................................................... 60
  *Tabea Runzheimer, Stefan Friesen, Sven Milde,*
  *Johannes-Hubert Peiffer, and Jan-Torsten Milde*

The Impact of Different Levels of Spatial Cues on Size Perception:
A Spatial Perception Study of Altered Conditions ........................ 74
  *Faezeh Salehi, Fatemeh Pariafsai, and Manish K. Dixit*

Modeling and Simulation Technologies for Effective Multi-agent Research .... 86
  *Kristin E. Schaefer, Ralph W. Brewer, Joshua Wickwire,*
  *Rosario Scalise, and Chad C. Kessens*

Optimizing XR User Experiences Through Network-Based Asset Bundles ..... 105
  *Maurizio Vergari, Tanja Kojić, Maximilian Warsinke,*
  *Sebastian Möller, Jan-Niklas Voigt-Antons, Osama Abboud,*
  *and Xun Xiao*

Enhancing Remote Collaboration Through Drone-Driven Agent
and Mixed Reality ..................................................... 116
  *Shihui Xu, Like Wu, Wenjie Liao, and Shigeru Fujimura*

Identifying Influencing Factors of Immersion in Remote Collaboration ........ 128
    *Yifan Yang, Xu Sun, Jie Gao, Ziqi Zhou, Sheng Zhang,*
    *and Canjun Yang*


**Sensory, Tangible and Embodied Interaction in VAMR**

Study of Perception and Cognition in Immersive Digital Twins for Robotic
Assembly Processes ................................................... 147
    *J. Cecil, Vasavi Gannina, and Sriram Kumar Tentu*

A Literature Review and Proposal Towards the Further Integration
of Haptics in Aviation ................................................ 159
    *R. D. de Lange*

Investigation of the Impression Given by the Appearance and Gestures
of a Virtual Reality Agent Describing a Display Product ................... 179
    *Michiko Inoue, Shouta Hioki, Fuyuko Iwasaki, Shunsuke Yoneda,*
    *and Masashi Nishiyama*

Assessing the Influence of Passive Haptics on User Perception of Physical
Properties in Virtual Reality .......................................... 191
    *Logan Kemper, Juan Lam, Matthew Levine, Aiden White Pifer,*
    *Seung Hyuk Jang, Markus Santoso, and Angelos Barmpoutis*

Collecting and Analyzing the Mid-Air Gestures Data in Augmented
Reality and User Preferences in Closed Elicitation Study ................... 201
    *Jieqiong Li, Adam S. Coler, Zahra Borhani, and Francisco R. Ortega*

Research on the Multisensory Feedback Representation of the Menu
Cards in VR Home Interface .......................................... 216
    *Shangge Li, Jing Zhang, Xingcheng Di, and Chengqi Xue*

Augmented Reality Compensatory Aid for Improved Weapon Splash-Zone
Awareness .......................................................... 230
    *Domenick M. Mifsud, Chris D. Wickens, Richard Rodriguez,*
    *Francisco R. Ortega, and Mike Maulbeck*

Augmented Virtuality–A Simplified, Scalable, and Modular Open-Source
Unity Development System for Tangible VR with the Meta Quest 2 ........... 241
    *Bjarke Kristian Maigaard Kjær Pedersen, Patricia Bianca Lyk,*
    *and Daniel Alexander Auerbach*

An Analysis of the Sense of Presence and Cybersickness in Virtual
Reality: The Influence of Content Type, Exposure Time, and Gender . . . . . . . . . .  263
  *Pedro Reisinho, Cátia Silva, Maria Ferreira, Rui Raposo,*
  *Mário Vairinhos, and Nelson Zagalo*

Proof-of-Concept MARG-Based Glove for Intuitive 3D Human-Computer
Interaction . . . . . . . . . . . . . . . . . . . . . . . . . . . . . . . . . . . . . . . . . . . . . . . . . . . . . .  283
  *Pontakorn Sonchan, Neeranut Ratchatanantakit,*
  *Nonnarit O-larnnithipong, Malek Adjouadi, and Armando Barreto*

An Effective Design on Locomotion and View Management
for an Immersive Analytics Platform in Everyday Use  . . . . . . . . . . . . . . . . . . . . .  298
  *Bo Sun and Benjamin Daniel Weidner*

**Author Index** . . . . . . . . . . . . . . . . . . . . . . . . . . . . . . . . . . . . . . . . . . . . . . . . . . . . . .  313

# Immersive Collaboration
# and Environment Design

# Navigating Real-To-Virtual Onboarding: A Holistic Exploration and Framework for Immersive Transitions

Priyanka Bharti[1]([✉]) [iD], Sanika Bhide[2], and Chirag Savaliya[3]

[1] Siemens Technology and Services Pvt. Ltd., Bangalore, India
pbharti.design@gmail.com
[2] Indian Institute of Science, Bangalore, India
[3] School of Planning and Architecture, Bhopal, India

**Abstract.** This research manuscript is dedicated to exploring the critical process of onboarding individuals from the tangible, real-world environment into the immersive realm of the virtual environment. It seeks to investigate the multifaceted nature of onboarding for a diverse group of users, with their experiences being differentiated based on their prior familiarity with the virtual environment and the tool employed for this study—the Virtual Reality (VR) device. This device serves as a transformative bridge, facilitating users' transition from the physical world to the virtual one. Within this overarching context, the study categorizes users into three distinct types: novices, intermediates, and experts. Each of these user types exhibits unique requirements and demands varying levels of guidance and support during the onboarding process.

At the core of this research lies a comprehensive exploration of users' journeys, encompassing both micro- and macro-level interactions within the virtual environment. These interactions are accompanied by related comprehensions, predictions, and assumptions as users navigate the intricate path from the real to the virtual world. The entirety of this journey is meticulously depicted in a descriptive manner, elucidating and accentuating the pain points encountered along the way. This journey also involves decoding key factors, including users' cognitive abilities, the dynamics of the learning curve they traverse, the relevance and significance of the information presented to them, and the triggers that facilitate comprehension. Moreover, it delves into the pivotal aspect of the interaction between the real world and virtual surroundings, a dynamic factor that significantly influences users' overall experiences. This interaction encompasses the seamless fusion of physical and digital elements, enabling users to navigate and interact within the virtual environment effortlessly. By comprehending the cognitive abilities of users and the nuances of their learning curves, we can gain valuable insights into what is still required to optimize the onboarding experience effectively. Identifying pertinent information while filtering out irrelevant details aids in streamlining the comprehension process, ensuring that users are not overwhelmed with extraneous information. These factors collectively contribute to crafting a more immersive and gratifying user experience that transcends the boundaries of both the real and virtual worlds.

To gather data for this research, a methodical approach based on the completion of a task is employed. This approach generates qualitative data, which is

J. Y. C. Chen and G. Fragomeni (Eds.): HCII 2024, LNCS 14707, pp. 3–15, 2024.
https://doi.org/10.1007/978-3-031-61044-8_1

further complemented by a structured questionnaire designed to elicit quantitative responses. The synergistic fusion of qualitative and quantitative data serves to provide a comprehensive and holistic understanding of the subject matter, enabling the acquisition of deeper insights into the intricacies of the onboarding process. The goal of this research project is to produce a complete framework that carefully encompasses the nuances inherent in the process of onboarding into virtual settings. This framework was carefully designed to improve the onboarding process and is distinguished by the combination of quantitative and qualitative data that it incorporates. This approach broadens its scope to include the complex interplay of social and emotional components, going beyond only addressing the technical aspects of onboarding, such as software training and system navigation. This comprises the growth of bonds and the nurturing of a strong sense of belonging, enhancing the user's trip through the digital environment.

**Keywords:** Virtual Reality · Onboarding · Framework · User experience · User journey First Section

## 1 Introduction

Onboarding is a process that has many phases to complete a step-in order to move from one context to another. In the case of the onboarding process with respect to device (moving from the real world to the virtual world), the transition of a user's feeling of the real tangible context to the virtual context, where the scenario is human-created and things can be felt or touched with the use of controllers or joysticks (depending on the device to device), is a crucial aspect. This transition requires the user to adapt to and familiarise themselves with the new interface and controls provided by the device. The onboarding process aims to make this transition seamless by providing clear instructions, tutorials, and interactive experiences that gradually introduce the user to the virtual world (Ashtari et al., 2020). It is important for the user to feel comfortable and confident in navigating and interacting within this new environment, ensuring a smooth and enjoyable transition from the real world to the virtual realm (Anthes, 2016; Kim et al., 2019). VR usage will definitely increase in the coming time, as most of the applications will be based on this, but mostly it is talked about the user experience (UX) within the VR device. Prior to assessing the UX in VR, it is much more crucial and evident to establish the foundation level for the user's, i.e., onboarding, so that it gets well established that it is as easy to access as we access things in the real world. One of the main agendas is to make users realise that the virtual world is not only for the tech-friendly or tech-navigation-friendly zone (Andersen et al., 2012; Ashtari et al., 2020; Rebelo & Noriega, 2012; Thoravi, 2019).

Nevertheless, UX takes into account reactions, including physiological ones, that take place during the interaction in addition to the user's responses, such as subjective assessments and action tendencies. Furthermore, it refers to their feelings and small gestures, which convey additional information in addition to their spoken replies. We attempted to capture and evaluate those microaspects in the process of building the framework, taking into account the influence of the user's expectations, beliefs, preferences, perceptions, feelings, emotions, and accomplishments on these responses and reactions. This will enable a remarkable study that will lay the groundwork for onboarding experience studies for researchers and practitioners (Thoravi, 2019; Whittaker, 2023).

## 2   Methodology

This study adopted a mixed-methods research design, commencing with user-task-based assessments. After that, the participants filled out a semi-structured questionnaire that had both (more) quantitative and (less) qualitative parts, as well as interview sessions to gather deeper insights into their experiences and perceptions.

The user-task-based assessments facilitated a methodical evaluation of participants' performance and interaction with the onboard process and the device. The semi-structured questionnaire yielded valuable insights regarding participants' preferences, satisfaction, and overall user experience. In addition, the interview sessions facilitated a more thorough examination of participants' thoughts, motivations, and recommendations for enhancement. This methodological approach allowed for a comprehensive understanding of user perspectives and behaviours, resulting in a thorough and detailed investigation of the research questions.

### 2.1   Participants

Regarding user categorization, we have classified users (Fig. 1) into three clearly defined levels of expertise, taking into account their level of skill, familiarity with the VR device, and knowledge in related fields. Here are the three levels of expertise we have classified users into, based on their skill level, familiarity with the VR device, and knowledge in related fields:

- Novice Users: Individuals who are inexperienced in using virtual reality (VR) devices. Novice users generally have a limited understanding of the tool and the domain. Providing assistance and direction is essential to ensuring their performance and the successful completion of a given task.
- Moderate Users: These individuals possess a fundamental level of experience and proficiency in a particular field, surpassing the initial stage of being a novice but not yet attaining the status of an expert. Users who are moderate exhibit a satisfactory level of familiarity with the device. They have a reasonable level of autonomy in completing tasks, but they may face difficulties that experts would handle more effortlessly.
- Expert Users: These users possess advanced proficiency, expertise, and a thorough comprehension of both the VR device and the specific domain. They demonstrate profound expertise, extensive practical know-how, and a sophisticated comprehension of the complexities within the field. They possess the ability to navigate intricate situations, effectively solve problems, and frequently make valuable contributions to the progress of the field due to their extensive knowledge and skills.
- Expert users who have extensive knowledge of a particular metaverse context with respect to the device have to go through a learning process and adjust their interactions when they encounter a newer metaverse context or device. It is essential to include these users in the study, as they possess preconceived notions and habits that influence

their behaviour in the virtual world, unlike other participants. Additionally, individuals who are experienced with VR devices desire a sense of assurance and are looking for adaptability and self-reliance during the initial training process. Understanding the differences among these users and how they impact the design requirements for onboarding is essential for the study.

**Fig. 1.** Users performing the assigned task with VR device

## 2.2 Task

During the task-based assessment, participants engaged in onboarding procedures for both Steam VR and Google Earth, employing a virtual reality (VR) device to achieve an immersive experience. Importantly, participants were not given any instructions before starting the assigned task. This meant that they had to use the controls on the VR device to explore and become familiar with the interfaces on their own. The onboarding assessments in Steam VR offer valuable insights into users' navigation throughout this multifaceted ecosystem and their interaction with different applications. In contrast, Google Earth in virtual reality provides a unique spatial exploration experience, where users are tasked with navigating a virtual depiction of the Earth. The evaluation of onboarding using Google Earth extends beyond assessing users' proficiency with virtual reality controls; it also examines their capacity to interact with geospatial data in a virtual environment. The primary objective was to assess users' natural understanding of VR features, with a particular emphasis on evaluating the effectiveness of onboarding procedures and the ease of use of VR controls in promoting user engagement on both the Steam VR and Google Earth platforms.

## 2.3 Questionnaires and Interview

The study utilised a comprehensive research methodology that integrated qualitative and quantitative data collection techniques. The collection of data was primarily conducted through the administration of a structured questionnaire to the participants. The survey, designed to elicit comprehensive responses, facilitated the gathering of qualitative data by capturing the participants' nuanced perspectives and experiences. A comprehensive interview was also undertaken with every participant in conjunction with the questionnaire to delve deeper into their perspectives and experiences. The interviews afforded the participants a chance to articulate their viewpoints in a more candid and intimate fashion, thereby facilitating a more profound comprehension of their inclinations. By using both qualitative and quantitative methods together, the topic was looked at in great detail and from many angles. This resulted in a dataset that was both diverse and useful for drawing conclusions.

### 2.4  User Journey

In order to develop the user journey, it was necessary to look at the patterns that emerged from the tasks that various user groups completed. The primary pattern identified was discovered through careful observation of user tasks and the qualitative data obtained from interviews. The resulting user journey encompasses different stages, similar to frameworks like controlled composition and uncontrolled decomposition.

It requires a careful approach and a deep understanding of the task at hand. As a result, it raises several important factors that need to be addressed in order to improve the user experience when moving from the physical world to the virtual world. The study was conducted by observing a user who was new to the task. This approach facilitated a comprehensive analysis of possible challenges and areas where the user might encounter difficulties. By gaining insights into the difficulties encountered by an inexperienced user, designers can make well-informed choices to streamline the task and offer intuitive support throughout the virtual experience. In addition, this approach prioritises the user experience, making sure that the shift from physical to virtual is smooth and enjoyable for everyone, regardless of their skill level.

## 3  Result and Discussion

The graph (Fig. 2) represents the onboarding journey evaluation scores for the different user types: novice, moderate, and expert. They were assessed based on six different factors: safety, understandability, usability, convenience, reliability, and a delightful experience.

(a) Safety: In the current context, safety refers to the act of guaranteeing that users are not subjected to detrimental or disorienting encounters within the virtual environment. This also involves reducing the likelihood of simulator sickness, discomfort, or any negative consequences linked to virtual reality interaction. Users who are inexperienced and users who are highly skilled have the highest safety ratings. Both Novice and Expert users perceive the onboarding process as relatively secure. In contrast, the moderate users obtained lower scores in terms of safety, suggesting potential concerns or anxieties regarding safety during the onboarding phase for this particular group.

(b) Understandability: It refers to the degree of clarity and intuitiveness in the instructions, navigation, and interactions within the virtual space. Both Novice and Expert users exhibit the highest levels of understandability scores, indicating that they perceive the onboarding process as reasonably straightforward to comprehend. Users with a moderate level of proficiency achieve lower scores, suggesting that they may encounter difficulties in comprehending certain aspects of the onboarding process.

(c) Usability: It refers to the degree of effectiveness, efficiency, satisfaction, ease of use, and overall user friendliness with which users are able to accomplish their objectives within the virtual environment. The usability scores exhibit a consistent trend, wherein Novice and Expert users assign higher ratings to the onboarding journey compared to Moderate users. Consequently, both inexperienced and experienced users find the onboarding process to be more user-friendly than moderate users.

(d) Convenience: It refers to the ease with which users can engage in and complete the onboarding process without unnecessary complications or interruptions. The convenience scores demonstrate a notable decline among moderate users, suggesting that they perceive the onboarding process as less convenient in comparison to novice and expert users. This implies potential areas for enhancement in order to enhance the convenience of the onboarding process for the moderate user demographic.

(e) Reliability: It refers to the device's ability to consistently and dependably interact with other systems or users. Novice users rank the onboarding process as the most reliable, while expert users rank it as the second most reliable. Users with moderate usage exhibit the least reliable score, suggesting possible problems or concerns regarding the consistency and dependability of the onboarding process for this particular group.

(f) Delightful experience: It refers to the positive engagement and emotional fulfilment experienced by users upon successfully accomplishing a given task. Novice users exhibit the highest levels of satisfaction throughout the onboarding process, while expert users demonstrate slightly lower satisfaction ratings. Users who engage moderately report the lowest levels of satisfaction, indicating a potential to improve the overall positive experience for this group during the onboarding phase.

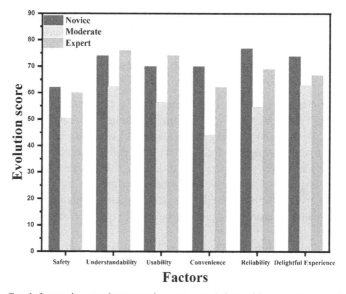

**Fig. 2.** Graph for novice, moderate, and expert users' data with respect to questionnaire

The information demonstrates differences in onboarding experiences among various user categories. Specifically, the moderate user group consistently assigns lower ratings for all aspects, suggesting possible areas for enhancing the onboarding process to align more closely with their needs and expectations. These results provide valuable insights for customising the onboarding experience, allowing adjustments to be made to cater to the distinct preferences and concerns of each user type.

A user journey (Fig. 3) was developed in order to accompany the revelations that were obtained regarding the responses of users at various stages of the task. The process of organising inferences about user sentiments that were derived from interviews made qualitative understanding easier to achieve. It is now abundantly clear that all user types encounter the same kinds of challenges at various points throughout the tasks they are performing. These challenges include problems with the pace and complexity of the instructions, as well as difficulties in leaving a space. In addition, distinct and contradictory problems were identified. For instance, experienced users expressed a desire for increased freedom of exploration, whereas novice users were looking for a companion to share the experience with as an instructor. In the process of refining particular aspects of the framework that was being developed, these particular findings from the study proved to be extremely helpful.

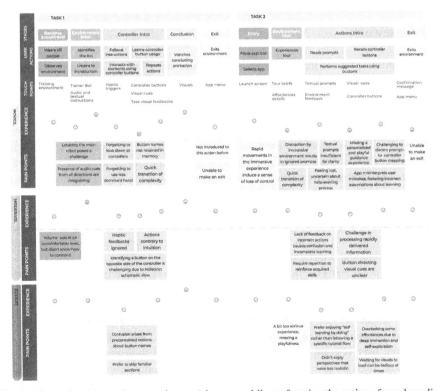

**Fig. 3.** User's (novice, moderate and expert) journey while performing the actions for onboarding

When examining the onboarding journey scores for different user types, such as novices, moderates, and experts (Fig. 3), interesting patterns emerge in their perceptions of various factors. Users with varying levels of experience consistently give higher ratings to the onboarding process in terms of safety, understandability, usability, convenience, reliability, and overall satisfaction. In terms of user proficiency, novice users tend to prioritise safety and enjoyable experiences, while expert users showcase their strengths in reliability and ease of use.

Moderate users consistently give lower scores for all evaluated factors, suggesting possible difficulties and areas for improvement in their onboarding experience. Concerns related to safety are particularly noticeable among moderate users, indicating the importance of addressing anxieties and improving the sense of security during the onboarding process. In addition, there are some challenges in terms of making the instructions and navigation more user-friendly for the moderate user group. This presents an opportunity to improve the overall understandability and usability for this particular proficiency level. Convenience and reliability show significant decreases among moderate users, indicating the importance of simplifying the onboarding process and resolving any concerns regarding consistency and dependability. The lower experience scores for moderate users suggest room for improvement in creating a more engaging and emotionally fulfilling onboarding process.

## 4  Framework

The onboarding process from the real world to the virtual world with immersiveness into this transition includes four phases, with two important junctions called nodes: the tangible realm, the arrival node, uncontrolled decomposition phase, controlled decomposition phase, the venture node, and virtual realm (Fig. 4). The tangible realm acts as the first stage of the onboarding process, where individuals physically reside in the real world. This is the phase where the user is introduced to the gadgets and the possible tangible interactions. Various things related to user safety must also be taken care of at this stage. The node that marks the entry to the next phase is the arrival node. This acts as a gateway to the virtual realm. This transition involves a gradual change in how people perceive and become aware of their surroundings as they disconnect from the physical world and fully engage in the digital realm. It becomes a responsibility of the designer of this space to ensure that the user feels safe in this new space and that the intended content is visible and understandable.

From this point starts the next phase, i.e. the uncontrolled decomposition. This phase is important for context setting. To facilitate seamless context establishment, we recommend guiding users through a transition from a detailed view of their environment to a bird's eye perspective, progressively minimizing clutter. This process should be entirely involuntary for users, akin to the experience of watching a movie unfold effortlessly.

Once the user is completely aware of the context of their environment, they can then be taken through the next phase, i.e. the controlled composition. During this phase the user makes the journey from the bird's eye perspective of their environment to the detailed view by performing actions thereby transforming their environment through these actions. These actions are introduced to them with different modes of instructions.

The culmination of this stage leads to the venture node. At this point, users possess full awareness of all actions and interactions, prepared to embark on their virtual journey. This node represents a significant milestone in the onboarding process as the person fully embraces the transformative potential of the virtual realm.

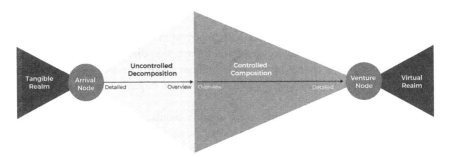

**Fig. 4.** Phases of onboarding process

A facilitator (elements that streamline and enhance the execution of tasks or processes) leads each phase, assisting users in navigating the one they are about to enter. These facilitators are essential (Figs. 4 and 5) in bridging gaps and improving the onboarding process to ensure a smooth and efficient experience for users. Basically, these facilitators serve as helpful guides, tackling any issues or roadblocks that users may face as they progress through each stage of the onboarding process. Through the identification and utilisation of these intervention gaps, the onboarding process can be optimised to enhance the transition for users, resulting in a more seamless and successful onboarding experience. Facilitators for each phase:

1 Tangible realm:

- Manuals and instructions: guides for the connections and starting devices, or for any other calibrations needed.
- Introduction to controls: knowledge of physical controls; visuals vs. haptics feedback
- Physical safety: Prior to entering a virtual world, it is crucial for users to ensure that they are in a safe physical environment and free from any potential hazards or factors that could lead to accidents or injuries. This precautionary measure helps to safeguard the well-being of users and minimize the risk of any untoward incidents while engaging with the virtual experience. Several areas of safety can be listed, such as problems with eye discomfort, spatial constraints, avoiding obstacles, avoiding use while running/ walking/cycling, motion sickness etc.

2 Arrival Node

- Proxemics: Virtual reality (VR) allows users to immerse themselves in virtual environments and experience a compelling sense of ownership over a virtual body. When an individual's virtual self is subjected to threats, the brain has the capacity to perceive these experiences as genuine threats. To ensure user safety in accordance with proxemics, designers can implement two key approaches:

– Ensure that the virtual space that a user is onboarding follows the rules of proxemics and that the intimate and personal space of a user is not infiltrated
– Ask for preferences regarding the user's comfort zones

- Orientation upon arrival: Orientation upon arrival in a virtual environment should be designed in a way that places essential information directly in front of the user. This approach ensures that important details are readily visible and easily accessible, enhancing the user's ability to understand and engage with the environment effectively.
- Quick action remediation: Since users identify themselves as their virtual selves, they tend to experience anxiety, distress or panic in threatening situations. They may also feel anxious when things don't turn out to be as expected. A designer should incorporate shortcuts or quick-action remediation techniques that empower users to swiftly exit challenging situations, preventing the escalation of adverse effects.
- Content Presentation with respect to location and anchoring: To ensure important content receives maximum visibility and attention, it is beneficial to position it within the user's line of sight and at the center of their field of vision. It can also be beneficial to orient important information, objects, or elements towards the user in the virtual environment. For generic information, it is recommended to avoid anchoring content solely to the wearer's head in virtual reality experiences. But this can create a sense of confinement and the perception of being constantly followed. Conversely, when content can be anchored to the ground or the virtual environment (in case of specific information), it provides users with a profound sense of freedom and agency.

3 Uncontrolled Decomposition

- Motion Guidelines: a seamless user experience with minimal disruption or inconvenience paired with fade effect to avoid sudden motions. For beginners and intermediate users, it is advisable to employ smooth, gradual movements to prevent any sense of disorientation or unease.
- Nudging elements: As this phase resembles an observational tour, it's crucial to craft effective prompts for users to focus on specific elements. Utilizing visual cues, haptic cues, or spatial audio as nudging elements is recommended. However, it's essential to ensure that these nudges are distinct from environmental noise and inputs.
- Context setting: explanation for the setting and the location. Commencing with detailed view and elements that characterize the location, and then zooming out to unveil the environment and surroundings, can invite individuals to immerse themselves in a broader narrative or experience.

4 Controlled Composition

- Character of Tutorials:

- Progressive complexity - Progressive complexity: Guiding users from simpler to more intricate tasks. This gradual learning curve ensures a smooth transition, empowering users to master the virtual environment step by step, enhancing their overall experience
- Interactive Practise: instructions via interactions,
- Flexibility and adaptability: Users have varying levels of prior experience and familiarity with VR. A good tutorial should be adaptable to accommodate different user backgrounds and allow users to progress at their own pace. Providing options for both beginners and more experienced users can enhance the onboarding experience.
- Accessibility considerations: Consider accessibility features in the tutorial design to cater to users with diverse needs. This includes options for text size adjustment, color contrast, audio alternatives for instructions, and customizable control configurations to accommodate different physical abilities.
- Enjoyability: the tutorial should strive to deliver an enjoyable and immersive experience. Integrating entertaining graphics, captivating characters, or engaging storylines can effectively enhance the overall appeal and user engagement.

- Display Timeline - Timeline: Display of timeline throughout the tutorial offer users a visual representation of sequential steps during onboarding in virtual reality
- Navigations like

  - Cues: visual cues, hand controllers or gesture cues, auditory cues, on-screen prompts, and physical feedback
  - Feedback: visual, auditory, and haptic feedback for a more realistic and interactive experience
  - Feedforwards: clear and intuitive feed forwards for the next interaction

## 5 Venture Node

- Codes of Conduct: Guidelines for appropriate behaviour and physical conduct, as well as the restrictions and limitations.

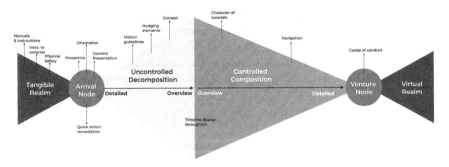

**Fig. 5.** Phases of onboarding process including facilitators

6 Virtual Realm: Ready to Explore

## 5  Conclusion

This study explores the complex process of transitioning users from the physical world to the virtual world, with a particular emphasis on the use of virtual reality (VR) devices as transformative tools. The study classifies users into different skill levels, acknowledging their specific requirements when they first start using the system. By thoroughly examining users' journeys in the virtual environment and analysing their interactions at different levels, valuable insights can be gained into the factors that impact the onboarding experience. The findings emphasise the importance of various factors in shaping users' perceptions during onboarding, including safety, understandability, usability, convenience, reliability, and the overall delightful experience. Less experienced users tend to focus on safety and having a good time, whereas more experienced users value reliability and user-friendliness. Users with moderate usage consistently give lower scores across these factors, suggesting room for improvement in onboarding processes that cater to their specific needs.

The proposed framework highlights six phases of onboarding, transitioning from the physical to the digital realm, with a focus on the crucial role of facilitators in each phase. Various resources, including manuals, instructions, and codes of conduct, are essential for helping users navigate the transition, overcome challenges, and enhance the onboarding experience. The chosen research methodology utilises a combination of methods, including task-based assessments, questionnaires, and interviews, to provide a comprehensive understanding of the onboarding process. The integration of qualitative and quantitative data enriches the depth of insights, laying the groundwork for future research and real-world applications.

While the essential facilitators have been listed in this paper, some of these can be studied and experimented with further to generate quantitative guidelines. This can add further comprehensiveness to the framework. Future research endeavors will focus on precisely quantifying these facilitators, thereby providing more specific and actionable guidelines.

In the end, the study seeks to make a valuable contribution to the creation of a holistic framework that takes into account not only technical aspects, but also the social and emotional elements of onboarding. Through a comprehensive understanding of user needs, this study aims to enhance the onboarding experience, promoting a greater sense of connection and belonging in the virtual environment. With the constant advancements in VR technology, it is becoming increasingly important to focus on improving the onboarding process. This will help make VR more accessible and enhance user engagement.

## References

1. Andersen, E., et al.: The impact of tutorials on games of varying complexity. In: Proceedings of the SIGCHI Conference on Human Factors in Computing Systems, pp. 59–68 (2012)
2. Anthes, C.: State of the art of virtual reality technology. In: 2016 IEEE Aerospace Conference, pp. 1–19 (2016)

3. Ashtari, N., Bunt, A., Mcgrenere, J., Nebeling, M., Chilana, P.K., Arbor, A.: Creating augmented and virtual reality applications: current practices, challenges, and opportunities. In: Proceedings of the 2020 CHI Conference on Human Factors in Computing Systems. pp. 1–13 (2020)
4. Kim, Y.M., Rhiu, I., Yun, M.H., Kim, Y.M.: A systematic review of a virtual reality system from the perspective of user experience experience. Int. J. Hum. Comput. Interact. **00**(00), 1–18 (2019)
5. Rebelo, F., Noriega, P., Duarte, E., Soares, M.: Using virtual reality to assess user experience. Hum. Factors J. Hum. Factors Ergon. Soc. **54**(6), 964–982 (2012). https://doi.org/10.1177/001 8720812465006
6. Thoravi, B.: TutoriVR: a video-based tutorial system for design applications in virtual reality. In: Proceedings of the 2019 CHI Conference on Human Factors in Computing Systems, pp. 1–12 (2019)
7. Whittaker, L.: Onboarding and offboarding in virtual reality: a user-centred framework for audience experience across genres and spaces. Convergence Int. J. Res. New Media Technol. 1–20 (2023). https://doi.org/10.1177/13548565231187329

# Research on the Benefits of Biophilia Effects in Virtual Environments

HsinChiao Chan[✉] and Yinghsiu Huang

Department of Industrial Design, National Kaohsiung Normal University, No.62, Shenghong Road, Yanchao District, Kaohsiung City, 82446, Taiwan

{611272005,yinghsiu}@mail.nknu.edu.tw

**Abstract.** Stephen Kaplan's attention restoration theory (ART) proposed that exposure to the natural environment can restore and replenish direct attention abilities [1]. With the advancement of technology, entertainment, work, and life in virtual environments have become a trend in the future. Therefore, this study wants to explore the difference between biophilia on attention recovery in real environments and virtual environments, and understand the difference in the recovery effects of two elements (plants, pictures) commonly used in biophilia environment design. The experiment uses the Sustained Attention to Response Test (SART) to test the participants' attention status, and uses the Perceived Restorativeness Scale (PRS) to understand the participants' restorative feelings about different biophilic environments. According to the results of the SART test, participants exposed to real plant and virtual plant environments achieved significant attention recovery, while other environments, although not as significant, also had a restorative tendency. The degree of improvement in the number of correct responses (CR) before and after exposure to the environment in the SART test is ranked as follows: Virtual Picture, $t = -2.57$, $p = 0.03$, Real Plants, $t = -1.79$, $p = 0.11$, Virtual Plants, $t = -0.87$, $p = 0.41$, Real Picture, $t = -0.17$, $p = 0.88$. The differences in the results of the SART test and the PRS scale in the four environments indicate that the virtual environment has a certain degree of impact on recovery, but it is currently uncertain which part caused the impact.

**Keywords:** Virtual reality · Directed attention · Restorative environments

## 1 Introduction

The term biophilia was coined by Erich Fromm in 1973 to describe a psychological tendency to be attracted by all living and dynamic things. Many studies have shown that staying in an environment with biophilia elements can bring physical and mental benefits, such as Kaplan's attention restoration theory (ART) [1], which suggests that exposure to the natural environment can restore and supplement the ability to direct attention. In addition to attention, the biophilia environment can also provide physiological benefits [2, 3], cognitive benefits [4, 5], and psychological health benefits [6]. Biophilia design is currently widely used in the field of architecture, by adding natural elements to the space as much as possible, such as placing plants or water features, using large windows to increase natural light exposure, using designs with biomimetic shapes,

© The Author(s), under exclusive license to Springer Nature Switzerland AG 2024
J. Y. C. Chen and G. Fragomeni (Eds.): HCII 2024, LNCS 14707, pp. 16–28, 2024.
https://doi.org/10.1007/978-3-031-61044-8_2

and also using natural materials to increase people's comfort in the space. In addition to the above examples, many experiments have also confirmed that viewing photos of natural landscapes can achieve a biophilic effect [7–9].

In this ever-improving era, as VR technology becomes more and more perfect, entertaining, working, and living in a virtual environments have become a future trend. For example, due to the Coronavirus in the past few years, many companies have adopted the method of working from home. Microsoft Research Institute has experimented with using VR to work in virtual reality environments. In the future, the use of virtual environments will be more extensive. Currently, experiments on the biophilia effect are mostly used in real environments. Therefore, this study wants to explore whether there is a difference in attention recovery between biophilia in real environments and virtual environments, and to understand the difference in the restorative effect of two elements (Plants, pictures) commonly used in biophilic environment design, it will help to better choose the application of elements when bringing biophilic design into the virtual environment in the future, so as to achieve the best benefits of biophilic design in the virtual environment.

## 2   Literature Review

The term biophilia was coined by Erich Fromm in 1973 and later used by Wilson in his work Biophilia [10], which describes a psychological tendency to be attracted to all living and dynamic things. Many studies have confirmed that staying in an environment with biophilic elements can bring physical and mental benefits, such as Kaplan's attention restoration theory (ART), It has been proposed that exposure to the natural environment can promote easier brain function, thereby restoring and supplementing its direct attention ability. In addition to attention, a biophilic environment can also improve stress and anxiety [2, 3], and even enhance creativity and problem-solving abilities [4, 11].

Ulrich's Psycho-evolutionary theory [12] and Kaplan's Attention Restoration Theory [1, 5] are the two major theories of biophilia. Both are based on the view that humans evolve in the natural environment. They believe that compared with the urban environments, there is less cognitive and physiological loss when interacting with the natural environment, because the brain is better able to process elements in nature, that is, the visual processing of objects in natural scenes is fast and efficient [13].

In the ART theory, Kaplan differentiates attention into voluntary attention (also called directed attention) and involuntary attention based on James' statement [14]. Voluntary attention is a kind of attention that requires effort and must be maintained to avoid distraction. Involuntary attention, on the other hand, refers to when people are naturally attracted to stimuli that are inherently fascinating, without having to work hard to stay focused, so Kaplan [1] also renamed it as fascination. Mental fatigue occurs when people are exposed to specific stimuli or perform tasks, and mental fatigue is related to voluntary attention. According to ART, exposure to and observation of nature can improve mental fatigue and restore attention. To achieve a restorative environment, it must be composed of four components: Being Away, Soft Fascination, Extent, and Compatibility. The combination of the four elements encourages involuntary attention and restores our directional attention.

Directed attention plays a key role in many aspects of cognitive function and behavior, including short-term memory [15, 16] or cognitive and executive functions. For example, Chiu and Algase's research explored the link between directed attention and getting lost behavior in early Alzheimer's disease [17]. In addition, directed attention also affects academic achievement [18] and work performance. Many working memory models propose a close relationship between working memory and attention [19].

Due to the benefits brought by biophilia benefits, biophilia elements are widely used in the fields of architecture and interior design. Many studies are also exploring the relationship between the natural landscape of residential areas and people's physical and mental health, such as Taylor, Kuo [20] Studies have shown that children living in an environment with more natural landscapes will improve their self-discipline performance. In other words, green landscapes outside their homes can help them live more effective and self-disciplined lives, and as the biodiversity of the landscape increases, the positive psychological benefits will also increase [21]. In order to achieve the biophilic effect, in addition to real contact with nature, there are many indirect ways to achieve it. In Kellert's book Nature by Design: The Practice of Biological Design, 3 experiences and 24 attributes of biophilia design are detailed [22]:

- Direct Experience of Nature: Light, Air, Water, Plants, Animals, Natural landscapes and ecosystems, Fire;
- Indirect Experience of Nature: Images of Nature, Natural materials, Natural colours, simulating natural light and air, Naturalistic shapes and forms, evoking nature, Information richness, Age, change and the patina of time, Natural geometries, Biomimicry;
- Experience of Space and Place: Prospect and refuge, organized complexity, Integration of parts to wholes, Transitional spaces, Mobility and wayfinding, Cultural and ecological attachment to place.

Although there is considerable evidence for the beneficial effects of exposure to natural environments, there is less evidence for other biophilic aspects, such as the use of natural materials [23]. The more common life friendly elements include plants [1, 4], window views [24], natural images [7–9], and so on.

## 3    Method

### 3.1    Study Process

The purpose of the experiment is to understand whether there is a difference in the effect of the biophilia effect on attention recovery between real and virtual environments. Therefore, this experiment designed four biophilic environments, namely real picture environment, real plant environment, virtual picture environment, virtual plant environment, to explore the relationship between virtual and real and two different biophilic elements. The virtual environment is built through Blender software and is experienced by participants through Unity software. The VR device is META Oculus Quest 2. Then, we searched for ten students aged between 18 and 25 at National Kaohsiung Normal University for experiments. The experiment mainly uses the Sustained Attention to Response Test (SART) to understand the attention recovery of participants, and this test can lead to cognitive fatigue. Participants will take two tests in total. After the first SART test, participants will move freely in a restorative environment for 6 min. After that, they will take the second SART test to observe the results of the two tests to understand the participants' recovery. Finally, participants will be asked to fill out the Perceived Restorativeness Scale (PRS) to understand the participants' recovery feelings about the biophilic environment. Each participant will experience four biophilic environments within 3 weeks, with intervals of 3 to 5 days between each experience to prevent participants from feeling fatigued or bored.

## 3.2 Stimulus Materials

Four restorative environments were designed in the experiment to understand the biophilia effects of real and virtual environments, namely real picture environment, real plant environment, virtual picture environment, and virtual plant environment. The real environment was arranged by the classroom located in National Kaohsiung Normal University, and the curtains of the classroom are closed, making it impossible to see the outside scenery. The virtual environment is built to simulate the real environment (see Fig. 1). We used Blender software to build two virtual biophilic environments and conducted VR experiences through Unity software in the experiment. The VR device was META Oculus Quest 2.

**Fig. 1.** Restorative environment with virtual plants and pictures, plants on the left and pictures on the right

## 3.3 Participants

Ten students (mean age = 20.7 years) from National Kaohsiung Normal University (Taiwan) participated in this experiment. Each participant will experience the experiments of real pictures, real plants, virtual pictures, and virtual plants in sequence, with an interval of 3 to 5 days between each experience.

## 3.4 Procedure

Participants entered a darkened classroom to perform the SART test. Before the test, the experimenter informed the participants of the test method and asked whether they would take a short version practice test. The formal test consists of 225 numbers. The short version consists of 27 numbers and is designed to familiarize participants with the test format. After participants became familiar with the test format, they took the formal test. After the test, participants were allowed to move freely in a restorative environment for 6 min. According to previous experiments, exposure to a restorative environment for 5 to 10 min can produce physiological and cognitive benefits [8, 25]. There are tables, chairs and biophilic elements (pictures or plants) in the environment. Participants can walk around or sit down and rest, but they are not allowed to use electronic products. The experiment in a virtual environment is conducted using VR, in which participants move through Teleport, using a wireless controller handle to jump from one point to another, and can also freely and fully experience the entire space. The second SART test will be conducted immediately after the environmental experience. And participants also need to fill out the Perceived Restorability Scale (PRS). Each participant will undergo experiments in four different environments, with the steps outlined above. The four experiments will be conducted with an interval of 3 to 5 days to avoid fatigue and boredom among participants.

### 3.5 Measures

Use the Sustained Attention to Response Test (SART) to test the attention state of participants before and after being in a restorative environment. SART is a measure of a person's ability to suppress responses to rare and unpredictable stimuli during rapid and rhythmic responses to frequent stimuli, and can also be explained as sustained attention. Robertson and Manly define it as "the ability to self-sustain mindful, conscious processing of stimuli whose repetitive, non-arousing qualities would otherwise lead to habituation and distraction to other stimuli [26]." During testing, we placed participants in a dimly lit room to avoid other distractions. The test is conducted via laptop computer. One of the numbers 1 to 9 was randomly displayed on the monitor at a regular rate of one every 1.15 s, and the entire test presented 225 numbers in a continuous sequence over 4.3 min. The task for participants is to press a spacebar every time a number appears, except for the specified forbidden area number (digit 3), and no response should be made to it. SART testing is easy to get started with and cannot be learned. And due to maintaining high concentration for a long time, participants will suffer from cognitive fatigue after the test.

Following that, the Perceived Restorativeness Scale (PRS) [27] is utilized to explore participants' restorative experiences in different biophilic environments. The PRS scale consists of 26 questions and is structured into four dimensions based on the measurement of the four restorative qualities of Attention Restoration Theory (ART): Being Away, Fascination, Coherence, and Compatibility. The questionnaire content is as follows:

- Spending time here gives me a break from my day-to-day routine (being-away);
- My attention is drawn to many interesting things (fascination);
- There is too much going on (coherence);
- I have a sense that I belong here (compatibility).

Because the restorative environment of the experiment is small and simple, it was determined that four questions related to the scope are not applicable to this experiment. The scale is conducted using the Likert 7-point scale (1 = strongly disagree; 7 = strongly agree).

# 4  Results

This experiment aims to investigate the restorative effects of four environments (real pictures, real plants, virtual pictures, virtual plants) on attention. The SART (Sustained Attention to Response Task) is employed as the assessment method, and the performance on the SART test is evaluated based on the following aspects:

- reaction times in seconds(RT): the time elapsed from the presentation of a number until the participant presses the spacebar;
- number of correct responses (CR): the number of times the participant did not press the target number (digit 3), and the participant should not respond to the target number;
- number of incorrect responses (IR): the number of times the participant presses the spacebar for the target digit; the sum of correct responses (CR) and incorrect responses (IR) is equal to 25;
- number of missing responses (MR): the number of times the participant misses pressing the spacebar for non-target digits; participants should strive to minimize omission occurrences.

The main objective of the experiment is to investigate whether attention recovers or improves after exposure to a restorative environment. Therefore, an analysis will be conducted comparing participants' performance (RT, CR, IR, MR) before exposure to the restorative environment (Session 1) and after exposure to the environment (Session 2). The Paired-Samples t-test will be employed to assess whether there are significant changes in these performance measures (see Table 1). It can be observed that there are significant changes in RT for real plants and in CR and IR for virtual pictures. Specifically, in the case of real plants, participants exhibited a tendency towards increased reaction time ($t = -2.36$, $p = 0.04$). Previous experiments have found a significant negative correlation between the average reaction time (RT) and the number of errors (IR) in SART tests. In other words, faster reactions are more likely to be associated with a higher number of mistakes. Therefore, the lengthening of reaction time observed may be attributed to participants consciously slowing down after detecting errors [28]. Although the IR of real plants did not reach statistical significance, there is indeed a noticeable decrease ($t = 1.79$, $p = 0.11$). Therefore, it indicates that exposure to a real plant environment does contribute to the restoration or improvement of participants' attention. In the case of virtual pictures, a significant increase is observed in CR, along with a significant decrease in IR. Since the sum of CR and IR is a fixed quantity (25), their values are complementary. For CR, $t = -2.57$, $p = 0.03$, and for IR, $t = 2.57$, $p = 0.03$. There is also a slight decrease in RT and MR. Therefore, participants do experience an improvement and restoration of attention after exposure to the virtual picture environment. Although not reaching statistical significance, there is a tendency towards increased correct responses (CR) in the other two environments as well.

**Table 1.** The mean and t-test results of SART at four levels (RT, CR, IR, MR) before and after exposure to four different environments

|  | Session | Real Picture | Real Plant | Virtual Picture | Virtual Plant | F | p |
|---|---|---|---|---|---|---|---|
| Reaction times (in sec) | 1 | 0.47 | 0.49 | 0.48 | 0.47 | 0.44 | 0.73 |
|  | 2 | 0.47 | 0.52 | 0.47 | 0.47 | 1.8 | 0.16 |
| t |  | 0.13 | −2.36 | 0.92 | −1.83 |  |  |
| p |  | 0.9 | 0.04* | 0.38 | 0.1 |  |  |
| Correct responses | 1 | 18.1 | 19.4 | 18.5 | 19.1 | 0.32 | 0.81 |
|  | 2 | 18.3 | 21.7 | 19.7 | 19.8 | 3.16 | 0.04* |
| t |  | −0.17 | −1.79 | −2.57 | −0.87 |  |  |
| p |  | 0.86 | 0.11 | 0.03* | 0.41 |  |  |
| Incorrect responses | 1 | 6.9 | 5.6 | 6.5 | 5.9 | 0.32 | 0.81 |
|  | 2 | 6.7 | 3.3 | 5.3 | 5.2 | 3.16 | 0.04* |
| t |  | 0.17 | 1.79 | 2.57 | 0.87 |  |  |
| p |  | 0.86 | 0.11 | 0.03* | 0.41 |  |  |
| Missing responses | 1 | 1.9 | 0.8 | 0.8 | 0.4 | 1.49 | 0.23 |
|  | 2 | 2 | 1.1 | 0.2 | 0.4 | 1.94 | 0.14 |
| t |  | −0.12 | −0.32 | 0.92 | 0 |  |  |
| p |  | 0.91 | 0.76 | 0.38 | 1 |  |  |

* represents statistical significance, $p < 0.05$.

The difference in recovery between the four environments is also a very interesting part. Through ANOVA, the RT, CR, IR, and MR before exposure to the environment (Session 1) and after exposure (Session 2) were compared in the four environments (see Table 1). It was found that the CR and IR after exposure to the environment (Session 2) reached significance ($F = 3.16$, $p = 0.04$). Therefore, Scheffé test was used to conduct post hoc tests and multiple comparisons on these two items (see Table 2). It was found that the mean CR of real plants was significantly higher than that of real pictures, indicating that in real environments, the restorability of plant environments is significantly better than that of picture environments. The relationship between IR and CR is corresponding, so IR is not discussed.

The restorativeness of participants' subjective experiences in four environments is measured by the average scores obtained through the Perceived Restorativeness Scale (PRS) questionnaire. The assessment is based on four dimensions of restorativeness derived from Attention Restoration Theory (ART) [1, 5, 29]:

- Being Away: psychologically detach yourself from your current worries and needs, and distract yourself from an environment that is depleting your attention and energy.
- Fascination: it can make one's attention being held without any effort expended. Kaplan divides fascination into two types. Hard fascination grabs your attention

**Table 2.** Scheffe Test results for CR after exposure to the environment

|  | (I) group | (J) group | difference-of-means(I-J) | SE | p |
|---|---|---|---|---|---|
| CR | Real Picture | Real Plants | −3.400* | 1.11 | 0.04* |
|  |  | Virtual Picture | −1.4 | 1.11 | 0.66 |
|  |  | Virtual Plants | −1.5 | 1.11 | 0.61 |
|  | Real Plants | Real Picture | 3.400* | 1.11 | 0.04* |
|  |  | Virtual Picture | 2 | 1.11 | 0.37 |
|  |  | Virtual Plants | 1.9 | 1.11 | 0.41 |
|  | Virtual Picture | Real Picture | 1.4 | 1.11 | 0.66 |
|  |  | Real Plants | −2 | 1.11 | 0.37 |
|  |  | Virtual Plants | −0.1 | 1.11 | 1.00 |
|  | Virtual Plants | Real Picture | 1.5 | 1.11 | 0.61 |
|  |  | Real Plants | −1.9 | 1.11 | 0.41 |
|  |  | Virtual Picture | 0.1 | 1.11 | 1.00 |

* represents statistical significance, p < 0.05.

dramatically and does not allow the attention to wander. Soft fascination grabs the involuntary attention moderately and allows it to wander freely.

- Coherence: There are no unusual or unexpected features in the environment, and you feel comfortable in the environment.
- Compatibility: it is about feeling enjoyment and congruence in your environment. The environment enables us to engage in activities that are compatible with our intrinsic motivations.

Looking at the overall results, the PRS scores of the four environments from high to low are (see Table 3): Virtual Plants (M = 4.94), Real Plants (M = 4.93), Virtual Picture (M = 4.79), Real Picture (M = 4.47), and the ranking of the degree of improvement in CR before and after exposure to the environment in the SART test (see Table 1): Virtual Picture, t = −2.57, p = 0.03, Real Plants, t = −1.79, p = 0.11, Virtual Plants, t = −0.87, p = 0.41, Real Picture, t = −0.17, p = 0.86, the rankings of the two are different. PRS represents the participant's subjective restorative feelings about the environment, while the results of the SART test represent the participant's actual recovery effect. In terms of subjective restorability, the plant environments are better than the picture environments. In terms of real restoration effect, the virtual picture environment is the best. There is a clear difference between the two restorative measurement methods in this part. As for the ranking difference between Virtual Plants and Real Plants, the mean difference in the total scores of the two in PRS is only 0.01. However, in the results of SART testing, the restoration effect of the real plant environment (t = −1.79, p = 0.11) is better than that of the virtual plant environment (t = −0.87, p = 0.41). Therefore, it is speculated that although the subjective experience of the two is similar, in terms of actual restoration, the real plant environment still has a better effect than the virtual plant environment.

Next, we will discuss the four restorative qualities separately (see Table 3). In the part of being-away, real plants got the highest score (M = 5.16), and the plant environments were higher than the picture environments. It is inferred that the plant environments can better detach people from current worries and needs. In the fascination part, the scores of the virtual environments are higher than those of the real environments, namely Virtual Picture (M = 5.16) and Virtual Plants (M = 5.14). In the real environment, the scores of the plant environment (M = 4.9) are significantly higher than picture environment (M = 4.2). Because the fascination part of the PRS question does not distinguish whether the charm is soft fascination or hard fascination, overall the virtual environment is more attractive. In the coherence part, the real picture environment has the highest score (M = 5.67), and both picture environments are higher than the plant environments, indicating that the picture environments are tidier and less distracting. In the compatibility part, the two plant environments are both higher than the two picture environments, and the scores are similar, namely Real Plants (M = 4.54), Virtual Plants (M = 4.44), Virtual Picture (M = 3.94), Real Picture (M = 3.88), indicating that the plant environment makes participants more integrated and feel consistent with the environment.

**Table 3.** The restorative quality scores of PRS in four different environments

| Environment | being-away | fascination | coherence | compatibility | total |
|---|---|---|---|---|---|
| Real Picture | 4.54 | 4.2 | 5.67 | 3.88 | 4.47 |
| Real Plants | 5.16 | 4.9 | 5.2 | 4.54 | 4.93 |
| Virtual Picture | 4.54 | 5.16 | 5.42 | 3.94 | 4.79 |
| Virtual Plants | 4.9 | 5.14 | 5.2 | 4.44 | 4.94 |
| $p$ | ns | ns | ns | ns | ns |

## 5 Discussion

The main purpose of this experiment is to explore the biophilic benefits of virtual and real environments. Analysis of the SART test results shows that although only the environments of real plants and virtual pictures are significant, all four environments have a tendency for attention recovery, which is consistent with the ART hypothesis. And also confirms that the biophilia effect is still useful for attention recovery in virtual environments. According to the results of SART, the virtual picture environment achieved the best recovery effect. However, according to the total score of PRS about subjective feelings, the virtual picture only ranks third (M = 4.79), but it achieves better restoration effect than the virtual plant environment (M = 4.94) and the real plant environment (M = 4.93) which are ranked higher in PRS. Referring to the four restorative scores of the virtual picture environment in PRS, it can be seen that there is only a relatively outstanding score in the fascination (M = 5.16). Therefore, it is speculated that this may be due to the bias caused by the participants' curiosity towards VR. Seven of the participants had not used VR devices before the experiment and showed strong curiosity about the virtual world and VR devices during the experiment. The virtual picture environment, as the first virtual environment experienced, may largely affect the results of SART.

Although the virtual plant environment also has a high score on fascination (M = 5.14), the results of the SART test are not as good as the virtual picture environment. From this point of view, the psychological state brought about by the "first time" may be freshness, curiosity, immersion, etc., which greatly affects the recovery of attention. This is a very interesting part, although it is a little outside the scope of biophilia. But if we can gain a deeper understanding of the psychological factors that affect the results in the future, there may be new breakthroughs in the way of attention recovery. And exclude virtual picture environment that may has experimental bias. It can be seen that the score ranking of the being away and compatibility parts is consistent with the restorative ranking tested by SART, indicating that these two restorative qualities may have a high correlation with attention recovery. The real plant environment, which has the best restorative effect after excluding virtual pictures, has a much higher score in being-away than other environments, indicating that this feeling of escaping from daily life and being away from all worries may greatly affect the restorative effect.

And for the difference between reality and virtuality. It can be found that the virtual environments received higher scores than the real environments in the fascination part of the PRS evaluation. This is probably because the participants are fresh and curious about VR. Half of the participants showed excitement and strong curiosity and high concentration towards the virtual world and VR devices during their first exposure to VR in the experiment. Although the reaction to experiencing the virtual environment for the second time was not as strong as the first time, there is still a certain sense of freshness and curiosity towards the virtual world. This may have significantly increased the PRS score of the virtual environments, resulting in the virtual plant environment achieving the highest score in PRS, but its restorative performance in SART testing is not as good as that of the real plant environment. This means that the real plant environment is actually more restorative than the virtual plant environment. This also indicates that the attractiveness brought by virtual environments may not always affect the attention recovery ability of biophilia effect. Real picture environment showed the worst recovery in both SART and PRS scores. However, in the SART test, the virtual picture environment achieved the best recovery effect (t = −2.57, p = 0.03), which shows that the virtual environment does have a certain degree of impact on recovery. However, it is currently uncertain which part of the virtual environment experience has affected the experimental results. If there are similar experiments in the future, it is necessary to examine the familiarity or adjustment level of participants with VR, in order to achieve the same situation as the real environment as much as possible.

Regarding the difference between pictures and plants. If the virtual picture environment affected by other factors is excluded, it can be seen that the real picture environment has the worst recovery performance in both SART and PRS. Referring to the scores of the four restorative qualities in PRS, it can be seen that the picture environments received higher scores in the coherence part, while lower scores were obtained in the being away and compatibility parts. The fascination part will not be discussed for the time being due to the influence of VR. Due to questions in the coherence part of the PRS questionnaire, such as "there is too much going on" and "it is chaotic here.", they are all discussing whether there are many things in the space that can attract attention. In ART theory, soft fascination is one of the important factors to achieve biophilia effect, which means that it can make people naturally interested and pay attention without effort. This may indicate that the picture environment arranged in this experiment is not attractive enough to effectively achieve the biophilia effect. Perhaps increasing the number or size of pictures can enhance attractiveness. The proportion of pictures and plants in space needs to be as consistent as possible to avoid experimental bias.

The experimental results confirm that the biophilia effect can indeed be achieved in the virtual environment. However, due to the significant differences between virtual and real environments, as well as the need to examine the office situation in virtual environment, there is still a lot of research space on how to carry out biophilia design in virtual environments. This study only explored two methods: pictures and plants. There are many other elements that can be tried in biophilia design, such as sound, natural light, window views, etc. Future experiments can also take these elements into consideration. And for the restorative difference between virtual and reality. Judging from the results of this experiment, if the virtual picture environment affected by the "first virtual environment experience" is excluded, the recovery of the real plant environment is still better than that of the virtual plant environment, even if the spatial design of the two is as close as possible to the same. According to the results of PRS, the real plant environment has the highest scores in being away and compatibility. It can be inferred that if you want to enhance the recovery effect of the virtual environment, you can try to make the virtual environment more in line with these two feelings: integrating with the environment and feeling liberated. For example, it is possible to consider increasing the immersion of the virtual environment, such as improving the realism of the virtual environment, or being able to touch elements in the environment, and so on. In view of possible experimental deviations that occur in the virtual picture environment, similar situations should be avoided in the future. The unexpected restorative effects brought about by deviant mental states can also be part of future development, and more advantages of the virtual environment in restorative effects should be explored.

# References

1. Kaplan, S.: The restorative benefits of nature: toward an integrative framework. J. Environ. Psychol. **15**(3), 169–182 (1995)
2. Ulrich, R.S., et al.: Stress recovery during exposure to natural and urban environments. J. Environ. Psychol. **11**(3), 201–230 (1991)
3. Yin, J., et al.: Effects of biophilic indoor environment on stress and anxiety recovery: a between-subjects experiment in virtual reality. Environ. Int. **136**, 105427 (2020)
4. Atchley, R.A., Strayer, D.L., Atchley, P.: Creativity in the wild: improving creative reasoning through immersion in natural settings. PLoS ONE **7**(12), e51474 (2012)
5. Kaplan, S.: Meditation, restoration, and the management of mental fatigue. Environ. Behav. **33**(4), 480–506 (2001)
6. Maller, C.J.: Promoting children's mental, emotional and social health through contact with nature: a model. Health Educ. **109**(6), 522–543 (2009)
7. Valtchanov, D., Ellard, C.G.: Cognitive and affective responses to natural scenes: effects of low level visual properties on preference, cognitive load and eye-movements. J. Environ. Psychol. **43**, 184–195 (2015)
8. Berman, M.G., Jonides, J., Kaplan, S.: The cognitive benefits of interacting with nature. Psychol. Sci. **19**(12), 1207–1212 (2008)
9. Berto, R.: Exposure to restorative environments helps restore attentional capacity. J. Environ. Psychol. **25**(3), 249–259 (2005)
10. Wilson, E.O.: Biophilia. Harvard University Press (1986)
11. Yin, J., et al.: Effects of biophilic interventions in office on stress reaction and cognitive function: a randomized crossover study in virtual reality. Indoor Air **29**(6), 1028–1039 (2019)
12. Ulrich, R.S.: Aesthetic and affective response to natural environment. In: Altman, I., Wohlwill, J.F. (eds.) Behavior and the Natural Environment, vol. 6, pp. 85–125. Springer, Boston, MA (1983).https://doi.org/10.1007/978-1-4613-3539-9_4
13. Rousselet, G.A., Thorpe, S.J., Fabre-Thorpe, M.: Processing of one, two or four natural scenes in humans: the limits of parallelism. Vision. Res. **44**(9), 877–894 (2004)
14. James, W.: Psychology. Henry Holt and Company (1892). https://doi.org/10.1037/11060-000
15. Jonides, J., et al.: The mind and brain of short-term memory. Annu. Rev. Psychol. **59**, 193–224 (2008)
16. Williams, R.A., et al.: Changes in directed attention and short-term memory in depression. J. Psychiatr. Res. **34**(3), 227–238 (2000)
17. Chiu, Y.-C., et al.: Getting lost: directed attention and executive functions in early Alzheimer's disease patients. Dement. Geriatr. Cogn. Disord. **17**(3), 174–180 (2004)
18. Diamond, A., et al.: Preschool program improves cognitive control. Science **318**(5855), 1387–1388 (2007)
19. Lepsien, J., Thornton, I., Nobre, A.C.: Modulation of working-memory maintenance by directed attention. Neuropsychologia **49**(6), 1569–1577 (2011)
20. Taylor, A.F., Kuo, F.E., Sullivan, W.C.: Views of nature and self-discipline: evidence from inner city children. J. Environ. Psychol. **22**(1–2), 49–63 (2002)
21. Fuller, R.A., et al.: Psychological benefits of greenspace increase with biodiversity. Biol. Let. **3**(4), 390–394 (2007)
22. Kellert, S.R.: Nature by Design: The Practice of Biophilic Design. Yale University Press (2019). https://doi.org/10.12987/9780300235432
23. Gillis, K., Gatersleben, B.: A review of psychological literature on the health and wellbeing benefits of biophilic design. Buildings **5**(3), 948–963 (2015)
24. Felsten, G.: Where to take a study break on the college campus: an attention restoration theory perspective. J. Environ. Psychol. **29**(1), 160–167 (2009)

25. Yin, J., et al.: Physiological and cognitive performance of exposure to biophilic indoor environment. Build. Environ. **132**, 255–262 (2018)
26. Robertson, I.H., et al.: Oops!': performance correlates of everyday attentional failures in traumatic brain injured and normal subjects. Neuropsychologia **35**(6), 747–758 (1997)
27. Hartig, T., Kaiser, F.G., Bowler, P.A.: Further development of a measure of perceived environmental restorativeness. Institutet för bostads-och urbanforskning (1997)
28. Manly, T., et al.: Not enough time or not enough attention? Speed, error and self-maintained control in the sustained attention to response test (SART). Clin. Neuropsychol. Assess. **3**(10), 1–12 (2000)
29. Kaplan, R., Kaplan, S.: The Experience of Nature: A Psychological Perspective. Cambridge University Press (1989)

# LimberUI: A Model-Based Design Tool for 3D UI Layouts Accommodating Uncertainty in Context of Use and User Attributes

Jamie W. Lee[1] and Kwang Lee[2]($\boxtimes$)

[1] United States Navy, Arlington, USA
[2] Computer Science, Slippery Rock University of Pennsylvania, Slippery Rock PA16057, USA
kwang.lee@sru.edu

**Abstract.** The designing of inclusive and immersive user interfaces (UIs) for virtual and augmented reality (VR, AR) systems is critical for providing a comfortable and efficient experience for all users and remains a challenge for the Human-Computer Interaction (HCI) community. This task is challenged by two key factors typically unknown at design time: 1) the context of use; and 2) the capabilities and attributes of the user. In this paper, we first use techniques from design engineering to systematically investigate the design parameters that dominate user performance and comfort when interacting with UI layouts. Second, we introduce *LimberUI*: a novel model-based 3D UI layout design toolkit that can create layouts that accommodate the context of deployment as well as the unique perceptual, cognitive, and physical capabilities of the user.

**Keywords:** Human-computer interaction · user interfaces · virtual and augmented reality · visualization techniques · and evaluation methods

## 1 Introduction

The designing of inclusive and immersive user interfaces for virtual and augmented reality (VR, AR) systems remains a challenge for the Human-Computer Interaction (HCI) community. Designing user interfaces (UI) for applications in head-mounted Augmented Reality (AR) exposes new challenges not encountered in conventional UI design for mobiles or computers. First, users in head-mounted AR are increasingly expected to perform arm, hand, and finger movements to interact with interface elements in mid-air. The way in which a UI is laid out thus has a significant impact on the ergonomic experience, general comfort, and speed of interaction for the user. Second, interface elements presented in head-mounted AR appear overlaid on the real background environment. This background context thereby has a potential influence on the legibility and general appearance of interface elements.

The first of the two challenges introduced above can potentially be addressed at design time by deriving a layout based on established performance and ergonomic models for mid-air selection. These ergonomic models, however, typically require initial assumptions about the average user and may deliver layouts that are unsuitable for a

J. Y. C. Chen and G. Fragomeni (Eds.): HCII 2024, LNCS 14707, pp. 29–40, 2024.
https://doi.org/10.1007/978-3-031-61044-8_3

user with outlying physiology (e.g. a person with short arms) or capability (e.g. a user with reaching difficulties due to a disability). The second challenge arguably demands an adaptive solution that updates the interface layout at runtime depending on the context of use. Addressing these two challenges in concert requires a unified process for capturing the general design goals of the designer and allowing these to inform UI layout generation conditioned on the background context and specific physiology and capabilities of the user. To this end we present *LimberUI*: a design tool for 3D UI layouts that accommodates uncertainty in context of use and user attributes.

LimberUI is designed to mitigate designer bias and facilitate the design, creation, and exploration of inclusively immersive 3D UI layouts. Specifically, our tool is flexible, or limber, to the various perceptual, cognitive, and physical capabilities of the user. LimberUI exploits a model-based approach to parameterize the various perceptual, cognitive, and physical factors which affect user performance and comfort when interacting with 3D UI layouts. The tool allows the designer to continuously choose and adjust the weights of these functions, which are then used in multi-objective weighted optimization to search for an optimal UI layout. This conceptual architecture, and its realization as LimberUI, represents the main novel contribution of this paper. We demonstrate LimberUI applied to the task of designing 3D user interfaces in Unity for the Microsoft HoloLens 2.

## 2 Related Work

Given the difficulty in extracting data in-situ from actual users or generating realistic data from proxy users, model-based approaches have been widely used in engineering to design systems, especially those that are complex and costly to validate. Unlike heuristic methods, this approach uses design knowledge in the form of user simulations, models, and/or heuristics as an objective function to model how users interact with and perceive such layouts. Todi et al. [16] adapts this method to develop Sketchplore, an interactive layout sketching tool with a real-time layout optimizer to generate usable and aesthetic layouts for conventional 2D interfaces. Their design tool uses predictive models to address the aesthetic and sensorimotor performance measures of generated layouts, such as visual clutter and search, grid quality, color harmony, and target acquisition, to define a multi-objective function. Multi-threaded optimization is then used to explore and exploit the design space.

Despite increased interest in the HCI community, the creation of inclusive VR/AR interfaces remains a challenge. As with many conventional consumer devices, such as computers and mobile phones, these systems are often designed with certain assumptions about the users' abilities. Despite ongoing research in accessible computing, many UIs designed for VR/AR systems fail to provide similar experiences for individuals with disabilities and/or centralize on the notion of disability, rather than ability. However, the abilities of a user can span across a vast spectrum and even fluctuate given the circumstance or environment they are in. Furthermore, anyone may face a reduction in abilities, even those who may not normally be considered disabled; for example, alcohol impairs the ability to drive and operate equipment, but only during the period of time the individual is in a state of drunkenness. Therefore, assumptions made about a user's (dis)abilities may make it more challenging to design more inclusive applications.

Therefore, to promote inclusive design, it is desirable to focus on *ability-based design* [19]. Systems developed through ability-based design may try to adapt and tailor themselves to the needs and preferences of a specific user or user group. For example, SUPPLE [7] is an ability-based system which generates different renditions in response to different user usage patterns. The system automatically constructs UIs using an optimization process that searches the design space for an interface that minimizes the users' movement time. Through this approach, SUPPLE generates UIs customized to a users' abilities which enables more efficient and accessible mouse interactions.

Numerous studies have been conducted to identify factors which make VR/AR systems more accessible to users of various capabilities. Interviews and quantitative studies are often employed in the understanding of user needs and behaviors when using interactive technologies. Blandford [2] addresses the principles for designing, conducting, and reporting on qualitative studies for the purpose of understanding current needs and practices and evaluating the effects of new technologies in practice. We see these principles reflected in many fields across HCI; for example, Dias et al. [4] interviewed patients with Parkinson's Disease (PD), physicians, and software/game developers to identify the most significant game-design factors in designing assistive serious games for PD patients. Furthermore, Mott et al. [14] conducted a semi-structured interview study with participants with mobility limitations regarding VR application usage, which reflected the need to consider the abilities of such users in the design process for VR systems.

## 3 Conceptual Architectures of LimberUI

LimberUI supports the design of user interfaces that can adapt to particular user needs and context of use. This adaptation capability is driven by four key components: (1) designer assigned constraints; (2) capture of user and contextual attributes; (3) predictive models of design objectives; and (4) optimization of design parameters. In this section, we briefly describe how these components relate to each other before examining each component in more detail.

There are certain aspects of the desired UI that are unalterable and constant across different settings of use, such as the number of UI elements and their required sizing—the designer must *assign* these constraints. Other aspects informing the layout adaption must be *captured* from the user and context of use, for example, the user's reachable space, current cognitive load, or the physical real background upon which the UI must be overlaid. In practice, these attributes may be inferred (e.g. inference of reachable space based on tracked motions), manually calibrated (e.g. the user specifies their reach limits), or directly captured (e.g. HMD camera captures images of the background context in real time). These constraints and attributes are fed to the *predictive models* which reflect the design objectives relevant to the performance and ergonomic comfort of the UI layout. Finally, the outputs of these predictive models must be unified in some way through an optimization process which determines the most suitable design parameters for the UI.

### 3.1 Designer Assigned Constraints

The designer specifies basic attributes about the UI that must be maintained. These attributes may be as simple as the number of elements and their size. Fuzzy constraints, such as the maximum or minimum sizing or spread of elements, may also be relevant, thereby constraining the design space.

## 3.2 Capture of User and Contextual Attributes

The UI adaption process proceeds with respect to uncontrollable aspects of the human-UI coupled system. These uncontrollable aspects are what we refer to as user and contextual attributes. User attributes relevant to mid-air UI adaptation may include the user's physiology, their motor control capability and their current cognitive load. Contextual attributes may include the current background scene and nearby free space available for UI objects and their placement. As described above, these various attributes may be inferred, calibrated, or directly captured depending on their 'visibility' to the system (Fig. 1).

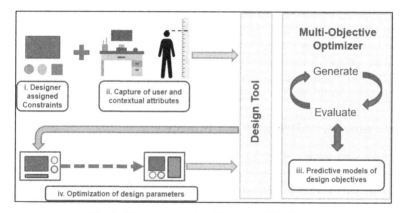

**Fig. 1.** The conceptual architecture of LimberUI

## 3.3 Predictive Models of Design Objectives

LimberUI seeks to incorporate a rich set of predictive models of design objectives to robustly adapt the UI to particular user needs and contexts of use. Conceptually, this set of predictive models can be extended to capture more and varied design aspects that are relevant to mid-air UI design. Below we describe the predictive models we have incorporated in the current implementation of LimberUI and how these are used to quantify the cost of various design objectives.

**Physical Ergonomics.** We adopt the approach used by Tolani et al. [17] to model the arm as a two-segment chain, in which the forearm and wrist constitute a single segment. While this method limits the number of possible arms poses available, it simplifies the complexity of inverse kinematic computations required to compute the ergonomic cost of each arm position. After computing the arm poses, we heuristically determine the ergonomic cost of regions in 3D space in terms of Consumed Endurance (CE) [10], muscle activation [1], and RULA [13].

**Target Acquisition Performance.** Fitts' law provides a predictive model for the time taken by a user to select (e.g. touch) an object given its size and displacement. By definition, Fitts' law models the performance of humans. However, human performance is dependent on human traits and factors such as age, visual health, previous exposure to certain technologies, cognitive abilities, and so forth [18]. Thus, factors such as tiredness, concentration, and cognitive load may have an effect on user performance. In the current implementation of LimberUI, however, we utilize a simple Fitts' law model to quantify the movement time given the size and displacement of interface elements.

**Text Legibility.** Prior work [5] has shown that users generally favor backgrounds of low variation in color and with minimal clutter when placing text labels in AR. These qualities are encoded in the system using established metrics such as colorfulness [9] and edgeness [15]. The background context is captured as described in Sect. 3.2 and these two metrics can be computed over the image.

**Coloration and Color Harmony.** The aesthetic appearance of the UI layout can also be informed by established models of appealing color combinations. We integrate harmonic color schemes developed by Matsuda [12] in the form of harmonic templates as described by Cohen-Or et al. [3]. We choose to use the V-type template, which consists of a sector of 26% of an HSV color wheel (or 93.6° of a 360-degree wheel). Colors in this 'wedge' consist of shades which are of the same or similar color. Colors are chosen for each element in the UI layout such that each color falls within this template.

### 3.4 Optimization of Design Parameters

The cost determined by the predictive models of the various design objectives must be aggregated in some way to derive a final *ideal* layout given the designer constraints and captured user and contextual attributes. Various approaches may be leveraged for this purpose. In the current implementation of LimberUI, we utilize an a priori articulation of designer weights which allows the optimization procedure to determine a single solution reflecting these implied preferences. Specifically, we take a weighted sum optimization approach [11] and minimize a weighted combination of the outputs of the different predictive models:

$$U \sum_{i=1}^{k} w_i F_i(\mathbf{x}) \tag{1}$$

where $w_i$ is the scalar weight for each objective function, and $F_i(\mathbf{x})$ is the cost of each function. Because all of the weights must be positive, minimizing the function for $U$ provides a sufficient condition for Pareto optimality, which means the minimum of this function is always Pareto optimal [8, 20]. We utilize the weighted sum method in the current implementation due to its simplicity.

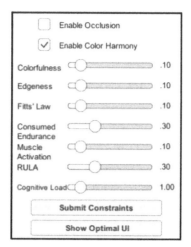

**Fig. 2.** LimberUI's objective function menu

## 4   Demonstrative Implementation of LimberUI

LimberUI was developed to target 3D UI layout design for the Microsoft HoloLens 2, an optical see-through HMD. We leveraged the method used by Belo et al. [6] and discretized the 3D interaction space into voxels: equal sized 3D cubes. These voxels are used to determine the optimal placement of UI elements in terms of physical ergonomics, text legibility and color harmony, as described in the previous section.

Three important simplifications are present in the current implementation of LimberUI to reduce computation and complexity: (1) we assume that the only interaction the user makes within the UI involve pressing interface elements with their finger (a touch-press); (2) we assume that the users' environment is static; and (3) we assume that the user is in a static position. We make these assumptions to demonstrate the potential of LimberUI but the underlying architecture can be extended to support fully dynamic adaptation of UI layouts in real time.

We evaluate the various design objectives for each voxel in the interaction space. The Fitts' law model is based on a dataset collected by one of the authors performing repeated reciprocal mid-air target selections. In practice, this model would be based on an aggregated sample of representative users or the most appropriate model for the current user could be pulled from this dataset.

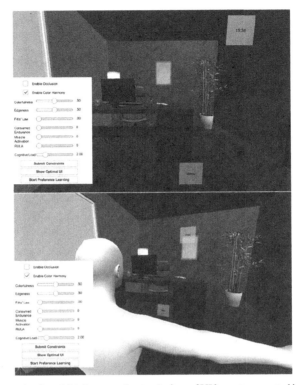

**Fig. 3.** First person (top) and third person (bottom) view of UI layout generated in Design Scenario 1.

### 4.1 LimberUI Workflow in Unity

In this section, we describe our envisioned designer workflow. The designer begins by adjusting the weights of the objective functions based on the factors which will be most impactful for the target user group. LimberUI allows the designer to specify the weights $w_i$ for each model using a slider scaled from 0 to 1. Using these weights, LimberUI iterates through each voxel in the interaction space to determine its overall cost $U$. The ergonomic costs (for consumed endurance, muscle reserve, and RULA models) are based on the ergonomics of the arm pose required to reach a particular voxel. For the colorfulness and edgeness models, the voxel positions (which are in world coordinates) are transformed using the camera intrinsics into pixel coordinates in order to find the patch in the 2D environment image corresponding to each voxel. Once $U$ has been computed for each voxel, LimberUI then chooses the voxel $v$ with the lowest $U$, $v_{min}$, and places the interface elements in the location of $v_{min}$. This process is repeated for each interface element in the UI layout until the layout has been completely optimized.

Once the UI is generated, the designer may further fine-tune the weights to continually adjust the UI layout. Once complete, the designer can record the optimal locations and colors of the UI panels and the weights. Figure 2 shows the LimberUI menu with

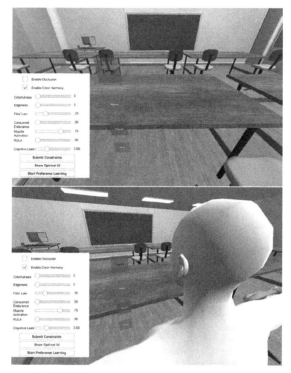

**Fig. 4.** First person (top) and third person (bottom) view of UI layout generated in Design Scenario 2.

sliders to adjust the weights of each design objective. The LimberUI inspector interface allows the designer to assign constraints for each interface element in the UI.

Due to the difficulty in quantifying the cognitive load of the user at a given instance, we enable the designer to manually specify the cognitive level through a slider widget in the Unity editor. Through manipulation of the cognitive level slider, the UI toolkit enables the designer to specify the level of detail and information displayed in interface elements in the context of potential environments the user may be in while interacting with such UIs.

## 5 Demonstration of LimberUI

In this section we demonstrate the application of LimberUI in three illustrative design scenarios. The three design scenarios are chosen to cover a range of design goals in terms of the intended purpose of the UI layout, different contexts of use, as well as different priorities attached to the various design objectives.

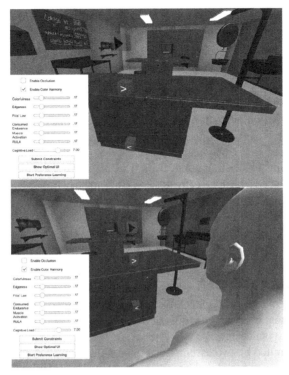

**Fig. 5.** First person (top) and third person (bottom) view of UI layout generated in Design Scenario 3.

### 5.1 Design Scenario 1: Basic Home Interface

The first hypothetical design scenario is the design of a basic AR home interface presenting simply a button to access the menu and a clock showing current time. Given the purpose of this UI, the designer is chiefly concerned with visibility given background context and assigns equal weights to the colorfulness and edgeness design objectives. The remaining weights are left at zero. The generated layout given the simulated background context is shown in Fig. 3. We can observe that LimberUI has placed the UI buttons over regions with low colorfulness and edgeness to promote legibility.

### 5.2 Design Scenario 2: Quick Launch Menu

The second hypothetical design scenario involves determining an appropriate UI layout for a quick launch menu with the goal of balancing comfort and efficiency. Four constraints are assigned by the designer in the form of the four elements of the quick launch menu. These are a button each for games, photos, maps, and news. In balancing comfort and efficiency, the designer sets a weight of 0.75 for the muscle activation model and 0.25 for the Fitts' law predictive model. The generated layout given these weights and the context is shown in Fig. 4. LimberUI has arranged the layout to be relatively low in the interaction space to reduce the amount of muscle activation required. At the same time, the interface elements are kept relatively close together to promote efficiency when selecting subsequent buttons.

### 5.3  Design Scenario 3: Task Sequence Interface

In this final design scenario, the designer's goal is to produce a UI that reflects a balance across all design objectives. The hypothetical interface under design is that of a basic navigation interface for moving through contextual instructions presented in AR related to an assembly task. The constraints specified the designer are the buttons required and their size: three buttons for play/pause, go to previous, and go to next. The designer assigns equal weights to all design objectives. The generated layout is shown in Fig. 5. LimberUI has produced a layout that avoids colorful and busy background regions while ensuring elements are centrally located.

### 5.4  Discussions, Limitations, and Future Work

While previous studies have commonly explored parameters related to physical ergonomics, visual aesthetics, or cognitive capabilities, this paper is the first to consolidate these relevant design aspects into a holistic architecture for supporting designers in producing adaptive mid-air UI layouts. We have demonstrated a model-based approach for converting these parameters into quantitative objective functions and determining a single final *ideal* layout design.

LimberUI is limited by two assumptions. First, it assumes that the only interaction type between the user and the UI elements is a touch-press. Realistically, UIs designed for VR or AR devices allow for a variety of interactions such as via dragging, pointing or gaze. Supporting such actions is a promising area to explore further. Second, LimberUI assumes that the users' body is static and the calculations for CE, muscle activation, and RULA only consider static arm poses. Supporting dynamic body movement is another fruitful avenue for future work.

In the future, LimberUI will be extended to support the creation of UI layouts that are truly adaptive given dynamic user attributes and contexts of use. For example, the user may move to another location or be in a setting where objects and/or other people in their environment are moving. Utilization of real-time visual and spatial information from the users' environment will allow the layouts to continually adjust to changes in scenery, objects, or locations.

## 6  Conclusions

LimberUI facilitates the design of mid-air UI layouts for deployment in AR. Rather than taking a universal design approach, which aims to develop systems for general use with a 'one size fits all' mentality, we have developed LimberUI based on the concept of ability-based design [19]. Using this design approach we address two of the major challenges encountered in AR user interface design: (1) the complex consequences of embodied interaction on ergonomic comfort and efficiency; and (2) the lack of information available to the designer about the context of use of their applications. LimberUI thus provides an effective tool for managing the high levels of uncertainty encountered in AR application development.

In the future, LimberUI will be extended to support the creation of UI layouts that are truly adaptive given dynamic user attributes and contexts of use. For example, the user may move to another location or be in a setting where objects and/or other people in their environment are moving. Utilization of real-time visual and spatial information from the users' environment will allow the layouts to continually adjust to changes in scenery, objects, or locations.

## References

1. Bachynskyi, M., Palmas, G., Oulasvirta, A., Weinkauf, T.: Informing the design of novel input methods with muscle coactivation clustering. ACM Trans. Comput.-Hum. Interact. **21**(6) (2015). https://doi.org/10.1145/2687921
2. Blandford, A.: Semi-structured qualitative studies (2013)
3. Cohen-Or, D., Sorkine, O., Gal, R., Leyvand, T., Xu, Y.-Q.: Color harmonization. ACM Trans. Graph. **25**(3), 624–630 (2006). https://doi.org/10.1145/1141911.1141933
4. Dias, S., et al.: Assistive HCI-serious games co-design insights: the case study of i-prognosis personalized game suite for Parkinson's disease. Front. Psychol. **11**, 612835 (2020)
5. Dudley, J.J., Jacques, J.T., Kristensson, P.O.: Crowdsourcing Design Guidance for Contextual Adaptation of Text Content in Augmented Reality. Association for Computing Machinery, New York (2021)
6. Evangelista Belo, J.A.M., Feit, A.M., Feuchtner, T., Grønbæk, K.: XRgonomics: Facilitating the Creation of Ergonomic 3D Interfaces. Association for Computing Machinery, New York (2021)
7. Gajos, K.Z., Weld, D.S., Wobbrock, J.O.: Automatically generating personalized user interfaces with supple. Artif. Intell. **174**(12), 910–950 (2010). https://doi.org/10.1016/j.artint.2010.05.005
8. Goicoechea, A., Hansen, D., Duckstein, L.: Multiobjective Decision Analysis with Engineering and Business Application. Wiley, New York (1982)
9. Hasler, D., Suesstrunk, S.: Measuring colourfulness in natural images. In: Proceedings of SPIE - The International Society for Optical Engineering, vol. 5007, pp. 87–95 (2003). https://doi.org/10.1117/12.477378
10. Hincapié-Ramos, J.D., Guo, X., Moghadasian, P., Irani, P.: Consumed endurance: a metric to quantify arm fatigue of mid-air interactions. In: Proceedings of the SIGCHI Conference on Human Factors in Computing Systems, CHI 2014, New York, NY, USA, pp. 1063–1072. Association for Computing Machinery (2014). https://doi.org/10.1145/2556288.2557130
11. Marler, R., Arora, J.: The weighted sum method for multi-objective optimization: new insights. Struct. Multidiscip. Optim. **41**, 853–862 (2010)
12. Matsuda, Y.: Color Design. Asakura Shoten (1995)
13. McAtamney, L., Nigel Corlett, E.: Rula: a survey method for the investigation of work-related upper limb disorders. Appl. Ergon. **24**(2), 91–99 (1993). https://doi.org/10.1016/0003-6870(93)90080-S
14. Mott, M., Tang, J., Kane, S., Cutrell, E., Morris, M.R.: "I just went into it assuming that I wouldn't be able to have the full experience": understanding the accessibility of virtual reality for people with limited mobility. In: ASSETS 2020. ACM (2020)
15. Stockman, G., Shapiro, L.G.: Computer Vision, 1st edn. Prentice Hall PTR, USA (2001)
16. Todi, K., Weir, D., Oulasvirta, A.: Sketchplore: sketch and explore with a layout optimizer, pp. 543–555 (2016). https://doi.org/10.1145/2901790.2901817
17. Tolani, D., Badler, N.: Real-time inverse kinematics of the human arm. Presence Cambridge, Mass. **5**, 393–401 (1996). https://doi.org/10.1162/pres.1996.5.4.393

18. Triantafyllidis, E., Li, Z.: The challenges in modeling human performance in 3D space with fitts' law. CoRR, abs/2101.00260 (2021)
19. Wobbrock, J.O., Kane, S.K., Gajos, K.Z., Harada, S., Froehlich, J.: Ability-based design: Concept, principles and examples. ACM Trans. Access. Comput. 3(3) (2011). https://doi.org/10.1145/1952383.1952384
20. Zadeh, L.: Optimality and non-scalar-valued performance criteria. IEEE Trans. Autom. Control 8, 59–60 (1963)

# XR Smart Environments Design and Fruition: Personalizing Shared Spaces

Meng Li[1]([✉]) [iD], Flora Gaetani[2] [iD], Lorenzo Ceccon[3] [iD], Federica Caruso[2] [iD], Yu Zhang[1] [iD], Armagan Albayrak[4] [iD], and Daan van Eijk[4] [iD]

[1] School of Mechanical Engineering, Xi'an Jiaotong University, Xianning Road 28, Xi'an 710049, People's Republic of China
limeng.81@xjtu.edu.cn
[2] Design Department, Politecnico Di Milano, Via Durando, 10, -20158 Milan, Italy
[3] Department of Architecture and Urban Studies (DAStU), Politecnico Di Milano, Via Bonardi, 9, -20133 Milan, Italy
[4] Faculty of Industrial Design Engineering, Delft University of Technology, Leeghwaterstraat 15, 2628CE Delft, The Netherlands

**Abstract.** The rise of urbanization, overpopulation, and resource depletion in recent years has triggered interest in developing more efficient solutions that could offer sustainable development and improve the quality of life in cities. The increasingly wider and more advanced availability of computational power throughout the anthropic space—which saw the emergence of the so-called "ubiquitous computing" paradigm—has opened new possibilities for the design of smart cities. In particular, the emergence of Extended Reality technologies (XR), such as Virtual Reality and Augmented Reality, has provided a new interface to bridge the gap between the physical and digital realms, enabling immersive experiences and interactions within Smart City environments. This paper, based on three case studies at different scales of smart environments, explores the current and prospected relevance of XR to both design and experience spaces enriched and characterized by layers of digital information and sensorial interactions.

**Keywords:** Ubiquitous Computing · Smart City · Smart vehicle · User Experience · Extended Reality

## 1 Introduction

The increasing individual use of connected smart devices, the rapid growth of the worldwide urban population, the gradual ageing of society in many countries, and the rising demand for sustainable energy resources have encouraged the research about Smart Cities and smart spaces [1]. However, even though the Smart City concept is an advanced solution for recent cities, the practical opportunity for smart cities is still to be revealed due to the different development of technology in various cities. Extended Reality (XR) has the potential to replicate or simulate the experience of smart cities and product-service systems [2], thus also helping future Smart City planning. This paper explores how XR technologies can support smart space design and fruition by providing three case studies.

J. Y. C. Chen and G. Fragomeni (Eds.): HCII 2024, LNCS 14707, pp. 41–59, 2024.
https://doi.org/10.1007/978-3-031-61044-8_4

## 2  Background Frameworks

### 2.1  Extended Reality

*Extended Reality.* (XR) is a term that encompasses several technologies, including Virtual Reality (VR), Augmented Reality (AR), and Mixed Reality (MR). To define XR, one must first understand what Milgram et al. [3] call the Reality-Virtuality Continuum to facilitate a better understanding of AR, MR, and VR and how these concepts are interconnected.

The continuum has two extremes: the fully real world and the fully virtual environment, i.e., Virtual Reality (VR). Everything in between, excluding the extremes, is defined as Mixed Reality (MR) [4]. Different types of MR can be defined differently depending on the degree of immersion and the mix between the virtual and real environments. In this fluid category, we can find technologies defined as Augmented Reality (AR, a mostly real environment augmented with some virtual parts), Augmented Virtuality (AV, a fully or partially immersive virtual environment to which a certain amount of reality is added), Mediated Reality [5] (XY-R, which refers to a technology that transforms reality for a specific purpose, for example, allowing color-blind people having a more accurate view of the environment) or Diminished Reality [6] (DR, which refers to the removal diminishing of real-world physical objects from users' perception). Thus, this definition shows that VR is not part of MR, and AR is only a subset of MR.

In the most recent publications, XR is defined as the combination of VR and all technologies referring to MR.

### 2.2  IoT, Ubiquitous Computing, and Smart City Design and Fruition

Internet of Things (IoT) is the concept of connecting everyday objects to the internet and enabling them to communicate and interact with one another, which is in turn powered by real-time digital connectivity (Ubiquitous Computing, a.k.a. UbiComp) and increasing bandwidths and lesser latency. IoT has opened new opportunities to tackle the challenges and trade-offs that rapid urbanization and anthropization have been causing to the global environment.

One significant area where the application of XR can have a profound impact is the design and development of smart cities. The concept of Smart City is to develop, deploy, and promote sustainable development practices to address growing urbanization challenges via an intelligent city information system. Some key areas related to the development and fruition of smart cities are urban intelligent Cyber-Physical Systems (CPS), intelligent vehicles, as well as user experience.

Challenges and prospected issues - from ethical to legal to technical - are numerous, but it is worth devising a conceptual approach to help steer such technologies in directions that align with global goals such as sustainability, efficiency, and inclusivity [7, 8].

### 2.3  XR Integration

While some challenges and trade-offs shall be solved and addressed by a combination of various technologies which are not the focus of this paper, the well-thought use of

XR as the interface between humans - including urban planners and designers, as well as the public within the urban spaces at large - and the data-enriched space of CPSs can allow for more efficient use of resources, achieving more personalized spatial fruition while using fewer resources, thus making it possible to share spaces among different users, yet providing a more tailor-made and attuned experience to all.

A well-designed XR experience, powered by a real-time data flow and on-the-fly AI data analytics tools, could indeed exploit the multimodal capabilities to channel the multidimensionality of data collected from the smart environments and from other data sources, as well as their interpretation by AI, in the most personalized and hence effective way to every user. As a significant example thereof, the learning environments [9], where the impact of XR technologies on spatial perception and cognition cannot be underestimated: in this context, the unique learning abilities of each student can be considered, bridging the notions and the personal cognition [10–12].

The Human-in-the-Loop (HitL) paradigm [13], a recent approach to AI whereby the user is not a passive recipient of the technology but an active participant in the AI workflow and in the decision-making processes which might stem therefrom, aligns well with the immersive design of smart cities using XR. Based on HitL processes, an increasingly efficient, tailor-made, and user-centric smart city design can be achieved by integrating XR technology.

## 3   Case Studies

The case studies will introduce the applications of XR in planning smart cities. They include three fields of smart city design, such as urban planning, intelligent vehicles, and user experience.

### 3.1   XR for Urban Planning and Public Space Fruition

Within the framework of BASE5G—Broadband InterfAces and services for Smart Environments enabled by 5G technologies research project, proposed by a consortium of public and private actors, including various departments at Politecnico di Milano and nation-wide industrial partners, such as Vodafone, a test bed was set up to evaluate the use of XR in the urban public space, along with many other converging and enabling technologies, as a foundational technology for "smart environments" [14]. These environments encompass diverse areas such as urban spaces, campuses, and learning environments, but also private or shared enclosed spaces, as we will see in the next case study.

More specifically, within Work Package 2 – Smart City, Smart Campus – we tested a workflow centered on the urban area of the campus Leonardo of Politecnico di Milano, in Milan, Italy, to evaluate the effectiveness of XR in supporting urban planning and design decisions, but also to better grasp the potential of such technologies for the fruition of public space by users, given designing a more inclusive, yet more personalized and engaging spatial experience [15].

The main underlying idea about the XR experience we wanted to enable to both urban planning professionals, including policymakers, designers, and academics, as well as the public, was to allow for a varying degree of immersion, from basic augmented reality experiences using mobile devices to fully immersive virtual reality experiences using head-mounted displays, but also device-less experience which could nonetheless become personalized for the single user. In other words, the underlying idea was the creation of a sort of "plug-in" toolbox allowing a nuanced use of XR technology, with a varying degree of interaction depending on the specific user devices and needs.

The project involved the creation of a virtual model of the campus, starting from a collection of different sources, ranging from the BIM models of the new campus buildings designed by ODB architects, based on an idea by Renzo Piano, to 3D models, GIS, and drone photogrammetry survey data (Figs. 1 and 2).

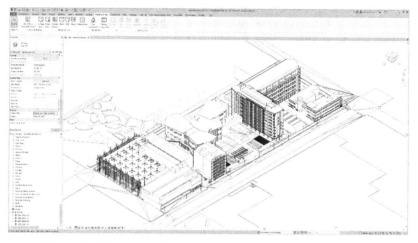

**Fig. 1.** The BIM model of Campus Leonardo of Politecnico di Milano.

The model had to be thought because of its fruition by a series of different software packages and devices, hence it was adapted for the potential "weak link" of the chain, i.e., low-end mobile devices, yet maintaining some of the informational dimensions from the BIM models and the survey. Spatial subdivisions - classes, corridors, courtyards - as well as other "semantic" elements were included so that meta-geometrical features could be used by the system to help interpret the contingent spatial context (Fig. 3).

This substrate of information would allow, for instance, the selective isolation of specific classes of elements in the model, or be used to calculate parameters of spatial fruition such as room crowdedness.

The main tool adopted for this aim was McNeel Rhinoceros 3D modeling package, enhanced by the Visual Programming Language (VPL) Grasshopper for Rhino, in turn with some relevant plugins installed, including Rhino-Inside-Revit for seamless integration of BIM geometries inside the NURBS modeler, as well as Fologram for Grasshopper, a package which enables the real-time sharing of a model across devices, including HoloLens visors and simple smartphones, and to even modify the model geometries and appearance according to the user gestures.

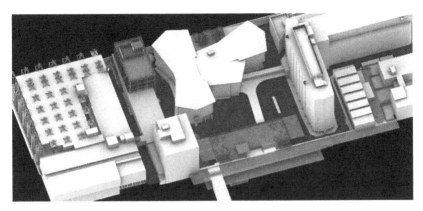

**Fig. 2.** The BREPS model of Campus Leonardo of Politecnico di Milano.

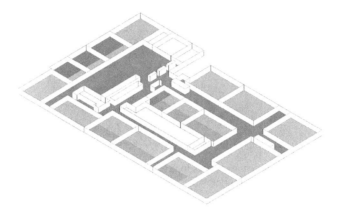

**Fig. 3.** The semantic subdivision of interior spaces – Campus Leonardo.

Moreover, the game engine "Unreal Engine" was also utilized for more realistic, immersive, and interactive visualization of the virtual campus model. One of the useful features of this platform was its ability to react to real-time inputs and even to simulate some "natural" behaviors through the embedded VPL "Blueprint", as well as through the inbuilt AI-powered behavior trees (Fig. 4).

Given the foreseen flow of real-time information – which would enrich the model of real-world data, as well as interact with the XR world based on the system responses – a series of actuators were also successfully installed along with the sensors (cameras), to test the feasibility of incorporating physical changes in the virtual campus model, and the I/O data flow.

A series of experiences by the research team, involving also students and contingent users, has successfully proven that an "asymmetrical" and multimodal XR experience can be set up to allow the real-time fruition by different audiences and determine a varying degree of engagement (and invasiveness), hence potentially providing a tailor-made

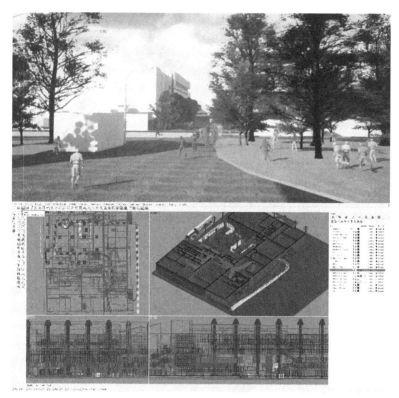

**Fig. 4.** The simulation of user's movements in space, both in the gaming engine and in BREPS modeler – Campus Leonardo.

experience for any user and user type, possibly avoiding a one-size-fits-all approach, with its ethical and personal implications.

Based on such flexible models and model fruition platforms, it was possible to achieve two main goals. On the one hand, we could share a simulated environment in real-time among teachers, researchers, and students, allowing them to collaborate and explore the virtual campus together – even at a distance – and even to conduct virtual experiments and simulations related to the public space, its design, and fruition, yielding different user experiences based on the tools available to each user (smartphone, in-ear wireless headphones, etc.). On the other hand, it was possible to simulate user behaviors, potentially adjusting the simulation based on real-time data, along the paradigm of the Digital Twin.

The data gathered from the simulated environment could then be analyzed and used to improve the design and functionality of the smart city, as well as the data acquired from the real users within the environment – as captured and analyzed by a series of cameras and AI-powered tools – could indeed enrich the model of real-time information and work as a feedback loop to continuously refine and enhance the virtual campus model [16–18].

The final aim of the research was also to demonstrate that—provided we create a flexible XR experience, based on a plug-in set of toolboxes each user may opt in for, and not limited to the use of immersive devices such as the HoloLens visors—a more nuanced and casual XR interaction is possible, which is both more customized and more inclusive. It appeared evident that the underlying mechanics of immersive design in smart city development can be significantly enhanced through the application of XR technology. It serves both as a means of visualization and interaction on the side of the planners and policy-makers and on the side of the users of the public space, which may opt for a personalized experience through the integration of XR technology (Fig. 5), along a new paradigm which in the project has been named "Smart Bubble".

**Fig. 5.** The simulation of XR-based adaptive space – Campus Leonardo.

In such spatial experience, based on Cyber-Physical Systems (CPS) and Ubiquitous Computing (UbiComp), XR is somewhat inherent to the idea of space itself, a space where the physical and the virtual merge and blend, creating a seamless and immersive environment for users to interact with, and navigate through, the smart city [19]. Very importantly, in the following approach, the layer of information and sensorial interaction characterizing the XR experience is a variable one – the Smart Bubble – based on the contingent user needs, preferences, and available tools, so to avoid imposing a standard spatial fruition experience top-down, and rather providing users, including planners and designers, with a customized level of immersivity, interactivity and, therefore, inclusivity [20, 21].

### 3.2  XR for Smart Vehicle

Concerning the XR applied to smart vehicles, the case study presented in this research refers to a hyper-connected car with a special focus on the interior and the in-car experience. The case study was developed as part of the BASE5G multidisciplinary research, specifically in Work Package 3, which identified new urban mobility scenarios and applied some of these to an interactive prototype car and simulated driving experience. The design followed an iterative process of testing design proposals in a virtual environment to simulate and assess the effectiveness of the concept. The BASE5G vehicle's design suggests a hyper-connected and shared mobility system experimenting with a new concept.

The research process consisted of four main phases:

1. *Research Framing:* This first phase deals with analyzing the specific state of the art using desk research, which was fundamental for understanding the trends in the automotive sector, analyzing competitors' landscape, and discovering new user behavior and needs.
2. *Concept Development:* The second phase translated the research into project actions through co-design activities during several structured workshops involving technology providers and technical project partners (such as automotive experts) to redefine the project objectives and outline directions to implement a prototype.
3. *Prototyping:* To validate the concept proposed, a virtual simulation was implemented on the iDrive driving simulator (Fig. 6) of Politecnico di Milano by assessing the effectiveness of the overall in-car experience.
4. *Testing:* A between-subjects design was planned in which subjects were divided into two groups. The subjects were asked to follow instructions from a pre-recorded neutral voice and interact with the driving simulator. Time and errors were monitored during the test using eye-tracking data. In addition, after the test, participants were asked to complete two questionnaires (Raw NASA-TLX and AttrakDiff) [22].

The final output of the design process was the prototype of a vehicle implemented on a driving simulator that reproduces an autonomous driving experience and thus allows testing of the human-machine interaction.

The research considers the main drivers reshaping the future of the automotive industry, which can be summarized in four main trends: 1) electrification to reduce reliance on fossil fuels, 2) autonomous driving technology, 3) connectivity of vehicles to the online world, and 4) sharing mobility. In this scenario, smart vehicles are becoming part of a complex ecosystem to simplify the driver's life, increase road safety, improve efficiency, and minimize environmental impact. Thus, a smart car can be delineated as a broader concept of a vehicle that is not only electric and self-driving but also connected and able to communicate and exchange data with the surrounding infrastructure and the people using it [23]. In this smart car concept, it has been suggested that future mobility should be considered in both physical and virtual form, with the physical bridging the virtual and the virtual emphasizing the physical [24].

In the BASE5G car, the interior has been reconfigured assuming that automation will change the driver's role and, consequently, the interior. Thanks to the possibility of diverting attention from the driving scene, the driver becomes a "passenger" [25, 26], who can perform different actions. Therefore, the space of future smart cars is essentially a space beyond the driving experience itself [27]. In the BASE5G project, this translates into a new dashboard model emptied of the superfluous: the steering becomes retractable, not eliminating it but appearing automatically according to the level of driving automation (Fig. 7).

**Fig. 6.** The prototype simulator during a demonstration event of the BASE5G project.

As mentioned, the project assumes that integrating IoT platforms and 5G connectivity would transform cars from only being modes of mobility into true digital platforms [28]. Cars are increasingly digitalized and are blurring the limit between the physical and digital dimensions, affecting the in-car configuration and how the user interacts with the vehicle. Considering this, the car is part of an integrated communication and data exchange known as the "Vehicle-to-Everything" [29], which includes communication with both infrastructure and people's devices in addition to vehicle-to-vehicle data exchange [30]. The smart infrastructure provided by the smart city enables the car to exchange dynamic information. This lets the user connect to the decentralized and proactive data exchange to personalize the driving experience. Users can bring their data into the vehicle and facilitate integration with personal devices and cloud storage using their digital identities, making the vehicle's interior highly personalized. The data users share under the terms and privacy consents provided may include details about status, preferences, health issues, and more.

The in-car experience then changes based on the driver's profile and data, adjusting the compliance of the environment as needed. In this way, augmented reality also augments or diminishes the experience. In other words, the technology should be able to use data to create an in-car environment that is as comfortable as possible for the driver, adopting changes such as driving parameter settings, light settings, seat layout, and interface accessibility settings, as well as data and device synchronization.

Moreover, to lessen the cognitive burden on the user and ensure that only the relevant information is presented on the interface at the proper moment, the automobile is proactive and adjusts to varied driving scenarios.

The car thus becomes a "Smart Bubble", a personal and customized space for the user, which communicates with the external environment to enrich the in-car experience. The car can isolate the user from the outside environment and allow him to concentrate as if they were in a smart office (Fig. 8) or become a space interacting with the outside world, providing information about the surrounding environment in a smart

**Fig. 7.** The new dashboard model of the smart vehicle in which the steering becomes retractable during autonomous driving.

entertainment scenario (Fig. 9). In this second case, Augmented Reality is essential for the in-car experience, providing continuous (synchronized with the car's movement) and multimodal access to information (Fig. 10).

In the BASE5G car, the interface is projected directly onto the windscreen thanks to a full-screen Head-Up Display (HUD), with which one can interact through a gesture-based control system implemented by haptic feedback. In addition, visual outputs and haptic and auditory feedback have been integrated to allow the user to interact with the vehicle. On the windshield, the user can activate communication with the environment through HUD that provides various kinds of information, for example, historical information about the building, useful information about the places of interest they encounter, or even on-demand information on businesses that might be useful during the journey.

**Fig. 8.** AR User Interface showing AR in the smart office scenario.

**Fig. 9.** AR User Interface showing AR in the smart entertainment scenario.

According to the literature [27], the HUD can improve speed control and reduce drivers' reaction time to emergencies. During assisted driving, the HUD allows information to be shown close to the driver's field of view, thus reducing eye movements and making important warnings more effective. This allows the XR to be used in an integrated manner, communicating directly with the environment through a 3D representation of the vehicle projected onto the interface, enabling the user to proactively control the state of the car about the road and surrounding vehicles.

**Fig. 10.** AR User Interface showing AR in the smart driving scenario.

As in the case study above, in the approach followed during the Smart Vehicle project, the level of information and sensory interaction must be carefully dosed to be effective without being invasive. Inclusivity is, also in the project described, a fundamental value and, in the amount of data that can potentially be exchanged between the car and the external environment, completely feasible.

## 3.3  XR for User Experience

Regarding the XR applied to user experience, the case study demonstrated in this research refers to a design protocol that enables designers to develop concepts of products and services in the context of a smart city. The previous case studies show the advantages of first-person immersion to check concepts from spatial experience and interaction aspects [14, 20, 31]. To develop a new concept of a smart city, designers need to translate human needs into targeted design qualities and design problems, define relevant design elements, and explore possible solutions to ensure these qualities, then fulfill the needs [32].

The design process model indicates the mind flow of designers across design processes [33]. A well-acknowledged design process model is the Double-Diamond Model (DDM) which describes two circles of a divergent-convergent process [34]. Since designing is a "solution-driven" activity, the designer's thinking is composed of iterative loops where they are continuously learning to understand the user's experience via "defining", "prototyping" and "testing" activities [32, 35, 36]. In this case study, the focus is thus on the effects of immersion to support the designer's thinking among design processes in the context of smart city design.

Designers showed a divergent way of thinking about the approaches to integrating XR experiences throughout their design processes. This case study aims to analyze the thinking styles of designers under immersion and thus develops a protocol that simulates realistic design processes following the Immersive Cycle aligning with the DDM [37] (Fig. 11). The protocol was developed on an XR platform -Tvori. co[1], which supports immersive prototyping and animating scenarios by using the Google Poly library or importing external files, like videos, audio, or 3D models. An HTC VIVE headset (1080 x 1200 pixels per eye with 6 degrees of freedom) was used to support navigating in the immersive environment and uses hand controllers to interact with virtual objects. The immersive environment was synchronized to a 19-inch LED display in front of a researcher and a 50-inch screen for the other team members.

Four design teams with seven design professionals participated in the study, representing different types of designers including corporate designers, senior designers, junior designers, and part-time designers [2]. Each team has a designated session to replicate a true-to-life design process:

1. *Design task definition:* A specific design task was defined together with each team and the researchers asked what they wanted to explore in the immersive session.
2. *Protocol customization:* The protocol was customized to include texts, videos, or models that could be used for the abovementioned design task.
3. *Protocol setup:* The start point was set at the "User" dock in the Tvori protocol.

---

[1] https://tvori.co/tvori.

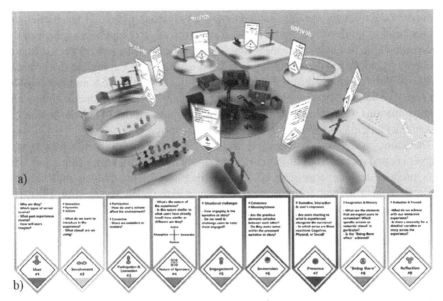

**Fig. 11.** The immersive design protocol is developed with the XR platform – Tvori. co. a) a bird's view of the immersive protocol that guides the sessions. b) the protocol is composed of nine phases.

Each immersive design session included four steps. 1) the researchers introduced the goal and the procedure of the session and then demonstrated how to move around and interact with the protocol. 2) One participant from each team put on the headset to try

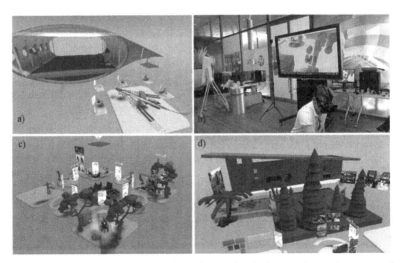

**Fig. 12.** The examples of the outcome of the immersive design sessions. a) conceptual safety training setup for crews; b) the configuration of a dialysis machine in hospitals; c) a conceptual scenario of a wheelchair for youths; c) a concept of a container house for a middle-aged couple.

out the protocol till he or she felt confident enough to interact with it. 3) The participant with the headset guided the team throughout the protocol to complete a concept of the design task within two hours. The team could decide whether to switch between different members to guide through the protocol. When a team couldn't complete the protocol in 140 min, the researcher asked the team to leave the design process and move to the final part. 4) The last part was a briefing where the team could give general comments, recommendations, or expectations on future XR design platforms. Then the researcher thanked the participants for their contribution to the study.

The teams created various concepts within 120 to 150 min (Fig. 12). The service designer created an airplane cabin to organize safety training for crews (Fig. 12a). The senior product designer team checked the configuration of the dialysis machine and reviewed reachability both from the patient's view and the nurse's view (Fig. 12b). The junior designer team built a 3D persona for youth and ideated an outdoor wheelchair in context (Fig. 12c). The part-time architect generated a container house for a middle-aged couple (Fig. 12d).

**Table 1.** The benefits and barriers of the XR design protocol

| Stages | Benefits | Barriers |
|---|---|---|
| *Discover* | + Prototyping is the key to discovering users' needs. Testing and observing (recording) are the key design activities<br>+ Creating personas in 3D is creative and fun, especially for young designers<br>+ Working with low polygon models is nice<br>+ The opportunity to share design proposals across mobile and PC | - Feel floating and nauseous<br>- Collaboration would be nice with two players<br>- Designers need to search for pictures inside the environment<br>- Teleport within the environment is difficult |
| Define | + The Environment has the function of being an experience<br>+ Designers could work in the real size<br>+ Posturing digital humans freely in the scene is useful and fun<br>+ By simulating realistic experience, it's a tool to observe users from different angles<br>+ Simulating scenes with people (like a crowd in a cabin)<br>+ Zoom in and out to check the layouts and scales | - Designers would be careful if they have real sizes<br>- Introducing eye-tracking could help to understand the designer's thinking processes<br>- Sketching is difficult<br>- Missing a whiteboard in the environment<br>- Similar functions with different controls in various XR platforms |
| *Develop* | + Opportunities for participatory design: people understand VR and concepts better if they create a bit of it themselves<br>+ Exploring the stories behind the use scenarios<br>+ The experience simulation can be both immersive or absorptive depending on use cases | - The difficult control of resizing objects<br>- Various challenges should be brought to the scene to build up the purposes and goals of XR applications<br>- An XR system should provide intuitive sketching while including different possibilities to explore user experience |
| *Deliver* | + Users feel better acceptance and ownership when designing together in XR<br>+ The opportunity to personalize user experience | - The heavy weight of the headset makes the neck discomfort<br>- Using a virtual camera is difficult |

Each team acknowledged the immersive session as engaging and creative. Learning basic interactions like navigation and object manipulation took 30 min to more than an hour, whereas junior designers took a shorter time to learn, and senior designers needed a longer duration to understand basic functions. The senior designers viewed the immersive protocol as a replacement for cardboard prototypes to explore different layouts and examine ergonomics; while junior designers appreciated creating personas with 3D polygons and showed interest in simulating interactions with animation. Both senior and junior designers naturally put digital humans in the scenes they created either to represent the human sizes or to indicate the target users. The benefits and barriers of this immersive design protocol are summarized in Table 1.

## 4 Discussion

This section deals with the commonalities among the foregoing case studies, both as regards the opportunities, and as to the envisaged limitations and criticalities of XR technologies.

The case studies, with their ample range of disciplines and applications, clearly show the inherent multidisciplinarity of XR technologies. Moreover, as highlighted mainly in the third case study, XR can be a back-bone technology throughout the design process, as well as in the subsequent phases, including the fruition by the final users.

Such a wide array of possible uses of XR is rooted in its key characteristic of working as a filter between the users and the environment, much like a pair of glasses that enhances or alters our perception [38]. In various types of environments, XR demonstrates the capability of merging the physical and digital layers of information and enhances sensorial interactions with spatial experiences [20]. XR bridges the physical and digital environments to create a seamless experience for the user and take advantage of both dimensions [24]. As shown in the "Smart Campus" case as well as in other space planning projects, XR can support design decisions and make the processes of both spatial design and spatial fruition more inclusive yet more personalized and engaging, along with the concept of "Smart Bubble" [15].

XR technologies span across a Reality-Virtuality Continuum [3], where its multimodal and multisensorial reach varies depending on the contingent technologies and user needs, as explained in the "Smart Bubble" concept in the smart case. Moreover, human understanding does not derive merely from impressions but from the interaction between the mind and the empirical world [39]. XR can naturally integrate proprioception within the spatial experience, making users' responses towards closure environments like cabins more intuitive and realistic [22, 31].

Drawing parallels from the notion of XR as a 'pair of glasses,' this technology can be considered an additional layer of 'sensibility'. It is an interactive framework that reshapes users' perception of the real world, providing a structured, novel, and augmented understanding of our surroundings [5, 6]. For example, in the user experience case, designers can check the overall layout from a bird-view and then review the details in the user's personas. XR technologies are becoming increasingly crucial in interacting with and understanding the digitalized environment. Soon, thanks to technological progress, XR will become more and more accessible and cross-sectoral, enabling physical and digital reality to be transformed for a specific purpose [5] where the user is not a passive beneficiary of technology but an active participant in the decision-making process [13].

## 5   Limitations and Future Work

These promising use case scenarios are nevertheless facing some issues and limitations. On the one hand, some major technological bottlenecks – such as still limited data bandwidth, as well as uneven multimodal and multisensorial capabilities of the available devices (typically, taste, smell, and touch are not yet well dealt with) – make the immersive experience still not on par with a more traditional experience in presence, as the (until now) failed promise of the Metaverse has clearly shown [40]. The possibility of overcoming spatial and sensorial barriers is still very limited, and the authors can only hypothesize that in the future the provided experience will be good enough to even "augment" the users' perceptions without limiting their sensorial experience. Once this is possible, in line with the presented case studies, the inclusivity of the experience could indeed be increased by connecting users in a network – even at a distance – where each user receives a customized "translation" of the shared environment.

On the other hand, the idea of a network based on the Ubiquitous Computing paradigm, where everything and everyone is present in a unified Cyber-Physical Space, raises some relevant ethical concerns. The impact on people's lives would arguably be quite different in case the adhesion to the network is on a truly voluntary basis or not. In a sense of data security, the choice between one/few central computing units or countless devices networked with no central computing and direction is critical. At the level of digital equality, whether the network and the data flow can be controlled and directed/blocked by any entity (including governments and corporations), as well as whether a legal mechanism is in place to guarantee transparency, accountability, and public scrutiny are of paramount importance.

## 6   Conclusion

When new technologies are invented, their adoption in real-life scenarios seems to require fine-tuning. Researchers shall avoid a priori acceptance or rejection of such technology, rather asking for a more nuanced and specific consideration of the key features such technology brings, its potential unique advantages and drawbacks, and possibly trying to find a good balance over time and for the contingent situations in the trade-offs its use may imply.

A truly immersive experience of smart environments requires a joint design integration of engineering and perceptual requirements stemming from human senses, cognition, and physiology [1].

**Acknowledgments.** The authors thank the support from Qiruo Su, Shucheng Zheng, and Yuxuan Xiao for preparing the outline and checking the format.

**Author's Contributions.** Lorenzo Ceccon, Flora Gaetani, Meng Li, and Federica Caruso completed the outline of the manuscript. All the authors wrote the introduction and the background frameworks. The case study on urban planning was written by Lorenzo Ceccon. The case study on the smart vehicle was written by Federica Caruso and Flora Gaetani. The case study on user experience was written by Meng Li, Daan van Eijk, and Armagan Albayrak. All authors completed the discussion and conclusion parts. All authors reviewed the manuscript critically.

**Disclosure of Interests.** The authors have no competing interests to declare that are relevant to the content of this article.

# References

1. Habibzadeh, H., Soyata, T., Kantarci, B., Boukerche, A., Kaptan, C.: Sensing, communication and security planes: a new challenge for a smart city system design. Comput. Networks **144**, 163–200 (2018)
2. Li, M., Houwing, D., Albayrak, A., Shidujaman, M., van Eijk, D.: Mapping XR platforms: analyzing immersion from the designer's perspective. In: Kurosu, M., Hashizume, A. (eds.) Human-Computer Interaction. HCII 2023. Lecture Notes in Computer Science, vol. 14013. Springer, Cham (). https://doi.org/10.1007/978-3-031-35602-5_32
3. Milgram, P., Kishino, F.: A taxonomy of mixed reality visual displays. IEICE Trans. Inf. Syst. **77**(12), 1321–1329 (1994)
4. Speicher, M., Hall, B.D., Nebeling, M.: What is mixed reality? In: Conference on Human Factors in Computing Systems - Proceedings (2019)
5. Mann, S., Furness, T., Yuan, Y., Iorio, J., Wang, Z.: All Reality: Virtual, Augmented, Mixed (X), Mediated (X,Y), and Multimediated Reality. arXiv:1804.08386 (2018)
6. Cheng, Y.F., Yin, H., Yan, Y., Gugenheimer, J., Lindlbauer, D.: Towards understanding diminished reality. In: Proceedings of the 2022 CHI Conference on Human Factors in Computing Systems (CHI 2022). ACM, New York, NY, USA, Article 549, pp. 1–16 (2022). https://doi.org/10.1145/3491102.3517452
7. Batty, M., et al.: Smart cities of the future. Eur. Phys. J. Spec. Top. **214**(1), 481–518 (2012). https://doi.org/10.1140/epjst/e2012-01703-3
8. Cardullo, P., Di Feliciantonio, C., Kitchin, R. (eds.): The Right to the Smart City. Emerald Publishing Limited (2019). https://doi.org/10.1108/9781787691391
9. Johnson-Glenberg, M.C., Birchfield, D.A., Tolentino, L., Koziupa, T.: Collaborative embodied learning in mixed reality motion-capture environments: two science studies. J. Educ. Psychol. **106**(1), 86–104 (2014). https://doi.org/10.1037/a0034008
10. Ragan, E.D., Sowndararajan, A., Kopper, R., Bowman, D.A.: The effects of higher levels of immersion on procedure memorization performance and implications for educational virtual environments. Presence Teleoperators Virtual Environ. **19**, 527–543 (2010)
11. Billinghurst, M., Duenser, A.: Augmented reality in the classroom. Computer **7**, 56–63 (2012)
12. Krajčovič, M., Gabajová, G., Matys, M., Grznár, P., Dulina, Ľ, Kohár, R.: 3D interactive learning environment as a tool for knowledge transfer and retention. Sustainability **13**(14), 7916 (2021). https://doi.org/10.3390/su13147916

13. Holzinger, A.: Interactive machine learning for health informatics: when do we need the human-in-the-loop? Brain Informatics **3**(2), 119–131 (2016). https://doi.org/10.1007/s40708-016-0042-6
14. BASE5G. https://www.base5g.polimi.it/progetto/
15. El-Jarn, H., Southern, G.: Can co-creation in extended reality technologies facilitate the design process? J. Work Appl. Manage. **12**(2), 191–205 (2020). https://doi.org/10.1108/JWAM-04-2020-0022
16. Ratcliffe, J., Tokarchuk, L.: The potential of remote XR experimentation: defining benefits and limitations through expert survey and case study. Front. Comput. Sci. **4**, 952996 (2022). https://doi.org/10.3389/fcomp.2022.952996J
17. Wang, K., Julier, S.J., Cho, Y.: Attention-based applications in extended reality to support autistic users: a systematic review. IEEE Access **10**, 15574–15593 (2022). https://doi.org/10.1109/ACCESS.2022.3147726
18. Elbasheer, M., et al.: Shaping the role of the digital twins for human-robot dyad: connotations, scenarios, and future perspectives. ICT Collab. Intell. Manuf. **5**, e12066 (2023). https://doi.org/10.1049/cim2.1206622
19. Grübel, J., et al.: The Hitchhiker's guide to fused twins: a review of access to digital twins in situ in smart cities. Preprints arXiv:2202.07104 (2022).
20. Farinea, C., Markopoulou, A., Sollazzo, A., Chronis, A., & Marengo, M, "Merging the Physical and Digital Layer of Public Space - The PobleJoc Installation Case Study", Proceedings of the 35th International Conference on Education and Research in Computer Aided Architectural Design in Europe (eCAADe) [Volume 2], 2017
21. Smaniotto Costa, C., Šuklje Erjavec, I., Kenna, T., de Lange, M., Ioannidis, K., Maksymiuk, G., de Waal, M. (eds.): CyberParks – The Interface Between People, Places and Technology. LNCS, vol. 11380. Springer, Cham (2019). https://doi.org/10.1007/978-3-030-13417-4
22. Bellani, P., et al.: Enhancing user engagement in shared autonomous vehicles: an innovative gesture-based windshield interaction system. Appl. Sci. **13**(17), 9901 (2023). https://doi.org/10.3390/app13179901
23. Kirk, R.: Cars of the future: the internet of things in the automotive industry. Network Secur. **2015**(9), 16–18 (2015). https://doi.org/10.1016/S1353-4858(15)30081-7
24. Lyons, G.: Future mobility. In: Lyons, G. (ed.) Transport Matters, pp. 381–400. Policy Press (2019). https://doi.org/10.1332/policypress/9781447329558.003.0016
25. Bengler, K., Rettenmaier, M., Fritz, N., Feierle, A.: From HMI to HMIs: towards an HMI framework for automated driving. Information **11**(2), 61 (2020). https://doi.org/10.3390/info11020061
26. Trubia, S., Severino, A., Curto, S., Arena, F., Pau, G.: Smart roads: an overview of what future mobility will look like. Infrastructures **5**(12), 107 (2020). https://doi.org/10.3390/infrastructures5120107
27. Liu, A., Tan, H.: Research on the trend of automotive user experience. In: Rau, P.L.P. (eds.) Cross-Cultural Design. Product and Service Design, Mobility and Automotive Design, Cities, Urban Areas, and Intelligent Environments Design. HCII 2022. Lecture Notes in Computer Science, vol. 13314, pp. 180–201. Springer, Cham (2022).https://doi.org/10.1007/978-3-031-06053-3_13
28. Guo, H., Zhao, F., Wang, W., Jiang, X.: Analyzing drivers' attitude towards HUD system using a stated preference survey. Adv. Mech. Eng. **6**, 380647 (2014). https://doi.org/10.1155/2014/380647
29. Arena, F., Pau, G., Severino, A.: An overview on the current status and future perspectives of smart cars. Infrastructures **5**(7), 53 (2020). https://doi.org/10.3390/infrastructures5070053
30. Coppola, P., Silvestri, F.: Autonomous vehicles and future mobility solutions. In: Autonomous Vehicles and Future Mobility, pp. 1–15 (2019). Elsevier. https://linkinghub.elsevier.com/retrieve/pii/B9780128176962000019

31. Li, M., Yao, X., Aschenbrenner, D., van Eijk, D., Vink, P.: Ergonomics 4.0: human-centered procedure for ergonomic design using virtual reality prototyping. In: INCOSE International Symposium, Virtual Event (2022)
32. Ball, L.J., Christensen, B.T.: Advancing an understanding of design cognition and design metacognition: progress and prospects. Des. Stud. **65**, 35–59 (2019)
33. Cross, N.: Design cognition. In: Design Knowing and Learning: Cognition in Design Education, pp. 79–103. Elsevier (2001). https://doi.org/10.1016/B978-008043868-9/500 05-X
34. Design Council: Eleven lessons: Managing design in eleven global companies-desk research report. D. Council (2007). www.designcouncil.org.uk
35. Buchenau, M., Suri, J.F.: Experience prototyping. In: DIS 2000: Proceedings of the 3rd conference on Designing Interactive Systems: Processes, Practices, Methods, and Techniques, Brooklyn, New York (2000)
36. Norman, D.: The Design of Everyday Things (Revised and expanded ed.). Basic books, (2013)
37. Lingan, C.L., Li, M., Vermeeren, A.P.: The immersion cycle: understanding immersive experiences through a cyclical model. Proc. Des. Soc. **1**, 3011–3020 (2021)
38. Azuma, R.T.: A survey of augmented reality. Presence Teleoperators Virtual Environ. **6**(4), 355–385 (1997). https://doi.org/10.1162/pres.1997.6.4.355
39. Kant, I.: Critique of Pure Reason. Cambridge University Press (1781/1998)
40. Stephenson, N.: Snow Crash. Random House Worlds (2000)

# Exploring VR Wizardry: A Generic Control Tool for Wizard of Oz Experiments

Tabea Runzheimer$^{(\boxtimes)}$, Stefan Friesen, Sven Milde, Johannes-Hubert Peiffer, and Jan-Torsten Milde

University of Applied Sciences Fulda, Leipzigerstr. 123, 36037 Fulda, Germany
{tabea.runzheimer,stefan.friesen,sven.milde,johannes-hubert.peiffer,
jan-torsten.milde}@ai.hs-fulda.de
https://www.hs-fulda.de/

**Abstract.** This paper presents a Virtual Reality (VR) simulation control tool developed for Wizard of Oz experiments, aligned with the CityBot project. The tool includes a VR simulation and a web-based interface to address security concerns during the testing phase of the CityBot, which is an experimental autonomous vehicle on the scale of a conventional car. The prototype of the tool underwent experimental setups to explore gestural and verbal inputs, and subsequent architectural adjustments were made to enhance its flexibility: The frontend has been updated to support multiple platforms, and compatibility with robotic systems has been improved by integrating the Robot Operating System (ROS). Backend improvements include the adoption of a MySQL database and stateless microservices for compatibility with Cloud-native technologies to improve persistence and scalability. The tool accommodates multi-user scenarios and customizable UI templates, making it a flexible platform for evaluating Human-Computer Interaction (HCI) aspects within robotic systems. Despite the increased complexity resulting from these changes, the tool provides a user-friendly interface. This tool has a wide range of applications in exploring HCI in robotic systems. It can be used for experimental simulations beyond the CityBot project and is relevant in various real-world and virtual environments.

**Keywords:** VR · HRI · Wizard of Oz · ROS

## 1 Introduction

The integration of VR technology has caused a significant change in the field of HCI in recent years. This intersection between VR and HCI not only introduces an innovative approach to HCI development but also presents a range of challenges and opportunities that make it a topic of great interest and significance. The investigation of HCI in VR provides captivating and immersive user experiences but also requires a robust framework to guarantee the reliability of user interactions. As we delve further into this subject, it becomes clear that the

J. Y. C. Chen and G. Fragomeni (Eds.): HCII 2024, LNCS 14707, pp. 60–73, 2024.
https://doi.org/10.1007/978-3-031-61044-8_5

primary need is not a complete product, but rather the creation of a secure and effective foundation for HCI development in the VR domain.

The study reported here comprises several simulations, i.e. tests conducted with the tool. This approach enables a comprehensive evaluation of the tool under various scenarios, providing valuable insights into its performance and reliability under different conditions. Additionally, the research broadens its scope by investigating the integration of real-life applications. This aims to bridge the gap between the virtual and physical realms and evaluate the practical implications of VR-based HCI solutions.

Essentially, the use of VR in HCI development is explored, with a particular emphasis on testing that is safe for subjects through simulations and integration with real-life applications. This represents a cutting-edge approach that not only enhances our understanding of immersive user experiences but also establishes the groundwork for the future evolution of interactive technologies.

## 2 Related Work

In this research landscape, a variety of studies contributes significantly to our understanding of key aspects within our domain. One noteworthy contribution is from Stadler et al. [21], who investigated the complex interaction between autonomous vehicles and pedestrians, using VR technology. Their research is notable for highlighting the significant role of VR beyond entertainment. It is a powerful tool for evaluating and refining communication dynamics in scenarios involving autonomous vehicles and pedestrians. Stadler et al. use VR to provide a controlled and immersive environment, allowing for a detailed examination of how individuals interact with autonomous vehicles. This advances our understanding of this critical intersection. Joundi et al's [16] work introduces a unique perspective on monitoring and controlling VR user tests. They not only incorporate desktop interfaces but also integrate physiological trackers, such as eye tracking and heart rate monitoring. This approach adds complexity to their investigations, allowing for a nuanced understanding of user reactions and responses within the VR environment. Both studies highlight the multidimensional nature of the research domain, emphasizing the physical and emotional engagement of individuals with the simulated scenarios. They highlight the important roles of VR not only as an evaluation tool but also as a medium that can capture the complexities of human interaction and responses.

Similarly, Dahlbäck et al. [14] stress the significance of thorough design of experiments in the field of HCI. They highlight the importance of creating authentic interactions to collect high-quality empirical data for developing user-friendly intelligent interfaces. The authors discuss various aspects of Wizard of Oz studies, including the selection of background systems, scenario design, the role of the wizard, and the necessity for dynamic focus management.

Due to the nature of the underlying CityBot project [2], which involves a robotic vehicle as the central entity, it is imperative to explore the Robot Operating System (ROS) for testing in VR environments and the actual operation of the robot. James Starkman's thesis, titled 'The Robot Operating System in Transition: Experiments and Tutorials,' [22] offers a comprehensive analysis of the evolution of ROS from its inception in 2007 to the development of ROS2. Stark-man examines the limitations of ROS1 and the trade-offs between ROS1 and ROS2, providing insights into the improvements made in ROS2 and its potential impact on robotics applications. This knowledge is crucial for our project, where the robot's effective functioning and communication in diverse scenarios, both in VR testing and real-world operations, heavily rely on the capabilities of the underlying ROS framework.

As discussed in previous research [15], the dynamics of human-robot interaction are multifaceted. Following the approach of open task specifications for experiments requires a tool that can react to a variety of different scenarios, especially since multimodal interaction is not always unambiguous and sometimes even contradictory [19].

## 3   Methods

### 3.1   Modalities and Interaction Concept

To define the aspects that require control and simulation, we began by analyzing typical use cases and developing an interaction concept for the CityBot. Figure 1 shows the CityBot tractor's front part, with one of its modules and the PeopleMover in the back. The tractor can be used with or without modules for transporting goods, watering, and collecting trash. The Avatar head, which is equipped with a display, microphones, and speakers, serves as the primary interface between the CityBot tractor and humans due to its design. Users can interact with the CityBot through speech, while animations on the display and gestures such as nodding the head of the CityBot enhance the interaction. The matrix at the front of the CityBot provides information for users who are further away, while the matrix at the back only provides regular driving signals, such as brake lights. As the CityBot is an electric vehicle, the driving sound itself also needs to be designed to communicate speed and distance. Additionally, we have included signal sounds, such as a horn and a warning sound for reversing.

These modalities comprise various design options that require testing and therefore need to be implemented in the simulation and control interface of the VR tool. The most crucial aspect is the driving of the CityBot in the VR simulation, as it is a vehicle. Additionally, basic usability testing functions should be provided, such as recording subject and wizard interactions for later in-depth investigation.

### 3.2   Experimental Setup and 1. Study on Gesture-Audio Integration for Enhanced Robot Driving

After defining the interaction concept, we developed an initial experimental setup. The VR simulation, which included the CityBot and three scenes (lobby, parking lot, and industrial area), as well as a passthrough mode, was implemented in Unity. To ensure a more natural user experience, a standalone Meta

**Fig. 1.** CityBot tractor with PeopleMover module

Quest 2 [5] with its existing hand-tracking system was used, instead of the customary hardware controllers. To facilitate navigation within the simulation, we added two colored markers that can be positioned by the wizard. The so-called webtool control system was set up locally using Node.js [6], and included both the backend and frontend, and ran on a standard laptop. To connect the webtool to the simulation via Open Sound Control (OSC) [11], the wizard had to enter the local IP addresses of the VR glasses and the webtool's hosts. Once the connection was established, the simulation running on the VR headset downloaded audio files containing pre-recorded voice commands for the CityBot from the webtool. To avoid cluttering the host's keyboard keys, we added support for separate MIDI controllers to trigger these audios. The audios were assigned values in advance and could be triggered by their corresponding MIDI buttons and keys. The frontend comprised various buttons, sliders, and input fields. These elements are used to trigger scene changes, teleport the CityBot to a specific position, or adjust the sound volume in the simulation. To address the difficulties encountered by the wizard when teleporting CityBot and user via coordinates, we added a top-down view map of every scene (see Fig. 2). This map allowed the wizard to click on the desired location for teleportation. The vehicle can be driven by using either the keyboard or a Nintendo Switch gaming controller [7]. A second screen was used to present the perspective of the user in VR to the assistant and presenter, using scrcpy to mirror the perspective. We utilized the MediaRecorder API [12] in JavaScript to capture both the wizards and the subjects views, which were downloadable as a zip file after the experiments. Additionally, we used a Nikon D750 [10] and a ZED 2i [8] camera to record the subject. The subjects as well as the moderator's voice were recorded using a Zoom H4 [4] and a RODE Wireless Go II [18]. To ensure that the various inputs were synchronized, participants were instructed to clap their hands three times at various points throughout the study.

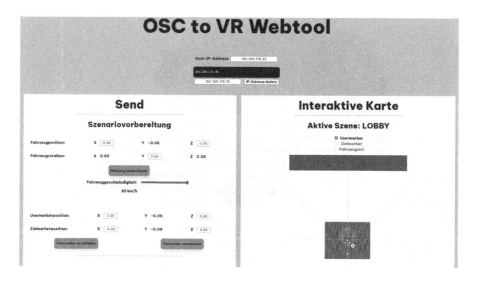

**Fig. 2.** First Experimental Iteration Of The Webtool

The study was conducted in three parts with 7 participants to investigate user interaction with the robot. Prior to the experiment, a brief interview was conducted to determine subjects' familiarity with VR, voice assistants, and mobility options. Following this, all subjects were introduced to the VR application and shown the guardian system [3] in passthrough mode, as well as the lobby scene. The guardian system is a blue grid that appears when the user approaches the boundaries of the game area and is designed to prevent the user from leaving the designated area. They were then given time to explore the scene and become familiar with it. Because of our simple setup and the need to record the gestures of the subjects from a front view, they were only permitted to walk around during this time. During the actual tests, subjects were directed to a fixed spot marked by one of the markers in VR and were required to face the CityBot, which meant facing the ZED camera head-on.

The experiment consisted of three parts. In the first part, participants were asked to communicate driving directions to the CityBot using only gestures. The second part was identical to the first, except participants were asked to use only voice commands. For the final stage, we utilized a parking scenario where participants were instructed to park the CityBot in a designated parking area marked with a cross. Participants were given the freedom to use both gestures and voice commands and were able to decide for themselves when they were satisfied with the outcome of the parking attempt. During the experiment, the CityBot reactions were controlled by the wizard, therefore according to their observations - the wizard was responsible for monitoring the participants and controlling the simulation. Following the experiment, participants were required to participate in a brief interview where they were asked about their experience during the test and given the opportunity to provide open feedback.

The pretest revealed significant time issues when attempting to enter multiple settings at once at the beginning of the tests in order to prepare the starting point of the simulation. Furthermore, it was nearly impossible for a single wizard to manage both driving and audio simultaneously.

The preparation for the experiments itself was also difficult because all functionalities, settings, and corresponding OSC messages were hardcoded. As a result, every new feature had to be added to the source code, which partially affected previous features and cluttered the code. In order to solve these issues, the tasks of the wizard were split between two persons, one for controlling audio responses and the other for controlling the driving and Avatar gestures. Through experimentation, it became apparent that the wizards required additional practice to improve their control actions for the robot and their reactions to the actions exhibited by the test subjects - in order to achieve the desired quality of the simulation. Additionally, some participants had trouble remaining stationary during the final phase of the test, possibly due to the natural inclination to move around the vehicle they were trying to park.

### 3.3   2. Experimental Setup and Study on Voice Interaction and Driving Assessment

For the second study, we kept the introduction to VR and the interviews from the first study and only modified the experiment. The study was conducted with 12 participants both female and male.

As voice interaction with the Avatar of the CityBot is a crucial modality of the CityBot, the first part focused on simulating a conversation between the participant and the CityBot. We prerecorded four different voices, each with 71 dialogue snippets, and made them switchable using the control tool. The CityBot initiated the conversation with the participants and posed several voice-based questions. The moderator intervened when the dialogue options were inadequate or when the participants misunderstood the CityBot. Additionally, we conducted an evaluation of driving and interaction, during which the wizard drove the CityBot towards the participant at varying speeds and angles. The participants were then instructed to stop the vehicle using either gestures, voice commands, or both. After each run, the CityBot inquired whether the participant was satisfied with the distance. If not, the test could be rerun. The third part aimed to identify specific keywords that would trigger a reaction from the CityBot when it was occupied with a task. To achieve this, we modified the Avatar display to show a busy mode, rotated it away from the participant, and added a dummy in VR to which the participants were supposed to seek assistance. When spoken to, the CityBot responded that it was busy, unless the predetermined keyword 'help' was used.

The final scenario examined a common street environment, where the City-Bot was in motion and a pedestrian wished to cross the road. To achieve this, we varied the speeds and distances at which the CityBot came to a halt or slowed down, signal sounds (such as a horn), and direct voice communication with the participant.

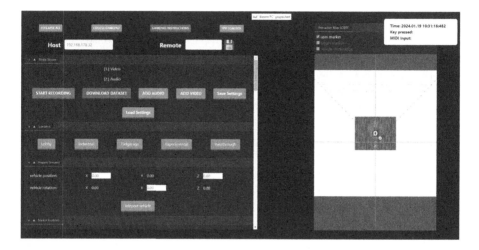

**Fig. 3.** Second experimental iteration of the Webtool

Learning from our previous study, we conducted a longer pretest to allow the wizards to become familiar with the script and interface. We also simplified the frontend by grouping similar settings and adding collapsible tabs which can be seen on the left side of Fig. 3, allowing both wizards to view what they needed. Additionally, we expanded the MIDI keyboard functions to include voice switching and signal sound buttons. To aid the wizards comprehension of VR events, we incorporated audio streaming. A lavalier microphone [9] was attached to the headband of the participants' VR glasses and connected to their RODE devices. The RODE receiver was then plugged into the webtool's host, where it could be added as an input source with the option to use one of the host's speakers as an output device. Headphones were used by the wizard to prevent feedback.

Instead of hardcoding scenario settings, we added buttons to save and name current settings, which were then saved locally on the device for future use. We also expanded gaming controller support to include PS4 controllers [1] for easier handling.

To ensure realistic driving, we included driving physics of the real CityBot for speed and braking, with options to enable or disable them. The vehicle was able to move without physics, resulting in abrupt changes in speed, relying only on acceleration or deceleration, or no physics at all. We also included options to control the maximum speeds for forward and backward driving, acceleration, deceleration, and rotation degree.

Options were added to test different levels of automation with various driving presets. These include deceleration, acceleration, and stopping at specific distances to the participant. Additionally, the Avatar head can automatically turn to look at the user within a range of distance. For the Avatar, we included additional control options, such as buttons that activate animations on the display for the following states: 'startup', 'busy', 'idle', 'thinking', 'shutdown', and 'teleoperation'. Additionally, we added gestures for nodding, shaking the head, and making eye contact with the user.

When evaluating both versions of the webtool in the two studies, we discovered multiple issues. Firstly, the UI was too complicated and cluttered, even with the applied changes. Although the experiments ran as planned and the wizards had enough practice, sufficiently quick reaction times to respond to a participant's actions were difficult. Audio files were assigned to keys on the MIDI keyboard in chronological order. However, due to unexpected participant reactions, it was difficult for the wizard to select the correct key for the desired response. On the other hand, the gaming controller was effective in controlling the driving, provided that the wizard had enough practice to become accustomed to the reactions in VR. However, it is important to note that both wizards mentioned difficulties due to the limited perspective from their point of view. A view from the CityBot would have been more helpful in providing a more objective evaluation.

Due to the original setup being planned for only one wizard, consistency issues arose, and the wizards had to restart the application to regain control over the simulation. This led to further issues because recorded streams were split into multiple files and had to be restarted after every reload. Additionally, synchronizing the different streams proved to be almost impossible due to the multiple sources with different settings and corrupted streams.

## 4    Results

Based on our experiences from the first two iterations, we decided to redesign our tools. Firstly, we opted to switch from OSC to a ROS-Bridge for communication. Although OSC worked well, we desired more flexibility to prepare our tool for other applications. ROS, being an industry standard for developing robots and vehicles [13], was identified as a suitable choice for compatibility. Following this principle, we split the backend and frontend. The frontend moved to a Flutter application, which enables multi-platform support [24] and offers great performance [23,24]. For the backend, we kept Node.js but split the application into multiple microservices. This approach aims to achieve better fault tolerance and scalability by allowing us to replicate the necessary services. The microservices are split by their functionality and consist of a logger, UI handler, experiment service, and control service. We also added a MariaDB database for persistence. Figure 4 illustrates the communication architecture. The microservices in the backend use Redis to communicate with each other. During an experiment, the logger service also subscribes to all ROS Topics to persist the sent messages.

Communication with the frontend is achieved through an API and simple HTTP requests. Communication with other applications, including VR simulation, as shown in Fig. 4, is done through the ROS Bridge. This ensures that all clients receive the necessary updates for their user interface during the experiment. For basic testing, everything can run in Docker with one instance of each service. However, we have also added Kubernetes support for running the application in a cluster and making use of its advantages such as scaling and fault tolerance [17, 20]. As ROS, like OSC, uses messages with topics and data, it is important to avoid hardcoding configurations and settings. Therefore, we have decided that these should be configurable in the frontend. Users can create different types of controllers, such as buttons, joysticks, or MIDI keys, as well as ROS messages. If the element is a ROS message, the user must define the topic and datatype for the message. The topic comprises a new scheme, consisting of the user-defined base topic and automatically applied endings '/state' and '/value' for subscribing and publishing. If the control tool only requests an update, it sends an empty message to the state topic, whereas the value topic is used to set values in the simulation. The simulation publishes to the state topic for updates.

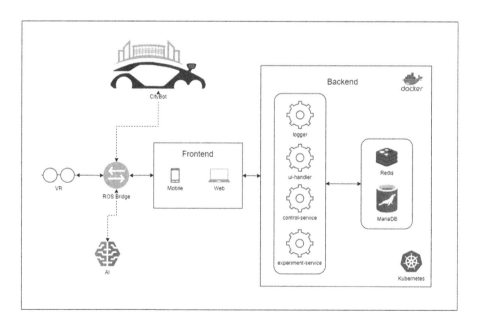

**Fig. 4.** Architecture and communication of the Webtool with its clients

Elements can also be members of other elements, allowing for grouping. For example, a game controller typically consists of multiple input devices, such as buttons and joysticks. The user can create a base element for the controller and then add the corresponding input devices. To enable the elements to perform actions, we added triggers for services. These services can publish to a ROS message or update the UI. These two foundations are connected through automations, which determine when the element triggers an action. Triggers can include incoming data, data differences, specific values or a range of values, application startup and shutdown, as well as a specific time or loop. Automations can be disabled, additional conditions can be added, and it can be specified whether the action is intended to receive or send something.

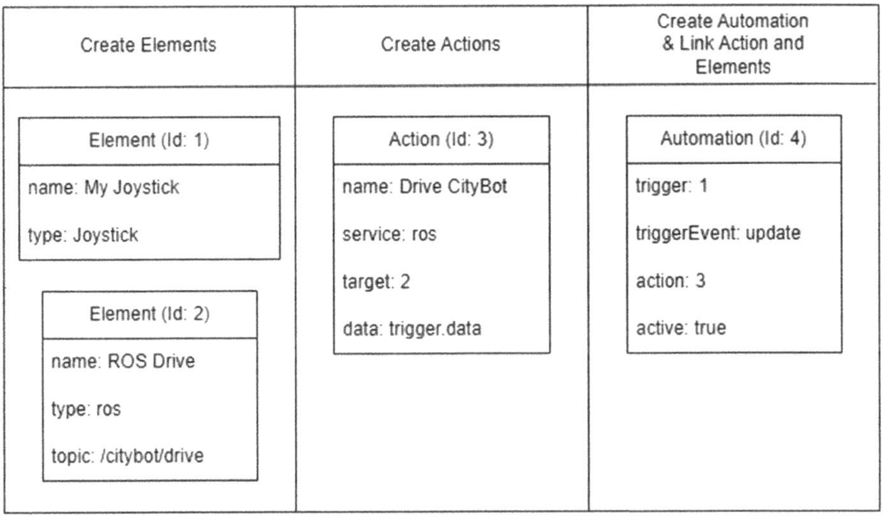

| Create Elements | Create Actions | Create Automation & Link Action and Elements |
|---|---|---|
| **Element (Id: 1)**<br>name: My Joystick<br>type: Joystick<br><br>**Element (Id: 2)**<br>name: ROS Drive<br>type: ros<br>topic: /citybot/drive | **Action (Id: 3)**<br>name: Drive CityBot<br>service: ros<br>target: 2<br>data: trigger.data | **Automation (Id: 4)**<br>trigger: 1<br>triggerEvent: update<br>action: 3<br>active: true |

**Fig. 5.** Example of creating controllable widgets linked with ROS

The diagram in Fig. 5 provides a straightforward example. The user creates two elements: 'My Joystick' with type 'Joystick' and ID 1, and 'ROS Drive' with type 'ros', ROS topic '/citybot/drive', and ID 2. Next, an action is defined with ID 3, named 'Drive CityBot' and service 'ros'. The 'target' links to the corresponding element, which must be of element type 'ros'; therefore, we set it to our 'ROS Drive' element's ID 2. Finally, we define the sent data to be the trigger's data. The data depends on the type of automation it is linked with, which is determined in the next and final step. To create an automation with id 4, set the trigger element to the 'My Joystick' element and specify that the automation should be triggered every time an 'update' occurs, meaning every time values are sent from the joystick. The automation is then linked to action 3, which updates the action to send the joystick data using ROS. Enabling the automation requires setting the active value to 'true'. All of these values are saved in the database and can be updated by using the frontend. Due to the action and automation system, one element can trigger multiple actions. For example, with the gaming controller, users can define their own actions. One user might apply driving actions to the controller's joystick, while another could use it to navigate a map.

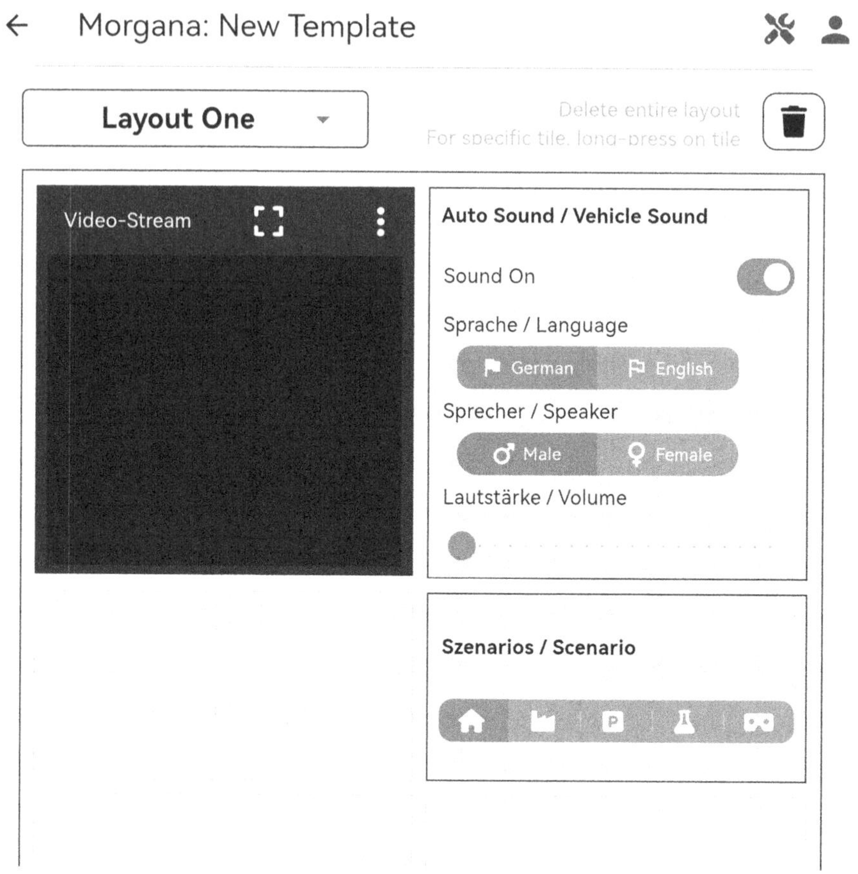

**Fig. 6.** Webtool templating view

To clean up the front end, we decided to let each user arrange their own UI. So, we added templates and widgets that can be configured by the user. Each template consists of several widgets. The widgets themselves can be scaled and positioned within the template. The widgets are also elements and their configuration is persisted by the backend. A user can create multiple templates for multiple experiments and then select what they need for the current test. Figure 6 shows a section of a sample template called 'Layout One'. In the top left corner is a video widget that links to a web stream of the VR application showing the subject's view. In the top right corner is a multi-element widget consisting of controls for the CityBot speaker's voice, gender and volume. Below these are icon buttons for scene selection and further areas for additional widgets.

# 5   Discussion

The final advancements of the VR tool described above, which result from insights gained in the reported experiments, have both positive and negative side effects. Starting with the Flutter application, using a template-based approach where users can choose their own elements allows for a more direct and flexible handling of the frontend itself, as well as the execution during the experiment. Users can decide for themselves which elements are necessary for their use cases, while still collaborating during the experiment. However, allowing users to choose their own UI does not guarantee that it is actually efficient and easy to use. Therefore, the actual usability of the tool during the experiment depends heavily on the preparation and training of the wizard. On the other hand, the multi-platform support provided leads to better overall usability.

Using microservices for the backend grants a better fault tolerance and scalability, as well as potential cloud deployment, but also increases the complexity of development, deployment and maintenance. Switching from OSC to ROS enables a wider range of use cases, as ROS is widely used in robotics applications compared to OSC, which is more commonly used in audio applications. By using the ROS bridge, it also allows the integration of (multiple) other applications for testing robotic systems simulated in VR or in real life, limited only by the processing power of the receiving device as well as the one hosting the ROS bridge.

It is also worth noting that this setup is completely mobile. The minimum requirements are a standalone VR headset and a device to host the backend, frontend and ROS bridge. For ease of use, we recommend using a separate network and separate devices for each working participant.

# 6   Future Work

Building on these foundations, we recommend further research into the adaptability of this tool for use with other domains, different applications and in conjunction with physical robots. In addition, a qualitative and quantitative analysis is essential to assess how easily untrained subjects can understand and use the webtool. This should include the preparation and execution of experiments.

In order for the webtool to be widely used, an analysis of IT-security concerns as well as accurate performance and monitoring tests are required. In order to improve the application, further research can also be carried out into the incorporation of other usability testing methods such as biological measurements including eye tracking, heart rate and the like.

# References

1. DUALSHOCK 4 Wireless-Controller für PS4 — PlayStation 4. https://www.playstation.com/de-de/accessories/dualshock-4-wireless-controller/
2. EDAG CityBot. https://www.edag-citybot.de/en/

3. Guardian System — Oculus Developers. https://developer.oculus.com/documentation/native/pc/dg-guardian-system/?locale=de_DE

4. H4 Support. https://zoomcorp.com/de/de/handy-recorder/handheld-recorders/h4/h4-support/

5. Meta Quest 2: Immersives all-in-one VR-Headset — Meta Store. https://www.meta.com/de/quest/products/quest-2/

6. Node.js. https://nodejs.org/en

7. Spielt wann, wo und mit wem ihr wollt. https://www.nintendo.de/Hardware/Nintendo-Switch-Familie/Nintendo-Switch/Nintendo-Switch-1148779.html

8. ZED 2 - AI Stereo Camera — Stereolabs. https://www.stereolabs.com/products/zed-2

9. Rode Lavalier GO. https://www.thomann.de/de/rode_lavalier_go.htm

10. Nikon D750 — Camera of the Year — FX-Format Wi-Fi Camera (2020). https://www.nikonusa.com/en/nikon-products/product/dslr-cameras/d750.html

11. OSC index (2021). https://ccrma.stanford.edu/groups/osc/index.html

12. MediaRecorder - Web APIs — MDN (2023). https://developer.mozilla.org/en-US/docs/Web/API/MediaRecorder

13. Bubeck, A.: ROS (Robot Operating System) für Automotive. https://publica-rest.fraunhofer.de/server/api/core/bitstreams/39ff4b71-a7a0-4055-8f99-3d6c3e1aecd5/content

14. Dahlbäck, N., Jönsson, A., Ahrenberg, L.: Wizard of Oz studies - why and how. Knowl.-Based Syst. **6**(4), 258–266 (1993). https://doi.org/10.1016/0950-7051(93)90017-N

15. Friesen, S., Runzheimer, T., Blum, R., Milde, J.T.: A VR based mobile usability lab to study multi modal human robot communication. In: 2022 45th Jubilee International Convention on Information, Communication and Electronic Technology (MIPRO), pp. 28–31. Opatija, Croatia (2022). http://www.mipro.hr/LinkClick.aspx?fileticket=vgJIHBtuOeE%3d&tabid=196&language=hr-HR

16. Joundi, J., et al.: ExperienceDNA : a framework to conduct and analyse user tests in VR using the Wizard-of-Oz methodology. In: Design, User Experience, and Usability : Design for Contemporary Technological Environments : 10th International Conference, DUXU 2021, held as part of the 23rd HCI International Conference, HCII 2021 : Proceedings : Part III, vol. 12781, pp. 171–186. Springer, Cham (2021). https://doi.org/10.1007/978-3-030-78227-6_13

17. Lehtinen, K.: Scaling a kubernetes cluster (2022). https://osuva.uwasa.fi/handle/10024/13971. Accepted 05 May 2022

18. Microphones, R.: Wireless GO II — Dual Wireless Mic System — RØDE. https://rode.com/de/microphones/wireless/wirelessgoii

19. Milde, S., et al.: Studying multi-modal human robot interaction using a mobile VR simulation. In: Kurosu, M., Hashizume, A. (eds.) Human-Computer Interaction, pp. 140–155. Lecture Notes in Computer Science, Springer Nature Switzerland, Cham (2023). https://doi.org/10.1007/978-3-031-35602-5_11

20. Shamim, S.I., Gibson, J.A., Morrison, P., Rahman, A.: Benefits, challenges, and research topics: a multi-vocal literature review of Kubernetes (2022). https://doi.org/10.48550/arXiv.2211.07032

21. Stadler, S., Cornet, H., Novaes Theoto, T., Frenkler, F.: A tool, not a toy: using virtual reality to evaluate the communication between autonomous vehicles and pedestrians. In: tom Dieck, M.C., Jung, T. (eds.) Augmented Reality and Virtual Reality. PI, pp. 203–216. Springer, Cham (2019). https://doi.org/10.1007/978-3-030-06246-0_15

22. Starkman, J.: The robot operating system in transition: experiments and tutorials. Ph. D. thesis, Case Western Reserve University (2018). https://etd.ohiolink.edu/acprod/odb_etd/etd/r/1501/10?clear=10&p10_accession_num=case1517240947102584
23. Sullivan, A.: Examining performance differences between native, flutter, and react native mobile development. (2018). https://thoughtbot.com/blog/examining-performance-differences-between-native-flutter-and-react-native-mobile-development
24. Sullivan, A.: Examining performance differences between native, flutter, and react native mobile development: take two. (2018). https://thoughtbot.com/blog/examining-performance-differences-between-native-flutter-and-react-native-mobile-development-take-two

# The Impact of Different Levels of Spatial Cues on Size Perception: A Spatial Perception Study of Altered Conditions

Faezeh Salehi[1]([✉]), Fatemeh Pariafsai[2], and Manish K. Dixit[1]

[1] Texas A&M University, College Station, TX 77843, USA
{faezehsalehi,mdixit}@tamu.edu
[2] Bowling Green State University, BGSU, Bowling Green, OH 43403-0001, USA
pariafsai@tamu.edu

**Abstract.** Spatial cognitive processing is a critical domain of human spatial cognition that involves studying how humans perceive their spatial environments and the relationship between different spatial objects that exist within them. Humans encode spatial relationships through egocentric processing in which they relate spatial objects with reference to their own body and through allocentric processing, which involves relating spatial objects with reference to other objects. Using this spatial encoding, whether egocentric or allocentric, humans stive to create a complete and accurate perception of a space. Other sources of information such as proprioceptive, somatosensory, and vestibular system further enhance the process of spatial perception. An accurate and complete spatial perception is critical to not only safely living and efficiently working in space but also navigating within and across the space. In other words, spatial perception impacts our everyday mundane and critical tasks.

Spatial cues emanating from spatial landmark objects in a spatial environment form one such a source of information that helps human brains to comprehend and perceive distance and size, which governs all major and minor decisions humans make in their routine lives. On earth, objects such as roads, buildings, trees, street poles, cars, and people act as visual landmarks to offer visual cues to help accurately determine size and distances that we use to make informed decisions. For instance, the judgment of the speed of an oncoming vehicle, decision of when to brake while riding a bike, and determining synchronized working with a piece of equipment rely heavily on our ability to perceive relative distances and sizes. The availability of these visual landmarks, therefore, could influence human ability to accurately and completely perceive distance and sizes.

Due to the advent of emerging technologies, the future workplaces are evolving faster and involving work conditions that may deprive humans of these essential visuospatial cues. For instance, polar regions and hot deserts of Earth may have no or very limited visual landmarks that may impact human spatial perception. Lunar conditions and environments on other planets such as Mars have landscapes that may not be familiar to humans. Moreover, such places do not have these spatial landmark objects, which may make perceiving distance and size a challenging task in such conditions. In fact, conditions of astronauts doing a spacewalk not only lack these visual landmarks but also the terrain that may offer some spatial cues. If the spatial perception is distorted due to the lack of visuospatial cues,

J. Y. C. Chen and G. Fragomeni (Eds.): HCII 2024, LNCS 14707, pp. 74–85, 2024.
https://doi.org/10.1007/978-3-031-61044-8_6

humans may not be able to understand distance, size, and speed accurately, which may jeopardize their health, safety, and work productivity.

The main goal of this paper is to examine how human spatial perception, specifically size perception, is affected by different levels of availability of spatial cues. To reach this goal, spatial environments of a city with all routine visual landmarks, Martian terrain with unfamiliar landscape with no familiar visual landmarks, and deep space with no base plane or terrain and no visual landmarks are simulated in Virtual Reality (VR) using Unity 3D game engine. VR can offer a powerful medium to simulate real-world conditions effectively and realistically, particularly those that cannot be experienced first-hand. The city, Mars, and space conditions are designated as control, (CG), experiment 1 (EX1), and experiment group 2 (EX2). Each condition is embedded with a size perception test that involves participants manipulating the length, width, and height of a cube-like object and make it a perfect cube. One hundred participants are recruited who completed the size perception task in the three conditions of the control and experiment groups.

The analysis of size estimations across various dimensions in different virtual reality (VR) environments has revealed intriguing patterns in participants' perceptual accuracy. In all three environments - CG, EG1, and EG2 participants consistently demonstrated a tendency to either overestimate or underestimate the dimensions of objects, including depth, height, and width. While the specific patterns varied among the dimensions and environments, the overall findings suggest that VR environments have a substantial influence on participants' perception of size.

Notably, depth and height estimations exhibited a consistent pattern of overestimation in the CG and EG1 Environments, indicating that participants generally perceived objects as closer or taller than they truly were. However, width estimations showed a more mixed pattern, with participants tending to overestimate in the CG and EG2 Environments but not in the EG1 Environment.

**Keywords:** Spatial perception · Virtual reality · Size perception test

# 1   Introduction

Recent scientific progress has empowered humanity to explore challenging terrains such as space, low Earth orbit, deep oceans, and polar regions, each presenting distinct visuospatial and gravitational conditions (Carroll 1993). These environments pose cognitive challenges, given the reliance of human perception on familiar spatial cues, like landmarks on Earth (Newcombe 2002). Landmarks, including roads, buildings, and trees, play a pivotal role in forming mental representations of spaces and aiding displacement perception (Ruddle, Volkova et al. 2011; Winter 2014). In the absence of such cues, as observed in altered visuospatial conditions like deep space or celestial bodies, spatial perception is profoundly affected (Oman 2007; Plumert, Kearney et al. 2005).

Deep space poses challenges with the absence of essential cues and even the foundational terrain, impacting spatial perception (Newman and McNamara 2022). Analogous altered conditions also exist on Earth, in regions like the Poles and deserts, where landmarks may be scarce (Ruddle, Volkova et al. 2011). These settings, serving as analogs for space exploration training, underscore the importance of spatial perception in extreme conditions (Kearney, Gorzel et al. 2012).

The consequences of altered spatial conditions extend beyond Earth, affecting human spatial perception, work productivity, and safety, potentially jeopardizing mission success. Accurate perception of distance, height, and size becomes crucial, especially in extreme environments like deep space (Kiefer, Giannopoulos et al. 2017). This study aims to explore the impact of absent visuospatial cues on size and distance perception using immersive Virtual Reality (VR) analogs, hypothesizing that object size perception improves with the availability of familiar visual cues.

## 2  Background

Over the past decade, the rapid integration of new technologies has orchestrated substantial transformations in our daily lives and the corporate arena, impacting communication methods and operational strategies (Folkierska-Żukowska et al., 2020). The newfound ability to explore once-inaccessible realms, including deep oceans, space, and polar regions, reflects the remarkable progress of humanity. Yet, venturing into these unexplored territories carries implications for the cognitive processing of spatial information in the human brain (Fukushima, Fukushima et al. 2013; Harris, Jenkin et al. 2017).

The dynamic evolution of work environments within these spaces raises concerns about potential disruptions to individuals' ability to effectively work and comprehend spatial relationships (Turgut, 2015). Particularly in scenarios involving the operation of rovers and quadcopters, precise judgment of distance, sizes, and speeds becomes paramount. Any deviation or distortion in spatial perception could compromise safety and overall well-being (Salehi, 2023). The confluence of technological advancement and exploration into novel frontiers introduces intricate challenges, necessitating a nuanced understanding of the cognitive implications for those navigating these uncharted territories.

Spatial cognition, a pivotal domain in cognitive science, investigates how humans perceive, mentally represent, and manipulate space, encompassing dimensions such as size, shape, depth, orientation, and position (Newcombe, 2002; Newcombe et al., 2013). Utilizing egocentric and allocentric encodings, individuals establish references to their body or other objects to encode object locations (Tuena, Mancuso et al. 2021). Spatial information, derived from visual, vestibular, and somatosensory systems, contributes to creating cognitive maps (Friederici & Levelt, 1987; Harris & Mander, 2014; Reschke et al., 1998).

## 3  Spatial Cognition and Size Perception Test:

Spatial perception, crucial for identifying spatial relationships, involves recognizing features, shapes, positions, and sizes (Carroll 1993, Brenner and van Damme 1999). It is deeply connected to exteroception and interception, contributing to awareness both within and outside our bodies (Peretz, Korczyn et al. 2011). Landmarks play a pivotal role in mental representations of space, acting as reference points for locating other objects (Higgins and Wang 2010). Additionally, spatial perception aids in anticipating changes and mentally representing spaces in 2D and 3D (Peretz et al., 2011).

Visuospatial perception, often discussed in spatial cognition literature, involves processing visual information about object positions in space (Höhler, Rasamoel et al. 2021). This aspect significantly influences daily functions, impacting our ability to navigate and manipulate spatial environments (Henry and Furness 1993). Visual perception, associated with the visual cortex, encompasses parieto-occipital regions for visual motion and spatial orientation and inferotemporal regions for object form and color processing (Kim et al., 1997; Kolb & Whishaw, 2009).

Landmarks, non-geometric spatial features like roads and buildings, contribute to distance, size, and direction perception (Casey et al., 1995; Kyttälä & Björn, 2014). Familiar objects provide perspective and scale, aiding accurate distance judgment (Naceri and Hoinville, Fennema, 1974; Newcombe, 2002). The absence of spatial cues from landmarks poses cognitive challenges, hindering spatial accuracy in altered environments (Parker 2003, Allred, Kravets et al. 2023).

Studies on spatial navigation emphasize the role of topological knowledge and metric representations in successful navigation (Schöberl, Zwergal and Brandt 2020). Factors like dimensions (2D vs. 3D), scales (vista-scale vs. large-scale), and visual landmark abundance impact spatial navigation (Harle & Towns, 2011). These aspects collectively contribute to our understanding of spatial perception, highlighting its intricate interplay with cognitive processes in diverse environments.

The ability of an observer to accurately assess distances between objects from any viewpoint is known as distance perception (Y. Sun et al., 2019). In the realm of object and surface perception, depth pertains to the distance directly in front of the observer's eye, involving gauging forward distances, akin to peering into a hole or tube (Kearney, Gorzel et al. 2012). Accurate distance measurements necessitate binocular stereoscopic vision (stereopsis), particularly for longer distances, along with other cues (Treisman 1962). Importantly, inaccuracies in size perception can result in corresponding inaccuracies in distance perception. Studies have revealed a correlation between distance and size perception, where objects located at a distance tend to be overestimated in size (Xinyue He et al., 2021). Overestimating the distance at which an object is seen leads to attributing a larger size to it, while underestimating the distance results in perceiving the object as smaller (Xinyu He et al., 2021).

The learned ability to perceive distances and sizes through repeated practice is crucial. However, in microgravity, linear perspective becomes less relevant due to the absence of gravitational reference and a visual horizon. Astronauts, with freely-floating eyes at varying distances from the floor, face challenges in using eye height scaling to determine their height (Xinyu He et al., 2021). These intricacies highlight the importance of understanding the interplay between distance and size perception, especially in environments with altered gravitational conditions.

Virtual Reality (VR) offers an immersive and versatile experience for users, making it a valuable tool in spatial cognition research and astronaut training. Studies have used VR to explore social dynamics, psychological functioning, and spatial challenges in environments like space stations. VR's ability to simulate extreme conditions with physiological responses akin to the real world is a valuable asset for research and training. Combining functional magnetic resonance imaging (fMRI) with VR enhances our understanding of how the human brain processes visual scenes and cues. The integration of VR technology in spatial perception research holds promise for gaining insights into size perception within simulated environments.

## 4  Materials and Methods

Through achieving these research goals and objectives, this study aims to deepen our understanding of how spatial cues, emerging technologies, and virtual environments influence human spatial perception, particularly in terms of size estimation. The findings may contribute valuable insights for various applications, from designing safer work environments to enhancing immersive experiences in virtual reality simulations.

**Research Goals and Objectives:**

– Investigate the Impact of Spatial Cues on Human Spatial Perception

  - Examine the role of egocentric and allocentric processing in shaping human spatial perception.
  - Explore how proprioceptive, somatosensory, and vestibular systems contribute to enhancing spatial perception.
  - Assess the significance of visual landmarks as spatial cues in accurately determining distance and size.

– Understand the Influence of Emerging Technologies on Spatial Perception

  - Investigate how evolving workplaces with altered visuospatial conditions may affect human spatial perception.
  - Examine the impact of technology-induced changes in spatial environments, such as those experienced in polar regions, deserts, lunar conditions, and spacewalk scenarios.

– Evaluate Size Perception in Varied Virtual Reality Environments

  - Simulate diverse spatial conditions (cityscape with familiar landmarks, Martian terrain with unfamiliar features, and deep space with no landmarks) in Virtual Reality using Unity 3D game engine.
  - Designate control (CG) and experimental groups (EG1 and EG2) to represent different levels of spatial cue availability.
  - Implement a size perception test within each VR environment, involving participants manipulating cube-like objects to assess their perceptual accuracy.

– Analyze and Interpret Size Estimations in Virtual Reality Environments

  - Recruit a sample of one hundred participants to complete the size perception task across the control and experimental groups.
  - Conduct a comprehensive analysis of participants' size estimations in three VR environments, considering dimensions such as depth, height, and width.
  - Identify patterns in participants' perceptual accuracy and explore variations in size estimations across different spatial conditions.

## 5  Participants

The research involved 100 participants, aged between 18 and 52, with a mean age of 24.74 and a standard deviation of 6.19 (refer to Fig. 1). The majority (74%) of the participants were male, and nearly half (40%) identified as gamers. All participants had either normal vision or vision corrected to normal. Recruitment occurred through bulk email announcements within Texas A&M University's student population, facilitated by the university's email system. The study received approval from the Institutional Review Board (IRB), and participants underwent a mandatory process of providing written consent before the commencement of the study.

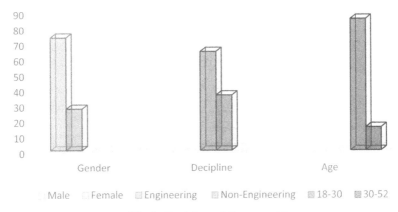

**Fig. 1.** Participants' Demographic

## 6  Study Environment

Unity 3D, a platform known for its versatility, was employed to craft Virtual Reality (VR) settings for both control and experiment conditions (Goldsmith et al., 2016). The scripting capabilities of Unity 3D allowed for tailored performance and functionality, essential for simulating distinct environments and interactions. The control group (CG) experienced a cityscape, rich in familiar landmarks and visual frames of reference (FOR), providing abundant cues such as roads, trees, cars, buildings, and people (Fig. 2). Experiment groups (EG1 and EG2) encountered altered visuospatial conditions, with EG1 representing a planet's surface (Mars or Moon) featuring an FOR and terrain but devoid of familiar landmarks. EG2 simulated outer space, lacking both FOR and terrain, akin to conditions faced during astronaut spacewalks. All environments maintained comparable visual quality for fair stimulus comparison. Participants engaged in size and distance perception tests in each setting (Fig. 3).

Size perception tests evaluate an individual's capability to accurately gauge object size in a spatial context (Haber and Levin, 2001). The distance perception test assesses allocentric spatial distance perception between objects (Plumert, Kearney et al., 2005)

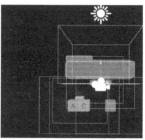

City Environment,
CG

Mars Environment,
EG1

Space Environment,
EG2

**Fig. 2.** Study environments

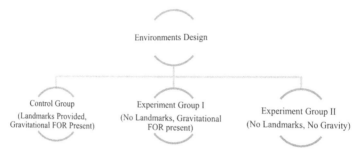

Environments Design

Control Group
(Landmarks Provided,
Gravitational FOR Present)

Experiment Group I
(No Landmarks, Gravitational
FOR present)

Experiment Group II
(No Landmarks, No Gravity)

**Fig. 3.** Experiments: Groups and Conditions

(Fig. 4). These tests drew inspiration from Clement's (2013) exploration of size and distance perception in microgravity environments (Clément, Skinner, and Lathan, 2013).

Control Group
(City Environment)

Experiment Group I
(Mars Environment)

Experiment Group II
(Space Environment)

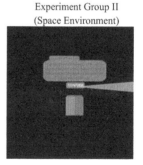

**Fig. 4.** SP in all 3 Environments

# 7   Limitations

Limitations in this study should be acknowledged. Firstly, prolonged use of VR headsets may induce participant fatigue, a factor not explored here but potentially affecting results. Despite efforts to create immersive microgravity simulations, participants still experienced gravitational feedback, introducing potential confounding effects. Secondly, the controlled lab setting may restrict the ecological validity of findings, as real-world spatial challenges often involve dynamic and unpredictable elements not replicated in controlled environments. Variables such as light quality, shadow patterns, and the absence of common spatial objects may impact results, reflecting a limitation in the study design.

# 8   Results

The study aimed to investigate how altered spatial conditions, represented by Control group (CG), Experiment group I (EG1), and Experiment group II (EG2) circumstances, influence participants' size perception, as assessed through the Size Perception (SP) test.

In evaluating the response accuracy across the different environments, a Friedman test revealed no statistically significant difference under Control group (CG), Experiment group I (EG1), and Experiment group II (EG2) circumstances ($\chi 2(2) = 0.740, p = 0.691$). This suggests that participants exhibited similar accuracy in size perception across these distinct spatial settings.

However, when examining response accuracy more closely, significant differences emerged (Friedman test, $\chi 2(2) = 9.500, p = 0.009$). Post hoc analysis using the sign test showed notable distinctions between SP responses under Control group (CG) vs. Experiment group I (EG1) ($p = 0.012$) and Experiment group I (EG1) vs. Experiment group II (EG2) ($p = 0.021$), with no significant difference between Control group (CG) and Experiment group II (EG2) ($p = 0.617$). Interestingly, SP responses under Control group (CG) and Experiment group II (EG2) were more accurate than those under Experiment group I (EG1).

Turning to response time, the Friedman test indicated no statistically significant difference under Control group (CG), Experiment group I (EG1), and Experiment group II (EG2) circumstances ($\chi 2(2) = 1.940, p = 0.379$). This suggests that participants exhibited similar response times in the SP test across the different spatial conditions.

Contrastingly, when scrutinizing response time differences, a significant finding emerged (Friedman test, $\chi 2(2) = 6.020, p = 0.049$). Post hoc analysis using the sign test revealed significant differences in SP response time under Experiment group I (EG1) vs. Experiment group II (EG2) ($p = 0.004$), while no significant differences were observed between Control group (CG) vs. Experiment group I (EG1) ($p = 0.484$) and Control group (CG) vs. Experiment group II (EG2) ($p = 0.368$). This implies that SP response time was longer under Experiment group I (EG1) compared to the Experiment group II (EG2) environment.

Examining the relationship between accuracy and response time, no linear association was found for the SP test under Control group (CG), Experiment group I (EG1), and Experiment group II (EG2) circumstances.

In summary, the Size Perception test results indicate that while overall accuracy remains consistent across different spatial settings, there are nuanced differences in both accuracy and response time, shedding light on the intricate influence of spatial cues on size perception in virtual reality environments.

## 9   Discussion

The exploration of size perception in varied spatial conditions has unraveled intriguing facets of human spatial cognition. The consistent accuracy across Control group I (CG), Experiment group I (EG1), and Experiment group II (EG2) settings, as revealed by the Friedman test, suggests a robust adaptability of human perceptual mechanisms in virtual environments. However, the nuanced differences in accuracy and response time prompt a deeper dive into the factors influencing size perception under different spatial cues.

One notable finding is the discrepancy in depth and height estimation between Control group I (CG) and Experiment group I (EG1) conditions, indicating potential influences of visual landmarks on perceived distance and height. The overestimation in these dimensions within Control group I (CG) and Experiment group I (EG1) environments may be attributed to the absence of familiar reference points in the Martian terrain, challenging participants to recalibrate their perception. In contrast, the absence of significant differences in accuracy between Control group I (CG) and Experiment group II (EG2) conditions suggests a distinct reliance on allocentric processing and spatial memory in the absence of Earthly landmarks.

The divergence in width estimation patterns across Control group I (CG), Experiment group I (EG1), and Experiment group II (EG2) conditions raises intriguing questions about the role of spatial cues in perceiving object dimensions. The overestimation in width within Experiment group II (EG2) conditions, contrary to Control group I (CG) and Experiment group I (EG1), may be linked to the absence of a base plane or terrain, altering participants' judgments of object proportions.

The longer response time observed in Experiment group I (EG1) conditions compared to Experiment group II (EG2) implies an additional cognitive load, potentially arising from the unfamiliar Martian terrain. The lack of a linear association between accuracy and response time suggests a complex interplay of cognitive processes in virtual size perception, challenging the notion of a straightforward trade-off between speed and precision.

## 10   Conclusion

In a world transitioning towards technologically advanced and spatially challenging environments, understanding the dynamics of size perception becomes paramount. This study, delving into the impact of spatial cues on virtual size perception, illuminates the intricate interplay between human cognition and altered spatial conditions.

The consistency in overall accuracy across Control group I (CG), Experiment group I (EG1), and Experiment group II (EG2) scenarios showcases the adaptability of human spatial perception, providing a foundation for designing immersive virtual environments. The nuanced differences observed in depth, height, and width estimations underscore the importance of considering specific spatial cues when crafting virtual reality simulations.

Beyond the realms of experimentation, the implications of this study extend to real-world scenarios. As workplaces evolve and individuals find themselves navigating unfamiliar terrains, the insights garnered from this research can guide the development of training programs, safety protocols, and ergonomic designs tailored to enhance spatial awareness.

In essence, this study not only enriches our understanding of human spatial perception but also pioneers a path towards creating more intuitive and adaptive virtual environments. By bridging the gap between theoretical insights and practical applications, this research contributes to the seamless integration of humans into ever-evolving spatial landscapes, ensuring a future where spatial challenges are met with informed, agile, and accurate perceptual responses.

**Acknowledgments.** The presented work has been supported by the U.S. National Science Foundation (NSF) through grant CNS 1928695. The authors gratefully acknowledge the support from the NSF. Any opinions, findings, conclusions, and recommendations expressed in this paper are those of the authors and do not necessarily represent those of the NSF.

# References

Allred, A.R., Kravets, V.G., Ahmed, N., Clark, T.K.: Modeling orientation perception adaptation to altered gravity environments with memory of past sensorimotor states. Front. Neural Circuits **17** (2023)

Brenner, E., van Damme, W.J.M.: Perceived distance, shape and size. Vis. Res. **39**(5), 975–986 (1999). https://doi.org/10.1016/S0042-6989(98)00162-X

Carroll, J.B.: Human Cognitive Abilities: A Survey of Factor-Analytic Studies. Cambridge University Press, Cambridge (1993)

Casey, M.B., Nuttall, R., Pezaris, E., Benbow, C.P.: The influence of spatial ability on gender differences in mathematics college entrance test scores across diverse samples. Dev. Psychol. **31**(4), 697 (1995)

Clément, G., Skinner, A., Lathan, C.: Distance and size perception in astronauts during long-duration spaceflight. Life (Basel) **3**(4), 524–537 (2013). https://doi.org/10.3390/life3040524

Fennema, E.: Mathematics, Spatial Ability and the Sexes (1974)

Fukushima, K., Fukushima, J., Warabi, T., Barnes, G.R.: Cognitive processes involved in smooth pursuit eye movements: behavioral evidence, neural substrate and clinical correlation. Front. Syst. Neurosci. **7**, 4 (2013). https://doi.org/10.3389/fnsys.2013.00004

Goldsmith, L., Hetland, L., Hoyle, C., Winner, E.: Visual-spatial thinking in geometry and the visual arts. Psychol. Aesthet. Creat. Arts **10**, 56–71 (2016)

Haber, R.N., Levin, C.A.: The independence of size perception and distance perception. Percept. Psychophys. **63**(7), 1140–1152 (2001)

Harle, M., Towns, M.: A review of spatial ability literature, its connection to chemistry, and implications for instruction. J. Chem. Educ. **88**(3), 351–360 (2011)

Harris, L.R., Jenkin, M., Jenkin, H., Zacher, J.E., Dyde, R.T.: The effect of long-term exposure to microgravity on the perception of upright. NPJ Microgravity **3**(1), 3 (2017)

Harris, L.R., Mander, C.: Perceived distance depends on the orientation of both the body and the visual environment. J. Vis. **14**(12), 17 (2014)

Henry, D., Furness, T.: Spatial perception in virtual environments: evaluating an architectural application. In: Proceedings of IEEE Virtual Reality Annual International Symposium (1993)

Higgins, J.S., Wang, R.F.: A landmark effect in the perceived dis-placement of objects. Vision. Res. **50**(2), 242–248 (2010)

Höhler, C., et al.: The impact of visuospatial perception on distance judgment and depth perception in an Augmented Reality environment in patients after stroke: an exploratory study. J. Neuroeng. Rehabil. **18**(1), 1–17 (2021)

Kim, C.K., et al.: Object-recognition and spatial learning and memory in rats prenatally exposed to ethanol. Behav. Neurosci. **111**(5), 985 (1997)

Kearney, G., Gorzel, M., Rice, H., Boland, F.: Distance perception in interactive virtual acoustic environments using first and higher order ambisonic sound fields. Acta Acust. Acust. **98**(1), 61–71 (2012)

Kiefer, P., Giannopoulos, I., Raubal, M., Duchowski, A.: Eye tracking for spatial research: cognition, computation, challenges. Spat. Cogn. Comput. **17**(1–2), 1–19 (2017)

Kolb, B., Whishaw, I.Q.: Fundamentals of Human Neuropsychology. Macmillan (2009)

Kyttälä, M., Björn, P.M.: The role of literacy skills in adolescents' mathematics word problem performance: controlling for visuo-spatial ability and mathematics anxiety. Learn. Individ. Differ. **29**, 59–66 (2014)

Newcombe, N.S.: Spatial cognition (2002)

Newcombe, N.S., Uttal, D.H., Sauter, M.: Spatial development (2013)

Newman, P.M., McNamara, T.P.: Integration of visual landmark cues in spatial memory. Psychol. Res. **86**(5), 1636–1654 (2022). https://doi.org/10.1007/s00426-021-01581-8

Oman, C.: Spatial orientation and navigation in microgravity. In: Mast, F., Jäncke, L. (eds.) Spatial Processing in Navigation, Imagery and Perception, pp. 209–247. Springer, Boston (2007). https://doi.org/10.1007/978-0-387-71978-8_13

Parker, D.E.: Spatial perception changes associated with space flight: implications for adaptation to altered inertial environments. J. Vestib. Res. **13**(4–6), 331–343 (2003)

Peretz, C., Korczyn, A.D., Shatil, E., Aharonson, V., Birnboim, S., Giladi, N.: Computer-based, personalized cognitive training versus classical computer games: a randomized double-blind prospective trial of cognitive stimulation. Neuroepidemiology **36**(2), 91–99 (2011)

Plumert, J.M., Kearney, J.K., Cremer, J.F., Recker, K.: Distance perception in real and virtual environments. ACM . Appl. Percept. (TAP) **2**(3), 216–233 (2005)

Reschke, M.F., Bloomberg, J.J., Harm, D.L., Paloski, W.H., Layne, C., McDonald, V.: Posture, locomotion, spatial orientation, and motion sickness as a function of space flight. Brain Res. Rev. **28**(1–2), 102–117 (1998)

Ruddle, R.A., Volkova, E., Mohler, B., Bülthoff, H.H.: The effect of landmark and body-based sensory information on route knowledge. Mem. Cognit. **39**(4), 686–699 (2011)

Salehi, F., Pariafsai, F., Dixit, M.K.: The impact of misaligned idiotropic and visual axes on spatial ability under altered visuospatial conditions. Virtual Real 1–15 (2023)

Salehi, F., et al.: How human spatial ability is affected by the misalignment of idiotropic and visual axes. In: Schmorrow, D.D., Fidopiastis, C.M. (eds.) HCII 2023. LNCS, vol. 14019, pp. 169–186. Springer, Cham (2023). https://doi.org/10.1007/978-3-031-35017-7_12

Schöberl, F., Zwergal, A., Brandt, T.: Testing navigation in real space: contributions to understanding the physiology and pathology of human navigation control. Front. Neural Circuits **14**, 6 (2020). https://doi.org/10.3389/fncir.2020.00006

Sun, R., Wu, Y.J., Cai, Q.: The effect of a virtual reality learning environment on learners' spatial ability. Virtual Real. **23**, 385–398 (2019)

Sun, Y., Xu, Q., Li, Y., Zhang, C., Li, Y., Wang, S., Sun, J.: Perceive where to focus: Learning visibility-aware part-level features for partial person re-identification. In: Proceedings of the IEEE/CVF Conference on Computer Vision and Pattern Recognition (2019)

Tachibana, K.: Workplace in space: space neuroscience and performance management in terrestrial environments. In: Organizational Neuroethics: Re-flections on the Contributions of Neuroscience to Management Theories and Business Practices, pp. 235–255 (2020)

Treisman, A.: Binocular rivalry and stereoscopic depth perception. Quart. J. Exper. Psychol. **14**(1), 23–37 (1962)

Tuena, C., et al.: Egocentric and allocentric spatial memory in mild cognitive impairment with real-world and virtual navigation tasks: a systematic review. J. Alzheimers Dis. **79**(1), 95–116 (2021)

Turgut, M.: Development of the spatial ability self-report scale (SASRS): reliability and validity studies. Qual. Quant. **49**, 1997–2014 (2015)

Winter, K.-F.R.S.: Chapter 1 (2014)

# Modeling and Simulation Technologies for Effective Multi-agent Research

Kristin E. Schaefer[1] ⓘ, Ralph W. Brewer[1(✉)] ⓘ, Joshua Wickwire[2] ⓘ,
Rosario Scalise[3] ⓘ, and Chad C. Kessens[1] ⓘ

[1] DEVCOM Army Research Laboratory, Aberdeen Proving Ground 21005, USA
{kristin.e.schaefer-lay.civ,ralph.w.brewer.civ}@army.mil
[2] Parsons, Omaha 20151, USA
[3] Oakridge Associated Research Universities, Oak Ridge 37831, USA

**Abstract.** Simulation technologies are increasingly essential for developing real-world agents throughout the product development cycle. Relevant phases include design, behavior development, prediction, training, and assessment, among others. This paper reviews current simulation technologies for advancing state-of-the-art research facilitating multi-agent teaming, considering strengths and weaknesses of current approaches as well as ideas for future development needs.

**Keywords:** Simulation · Multi-Agent · Modeling · Teaming · Robotics · Autonomy

## 1 Introduction

Simulation technologies are a critical resource for robotics, from design of the system to integration into a world (physics modeling), learning (artificial intelligence and machine learning approaches), human-robot interaction, and more recently multi-agent collaborative behavior development. While several reviews of simulation technologies for robotics have been conducted over the years defining many benefits and barriers [1, 2], the driving research needs for integrating live, virtual, and constructive simulation capabilities for multi-agent autonomy research require an integrative technology approach bridging the gap from physics modeling to game-based virtual environments.

### 1.1 Live, Virtual, Constructive Simulation for Multi-agent Autonomy

Simulation technologies can be used to support live, virtual, constructive (LVC) research, as well as a combination of LVC simulation approaches for research spanning vehicle design and engineering, autonomy and artificial intelligence (AI) development, machine learning (ML) principles, networking, and data management, to name a few. But when considering a simulation testbed for multi-agent autonomy, which may include coordinated integration of unmanned aerial, ground, and surface robotics operating with humans either in or on-the-loop, there is currently no single simulation technology that addresses all requirements. Therefore, a multi-faceted approach is required.

© The Author(s), under exclusive license to Springer Nature Switzerland AG 2024
J. Y. C. Chen and G. Fragomeni (Eds.): HCII 2024, LNCS 14707, pp. 86–104, 2024.
https://doi.org/10.1007/978-3-031-61044-8_7

Developing the underlying science and technology (S&T) for collaborative behaviors and coordinated maneuver on actual platforms requires significant cost, time, and resources. Given these costs, the integration of game-based simulation technologies with specific hardware and software provides a testbed to assess multiple scenarios to develop novel algorithms, behaviors, and mission sets prior to field operations. Current S&T applications are often developed for a specific platform, mission, or capability. However, with multi-agent autonomy moving forward, LVC simulation testbeds need to account for a variety of potential autonomous behaviors, heterogeneous robotic morphologies, terrains, and dynamics regimes.

**Definitions.** This section provides reference point for definitions to level set the discussions below.

*Live, Virtual, and Constructive (LVC) Simulation.* LVC is a taxonomy used to classify simulation types [3] whereby *live simulation* involves real people operating real systems. *Virtual simulation* involves real people operating simulated systems. *Constructive simulation* involves simulated people operating simulated systems. It is important to note that in the area of multi-agent research and intelligent robotics, a combination of LVC simulations is often leveraged for improved fidelity, sim-to-real transition, and rapid prototyping.

*Agent.* For the purpose of this work, agent can refer to any member of the team, including a human agent, a robotic agent (embodied), or an intelligent computer agent (not embodied). Autonomous agents work toward their given goal and interact with their environment and other systems without immediate help from humans, typically using artificial intelligence (AI), machine learning (ML) or deep learning (DL) to accomplish goals [4].

*Autonomy.* Autonomy is on a spectrum that results in the system's ability to accomplish tasks with varying levels of human input. While many definitions exist, a common direction is focused on the minimization of human input so that the robot or autonomy-enabled system can carry out its own actions, refine or modify the task and its behaviors [5] with the ability to accommodate variations in the environment [6], and achieve goals given a specified level of uncertainty [7]. It is important to understand that an autonomy-enabled system, such as an intelligent robot, can go through multiple stages or levels of autonomy under different situations or interactions [8].

*Artificial Intelligence.* In 1956, at a conference at Dartmouth University, scholars formally proposed the term *artificial intelligence.* That moment was the first step in a new topic of studying how machines simulate human intelligent activities. AI is a compilation of computer science, logic, biology, psychology, philosophy, and many other disciplines that impact research in expert systems, ML, robotics, decision support systems, and even pattern recognition [9].

*Research Requirements and Current Simulation Gaps.* An LVC simulation testbed for multi-agent autonomy research has a number of research requirements that a single simulation technology will not be able to support. A large portion of the robotics simulation research to date is directed at either single agent design, physics, algorithm development, testing, or learning. Andrews [10] describes robotic simulation as enabling "virtual training and programming that can use physics-based digital representations of environments, robots, machines, objects and other assets." However, within the concept of LVC simulation, connections must be made beyond that of a virtual robot in a virtual environment. The following research requirements need to be addressed in an LVC simulation testbed.

*Big Data Processing.* Big Data is a term that often references Internet of Things research applications and is a perquisite for AI [11] to describe the collection of methodologies for not only accessing large amounts of data, but also extracting meaningful information. The five characteristics are volume (amount), variety (structured vs unstructured), velocity (speed), variability (changing data), and veracity (differing data), making it challenging in the areas of accuracy, power consumption, and cost [12]. Robotic systems have the potential to collect and generate large data sources, yet data fusion and data management processes are still being developed. In addition, for best sim-to-real transition, managing and matching these data management processes should be as seamless as possible.

*Test, Evaluation, Verification, and Validation (TEVV).* Traditionally TEVV processes are thought about as a final stage in robotic system development. However, there is a more recent push to integrate these processes earlier in the S&T life cycle. For autonomy or AI-enabled systems where change and learning are expected, novel methods for TEVV need to be developed. It is more than just for safety. Ten challenges for TEVV for autonomy and AI-enabled systems [13] should be considered when developing LVC simulation testbeds for multi-agent coordinated operations:

- Instrumenting machine thinking
- Linking system performance to autonomous behaviors
- Comparing AI models to reality
- Concept of Operations and training as design features
- Human trust in autonomy
- Elevated safety concerns and asymmetric hazard
- Exploitable vulnerabilities
- Emergent behavior
- Post-fielding changes
- Verification and validation of training data

*Networked Communication.* In a multi-agent team, networked communication becomes a priority for coordinated behavior [14], as it advances intent sharing, team trust, and team situation awareness [15]. A many-to-many paradigm of grid networked systems that have a multi-directional flow of information can result in system latency paralleling the behavior of malicious attacks on a system [16]. However, scalability and observability become important variables in network approaches for multi-agent communication and learning [17]. Integrating network architectures into virtual or LVC simulation is very difficult to initiate, integrate, and coordinate.

*Sim-to-Real.* The goal of aligning the simulation of an autonomous agent and simulated environment so that the simulated outputs match the real sensor data as closely as possible. However, this results in many considerations [18, 19]:

- Cost: The cost of creating a simulation environment must also be weighed with balancing compute requirements with appropriate levels of fidelity.
- Transferability of data or research outcomes: Sim-to-real decisions can directly impact the coordination and transition between LVC environments.
- Dealing with the unknown: Complexity and uncertainty are two givens in robotic operations in the real world. Simulation often artificially injects methods to reduce complexity and uncertainty. Understanding what is "pre-programmed" or "simulated" to identify variables that will impact performance in the real world.
- Reality gap: The performance of systems in real life must be compared to that of the simulation. This includes the stochastic nature of activities performed in the real world in order to know that the simulation adequately represents the necessary qualities of real life. Among other factors, system safety when operating in the real world must be guaranteed.
- Agent collaboration: Suh and colleagues [20] argue that system issues may raise an additional reality gap in the two execution environments of the simulator and the real world. It originates from an inconsistency of assumptions and constraints imposed on the two execution environments.
- Environment synchronization: We need an accurate model of the real robot and the environment to improve accuracy in the sim-to-real [21]. Inherent mismatches with the real-world setting can negatively impact reinforcement learning and training [22].

*Dynamic Environments.* An environment that is characterized by rapid changes, uncertainty, complexity, with a mix of risks and opportunities. In simulation, this may include temporal changes for time of day, weather events, non-player character behaviors, among others. Dynamism, which is the evolution of a simulated environment over time, should be modeled explicitly as part of the simulated environment [23].

### 1.2   Simulation for Robotics

Simulation is a critical part of robotics across the research and development (R&D) lifecycle. However, many developed simulation technologies are limited to a specific use case or application. This makes it difficult to develop an integrative simulation testbed to support LVC multi-agent research. Figure 1 is a conceptual depiction showing the relationship and importance of modeling (mathematical modeling, physics modeling, dynamical modeling, and world modeling) and the associated intersections with simulation from particle simulation to physics simulation, and onto game-based simulation. Developing, testing, and validating robotic features, capabilities, and team dynamics is a cyclical process that may include part or all of these modeling and simulation approaches.

**Why Simulation?** While simulation will not be the end-all-be-all for multi-agent autonomy research, it can provide several benefits to the research process. Simulation is often one of the first steps to assess theoretical methods. It is convenient and supports rapid prototyping, resulting in a tighter development-test loop. Simulation can also provide cost savings in that virtual testing often has fewer personnel requirements, lower associated fees, and by controlling for different variables, system evaluations can occur without a fully functioning system. Simulations can also adapt speed to run faster than real-time

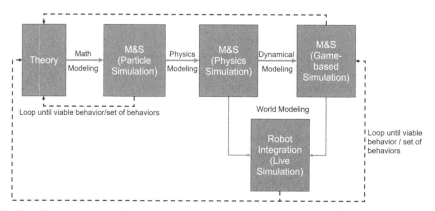

**Fig. 1.** Initial conceptual diagram on the intersections between modeling and simulation approaches that feed into a multi-agent simulation testbed.

with parallel processing (increasing throughput of the simulations) with access to on-line processing or even high-performance computing resources. In addition, simulation can generate datasets at scales which are currently unachievable with real robots.

Choi et al. [24] outlined the critical benefits and barriers to simulation. Benefits include generation of large training datasets for ML, accelerating the engineering design cycle, and accelerated, controlled virtual testing and verification that can facilitate the development of more intelligent robots and improved human-robot interaction. However, producing simulation testbeds requires broad multidisciplinary expertise and sustained software development commitment. In addition, existing modeling languages are immature at a time when a robotics simulation ontology is just now emerging, model composability needs improvements, and uncertainty, complexity, and integrated teaming is marginally handled given compute and graphics requirements. Given these well-defined benefits and barriers, it is critical to develop an integrative simulation approach for multi-agent autonomy research. This requires a thorough understanding of the theoretical principles and considerations for robotics simulation.

**Underlying Theoretical Principles and Considerations.** Science and mathematics have identified many underlying theoretical principles that impact simulation technologies. These are critical variables that can directly impact an integrated multi-simulation system approach.

*Rotation Transformations.* In simulation, rotation transformations provide the basic relationships between reference frames (e.g., how does the robot appear in space). Rotation representations aligned with relative transformations are critical calculations to simulate movement through space. However, different game engines use varying methods (e.g. matrices, quaternions, Euler angles) for representing rotational transformations, leading to difficulties communicating data from one model or simulation technology to another. This was seen when Schaefer et al. developed the Wingman software-in-the-loop simulation testbed which use a combination of OGRE 3D and Unity 3D engines for visualization of different subsystems [25].

*Kinematics.* Kinematics describe the motion of objects without considering the forces and torques that cause the motion. For robots consisting of multiple parts (e.g. limbed systems), kinematics determines the position and orientation (pose) of each body part relative to the others, subject to system constraints. This is important for determining the end effector pose given manipulator joint angles, also known as forward kinematics. It is also important for solving the inverse kinematics problem – determining what joint angles to command in order to locate and orient the end effector as desired. For multi-agent simulations, accurate kinematic simulations are essential for collision avoidance and interaction.

*Dynamics.* Dynamics modeling considers how mass and applied forces and torques affect the evolution of motion within a system. A variety of dynamics solvers are used by different simulators, and the choice of which solver to use can significantly affect the fidelity and speed of the simulation, usually trading against one another.

*Collision Detection and Modeling.* Collision detection and modeling is critical to interaction. Convex contact models (e.g. in MuJoCo) is often used in manipulation to allow for planning to grasp, move, or interact with objects in the world [26]. From the virtual simulation perspective, models of the terrain, world, and object features are critical to preventing the robotic agent from traveling through an object that should be solid. However, fully modeling every object in a virtual environment is computationally expensive and can drastically slow the processing speed of the simulation, suggesting the value of using multi-fidelity models [27].

*Friction.* Friction models are also important whenever an agent is interacting with objects in the world, including the ground. Like contact modeling, friction model fidelity can vary considerably, representing trade-offs between accuracy and speed. Specifically, simulation of terrain features and textures may or may not capture how sand or soil changes in reaction to driving over it, how an agent will move when in contact with the road versus sliding on ice, and whether a grasped object will slip from the hand if it is rotated. The need for modeling dynamic friction (i.e. sliding) and its fidelity must be considered based on the desired application.

*Differentiable Simulators.* Presently, the standard procedure for simulators is to assume that once the models they represent are loaded, they remain unchanged throughout the lifetime of the simulation. That is, information only flows from the simulator to an external process, never in the reverse direction. This is sufficient for many of the common simulator use cases. However, when simulation is tightly coupled to a process that improves the behavior of a robot, it can become restrictive to stick to the "initial" assumptions of the model. A weak form of allowing some feedback includes system identification (SysID), but a more general framework that readily accepts model feedback via gradient signals is known as "differentiable simulation".

Advantages: Enabling differentiability means the entirety of the simulator can be included as part of the model parameters when using machine learning to obtain better robot behaviors. This implies that we can blend our model-based priors with data obtained from the real systems (that might not completely obey the priors). Because of this, we have a new flexibility to fine-tune for specific contexts as well as different hardware characteristics. This paradigm also naturally admits a specific subset of reinforcement learning known as model-based reinforcement learning (MBRL), which uses the learning process to simultaneously update both the robot behavior policy and the dynamics model. This often leads to greater update accuracy and is therefore a significantly more efficient class of algorithms. Differentiability also opens the possibility of more natural parallelism in the model space, something that is not as straightforward (or in some cases even possible) with traditional simulators. Once again, this can lead to significant increases in accuracy and learning efficiency.

Disadvantages (caveats): The machinery required to perform differentiable simulation is more involved. In some cases, simple assumptions cannot be always made when computing simulator updates. For example, if a non-differentiable simulator is used underneath, the acquisition of gradient information will require finite-difference approximations which can become numerically unstable if modeling discontinuous phenomena. In other cases, simplifying assumptions are required to make the computation tractable. As with simulators in general, striking the right balance between computational feasibility and the appropriate simulation fidelity remains a challenge, and requiring the computation to be differentiable adds an extra dimension to the design considerations, restricting the kinds of assumptions and algorithms that can be used within the physics engine.

## 2   Review of Simulation Systems for Robotics

Simulation is a critical tool for robotics but is continually developing. In 2016, Dr. MaryAnne Fields led an effort to evaluate the pros and cons of simulation systems for four areas of robotics: perception, intelligence, human–robot interaction, and dexterous manipulation. The team evaluated open source (e.g., Gazebo, Moby), commercial (e.g., Simulink, Actin, LMS), government (e.g., ANVEL/VANE), and other simulation systems for tradeoffs [1]. Since that time, some of these technologies have deprecated and new technologies have been developed, but many of the critical findings still hold true:

- No single robotic simulation environment adequately covers the needs of the robotic researcher in all domains.
- Unique constraints of specific robots (e.g., unmanned aerial systems or robotic manipulators) require physics-based models that can be computationally heavy.
- Dynamic motion is reliant on the accuracy of computational models.
- Perception remains problematic for adequate simulation performance due to computer rendering and inadequate realism.

In 2021, Collins and colleagues conducted a comparative review to identify the best physics simulation tools for robotics based on domain of operations. These included:

- Mobile Ground Robotics: CARLA, CoppeliaSim, Gazebo, MaloCo, PyBullet, SOFA, UWSim, Project Chromo, Webots
- Maritime Robotics: UWSim, UUV, Stonefish, URSim, USVSim
- Aerial Robotics: AirSim, Flightmare, Gazebo, Webots
- Manipulation Robotics: SimGrasp, Gazebo, CoppeliaSim, PyBullet, MaloCo, NVIDIA ISAAC

- Learning Robots: Raisim, Gazebo, NVIDIA ISAAC, MuJoCo, PyBullet, CARLA, Webots, CoppeliaSim

From this, it is clear some simulation technologies are cross-domain. The most popular simulation technologies per a citation count evaluation from 2016–2020 by Collins et al. [2] include Gazebo, MuJoCo, CoppeliaSim, CARLA, Webots, AirSim, and PyBullet. While physics simulation is of critical importance to robotics, it must be used in conjunction with other integrated models and simulation technologies. Therefore, we extend this foundational research in simulation for robotics to review novel advancements from physics-based simulations to integrated game-based environments for multi-agent LVC research.

## 2.1  Physics Modeling and Robotic Dynamics

Modeling physics and robot dynamics is a critical step in systems engineering. Understanding how a robot will and should move, function, and interact with the world is paramount for integration with autonomy stacks, networked communication, mission planning, and execution that will feed into the LVC simulation testbed for multi-agent autonomy research. Here we introduce some of the most common physics simulations for robotics.

**MuJoCo.** MuJoCo is a free, open source, advanced physics simulator developed at the University of Washington and now maintained by Google's DeepMind. It is primarily used to train policies for robotic manipulation (e.g., solving a Rubik's cube [28]), biomechanics, graphics, and animation. MuJoCo can be used to implement model-based computations such as control synthesis, state estimation, system identification, mechanism design, data analysis through inverse dynamics, parallel sampling for machine learning applications [29] but lacks contact stability or support for inverse kinematics and path planning.

**Drake.** Drake is a C++ toolbox started by the Robot Locomotion Group, MIT Computer Science and Artificial Intelligence Lab. This design and analysis tool is well suited for analyzing robot dynamics and building control systems. It is known for its ability to simulate complex dynamics, such as friction, contact, etc., while aligning with the governing equations, including sparsity, analytical gradients, and polynomial structure, among others [30]. However, it does not support ROS 2 at the time of this writing.

**Open Dynamics Engine (ODE).** ODE is a free, open source, high performance library for simulating rigid body dynamics (e.g., collision detection), especially articulated structures such as serial, open-chain linkages [31]. This makes it a viable platform for robotic manipulation. However, it has significant limitations when it comes to friction approximation and joint-damping and is not designed for soft contact.

**Bullet.** Bullet is another free, open-source physics engine and library. It is capable of simulating both rigid body and soft body (e.g. rope, cloth) dynamics, and has been used extensively for video game development, visual effects in movies, robotics, and reinforcement learning. It handles both discrete and continuous collision detection. Developers often use PyBullet [32], which is a Python module based on the Bullet Physics Software Development Kit (SDK).

**Dynamic Animation and Robotics Toolkit (DART).** DART is a collaborative, cross-platform, open-source library developed at the Georgia Institute of Technology, with ongoing contributions from the University of Washington and the Open-Source Robotics Foundation [33]. It provides data structures and algorithms for kinematic and dynamic applications in robotics and computer animation. DART stands out due to its accuracy and stability, which are achieved using generalized coordinates to represent articulated rigid body systems and the application of Featherstone's Articulated Body Algorithm to compute motion dynamics.

**RaiSim.** RaiSim, developed by ETH Zurich, is a rigid-body physics simulator that is aligned to research in learning dynamic policies for legged robotics. It includes high fidelity contact dynamics models with uneven terrain models [2], and has proven useful for simulating complex, high degree of freedom robots such as ANYmal [34].

**Brax.** Brax is an open-source library for rigid body simulation [35]. This simulation technology is written in JAX, and specifically designed to support reinforcement learning. It can integrate with MuJoCo to facilitate training on performance policies. A highlight of Brax is that it is designed to be fully differentiable, meaning gradient information can be propagated through arbitrary layers of the physical computation. This is generally challenging to achieve in simulators that are not designed to do this from the ground up.

## 2.2 Network Modeling

Multi-agent communication requires network modeling. The Extendable Mobile Ad-hoc Network Emulator (EMANE) is a next-generation framework for real-time modeling of mobile network systems allowing network protocol and applications to be experimentally assessed and connected to both real and virtualized network stacks [36].

## 2.3 Interfacing with Deep Reinforcement Learning Libraries

The term "gym" is often appended to software abstractions that require a "gym-like" API. This is most useful in the context of reinforcement learning, but also other approaches including imitation learning, motion planning, etc. It simply means there is an interface defined which includes a 'step ()' function that returns a specific signature. The step function takes a current state (or observation) and action, forward simulates physics for one timestep, and returns a next state (or observation) as well as a reward for this step. Examples include Unreal Gym, Soft-body Gym, and Isaac Gym.

## 2.4 Integrating Physics and Sensor Simulations

Transition of physics models and simulation requires interaction with a world. The following simulators have lower fidelity virtual environments but provide the next level of validation and verification of robotic physics and sensors.

**Gazebo.** Gazebo, developed by Open Robotics, is a highly leveraged open-source robot simulator. Beyond physics, Gazebo can simulate a variety of sensors (e.g. RGB-D cameras, 3D LiDAR, GPS, IMU) and other plug-ins to validate algorithms for land, air, and water robotics [37, 38]. It is known for its integration with ROS, making it a preferred tool for testing control software in simulation and transferring it onto physical systems [2]. However, it has accuracy limitations due to rendering capability.

**CoppeliaSim.** CoppeliaSim (formerly V-REP) from Coppelia Robotics [39] is a robotics simulator similar to Gazebo that can simulate multiple ground-based mobile robots in real-time, making it a versatile tool for fast algorithm development [2]. This simulation is based on a distributed control architecture allowing each individual object or model to be controlled through an embedded script, plugin, ROS node, remote API client, or custom solution. It can support multiple physics engines (e.g. MuJoCo, ODE, Bullet) to simulate soft bodies and some sensor modalities.

**CARLA.** The CARLA simulator is built on the Unreal Engine and was designed to support system development, training, and validation for autonomous self-driving vehicles with the goal of transitioning trained policies to the real world. It is scalable for multi-robot scenarios using a server and multi-client architecture, and is viable for planning and control, map generation, traffic simulation, and autonomous driving baselines. It supports multiple sensor modalities including RGB-D cameras, LiDAR, IMU, Radar, and collision detectors, among others [40].

**Webots.** Webots, from Cyberbotics, is an open source and multi-platform desktop application used to simulate robots. It provides a complete development environment to model, program and simulate robots [41]. It is popular for fast prototyping and multi-system applications (robotic arms, legged, modular, automobile, underwater, tracked, or aerospace) in indoor or outdoor environments.

**AWS RoboMaker.** From Amazon, AWS RoboMaker is a cloud-based simulation service enabling robotics development to run, scale, and automate simulation without managing infrastructure. It is well suited for automated regression testing, training reinforcement models, and multi-robot testing [42].

### 2.5 Game-Based Virtual Environments

A virtual environment is a computer-simulated domain that is accessible by one or more clients (users). Game engines provide an advantage to developers as they are typically outfitted with graphics, artificial intelligence, physics, and other modules [43]. Two of the most prominent game engines for robotics simulation include Unity and Unreal. Each have advantages and disadvantages for the research community. Table 1 is a compilation of Unity and Unreal comparative analyses from the community at large [44–52].

**Unity.** Unity is a powerful and popular cross-platform game engine that enables developers to create 2D and 3D applications. Its advantages include powerful mobile features; a user-friendly editor; the integration of Unity Playmaker for visual scripting; excellent scripting support through C#, custom plug-ins, and framework; fast compiling; support tutorials. The disadvantages include limited AI support, and it does not match the capabilities of UE regarding performance scalability—especially when dealing with large and graphically demanding projects. Unity can be used in conjunction with Flightmare (aerial), RaiSim, and NVIDIA Isaac for realistic rendering and deep reinforcement learning.

**Table 1.** Comparison of Unity and Unreal.

| Topic | Unity | Unreal |
|---|---|---|
| Software documentation and support | Well-documented online, up to date | Transition to Unreal 5 has made much online information obsolete |
| Operating systems | Windows, macOS, Linux (well-supported) | Windows# (preferred), macOS, Linux |
| Graphics | Stylized | Realistic |
| Languages | C# | C+ + |
| Dimensions | 2D and 3D | 3D, less support for 2D |
| Features: Plug-ins/assets | 65,000 + assets | 16,000 + assets |
| Features: AR/VR | Ray casting, Face tracking, 2D image tracking | Motion capture, Face tracking, 3D object detection |
| Features: Docker | Supported via NVIDIA Docker | Supported via NVIDIA Docker |
| Architecture | Client-server | Client-server |
| Coordinate system (X, Y, Z) | Left-handed, Y-up | Left-handed, world Cartesian |
| Source code | Not open source | Source available |
| Scripting | Unity visual scripting | Blueprint visual scripting |
| Development focus | Leader of AR/VR development | Renowned for high-quality 3D graphics |

**Unreal Engine (UE).** UE is a powerful game engine developed by Epic Games, known for its versatility and graphical capabilities. Recently, more companies have been moving from Unity to UE due to its impressive features, realism, and performance. Microsoft Airsim, NVIDIA Isaac, and CARLA have all been used in conjunction with UE. Overall advantages include real-time rendering capabilities, blueprint visual scripting system, use of object-oriented programming, node features, and realistic graphics. Disadvantages include limited capabilities for supporting 2D projects as well as its AR/VR features, and fewer plug-ins than Unity.

## 2.6 Multi-simulation Integration

In efforts to integrate multiple software components, NVIDIA developed several simulation capabilities. NVIDIA Omniverse is an umbrella term for a family of software solutions and applications resulting in an innovative platform that changes the way developers can work with different software. Its Omniverse connector has built-in plug-ins for both Unity and UE, which should allow them to work together and communicate with each other, leading to massive potential in enhancing the communication framework between Unity and Unreal.

**Isaac Sim.** Isaac Sim is a simulation engine that aims to accelerate graphics and physics computation on NVIDIA / CUDA platforms – namely graphics processing units (GPUs). Traditionally, physics simulation is performed using multi-threaded, multi-core CPU computation (i.e. one CPU thread per agent). Due to architectural differences, GPUs can typically simulate physics for up to 100x more agents simultaneously. This is especially advantageous when algorithms require significant amounts of simulated data (for example, using deep reinforcement learning algorithms to develop robot policies). Additionally, Isaac Sim aims to provide an entry into high-fidelity graphics that utilize ray-tracing hardware accelerators and other specialized physics simulation paradigms that depart from the typical rigid-body dynamics, including soft-body, cloth, and fluid dynamics simulation.

Aside from simulating dynamics in a hardware-accelerated manner, Isaac Sim (and Omniverse more broadly) aims to provide a next-generation community of support for interfacing with robotic hardware systems. This includes support for sensors like RGB cameras, depth cameras, LIDAR, IMUs, force sensors, contact sensors, etc. There is a growing set of resources from robotics manufacturers for integrating their systems into Isaac Sim including bridges to ROS 1 and ROS 2. For this reason, a secondary use-case for Isaac Sim is simply functioning as a digital twin that can be used to view robot status and issue controls in a bidirectional manner. As an example, industries have begun adopting Isaac Sim as a sort of "mission-control" visualizer for the robots currently in their inventory and on factory floors.

## 3   Concepts for Developing a Multi-Agent Simulation Testbed

The above listed simulation systems provide critical capabilities to the robotics R&D process; however, methods to develop an integrative simulation approach will be needed to develop, test, and validate multi-agent autonomy within the LVC domains. To address the simulation requirements for multi-agent teaming, a primary theoretical concept that needs to be addressed is context, because without context, robotic capabilities will remain limited in uncertain and dynamic environments [15]. Integration of context for intelligent robots is integral in the formulation of shared situation awareness, mutual trust, and improved multi-agent coordination [53].

### 3.1   Context-Aware Autonomy in Simulation

Context in AI and autonomy-enabled systems is critical for classifying and quantifying states, situations, and world information required to feed decision-making and behavior. Therefore, multi-agent simulation technologies will need to incorporate features related to space, time, mission, and history of the robot. Table 2 leverages previous large scale literature reviews on context-driven AI and autonomy in team dynamics [15, 53] to identify critical simulation features that inform behaviors.

**Table 2.** Simulation features for multi-agent context

| Multi-agent concept | Simulation Feature | Behavioral Outcome |
|---|---|---|
| **Spatial Context:** Location of objects or agents | Geospatial information: topologies, distances, routes, fixed features, and observations | Conceptualization and reasoning about the world for coordinated maneuver |
| **Spatial Context:** Semantic mapping and classification | Environmental feature fidelity with access to training datasets; integration of real or simulated sensor technologies | Feature detection, resolution of sensed object; error reduction in scene detection and inference processing |
| **Temporal Context:** Recognizing and tracking consecutive scenes | Integration of location and time | Realistic interaction with dynamic events or characters |
| **Temporal Context:** Time-critical decision-making based on rapid assessment | Meaning from the scene, task, or mission: Access to prior knowledge, plug-in, or harness to incoming information from team members | Real-time or close to real-time decision-making |
| **Temporal and Environmental Context:** Assessing a current situation | Observing partial or entire state history; Dynamic events and characters | Integration of learning approaches for robot/team behaviors |
| **Environmental Context:** Infer optimal maneuver | Integration of additional sensors or models (temperature, humidity, smell, audio) with physics models; simulated terrain density | Weather inference can direct the capability to deploy a payload, operate a system, or maneuver in a given environment |
| **Mission Context:** Conduct team-based task operations | Integration of Mission Planners: Be able to support active decision-making; account for rules of engagement and social norms given vehicle physics capacity | Goal prioritization |
| **Social Context:** Collaborative decision-making | Advanced robot awareness: pose, location, social behavior tracking; integration with computational models for social interactions | Deep learning |

## 3.2   Autonomy Integration with Simulation

A multi-agent simulation testbed should be agnostic to a particle autonomy stack. However, it is paramount to understand the simulation features that are unique to ground, aerial, and surface vehicles. Thus, the vehicle matters, the world matters, and the networked coordination of agents matters.

**Ground Vehicle Autonomy.** Ground vehicle autonomy has a range of vehicle dynamics factors including size, ground contact (e.g. wheels vs treads vs legs), and on to unique capabilities for maneuver and payload. The following features are considerations for simulation:

- Simulated terrain variation (soil density and types), littoral transition, obstacles (lethal vs non-lethal)
- Environmental features that impact vehicle dynamics and autonomy behaviors: weather, lighting, temperature, humidity, air quality
- Localization: GPS vs GPS denied
- Sensor Perception: Particle simulations for dust, obscurants, weather

**Aerial Vehicle Autonomy.** Aerial vehicles range across Group 1 (0–20 lbs.), Group 2 (21–55 lbs.), and Group 3 (<1320 lbs.), wing type (rotary versus fixed wing), and vertical takeoff and landing capability. All these unique features are directly relational to how the vehicle operates in given wind gusts, atmospheric phenomena, and lighting.

- Simulation systems should have the ability to integrate real-world models of wind, atmospheric (weather), and lighting.
- Simulation systems should be able to directly integrate with the actual controller (e.g., PX4).
- Navigation and maneuver are not locked to the ground.

**Surface Vehicle Autonomy.** Surface vehicle autonomy is incredibly complex in that the water surface is always moving. Simulation features include:

- Models of buoyancy, surface tension, salinity
- Environmental models: wind, wave height, temperature
- Waterproof / resistant sensors

# 4    Connecting the Pieces

The dynamics and requirements for multi-agent autonomy change how simulation technologies are integrated and used as they move through the R&D lifecycle. The critical factor for this change is the requirement for uncertainty and complexity. Robotic systems need to learn and dynamically adapt behavior. Context drives decision-making and feeds the underlying requirements. The lifecycle then further drives the simulation features and considerations to quantify the degree of simulated inputs, further adding complexity to developing a testbed. Here we provide an initial conceptual framework that addresses the identified considerations for developing integrated LVC simulation technologies for multi-agent autonomy research.

## 4.1    Conceptual Design for Multi-Agent Simulation Testbed

The development of a multi-agent simulation testbed that can integrate and support live, virtual, and/or constructive research requires a harnessed, plug-in approach to support research across the R&D lifecycle. Figure 2 depicts the intersection of a perception layer that leverages real-world models (either live or previously modeled), vehicle physics models and autonomy stacks, with links to a human-machine integration (HMI) layer for integration with live human agents. All layer connections require feature upgrades within a virtual environment to support dynamic, multi-agent behaviors to occur.

## 4.2   Simulation Features and Considerations

Throughout the R&D lifecycle of multi-agent autonomy, a simulation testbed will need to adapt and transition new capabilities and enhancements. However, trade-offs in development time, computational resources, graphics card requirements, and other factors must be considered. Further, each additional agent integrated into a testbed impacts computational resources.

**Dynamic Features vs Repeatability.** A simulation testbed should be able to transition from repeatable tests to dynamic features. Simulation features for repeatability allow the autonomous agent(s) to face the same environment, events, non-player character behaviors, and timing sequences. These features can be considered "pre-programmed" through use of event and trigger functions. This allows a decision tree type architecture for decision-making – if Agent A enters Zone B, the agent executes the Behavior C sequence. However, as the R&D lifecycle continues through validation and verification processes, the importance of dynamic features increases. This adds an AI layer onto the environmental features and non-player character behaviors.

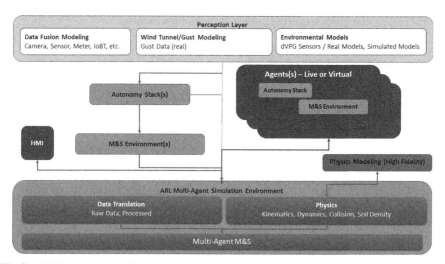

**Fig. 2.** Initial conceptual diagram on the intersections between modeling and simulation approaches that depict the intersections between vehicle models, environmental models, and autonomy.

**Model-fed Simulation Approaches.** System engineering approaches highlight the value of linking vehicle dynamics with world dynamics to improve the sim-to-real transition. This can be accomplished by integrating vehicle models and physics with the simulated world. This requires a method for integrating the vehicle models, as well as adding higher fidelity terrain and environment models in the virtual environment. Some of this model integration, such as wind gust generation and atmospheric modeling, can vary from a look-up table approach calculated from real-world data to live integration. While this approach requires specific technology, software, or hardware to function, it will increase real-world fidelity and system TEVV.

**Data Management and Networked Communication.**  An LVC integrated simulation approach requires a method to move and integrate data, from sensor processing and perception (through simulated or hardware-in-the-loop processes), coordinated behavior and networked communication, and on to data fusion, processing, and interpretation. The ROS 2 [54] library supports multi-agent, multi-domain operations across platform and environment, but should be used in conjunction with a networked communication model (e.g., EMANE) within a multi-network approach for integrating the virtual and real world.

**Multi-simulation Integration Approach.**  Different simulation testbeds each have their unique benefits and limitations. For effective multi-agent teaming in a complex, dynamic environments, a layered simulation approach will be required to leverage unique simulation features such as cyber resiliency and large-scale mission behaviors, integration with external graphical user interfaces for human-machine integration, and individual and team behaviors. This will require a plug-in, harness approach to effectively move data.

**Acknowledgments.**  The authors thank Dr. Derrik Asher, DEVCOM Army Research Laboratory for his technical review, and University of Maryland students Hersh Chawla, Henry Reimert, Will Sheesley, and Jason Appiah-Kubi for their exploration of Unity and Unreal Engine for robotics simulation. The views and conclusions contained in this document are those of the authors and should not be interpreted as representing the official policies, either expressed or implied, of the DEVCOM Army Research Laboratory or the U.S. Government. The U.S. Government is authorized to reproduce and distribute re-prints for Government purposes notwithstanding any copyright.

**Disclosure of Interests.**   The authors have no competing interests to declare that are relevant to the content of this article.

# References

1. Fields, M., et al.: Simulation tools for robotics research and assessment. In: Proceedings SPIE 9837, Unmanned Systems Technology XVIII, vol. 98370, pp. 156–171 (2016)
2. Collins, J., Chand, S., Vanderkop, A., Howard, D.: A review of physics simulators for robotic applications. Access **9**, 51416–51431 (2021)
3. Military. Live, virtual, and constructive. https://military-history.fandom.com/wiki/Live,_vir tual,_and_constructive. Accessed 25 Jan 2024
4. Iosifidis, A., Tefas, A.: Introduction. In Deep Learning for Robot Perception and Cognition, pp. 1–17. Academic Press, San Diego CA (2022)

5. Alami, R., Chatila, R., Fleury, S., Ghallab, M., Ingrand, F.: An architecture for autonomy. Int. J. Robot. Res. **17**(4), 315–337 (1998)

6. Thrun, S.: Toward a framework for human-robot interaction. Hum.-Comput. Interact. **19**(1–2), 9–24 (2004)

7. Antsaklis, P.: Autonomy and metrics of autonomy. Annu. Rev. Control. **49**, 15–26 (2020)

8. Beer, J.M., Fisk, A.D., Rogers, W.A.: Toward a framework for levels of robot autonomy in human-robot interaction. J. Hum.-Robot Interact. **3**(2), 74–99 (2014)

9. Zhang, C., Lu, Y.: Study on artificial intelligence: the state of the art and future prospects. J. Ind. Inf. Integr. **23**, 100224 (2021)

10. Andrews, G: What is robotics simulation? nVIDIA (2023). https://blogs.nvidia.com/blog/what-is-robotics-simulation/. Accessed 23 Jan 2024

11. Kumari, A., Tanwar, S., Tyagi, S., Kumar, N., Maasberg, M., Choo, K.K.R.: Multimedia big data computing and Internet of Things applications: A taxonomy and process model. J. Network Comput. Appl. **124**, 169–195 (2018)

12. Kumar, P.: Understanding big data processing: 2024's ultimate guide (2022). https://hevodata.com/lear/big-data-processing/. Accessed 23 Jan 2024

13. Haugh, B.A., Sparrow, D.A., Tate, D.M.: The status of test, evaluation, verification, and validation (TEV&V) of autonomous systems (P-9292). Institute for Defense Analysis, Alexandria, VA (2018)

14. Kim, W., Park, J., Sung, Y.: Communication in multi-agent reinforcement learning: intention sharing. In: International Conference on Learning Representations (2020)

15. Schaefer, K.E., Straub, E.R., Chen, J.Y.C., Putney, J., Evans, A.W.: Communicating intent to develop shared situation awareness and engender trust in human-agent teams. Cogn. Syst. Res. **46**, 26–39 (2017)

16. He, W., Xu, W., Ge, X., Han, Q.-L., Du, W., Qian, F.: Secure control of multiagent systems against malicious attacks: A brief survey. IEEE Trans. Ind. Inf. **18**(6), 3595–3608 (2022)

17. Du, W., Ding, S.: A survey on multi-agent deep reinforcement learning: from the perspective of challenges and applications. Artif. Intell. Rev. **54**, 3215–3238 (2021)

18. Candela, E., Parada, L., Marques, L., Georgescu, T.A., Demiris, Y., Angeloudis, P.: Transferring multi-agent reinforcement learning policies for autonomous driving using sim-to-real. In: International Conference on Intelligent Robots and Systems (IROS), pp. 8814–8820. IEEE (2022)

19. Daza, I.G., Izquierdo, R., Martínez, L.M., Benderius, O., Llorca, D.F.: Sim-to-real transfer and reality gap modeling in model predictive control for autonomous driving. Appl. Intell. **53**, 12719–12735 (2023)

20. Suh, Y.H., Woo, S.P., Kim, H., Park, D.H.: A sim2real framework enabling decentralized agents to execute MADDPG tasks. In: Proceedings of the Workshop on Distributed Infrastructures for Deep Learning, pp. 1–6 (2019)

21. Salvato, E., Fenu, G., Medvet, E., Pellegrino, F.A.: Crossing the reality gap: a survey on sim-to-real transferability of robot controllers in reinforcement learning. IEEE Access **9**, 153171–153187 (2021)

22. Zhao, W., Queralta, J.P., Westerlund, T.: Sim-to-real transfer in deep reinforcement learning for robotics: a survey. In: IEEE Symposium Series on Computational Intelligence (SSCI), pp. 737–744. IEEE (2020)

23. Helleboogh, A., Vizzari, G., Uhrmacher, A., Michel, F.: Modeling dynamic environments in multi-agent simulation. Auton. Agents Multi-Agent Syst. **14**, 87–116 (2007)

24. Choi, H., et al.: On the use of simulation in robotics: opportunities, challenges, and suggestions for moving forward. In: Proceedings of the National Academy of Sciences of the United States of America, vol. 118 (2020)

25. Schaefer, K.E., Brewer, R.W., Pursel, E.R., Zimmermann, A., Cerame, E., Briggs, K.: Outcomes from the First Wingman Software-in-the-Loop Integration Event: January 2017 (2017). First wingman software-in-the-loop integration event: January 2017 (ARL-TN-0830). US Army Research Laboratory, Aberdeen Proving Ground, MD (2017)
26. Todorov, E.: Convex and analytically-invertible dynamics with contacts and constraints: theory and implementation in MuJoCo. In: International Conference on Robotics and Automation (ICRA), pp. 6054–6061. IEEE (2014)
27. Tordesillas, J., Lopez, B.T., Carter, J., Ware, J., How, J.P.: Real-time planning with multi-fidelity models for agile flights in unknown environments. In: International Conference on Robotics and Automation (ICRA), pp. 725–731. IEEE (2019)
28. Akkaya, I., et al.: Solving Rubik's Cube with a Robot Hand (2019). https://openai.com/research/solving-rubiks-cube. Accessed 23 Jan 2024
29. Weng, J., et al.: EnvPool: a highly parallel reinforcement learning environment execution engine. Adv. Neural. Inf. Process. Syst. **35**, 22409–22421 (2022)
30. Drake: Model-Based Design and Verification for Robotics. https://drake.mit.edu/. Accessed 18 Jan 2024
31. Open Dynamics Engine. http://ode.org/. Accessed 18 Jan 2024
32. Bullet Real-Time Physics Simulation. https://pybullet.org/wordpress/. Accessed 18 Jan 2024
33. DART: Dynamic Animation and Robotics Toolkit. https://dartsim.github.io/. Accessed 18 Jan 2024
34. Shi, F., et al.: Circus ANYmal: a quadruped learning dexterous manipulation with its limbs. In: International Conference on Robotics and Automation (ICRA), pp. 2316–2323. IEEE (2021)
35. Freeman, C.D., Frey, E., Raichuk, A., Girgin, S., Mordatch, I., Bachem, O.: Brax - A differentiable physics engine for large scale rigid body simulation. ArXiv Preprint https://arxiv.org/abs/2106.13281 (2021)
36. US Naval Research Laboratory: Extendable Mobile Ad-hoc Network Emulator. https://www.nrl.navy.mil/Our-Work/Areas-of-Research/Information-Technology/NCS/EMANE/. Accessed 23 Jan 2024
37. Sixt, A.: Best Robot Simulators. https://formant.io/news-and-blog/2023/08/23/community/best-robot-simulators/. Accessed 23 Jan 2024
38. Gupta, G.: Migration from Gazebo Classic to Ignition with ROS 2. Black Coffee Robotics (2023)
39. Coppelia Robotics. https://www.coppeliarobotics.com/. Accessed 18 Jan 2024
40. CARLA. http://carla.org/. Accessed 28 Jan 2024
41. Cyberbotics. https://cyberbotics.com/#webots. Accessed 18 Jan 2024
42. AWS. https://aws.amazon.com/robomaker/. Accessed 18 Jan 2024
43. Vohera, C., Chheda, H., Chouhan, D., Desai, A., Jain, V.: Game engine architecture and comparative study of different game engines. In: 12th International Conference on Computing Communication and Networking Technologies (ICCCNT), pp. 1–6. IEEE (2021)
44. Johns, R.: Unity vs Unreal: Which game engine should you choose? https://hackr.io/blog/unity-vs-unreal-engine. Accessed 23 Jan 2024
45. Senycia, T.: Unity vs Unreal: How to choose the best game engine? https://youteam.io/blog/unity-vs-unreal-how-to-choose-the-best-game-engine. Accessed 23 Jan 2024
46. Buckley, D.: Unity vs Unreal – the ultimate game engine face off. https://gamedevacademy.org/unity-vs-unreal/. Accessed 23 Jan 2024
47. Sibony, J.: Unity vs Unreal – what kind of game dev are you? https://www.incredibuild.com/blog/unity-vs-unreal-what-kind-of-game-dev-are-you. Accessed 23 Jan 2024
48. Chauhan, A.: Unreal Engine vs Unity: Which game engine would be productive for your business? https://www.appventurez.com/blog/unreal-engine-vs-unity. Accessed 23 Jan 20243

49. Davidson, A.: Unreal Engine vs Unity: choose best game engine. https://codersera.com/blog/unreal-engine-vs-unity-choose-best-game-engine. Accessed 23 Jan 2024
50. Kevuru Games. Unity – what makes it the best game engine? https://kevurugames.com/blog/unity-what-makes-it-the-best-game-engine/. Accessed 23 Jan 2024
51. Geeks for Geeks: Unity vs Unreal Engine. https://www.geeksforgeeks.org/unity-vs-unreal-engine/. Accessed 18 Sept 2023
52. Dealessandri, M.: What is the best game engine: is Unreal Engine right for you? https://www.gamesindustry.biz/what-is-the-best-game-engine-is-unreal-engine-4-the-right-game-engine-for-you. Accessed 23 Jan 2024
53. Schaefer, K.E., Oh, J., Aksaray, D., Barber, D.: Integrating context into artificial intelligence: research from the Robotics Collaborative Technology Alliance. AI Mag. **40**(3), 28–40 (2019)
54. Github. Programming multiple robots with ROS 2. https://osrf.github.io/ros2multirobotbook/. Accessed 25 Jan 2024

# Optimizing XR User Experiences Through Network-Based Asset Bundles

Maurizio Vergari[1(✉)], Tanja Kojić[1], Maximilian Warsinke[1],
Sebastian Möller[1,4], Jan-Niklas Voigt-Antons[3], Osama Abboud[2],
and Xun Xiao[2]

[1] Quality and Usability Lab, TU Berlin, Berlin, Germany
maurizio.vergari@tu-berlin.de
[2] Advanced Wireless Technologies Lab - Munich Research Center,
Huawei Technologies Duesseldorf GmbH, Munich, Germany
[3] Immersive Reality Lab, Hamm-Lippstadt University of Applied Sciences,
Lippstadt, Germany
[4] German Research Center for Artificial Intelligence (DFKI), Berlin, Germany

**Abstract.** Even though XR apps are becoming more widely used, one common issue is the need for more processing power on hardware to handle the complexity of the objects that need to be rendered. This study tests a system that shifts the computational load to the network and transfers information from a server to an XR device to maximize different aspects of user experience (e.g., innovativeness, consistency and control).

The technical implementation utilizes the Unity 3D Engine to create and construct a Virtual Reality (VR) environment that embeds a communication mechanism between the server and the XR device. It uses distributed assets kept on a server as Asset Bundles. Asset Bundles provide a technique that enables dynamic loading at runtime. This allows for the minimization of local processing demands. The chosen application exemplifies this methodology in a "Pirate Game", where players incrementally render ships.

The "Surge.hs" was selected as the remote server in this process due to its seamless integration with the Unity editor, facilitating the storage and retrieval of 3D models. The study's core contribution lies in testing the proposed solution and reporting loading times for 3D models from the network. Empirical results show the solution's effectiveness, revealing initial loading times of approximately 800ms, followed by subsequent loading times experiencing a notable 60 to 80% reduction.

This demonstrates the practicality of the suggested technique by giving an interesting method for displaying 3D models from a network, hence increasing the XR user experience.

**Keywords:** Virtual Reality · User Experience · Network Communication System

© The Author(s), under exclusive license to Springer Nature Switzerland AG 2024
J. Y. C. Chen and G. Fragomeni (Eds.): HCII 2024, LNCS 14707, pp. 105–115, 2024.
https://doi.org/10.1007/978-3-031-61044-8_8

# 1   Introduction

As part of our natural environment, digital objects are now nothing out of the ordinary. What was hardly imaginable a few years ago is now normality. Hardware making this possible is becoming more comfortable, cheaper, and accessible. The technology that makes this possible is called Extended Reality (XR) and is used in many different areas. XR is an umbrella term that includes the specific technologies of virtual reality, augmented reality, and mixed reality. Each enables a different level of representation of reality.

The Swiss Society of Virtual and Augmented Reality (SSVAR) defines the technologies as follows:

## 1.1   Augmented Reality

"Augmented reality (AR) overlays digitally created content onto the user's real-world environment. AR experiences range from informational text overlaid on objects or locations to interactive photorealistic virtual objects. AR differs from mixed reality in that AR objects (e.g., graphics, sounds) are superimposed on, and not integrated into, the user's environment[1]".

## 1.2   Mixed Reality

"Mixed reality (MR) seamlessly blends a user's real-world environment with digitally created content, where both environments coexist to create a hybrid experience. In MR, the virtual objects behave in all aspects as if they are present in the real world. E.g., they are occluded by physical objects; their lighting is consistent with the actual light sources in the environment, and they sound as though they are in the same space as the user. As the user interacts with the real and virtual objects, the virtual objects will reflect the changes in the environment as would any real object in the same space (see footnote 1)." Knowing the difference between AR and MR is essential, as both technologies seem similar initially. However, the difference is that "AR objects (e.g., image and sound) overlay the user's environment and are not integrated into it (see footnote 1)". The digital objects of augmented reality merely overlay the real objects, while in mixed reality, the virtual objects interact with the real objects, allowing interaction with both worlds.

## 1.3   Virtual Reality

"Virtual reality (VR) is a fully immersive user environment affecting or altering the sensory input(s) (e.g., sight, sound, touch, and smell) that can allow interaction with those sensory inputs based on the user's engagement with the virtual

---

[1]    https://courses.minnalearn.com/en/courses/emerging-technologies/extended-reality-vr-ar-mr/introduction-to-extended-reality-ar-vr-and-mr/.

world. Typically, but not exclusively, the interaction is via a head-mounted display, use of spatial or other audio, or motion controllers (with or without tactile input or feedback) (see footnote 1)". More and more applications are integrating and adopting XR technology. Nevertheless, problematically, the computing power on the hardware side needs to be increased to support most of the unique content enabled by XR technologies. Moving most of the computational power to the network and transmitting information over the network instead of head-mounted devices (HDMs) or smartphones represents a more than promising solution to this problem.

This paper aims to report results on the test of a communication system between a server and an XR device (client), in our case, a Meta Quest, that can successfully transmit different types of information with minimal delay. The purpose is to improve user experience on different dimensions, such as innovativeness, consistency and control.

After initial research on the existing state of the art, we developed a prototype that meets the requirements of the solution approach. In addition, testing was conducted to demonstrate that the transfer to a network can be performed smoothly and that an improved user experience is achieved.

## 2    Related Work

Our research on this topic led us to some relevant literature. As XR has gained popularity in recent years and will continue to do so, and as our end-user devices become smaller and smaller and the applications for them more and more complex, more people are looking into the topic. Qcarfordt et al. discuss which qualitative requirements must be met to outsource part of the virtual reality processing to cloud servers. They already outline the possibilities of deployment on the 4G and 5G mobile networks [4]. Following a similar line of research, Cheng et al. present additional requirements that XR should fulfil and discuss existing platforms and their development for virtual social reality (especially the Metaverse) [1]. Moreover, a list of possibilities and future directions for further innovations in Extended Reality is presented. When it comes to the technological side of network communication, an interesting work was done by Vikberg, who focused on using WebRTC streaming technology for Cloud XR [5]. "WebRTC is a multi-purpose technology that enables low-latency peer-to-peer connections between clients over the Internet. In addition to low latency, it enables signalling and transmission of both binary data messages and multimedia content, making it a powerful tool for streaming extended reality (XR) content." Of particular note is the knowledge shared about transferring video using WebRTC over a cloud server and how this technology can be applied to XR content. Kurt et al., with their work, presented a tool through which network-ready XR applications can be built [3]. Specifically, their "ARgent" is discussed, including the means and steps needed to implement such software. It is an AR-authoring tool developed in Unity to create and maintain AR applications through a graphical user interface. It also provides a server, a web interface and a mobile application.

# 3   Method

## 3.1   Design and Implementation

This section briefly describes our solution for the problem and the critical steps in the implementation process. Our solution prototype builds on Meta Quest 1, a VR Head Mounted Device (HMD) that enables the development and use of VR applications. Using controllers, the Meta Quest enables users to interact with objects in a simulated environment.

To address the project objectives explained in the first section, we considered the scientific background of the underlying problem. We built our prototype using distributed assets on a remote server (Asset Bundles). These assets can be loaded at run time when a particular event is triggered - in our case, that event is a button click. Therefore, we can shift the computational power from the VR device to the remote server that handles all the heavy processing and rendering needed.

We will review the essential steps, milestones, and technology tools used during our implementation phase.

**Unity and Asset Bundles.** Unity is a cross-platform game engine considered easy to use for beginner developers [2]. It can be used to create interactive simulations and has been adopted by industries outside video gaming, such as film, automotive, architecture, and engineering. First, we had to familiarise ourselves with Unity, its frameworks, Software development kits (SDKs), and how to implement our solution. Secondly, we explored the different model file formats and checked which is supported by Unity[2]. Finally, before adding our scene or importing any heavy 3D models, we developed our prototype with no functionalities. However, the goal was to adjust our unity project and make it compatible with Android development so that it would work and be appropriately displayed on the Meta Quest. Therefore, we downloaded the correct unity modules by upgrading to a newer version (2022.1.7f1) with Android Build Support and all the needed SDKs. Thus, we could enable Unity VR Support[3] and adjust player and quality settings in the Unity editor accordingly.

An Asset Bundle is a content stored separately from a primary game or application and loaded (or downloaded, in the case of mobile and online apps) at runtime (see Fig. 1). Individual storage helps minimize the impact on network and system resources by allowing customers to download and install only the parts they need. It can also be used to update or add to content post-release[4].

Therefore, Asset Bundles appear to be the best solution for our problem. It will allow us to store the heavy 3D models we want separately and load them at runtime, shifting most of the processing and rendering Load to the network and hopefully making our application faster. Although implementing Asset Bundles

---

[2] https://docs.unity3d.com/2020.1/Documentation/Manual/3D-formats.html.
[3] https://docs.unity3d.com/540/Documentation/Manual/VROverview.
[4] https://learn.unity.com/tutorial/introduction-to-asset-bundles.

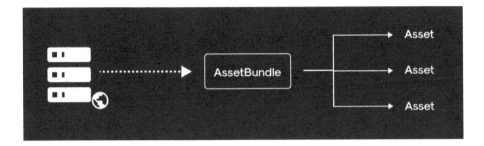

**Fig. 1.** Asset Bundles

is a straightforward process, one must consider that Asset Bundles are platform-specific. Thus, creating Asset Bundles for the correct build target for the stored file to be uploaded is essential.

We followed the following four simple steps to create and load Asset Bundles:

1. Build Asset Bundles: Create Asset Bundles in the Editor using the Assets in the scene, create Asset Bundles using a C# (see Fig. 2) and then from the Assets tab, click on Build Asset Bundles.
2. Upload Asset Bundles to external storage: we set up a remote server (Surge) and uploaded our 3d-models to it, which can be loaded on demand when the respective buttons are clicked.
3. Download Asset Bundles at run time from the application: This is done from the Script within a Unity Scene (see Fig. 3), and Asset Bundles are loaded from the server on demand.
4. Load GameObjects from Asset Bundles: once the Asset Bundles are downloaded, the needed asset can be loaded at runtime as if it were locally stored on our device (see Fig. 4).

**Remote Server.** Surge.hs is a free static website host where the interaction happens from the command line. It makes it quick and easy to get new sites and apps online, either manually or as part of the CI build process[5]. We managed to use Surge.hs as our remote server where we stored our 3d-models, from which we then loaded them at runtime when needed. One of the main reasons we decided to use Surge.hs, in particular, is the relatively easy interaction between the server and unity editor, where we only had to find the right path for our 3D models to be able to access and load them correctly.

### 3.2 Design Choices

Since our main goal was to reach and analyze the limitations of our solution, we brainstormed an efficient and aesthetic design choice. After considering multiple

---

[5] https://www.howtogeek.com/devops/how-to-deploy-static-websites-for-free-with-surge sh/.

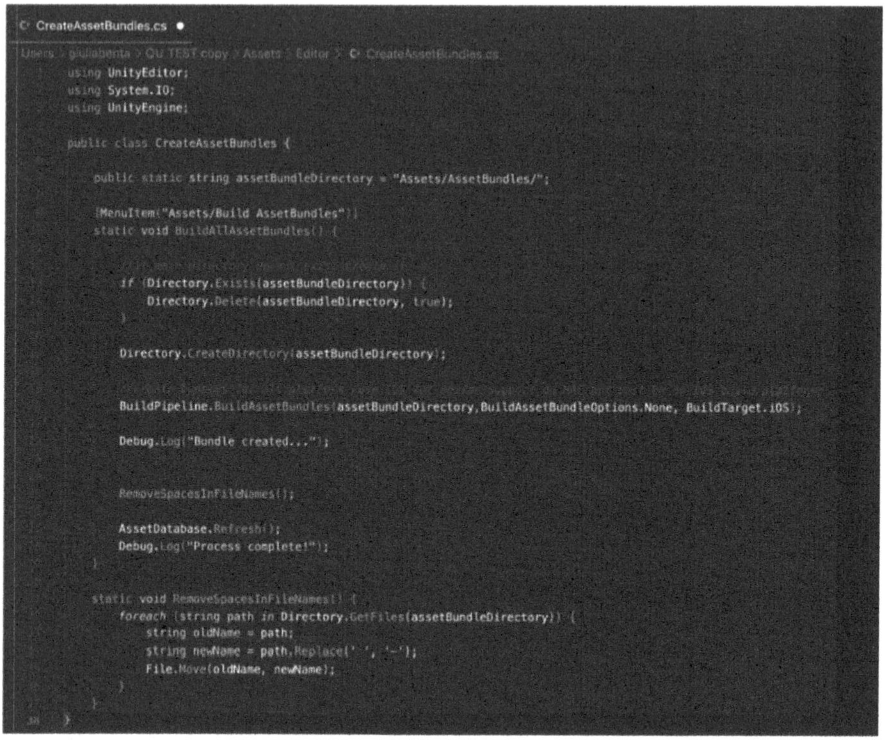

```
C: CreateAssetBundles.cs  •

Users > giuliabenta > Qu TEST copy > Assets > Editor > C: CreateAssetBundles.cs
    using UnityEditor;
    using System.IO;
    using UnityEngine;

    public class CreateAssetBundles {

        public static string assetBundleDirectory = "Assets/AssetBundles/";

        [MenuItem("Assets/Build AssetBundles")]
        static void BuildAllAssetBundles() {

            if (Directory.Exists(assetBundleDirectory)) {
                Directory.Delete(assetBundleDirectory, true);
            }

            Directory.CreateDirectory(assetBundleDirectory);

            BuildPipeline.BuildAssetBundles(assetBundleDirectory,BuildAssetBundleOptions.None, BuildTarget.iOS);

            Debug.Log("Bundle created...");

            RemoveSpacesInFileNames();

            AssetDatabase.Refresh();
            Debug.Log("Process complete!");
        }

        static void RemoveSpacesInFileNames() {
            foreach (string path in Directory.GetFiles(assetBundleDirectory)) {
                string oldName = path;
                string newName = path.Replace(' ', '-');
                File.Move(oldName, newName);
            }
        }
    }
```

**Fig. 2.** Rendering test results

options and creating initial prototypes for them in Blender, we settled on the option of a "Pirate Game" (see Fig. 5), where the player would be able to render more and more boats in increments of 1, 3, 10, and 50 boats by tapping buttons in front of them. The work for the final product started in Blender, where the main objects for the environment were created and exported into Unity to create an initial working prototype that we could start testing. We used objects and materials created in Blender and exported to Unity or pre-made Unity Asset Packs that fit our vision to create our environment. When the environment was ready, we created the ships that would be our Asset Bundles. Each Asset Bundle was unique and stored individually as a prefab.

While working towards successfully loading the, the product underwent a continuous usability testing process. The tests helped us focus on more design choices to create a more interactive and enjoyable experience for the user.

We decided that the player's position in the environment should be at the highest point of the main island to have a full view of the ships that were going to be loaded and the rest of the surroundings.

The position of the buttons panel was also deliberate, as it should not obscure the area where the ships will appear but should also be within reach for the player, and their purpose should be easily understood.

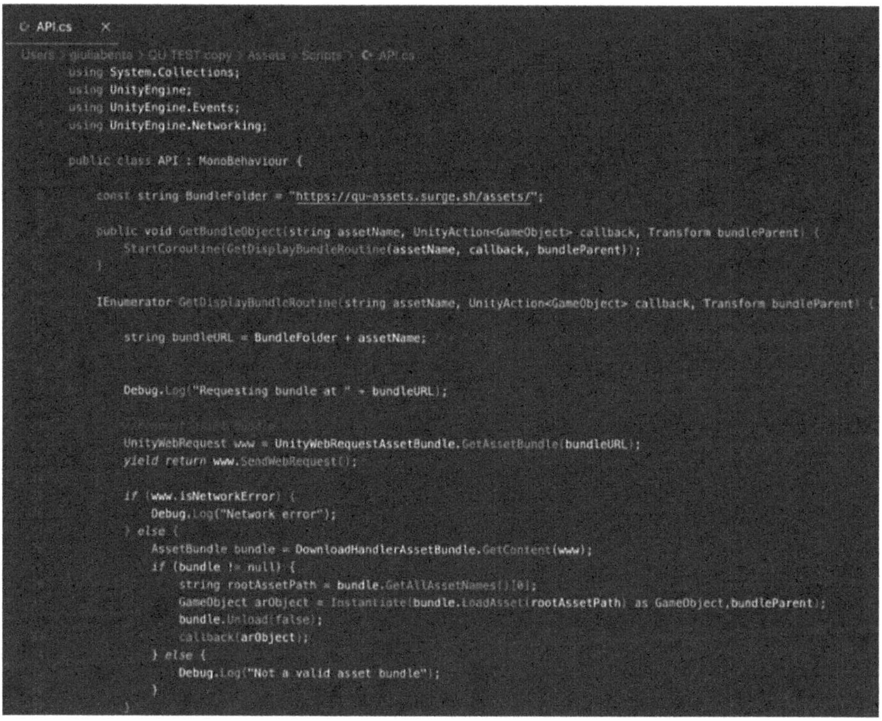

**Fig. 3.** API

For usability reasons, as well as for our rendering tests and debugging, we added a timer underneath the buttons that would provide the user with feedback that pressing the button was successful.

Furthermore, the ships were rendered in randomized positions within the user's field of view. They were animated to continuously move to provide more complexity to our tests and make the end product more realistic and immersive. The randomization of the position took place by setting a range for the coordinates and creating two random vectors within the respective ranges for the positions on the X and Z-axis. The position on the Y-axis stayed the same since we wanted to keep the ships at the same height above the water. The animation was made possible by constantly updating the position and multiplying it with time and a previously set speed.

Other minor design choices were made to create a beautiful experience, such as keeping accessibility and aesthetics in mind when picking our Color Palette, adding a background sound, and animating the water.

```
public class ContentController : MonoBehaviour {

    public API api;
    public TextMeshProUGUI spanValue;

    System.DateTime startTime;
    System.DateTime endTime;

    float speed = 10.0f;

    public void LoadContent(string name) {

        startTime = System.DateTime.Now;
        api.GetBundleObject(name, OnContentLoaded, transform);

    }

    void OnContentLoaded(GameObject content) {

        int pX = Random.Range(-1061, 621);
        int pZ = Random.Range(-889, 455);
        if (content.name == "StylShip_Unity(Clone)"){
            content.transform.position = new Vector3(pX, 12, pZ);
        } else if (content.name == "1d_ships(Clone)") {
            content.transform.position = new Vector3(pX, -2, pZ);
        }
        else
            content.transform.position = new Vector3(pX, 90, pZ);

        endTime = System.DateTime.Now;
        Debug.Log("Loaded: " + content.name);
        Debug.Log("start time is : " + startTime);
        Debug.Log("end time is : " + endTime);

        System.TimeSpan span = endTime - startTime;
        Debug.Log("span is : " + span.Milliseconds + " ms");
        spanValue.text = "time span value: " + span.Milliseconds + " ms";

    }

    void Update()
    {
        transform.position += transform.forward * Time.deltaTime * speed;
    }
}
```

**Fig. 4.** Content Controller

**Fig. 5.** Game Prototype

## 4   Results and Discussion

This section summarises the results of our product test and its limitations. We also discussed how the testing process aided the product's development and showed us the incremental improvements to our solution. We settled on two tests: one to test the speed at which they get rendered and one to test and improve the usability of our product.

## 4.1  Rendering Tests

Since our solution to the initial problem was to load 3D Models from the network, one of the most critical aspects of the project was testing our solution and proving that it was a good candidate for solving the issue. We decided to do so by gathering data about the timespan it takes for each asset to load from the network the first time such a request is sent and comparing this timespan to the average timespan it takes for the asset to load on subsequent requests.

The expected and ideal result for us would have been that both loading times are relatively short and the delay would be barely noticeable to the average user. That is what we worked towards.

The timespan was calculated in the ContentController.cs script by subtracting the date when the request was sent to load the content from the date when the content was loaded. The timespan result will show up in our Console and the project as visual feedback for the user.

After multiple quantitative tests we wrote down, we calculated the average for the initial and subsequent loading time for each of the four Assets and analyzed our numbers (see Fig. 6)

| Model Type | Initial Loading(sec) | Subsequent Loadings(sec) |
|---|---|---|
| 1 ship | 863ms | 156ms |
| 3 ships | 877ms | 274ms |
| 10 ships | 905ms | 339ms |
| 50 ships | 967ms | 378ms |

**Fig. 6.** Rendering test results

Our results show that even if the minor initial loading average is around 800ms, which is noticeable to the user, the subsequent loading time drops by approximately 60 to 80% and becomes almost unnoticeable and a valid solution for our problem according to our previously set expectations.

Therefore, after looking at our numbers, our project and its execution successfully delivered a solution for rendering 3D models from a network.

## 4.2  User Experience

The second set of tests we conducted were the user experience tests that aided in refining the whole experience and creating an interface that would respect a pre-established set of specifications. Our list of specifications was:

- Intuitive: Is the interface easy to use and understand for the user? Are all the elements functioning correctly?
- System status visible at all times: Can the user tell when an action takes place? Is the user aware if an error occurred?
- Consistency: Do all the elements in the interface follow the same conventions?
- Efficiency: Is the interface achieving its purpose of showcasing the rendering solution without getting in the way?
- User is in control: Are errors prevented? Is the user stuck when they make a mistake? (e.g., clicking on the wrong button)
- Aesthetic design: Is the interface cluttered? Is any irrelevant information displayed?
- Overall feedback and suggestions

To give questions to participants, we created a Typeform Survey using the questions mentioned above throughout the process until we eventually reached a point where we were satisfied with the result. We conducted a "small-scale user testing round" where we asked fellow students to test our interface and fill out the document with their personal experiences and suggestions for us moving forward. Typeform is a platform where users can create surveys for their testing rounds. We got 10 responses to our survey. All the data was collected in a Google Sheets document so that we could see our next steps easily.

The results reported that the final product respected most of our specifications, with only a few exceptions. A feature that would have given the user more control over the experience would have been the ability to delete ships they rendered by mistake. Aside from minor changes, our product was described as intuitive, consistent, efficient, having an aesthetic design, and offering the user control and feedback. In particular, the interface was rated as easy to use and understand, with a mean score of 4.9 out of 5 $(SD = 0.32)$. Also, 90% of participants reported the interface elements to be consistent with a mean score of 4.5 out of 5 $(SD = 0.85)$.

## 5    Conclusion

The 3D-model project is Product Development oriented. The overall objective was also to successfully develop a VR application that transfers different kinds of information with minimum delay and is usable and enjoyable. Our solution was to implement a simple product that communicates with an XR device across a remote server and is used as a Package Manager to archive files and 3d-models that can be loaded at run time when a particular event is triggered (Button click). Therefore, we conducted two tests: a rendering test that calculated how much time it took a certain 3d-model to be loaded from the remote server, measuring initial as well as subsequent loading time for four 3d-models (1 ship, 3 ships, 10 ships, 50 ships). A second user experience test has been conducted to ensure that the application and its user interface fulfil the required specifications, being, first and foremost, easy to use, consistent through all phases, and intuitive for the user. We maintained a compelling aesthetic design and tried to make the application interactive, adding buttons, interactions with controllers, background sounds, and animations.

This study comes, of course, with some limitations. First, the added delay to transfer from the utilized server cannot be exactly quantified. Faster servers could bring improvements or, in general, variations of such results. Second, this study tackles the transfer of just a kind of object, so different results could emerge when transferring different objects.

**Acknowledgements.** This work would not have been possible without the effort of Giulia-Marielena Benta, Albnor Sahiti, and Obadah Mohamed Aleem, who contributed to the design and development of the solution shown. This work was partly funded by the Federal Ministry of Education and Research (BMBF) and the state of Berlin under the Excellence Strategy of the Federal Government and the Länder.

# References

1. Cheng, R., Wu, N., Chen, S., Han, B.: Will metaverse be NextG internet? Vision, hype, and reality. IEEE Network **36**(5), 197–204 (2022)
2. Dealessandri, M.: What is the best game engine: is unity right for you. Preuzeto **7**(7), 2022 (2020)
3. Gökhan, K., Gökhan, İ.: Argent: a web based augmented reality framework for dynamic content generation. Avrupa Bilim ve Teknoloji Dergisi, pp. 244–257 (2020)
4. Qvarfordt, C., Lundqvist, H., Koudouridis, G.P.: High quality mobile XR: requirements and feasibility. In: 2018 IEEE 23rd International Workshop on Computer Aided Modeling and Design of Communication Links and Networks (CAMAD), pp. 1–6. IEEE (2018)
5. Vikberg, E., et al.: Optimizing webRTC for cloud streaming of XR (2021)

# Enhancing Remote Collaboration Through Drone-Driven Agent and Mixed Reality

Shihui Xu$^{(\boxtimes)}$ (iD), Like Wu(iD), Wenjie Liao(iD), and Shigeru Fujimura(iD)

Graduate School of Information, Production, and Systems, Waseda University, Kitakyushu, Japan

shxu@toki.waseda.jp, wulike@fuji.waseda.jp, jie3040@akane.waseda.jp, fujimura@waseda.jp

**Abstract.** Mixed Reality (MR) and Augmented Reality (AR) technologies have been used to improve remote collaboration. However, existing MR- or AR-based remote collaboration systems lack of a fully independent view sharing between the local user and remote user. This research propose a novel approach to enhance the remote collaboration using a drone and MR technology. By augmenting a virtual 3D avatar on the drone in the local environment, we propose the drone-driven agent to embody the remote user. And the view sharing between local and remote user is achieved by sending a real-time video stream of the local environment captured with the drone. There are three novelties including 1) fully independent view sharing, 2) augmenting virtual character on the drone to embody remote user, and 3) 3D AR sketching o facilitate communication between local and remote users. We implemented a proof-of-concept prototype to illustrate our design using a see-through type head-mounted display and a small-size drone. In addition, we provide discussion and implication for the future work to design drone-based remote collaboration systems.

**Keywords:** Remote collaboration · Mixed reality · Augmented reality · Drone · Embodiment using character

## 1 Introduction

Mixed Reality (MR) and Augmented Reality (AR) technologies have been verified to be effective in remote collaborative work. Many researchers proposed architectures, models, methods, and systems to improve task performance and user experience of remote collaboration [1–5,21]. However, in existing MR- or AR-based remote collaboration systems, the remote users heavily rely on the local users. For instance, most systems often employ cameras worn by local users to transmit the local environment, thereby limiting remote users to the first-person perspective of the local users. How to provide remote users with greater freedom remains unsolved.

© The Author(s), under exclusive license to Springer Nature Switzerland AG 2024
J. Y. C. Chen and G. Fragomeni (Eds.): HCII 2024, LNCS 14707, pp. 116–127, 2024.
https://doi.org/10.1007/978-3-031-61044-8_9

A drone, also known as an unmanned aerial vehicle (UAV), is an aircraft that operates without any humans on board [6]. Drones are increasingly used to support industrial and agricultural tasks, aerial telepresence, remote collaborative work, and social interactions, especially events that involve dangerous or costly tasks [7]. For example, companies like Amazon and Google are testing drones for delivering packages, in particular in remote or hard-to-reach areas to reduce delivery times and costs [8,9]. Firefighters employed drones to monitor the progression of the Notre Dame fire and to identify optimal locations for directing fire hoses [10].

To address the problem that remote users are heavily depended on the local users in the remote collaboration systems, we propose to combine Drone and MR technology, enabling the remote user to have a drone-driven agent in the local environment. The remote user can have a independent view of local environment through drone. Besides, we embodied the drone-driven agent using MR to enhance the collaboration.

In this research, we explore how the MR technology and a drone can enhance remote collaboration, especially for the physical tasks. Compared with prior remote collaboration system using MR or drones, the novelties of our system locate in three aspects:

1. View Independence: The perspective of remote users typically relies on the viewpoint of local users. For instance, current systems often employ cameras worn by local users to transmit the local environment, thereby limiting remote users to the first-person perspective of the local users. Remote user can detach themselves from the viewpoint of local users and utilize camera-equipped unmanned aerial vehicles (UAVs) to explore the local environment. This enables remote users to have enhanced mobility and greater freedom in navigation.
2. Embodiment of Remote User: In previous remote collaboration systems, it was challenging to depict remote users due to the difficulty of representing their actions. Recent research has explored the use of augmented reality (AR) technology to convey the head movements of remote users to local users. However, such embodied representation is limited to rotational movements in the original position and fails to depict displacement or movement. This study employs unmanned aerial vehicles (UAVs) as a medium for instantiating remote users. We utilize AR technology and UAVs as carriers to represent the navigation and manipulation of remote users within the local environment, aiming to enhance the sense of presence between users.
3. Communication Cues: Sharing 3D sketching is challenging in remote collaboration because of spatial mismatching. With the drone as a spatial medium, our system implements AR 3D sketching as communication methods in addition to auditory and visual channels. Remote users can convey information to local users through sketching, facilitating improved collaboration between them.

The main contributions of our work include:

1. The design and implementation details of a remote collaboration system that combines MR with drone technologies, including the framework and specific interaction methods.
2. Providing discussions for designing future remote collaboration systems using MR and drone technologies.

In the following parts of this paper, a related literature review is firstly provided. Then we describe the system design and implementation details in Sect. 3 and Sect. 4. In Sect. 5, we discuss the findings and provide some implications for future work. Finally, we give a conclusion of this paper in Sect. 6.

## 2    Related Works

We built our research on several areas of research domains, in terms of MR/AR-based remote collaboration, embodiment in remote collaboration, and collaborative experience using drones.

### 2.1    MR/AR-Based Remote Collaboration

Remote collaboration is the process of working together to achieve a specific goal from geographically separated locations, usually using digital techniques to support communication and coordination [21]. With the rapid development of Virtual Reality (VR), AR, and MR technologies, there are many compact devices, such as Microsoft's HoloLens[1], Meta Quest[2], Magic Leap[3], HTC Vive[4], Oculus Rift[5], etc., that benefit the collaboration process and attract the attention of academia and industry, yielding positive results. For instance, in terms of perspective sharing and environmental perception, traditional systems utilize 2D video to share the first-person perspective of local users, which heavily relies on the local users and limits the field of view for remote users, resulting in inefficient information acquisition for remote users. To solve the problem, Lee et al. [1] has employed panoramic cameras to share the viewpoint of local users and employed VR technology to visualize it for remote users, so that the remote user can observe the surroundings of local users, allowing perspective independence of local users to a certain extent. In research of Teo et al. [4], the scanned local environmental model is shared with remote users, enabling them to have the imagery of the local environment. However, the scanned models are typically coarse and may even hinder remote users. To address the issue of perspective limitations caused by mobility constraints, researchers have employed Mobile

---

[1] https://www.microsoft.com/en-us/hololens/.
[2] https://www.meta.com/quest/.
[3] https://www.magicleap.com/en-us/.
[4] https://www.vive.com/us/.
[5] https://www.oculus.com/rift-s/.

Robotic Telepresence (MRP) systems to enable remote users to physically move within the same range as local users. MRP systems integrate video conferencing equipment onto mobile robot devices that can be remotely controlled and navigated [11,12].

## 2.2  Embodiment in Remote Collaboration

Embodiment refers to the representation of remote users in a way that provides a sense of physical presence in the collaborative environment. It involves creating virtual or augmented substitutes for remote users that facilitate them to interact and engage with others in collaborative work. Embodiment techniques may change how individuals present themselves and have a significant influence on experiencing the physical distance between remote participants. Previous research has shown that the embodiment of users can improve co-presence and social presence in remote collaboration [13].

Many researchers have shed light on embodying remote users with humanoid avatars. Piumsomboon et al. [2] presented Mini-Me, an adaptive avatar that can reflect the remote user's gaze direction and body gestures, to improve the user experience in MR remote collaboration. Yoon et al. [13] conducted user studies to investigate the effect of avatar appearance on social presence and user perception in an AR remote collaboration system. And they found that a realistic whole-body avatar was rated best by the users. In addition to embodying remote users with virtual or AR avatars, some research focused on the physical embodiment. Paulos and Canny proposed Personal Roving Presence [14], which is one of the earliest contributions in this category. Many studies have followed, ranging from tabletop-sized robots [15] to human-scale devices capable of physical movement [16]. These robots have been widely used in home care, education, and working space. Bae [17] introduced "Avatar Drone" to illustrate the potential of a drone as a medium of embodiment. But these systems require a high cognitive load for remote users to control them manually. Recently, Sakashita et al. [18] proposed RemoteCoDe to track a remote user's attention using a depth camera on the smartphone and render it to a local articulated display. However, it is fixed on the desktop, limiting the mobility and navigation of remote users.

## 2.3  Collaborative Experience Using Drones

How to interact with drones and make use of drones to enhance interaction between humans has garnered the interest of the HCI community. Compared with other telepresence robots, the drone has the potential to provide mobility and navigation beyond the reach of human beings, which enhances collaborative work. Jones et al. [19] investigated the use of semi-autonomous drones for video conferencing, enabling an indoor desktop user to explore the outdoor environment from the drone's perspective. A view that is decoupled and manipulated was provided for the desktop user. Sabet et al. [7] extended Jones et al.'s work by expanding collaborative sharing from one-to-one to multiple users, employing panoramic cameras to capture outdoor environments. Teledrone [20] is another drone-based video conferencing system to foster shared outdoor activities over distance. Although there are existing collaboration systems using drones, the level of interaction and manipulation is relatively low, which is insufficient for complex tasks. In their systems, the local users manipulate the drone, and the video captured by the drone will be transmitted to remote users. The remote users can only view the received video.

We focus on remote collaborative physical tasks in industrial scenarios. This type of task requires relatively frequent and complex interactions. We aim to explore further the potential of drones in remote collaboration.

## 3   System Design

In this section, the design of our remote collaboration system using drone and MR technology is described.

### 3.1   System Overview

The system overview is shown in Fig. 1. The local worker wears an MR head-mounted display (HMD) and performs physical tasks indoors. The remote expert operates a PC to control the drone which is located with the local worker. The drone comes with a camera that can capture video of the local environment, and our system streams real-time video of the local environment to the remote PC. The remote expert can look around the local environment by controlling the navigation of the drone, independent of the local worker's perspective. The remote expert can sketch on the PC to give an illustration. Our system will transfer the sketch to the local worker and visualize the sketch in the real local environment using MR technology. Besides, we propose a new method to embody the remote expert in the local environment to increase the co-presence of both users and enhance collaboration. We propose a drone-driven agent, which combines drone and MR technology. We superimpose a virtual 3D character on the drone using MR technology, embodying the remote expert from both physical and virtual aspects.

**Use Case.** A local user, usually a novice without much experience, needs to perform some physical tasks, such as common assembly tasks or finding tasks in factories, or visual inspection tasks. Due to a lack of experience, the local user may encounter some obstacles and difficulties that make the task difficult to proceed. At this time, the local user can use our system to connect with a remote user who is usually an experienced expert, and work together to complete the task. The local user wears HoloLens to enter our system. There is a drone embedded with a camera in the local environment. By controlling the drone, the remote user can obtain local environmental information and the work status of the local user. We provide remote users with an interface to operate the drone, and the remote user can adjust the rotation angle of the drone, and make the drone fly up, down, left, and right to visit the surroundings of the local

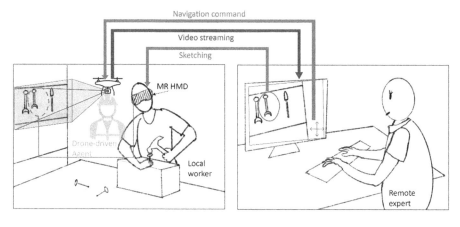

**Fig. 1.** System overview.

environment. Remote users can also make guidance and instructions to local users by marking and sketching on the PC interface. We will synchronize these guidance and instructions with the local user and use AR technology to display them in 3D in the local environment. Local users can see 3D marks and sketches in HoloLens. We also use a drone as a medium to embody remote users in local environments. The local user can see that at the location of the drone, there is an avatar of the remote user. This is done to enhance social presence.

### 3.2    Independent View Sharing Using Drone

The drone, equipped with a high-definition camera, provides a unique aerial perspective of the local environment, which is fundamentally different from the first-person viewpoint of the local worker. This capability allows the remote expert to navigate and explore the local environment independently, without being constrained to the local worker's field of view. Our system provides a manipulation interface for the remote user to control the drone in real-time, ensuring a comprehensive and dynamic assessment of the local environment. Figure 2 shows the interface for the remote user. The main image is the view captured by drone. The right-bottom small image is the top view of drone's route. The remote user can make the drone fly forward, backward, left, right, up, and down and make the drone rotate to a degree by pushing buttons on the keyboard. The route of the drone is visualized using a top view with coordinate values. The green point stands for the current position of the drone and the red line stands for the route that the drone has traveled.

**Fig. 2.** Third person view of drone and corresponding interface for remote user.

### 3.3    Embodiment of Remote User Using Drone and Mixed Reality

The drone acts as a physical proxy for the remote expert in the local environment. Through mixed reality, we overlay a half-body 3D avatar onto the drone, representing the remote expert's presence. The head position and rotation of the 3D avatar are aligned with the drone's camera. The 3D avatar can move according to the manipulation of the remote user. This feature enhances the sense of presence and engagement, allowing the local worker to interact with the remote expert as if physically co-located, as Fig. 3 shows. The embodiment through a drone-driven agent provides a more intuitive and natural way for the local and remote users to collaborate, especially in complex tasks requiring precise coordination.

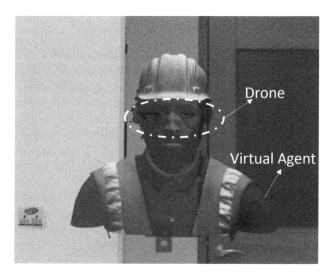

**Fig. 3.** Drone-driven agent.

### 3.4    Communication Cues

Apart from traditional audio-visual communication channels, our system incorporates advanced AR-based techniques like 3D sketching and gaze tracking. The drone is a medium to transfer the communication cues between the remote expert and the local worker. For instance, the remote expert can draw sketches or annotate objects in the desktop interface using keyboard, which are then rendered in real-time in the local environment through the MR head-mounted display worn by the local user. This method provides a more interactive and effective way to convey complex instructions or feedback. Additionally, the system includes gaze tracking technology to indicate the remote expert's focus, offering a more intuitive understanding of their intentions and enhancing collaborative efficiency.

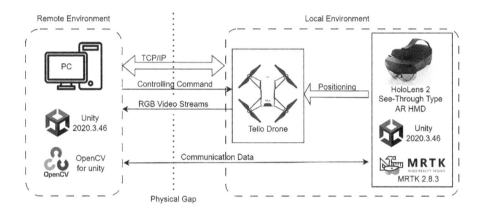

**Fig. 4.** Implementation Framework

## 4    Implementation

The implementation of our prototype system includes three components:

- A local side where the user wears an MR head-mounted display to receive and follow the guidance to accomplish tasks.
- A drone that is located on the local side but acts as an embodiment of a remote user and can capture the local environment in real time.
- A remote PC side where the user can access the video captured by the drone synchronously and control the navigation of the drone by manipulating the PC.

Fig. 4 shows the implementation framework of our prototype system. Overall, the implementation is divided into remote side and local side with hardware and software.

The hardware used in the prototype includes Microsoft HoloLens 2 which is a see-through-type MR head-mounted display, a PC with Intel i9 CPU and 32 GB RAM, and a Tello drone which is embedded with a micro camera[6]. The camera features a 5-megapixel photo resolution and an 82.6-degree field of view, capable of recording HD720P30 video in MP4 format. Additionally, it supports electronic image stabilization to ensure steady footage. We chose Tello because it is small, its size is only $98 \times 92.5 \times 41$ mm, and its weight is only about 80 g, which is very suitable for indoor flying such as industrial physical tasks.

The prototype system was developed based on the Windows 10 operating system using the Unity 3D[7] 2020.4 game engine. The MixedRealityToolkit[8] was used to develop the local user's MR application of HoloLens and the remote user's manipulation application. The OpenCV for unity was used to visualize the sketching communication cues. The communication between remote and local environment was done by TCP/IP protocol, including controlling command from remote side to local drone, RGB video streams from drone to remote PC, and communication data between the remote and local sides.

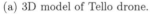

(a) 3D model of Tello drone.                    (b) Tracked QR code.

**Fig. 5.** Calibration of coordination using QR code.

The coordination of the drone, local MR environment, and remote manipulation need to be calibrated. To calibrate the drone and local MR environment, we use a QR code that is placed on the floor of the local physical world. By scanning the QR code, the MR device knows the position of the QR code, and a virtual 3D model of the Tello drone is shown on the QR code. Then we place the drone onto the QR code to make the QR code the origin of coordination (Fig. 5).

---

[6] https://www.ryzerobotics.com/.
[7] https://unity.com.
[8] https://github.com/microsoft/MixedRealityToolkit.

# 5   Discussion and Future Work

In this paper, we present a remote collaboration system using drone and MR technology. We propose the drone-driven agent to embody the remote user in the local environment and share the local environment through a drone-embedded camera to provide a fully independent view sharing. The communication cues are provided to facilitate instruction and communication between collaborators. By combining drone and MR technology, we intend to explore a new direction of remote collaboration.

The view sharing using drone provides a more independent way of sharing compared with previous camera based sharing. However, the manipulation of drone from remote space is sometime not stable because of the delay of network. In addition, the drone used in this paper is a small-size drone, and its flight direction is easily affected by airflow and other factors in the environment. Future work needs to consider the above issues and overcome them when designing remote collaboration systems with drones. For example, the drone-involved system can work well in the indoor workspace, but may not be as good outdoors.

Augmenting a 3D virtual character to the drone provides a new embodiment method of remote user. However, the alignment of virtual character and real drone is depend on the situation of drone. In our system, the position of drone and virtual character is calculated by command from the remote user. Future system can consider to detect the drone directly so that the alignment will be more precise.

Our current system primarily focuses on one-to-one collaboration scenarios. Future work should enable multiple users to collaborate simultaneously. This could involve multiple drones or advanced MR techniques to represent multiple remote users in the local environment.

For the safety concerns, as drones become more integrated to the collaborative workspace, there are issues that drones may collide with physical objects. Future systems should consider intelligent security mechanisms to protect users from hurt.

Formal user studies are needed to evaluate drone-driven agents in remote collaboration systems. To measure the effectiveness and user acceptance of drone-driven agents in remote collaboration environments, comprehensive user research is needed. User research should evaluate the technical performance of the system and should also collect user feedback on usability, engagement, and overall satisfaction to guide further improvements to the system to make it more user-friendly and efficient in practical applications.

# 6   Conclusion

In summary, this paper proposes a new remote collaboration system integrating drones and mixed reality technology. Our system provides remote users with greater independence and enhanced presence in the local environment through augmented drone using a 3D virtual avatar. Drone-driven agents and independent view sharing via drone-embedded cameras help remote collaborative work a lot, especially for physical tasks.

Although combining MR and drone technologies has great potential, our system still faces some challenges, such as network latency, drone environment limitations, and user interface. Future research is needed to refine the system and expand its applicability to these challenges. For future work, we plan to conduct a formal user study to evaluate the proposed system.

**Disclosure of Interests.** The authors have no competing interests to declare that are relevant to the content of this article.

# References

1. Lee, G.A., Teo, T., Kim, S., Billinghurst, M.: Mixed reality collaboration through sharing a live panorama. In: SIGGRAPH Asia 2017 Mobile Graphics & Interactive Applications, New York, pp. 1–4. ACM (2017)
2. Piumsomboon, T., et al.: Mini-me: an adaptive avatar for mixed reality remote collaboration. In: Proceedings of the 2018 CHI Conference on Human Factors in Computing Systems, New York, pp. 1–13. ACM (2018)
3. Bai, H., Sasikumar, P., Yang, J., Billinghurst, M.: A user study on mixed reality remote collaboration with eye gaze and hand gesture sharing. In: Proceedings of the 2020 CHI Conference on Human Factors in computing systems, New York, pp. 1–13. ACM (2020)
4. Teo, T., Lawrence, L., Lee, G. A., Billinghurst, M., Adcock, M.: Mixed reality remote collaboration combining 360 video and 3d reconstruction. In: Proceedings of the 2019 CHI Conference on Human Factors in Computing Systems, New York, pp. 1–14. ACM (2019)
5. Kim, S., Lee, G., Huang, W., Kim, H., Woo, W., Billinghurst, M.: Evaluating the combination of visual communication cues for HMD-based mixed reality remote collaboration. In: Proceedings of the 2019 CHI Conference on Human Factors in Computing Systems, New York, pp. 1–13. ACM (2019)
6. Hassanalian, M., Abdelkefi, A.: Classifications, applications, and design challenges of drones: a review. Prog. Aerosp. Sci. **91**, 99–131 (2016)
7. Sabet, M., Orand, M., McDonald, D.W.: Designing telepresence drones to support synchronous, mid-air remote collaboration: an exploratory study. In: Proceedings of the 2021 CHI Conference on Human Factors in Computing Systems, New York, pp. 1–17. ACM (2021)
8. Amazon Prime Air prepares for drone deliveries. https://www.aboutamazon.com/news/transportation/amazon-prime-air-prepares-for-drone-deliveries. Accessed 24 Dec 2023
9. Drones Survey Services. https://dronesurveyservices.com/do-drones-deliver-packages/. Accessed 24 Dec 2023
10. DJI drones helped track and stop the Notre Dame fire. https://www.theverge.com/2019/4/16/18410723/notre-dame-fire-dji-drones-tracking-stopped-thermal-cameras. Accessed 24 Dec 2023

11. Biehl, J.T., Avrahami, D., Dunnigan, A.: Not really there: understanding embodied communication affordances in team perception and participation. In: Proceedings of the 18th ACM Conference on Computer Supported Cooperative Work & Social Computing, New York, pp. 1567–1575. ACM (2015)

12. Kristoffersson, A., Coradeschi, S., Loutfi, A.: A review of mobile robotic telepresence. In: Advances in Human-Computer Interaction 2013, p. 3 (2013)

13. Yoon, B., Kim, H., Lee, G.A., Billinghurst, M., Woo, W.: The effect of avatar appearance on social presence in an augmented reality remote collaboration. In: 2019 IEEE Conference on Virtual Reality and 3D User Interfaces (VR), New York, pp. 547–556. IEEE (2019)

14. Paulos, E., Canny, J.: PRoP: personal roving presence. In: Proceedings of the SIGCHI Conference on Human Factors in Computing Systems, New York, pp. 296–303. ACM(1998)

15. Neto, I., Johal, W., Couto, M., Nicolau, H., Paiva, A., Guneysu, A.: Using tabletop robots to promote inclusive classroom experiences. In: Proceedings of the Interaction Design and Children Conference, New York, pp. 281–292. ACM (2020)

16. Gealy, D.V., et al.: Quasi-direct drive for low-cost compliant robotic manipulation. In: 2019 International Conference on Robotics and Automation (ICRA), New York, pp. 437–443. IEEE (2019)

17. Bae, I. H.: Avatar drone: drone as telepresence platform with 3D mobility. In: 2016 13th International Conference on Ubiquitous Robots and Ambient Intelligence (URAI), New York, pp. 452–453. IEEE (2016)

18. Sakashita, M., Ricci, E. A., Arora, J., Guimbretière, F.: RemoteCoDe: robotic embodiment for enhancing peripheral awareness in remote collaboration tasks. In: Proceedings of the ACM on Human-Computer Interaction, New York, vol. 6, no. CSCW1, pp. 1–22. ACM (2022)

19. Jones, B., et al.: Elevating communication, collaboration, and shared experiences in mobile video through drones. In: Proceedings of the 2016 ACM Conference on Designing Interactive Systems, New York, pp. 1123–1135. ACM (2016)

20. Shakeri, H., Neustaedter, C.: Teledrone: shared outdoor exploration using telepresence drones. In: Conference Companion Publication of the 2019 on Computer Supported Cooperative Work and Social Computing, New York, pp. 367–371. ACM (2019)

21. Lee, G., Kang, H., Lee, J., Han, J.: A user study on view-sharing techniques for one-to-many mixed reality collaborations. In: 2020 IEEE Conference on Virtual Reality and 3D User Interfaces (VR), New York, pp. 343–352. IEEE (2020)

# Identifying Influencing Factors of Immersion in Remote Collaboration

Yifan Yang[1,2(✉)] ⓘ, Xu Sun[1,5] ⓘ, Jie Gao[3], Ziqi Zhou[4], Sheng Zhang[1,2],
and Canjun Yang[2]

[1] Faculty of Science and Engineering, University of Nottingham Ningbo China, Ningbo, China
Yifan.Yang@nottingham.edu.cn
[2] Ningbo Innovation Center, Zhejiang University, Ningbo, China
[3] Singapore-MIT Alliance for Research and Technology, Singapore, Singapore
[4] College of Computer Science and Technology, Zhejiang University, Ningbo, China
[5] Nottingham Ningbo China Beacons of Excellence Research and Innovation Institute,
University of Nottingham Ningbo, Ningbo, China

**Abstract.** Working remotely and collaborating with colleagues online has become a prevailing trend. The user experience with various collaboration tools, such as teleconferencing platforms, online whiteboards, and virtual reality, plays a pivotal role in facilitating effective communication. This paper aims to explore the social factors that influence immersion in remote collaborative meetings. Through the analysis of data collected from a series of semi-structured interviews, themes were categorized into three dimensions, namely system, context, and human factors. Compared to earlier research into the relevant influencing factors, the social dimension is emphasized in our findings, and all the factors are described from a social perspective. We conclude by discussing the possible implications of these factors on system and platform design.

**Keywords:** Influencing factors · Immersion · Social Immersion · Collaborative work · Design Application · User Experience · Virtual Reality

## 1 Introduction

In today's workplaces, there is an increasing trend towards collaborative, social, and virtual modes of work, encompassing both short-term and long-term perspectives [1, 2]. The number of workers who are choosing to telecommute and collaborate online is increasing, especially in the context of the COVID-19 pandemic [3], while workers have become more reliant on web-based tools to communicate and organize their tasks. Information technology also benefits workers to a significant degree in facilitating remote collaborative work, such as supporting communication, helping to share knowledge, and improving processes, which could, in turn, improve their work efficiency and outcomes [4, 5].

Today's workers are making decisions about which information technologies to use based on how they feel about them [6]. Thus, user experience plays a vital role during

J. Y. C. Chen and G. Fragomeni (Eds.): HCII 2024, LNCS 14707, pp. 128–144, 2024.
https://doi.org/10.1007/978-3-031-61044-8_10

the remote collaboration process in the virtual environment, and user experience theories have been proposed to better understand and provide users with such experiences, including immersion.

Immersion has been defined as a psychological state "characterized by perceiving oneself to be enveloped by, and interacting with, an environment that provides continuous stimuli" [7]. The investigation of factors influencing immersion has been ongoing since the 1990s. However, the social aspects of immersion have been assigned a marginal role, and the features and influencing factors of social immersion remain unclear [8]. In this study, we aim to investigate the influencing factors of immersion in the context of remote collaborative meetings using qualitative methods. The research questions include:

1. What are the influencing factors of social immersion?
2. How important are these influencing factors in remote collaborative meetings?
3. How could a design application use these factors to improve user experience?

Our research extends the field of immersion by providing its social aspect. It could form the foundation for understanding and analyzing the influencing factors of information and social technology, such as social networking or collaboration tools, and could be used to analyze the various phenomena of user experience, such as the reasons for collapses in collaboration. The influencing factors could also guide designers and engineers to develop corresponding functions when practicing. It also contributes to a recent call for the investigation of remote working, to better understand what influences the experience of remote collaborative work.

## 2   Theoretical Background

### 2.1   Immersion and Influencing Factors

In the previous studies, the concept of immersion has two main categories: system-focused (also a technological-based method, and sensory immersion) and user-focused (also a perspective-based method, the sense of immersion, and perceived immersion, psychological immersion) [9–11]. The system-focused dimension considered the technological qualities of immersion, in which the use of the system and the way the content is displayed determined the level of immersion [12]. Namely, the more the system displays, the more it is perceived as "immersive" [13]. The type of medium itself is one of the significant factors in characterizing immersion [14]. Studies have shown that immersion could be improved by a larger screen and better audio quality [15]. Slater and Wilbur proposed that the immersive capability of a virtual environment depends on the degree to which it is inclusive, extensive, surrounding, vivid, and matching [13]. Miller & Bugnariu [10] classified immersion in virtual environments as either low, moderate, or high-level immersion according to the field of view, the fidelity, the motion capture, the sensory modality, and the signals. In addition, when describing users' experience together with other concepts, such as presence and flow, immersion usually represents the characteristics of the technology [10, 16]. Dengel & Mägdefrau [17] summarized immersion as objective factors that are provided by the technology, in contrast to subjective factors in an immersive virtual environment.

Some researchers have criticized these technology-based methods, since they ignore the content, the context, and users' preferences [11], and have now begun to accept and use a user-focused approach [9]. The user-focused dimension recognizes immersion as a user's psychological state and the subjective sense of being surrounded by technological stimulation [11, 18]. It is defined as a psychological state "characterized by perceiving oneself to be enveloped by, and interacting with, an environment that provides continuous stimuli" [7]. Brown & Cairns [19] found that immersion is influenced by a user's attention, thoughts, and goals within a game. Some researchers have focused on the users' demographic characteristics, including age, motivation, and emotion could both become critical influential factors for a user's perception of immersion [20–22]. Seo & Corness [23] tried to understand the immersion experience with culture, society, environment, and history and built the immersive consciousness. Witmer & Singer [7] even proposed the Immersive Tendencies Questionnaire to predict an individual's ability to predisposition immersion from three subscales: involvement, focus, and games.

In recent years, some researchers have also accepted the interrelation between the two conceptualizations, which means immersion relies both on the quality of the technology and the user features [9]. Indeed, the two concepts reinforce each other. A higher quality of technology improves the levels of engagement, presence, and cognitive absorption, which in turn affects the sense of immersion [24, 25]. Mütterlein [26] stated that a user's immersion is restricted by the technological quality (system-focused immersion), but has to be measured on a subjective level. In this research, we have adopted Mütterlein's idea that immersion is a psychological state, but it is a state that could be influenced by technological quality.

## 2.2 Immersion and Social Collaboration

Research shows that the results concerning individual user experience may not be suitable to transfer to collaborative contexts [27]. Thus virtual collaborations should be taken seriously and researched separately [28]. Furthermore, although researchers have begun to focus on immersion in social contexts, such as in remote collaboration, many have focused on games and online learning, or combining games and learning [29]. While immersion has hardly been explored in the context of remote collaborative work. Previous studies have mainly used social presence, social flow, and sociability to explain and describe the social collaborative phenomenon, while immersion has been ignored [30].

Distributed work is becoming more common across the world, especially after the COVID-19 crisis. Researchers have found that immersion influences work performance in a virtual environment, including team performance, individual performance, and group behavior [31]. Narayan et al. [32] also proved that different immersion levels would determine the level of performance in collaborative work, where the use of stereo displays has a positive effect. Immersion is characterized as a level of fidelity in this research, which includes the use of head tracking, stereo displays, the field of view, and haptic feedback, among others. Oprean et al. [33] explored the use of VR technology in geographically distributed collaborations and found that immersion could promote co-presence and self-location. The state of immersion here also refers to the degree of technology employed, where a 360° camera, combined with more immersive displays, could provide better situational awareness and cultivate the level of awareness of team members. This research shows the possibility of using immersive technology in distributed collaborative work.

Regarding immersion as a psychological state of mind, Mütterlein et al. [27] found that interactivity and trust could promote the sense of immersion, which could drive users' intentions to collaborate. Similarly, Schouten et al. [34] found that 3D virtual environments offer greater immersion than text-based communication, which could better facilitate team collaborations and decision-making by offering better levels of consensus, satisfaction, and cohesion.

Overall, there is an indication that social influence alters user experience in the virtual environment. However, when it comes specifically to immersion in the context of collaborative work, social aspects play a marginal role, and there is little evidence in studies that shows systematically what human factors and social influences will impact immersion [10, 11, 35–37]. Thus in this paper, considering immersion as a psychological state of mind, we tried to explore the factors that influence the social aspect of immersion in the context of remote collaborative work and offer implication instructions for design and management projects.

## 3  Methods

### 3.1  Participants

34 participants were recruited online from around the world through social networking platforms or by email. All the participants had remote collaboration experience. The goal of the recruitment process was to maximize heterogeneity in terms of age, occupation, role, and tenure. Among 34 interview participants, 15 participants recalled their experience through VR, 18 used video or audio conferencing systems and 1 only used text. Aside from four PhD students, the working experience of participants ranged from 1 year to 28 years, with a median job tenure of 5 years. Their occupation includes professors, engineering, white-collar workers, service personnel, sales, and freelancers.

The study was approved by the University Ethics Committee. The participants were provided with information about the goals and procedure of the research and agreed to be recorded during the interview process.

### 3.2  Procedure

We adopted the semi-structured interview method to explore the influencing factors since this method allows the collection of participants' experiences, feelings, and thoughts during their collaborative work, and it is an established method often used to guide software development [38].

Before the formal interviews, two pilot studies were carried out. In line with the feedback gained, the interview questions were revised and subsequently used in the present study. Since we found the data in the pilot study to be both unique and useful, after seeking permission from the interviewees, such data was also used in the analysis.

The interview questions were made based on prior research [19, 39] and were designed to prompt the interviewees to talk about their feelings and thoughts. The interview would initially guide the interviewees to recall a specific collaborative experience. The questions were focused mainly on their feelings concerning the social aspects of collaborative work. The questions were focused mainly on their feelings concerning the social aspects of collaborative work. The detailed interview protocol is in Appendix. The formal interviews were carried out mainly through audio calls or telephone as the participants were located in different cities. Each interview lasted from 30–60 min and was recorded with permission from the participants.

### 3.3 Data Analysis and Trustworthiness

The interview data were analyzed based on Grounded Theory [40] and thematic analysis methods [41]. Thematic analysis was used to identify and analyze patterns in data since it is flexible and suitable for analyzing qualitative data. The analysis process is inductive and has six steps according to Braun and Clarke's theory [42]. Namely familiarization with the data, generating initial coding, searching for themes, reviewing the themes, labeling themes, and writing the report.

The interview was first transcribed in Microsoft Word. Team members first familiarized themselves with the interview content, and then coded the data in Word. The aim of the coding is to understand factors affecting immersion in the social aspect. Then the codebook was created in Microsoft Excel, where the themes were discussed and summarized iteratively by the three researchers. Finally, the codes were sorted under the three dimensions of system, context, and human factors, in which there were 13 subcategories.

The importance of different factors and allocated weights was measured with the assistance of the Analytic Hierarchy Process (AHP) methodology and the Delphi technique. AHP, relying on the judgments of experts, was found to be useful because of its ease of applicability [43, 44]. Moreover, it can be performed with a small sample size to achieve useful models, where a variety of research uses sample sizes ranging from four to nine [45]. After the hierarchical structure was built based on the exploration from semi-structured interviews, four experts, who are professors in the area of HCI, were invited to assign ratings to calculate the weights by pair-wise comparison of each subcategory in Saaty's 9-point scale [44]. The data was analyzed according to the calculation method of AHP and the consistency ratios in Excel. The consistency ratios are less than 0.1, showing that the experts were consistent in giving their judgments and the judgments were acceptable.

Triangulation was used to increase the validity of the results. To avoid misinterpretation of the data, the codes and themes were generated independently by three researchers in human-computer interaction. After discussion and iteration of the themes by three researchers, the results were reported to external experts, who evaluated the weight of each factor. Finally, we compared the results with previously published studies and found that the final categories corresponded with existing research concerned with influencing factors on experience [46, 47]. Our research verified the previous research since immersion is a subcategory of user experience. Compared to these earlier frameworks, each factor was described from the social perspective in the context of collaborative work.

# 4   Results

The influencing factors of social immersion revealed by the interview data were categorized into three dimensions with 13 subcategories. According to the judgments from experts, social motivation (0.137) is regarded as the most important factor that influences participants' sense of social immersion, namely one's motivation to collaborate and communicate with others. Then followed by personality and background (0.109), role in the collaboration (0.080) and collaboration form get the same weight (0.080). Unexpectedly, collaboration platforms are regarded as unimportant for the sense of social immersion during the collaboration process. Figure 1 describes the influencing factors and weights of each sub-category.

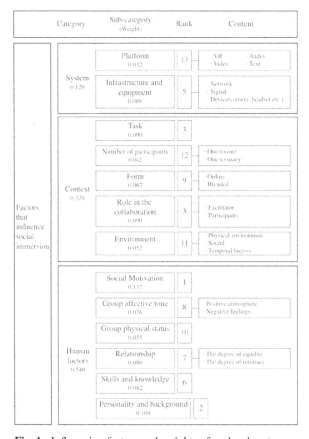

**Fig. 1.** Influencing factors and weights of each sub-category.

## 4.1   System

**System.** The way platforms affect immersion mainly relies on different ways of interaction, including text-based interaction, audio communication, video communication virtual reality, etc. Besides, there are some new supporting functions available in an online conference such as whiteboard, screen sharing, and tools that help with transcription, voting, and distributing tasks, which could help them considerably in their communication (P2, 3, 6, 8, 12, 14 & 15).

Opening a video could improve participants' sense of immersion and thereby provide them with a better experience. However, for some participants, even the use of video connection could not convey clearly the necessary information from their partners, and make them not that "immersed" in the communication (P1, 13, 16 & 18). First, the field of view available on a video call is limited, and it is difficult to perceive partners' facial expressions, gestures, and the working content at the same time, which will to a great extent reduce the level of mutual awareness, and then affect the users' experience. Second, the interactions between the partners are still limited. For example, there is a lack of visualizations of the ideas being expressed, and according to one respondent "I have no way to express myself" (P4). Third, there is a lack of small talk. "Because it is not as casual as it would be in person… and I will have fewer topics to discuss" (P8).

VR has different interaction methods. The various methods of interaction could support the communication process, helping participants enter into social immersion. However, three participants complained about the motion sickness, and lack of emotions and feedback since the avatars had no facial expressions (P25 & 26). Thus, the lack of social cues may lead to a lower level of social immersion in VR than in a video conference.

Previous researchers believe that a head-mounted device, such as VR, offers better immersion than a computer screen [10, 11]. However, in this research, we have found that VR is sometimes less effective, and provides less social immersion, than a video conference, since it has fewer functions, limited capacity, and participants can not see others' facial expressions. Although it can capture body gestures and simulate a scene realistically [36], more research is necessary to determine whether or not this overweighs the information expressed by the facial expressions and thereby offers better social immersion.

**Infrastructure and Equipment.** Group collaboration requires better infrastructure and equipment, because if one person has a hardware or systems problem, the others also need to spend time waiting for their teammates to fix the problem, and the progress of the entire team will be affected (P21). Nine participants complained that signal delays, network problems, and poor sound and image quality would decrease the efficiency of communication. Five participants who use VR also face bad networks, limited capacity of the platform, and technical problems with avatars. They have to leave the room and rejoin again, or their partners' avatars disappear during the collaboration, which could both break up the communication process and break down the sense of social immersion.

### 4.2  Context

**Task.** Task context could directly influence the user's interaction and level of concentration, so as to relate to the sense of social immersion. Five participants said they are more focused if the task is something in which they have an interest. One participant reported that his sense of immersion, satisfaction, and experience depends on the task, not on the equipment used in the collaboration. P12 complained about the boring task, where the participants simply reported their work to the leader, so there was less interaction between the participants and less social immersion.

**Number of Participants.** The number of attendants will influence engagement and the sense of social immersion, since "The more the number of people in a discussion, the fewer the number of people who will speak" (P3). Thus, they prefer to split the participants into small teams to encourage better communication. "During a small group discussion, I have to understand each sentence and each word said by my partner(s) and give instant feedback". Participants found that one-to-one communication is comfortable and easy. P7 mentioned one particular form of collaboration: interaction–turn ("话轮"), in which she felt she was in the state of flow, and she felt that this format made a conversation more efficient. P3 thought that it was more immersive when splitting a large group into small groups for discussion.

The monologue was commonly described as an uncomfortable interaction form. When there are several people, it is easier to enter a certain type of monologue. Sometimes, P12 complained that each in the conference only completed their own business and there was less interaction and information exchange, while at other times, reported information was only useful for some of the participants, and others had to wait. In addition, some participants hold on to one question, for example, "one participant kept on expressing his thoughts irrelevant to the task" (P2) or they will "keep asking questions and want to get to the bottom of a problem" (P13). Such behavior will reduce rapidly other participants' sense of social immersion and will test their patience.

**Form.** The form of collaboration, which means whether the participants are all online, or blended, also influences the social sense of immersion. Five participants stated that the blended option is unfair for those who join the collaboration online, since those who are offline have more social cues and interactions, and those who are online tend to be listeners and will have less engagement. They explained that for the same content, online participants would accept less information. Researchers also discovered that remote participants sometimes could not follow the activities of the offline participants [48].

**Role in the Collaboration.** To join a collaboration as a facilitator or a participant is vital for the sense of social immersion. Participants reported that they are less immersed as facilitators since they need to consider many other aspects besides the collaboration content, including controlling the time, facilitating other participants, or taking the meeting minutes, this will cause them to focus and interact differently as participants. P10 stated, "Although I am focused, I am not immersed because I need to keep looking at the clock since I am the facilitator".

**Environment.** We have found that the environment of the partners will influence the participants' sense of social immersion, including their physical situation, sounds, and temporal factors.

Physical situation. Users are not limited to sitting at home when collaborating remotely. They may also work in the field (P5), on a train (P15), or in a café (P12), among other place. However, the location could offer different images to collaborative partners. P8 and 10 felt that their partners were not in working status if they discovered that they were attending the meeting while in a car. Similarly, three participants found their social immersion was interrupted if their partners' children or parents interrupted the meeting because the scene suddenly changed from work to life. P21 found it interesting since she could see another side of a colleague's life outside of his job, but she agreed that this did not constitute the status of being at work.

Surrounding sounds. Noise would have a negative impact on the meeting experience. "If there are too many people in the environment, I may not be fully concentrated on listening to the content of meetings" (P15). On the other hand, the lack of social sounds during a period of remote collaboration. "If it is face-to-face communication, someone murmured how can this be, then I will know he doesn't understand. I can feel them muttering something, or whatever…But this is impossible online since if all participants open their microphones, it will become too noisy and we would not be able to hear the speaker clearly, so the others have to be muted, and it is embarrassing (P21)."

Temporal factors. Time differences may also have an impact on remote online collaboration and the sense of immersion. This would happen when team members are located in different continents or time zones (P00, P8 & 14). Participants may worry about whether their partners are working. "I was having a meeting with colleagues in Europe. It's still the day for me, but it's night for them. I would feel embarrassed (P00)." Furthermore, different arrangements and schedules create a form of "invisible jet lag" between the participants. As P20 noted, "Originally, I thought it was the problem of the jet lag. But now there is only a one-hour time difference between us, so it can't be considered a time difference. It's still due to a different schedule."

## 4.3 Human Factors

**Social Motivation.** Social motivation refers to the seeking of social information and collaboration [49]. When personal motivation is different from the team goals, social motivation will decrease or even lose, which leads to the reduction of involvement and engagement, and may affect team performance. On the other hand, the same interest with partners could increase the participants' sense of social immersion. Seven participants said that they are more focused when the topic is related to themselves, otherwise they may become distracted. "I will be focused on what I am most concerned about, such as future planning, the future direction of work, and my personal career development" (P3). When the group aim matches their personal motivation, participants will pay more attention and dedicate more effort to the collaboration (P3 & 4). Therefore, a clear common goal could also help participants to become and remain focused (P2, 16 & 21).

**Group Affective Tone.** Emotion plays a crucial role in communication, builds mutual understanding and empathy, provides feedback, and coordinates relationships, and interactions with others [50]. Four participants indicated that their partners' emotions could both increase or decrease attention and influence the sense of social immersion. It was also noted that the negative feelings spread easily among team members, which mainly include anger, anxiety, embarrassment, frustration, nervousness, and uncomfortable. Participants reported that they would also be anxious when their partners become anxious or stressed (P3). Embarrassment also easily happens during remote collaboration when suddenly no one talks. "if I say something and nobody answers, it's hard for me to tell if they didn't hear me, or if they were thinking, or if they are offline P3."

. The consistent emotion reflected by the group members forms the group's affective tone [51]. Five participants expressed that the collaboration is more fluent if the atmosphere is relaxed. For example, there are small informal talks before the formal collaboration (P14). The process should be adjusted according to the group atmosphere and the group emotion, for example, "to tell a joke or open the window when I feel the atmosphere become embarrassed (P3)".

**Group Physical Status.** A negative physical state could make participants distracted. Fatigue is the primary physical state that influences collaboration and decreases the sense of social immersion, especially after a long time meeting (P1, 2, 4, 6, 8 & 12). Four participants pointed out that one's energy is limited, thus the participants may get tired and become distracted after a long time of working, which will lead to a decrease in attention and team effectiveness. Thus time control is essential, online collaboration needs to be broken to let attendances relax and better focus. For VR collaboration, participants complained that they felt more tired in VR than in video conferencing and some participants suffered especially from sore neck and eye fatigue, and motion sickness, which made them distracted and non-immersed.

**Relationship.** Proximity makes collaboration easier. A good relationship can promote interaction, and bad relationships hinder interaction [52]. Participants tended to be more comfortable and active interacting with partners they already know and was easier to enter the sense of social immersion. P19 noted that his impression of students did not come from their avatars in VR, but rather from whether or not they were already known to him in the real world. On the other hand, if the participants are unfamiliar or not comfortable with each other, they may feel nervous and afraid (P6).

In particular, it has been pointed out that proximity and relationship may vary in online collaboration. Three participants said that their relationship with partners becomes distant in an online collaboration due to the lack of social cues. P0 reflected that remote collaboration will lead to greater inequality of status, while there's more sense of differences and the students speak less, which makes her feel less immersed in the communication. On the other hand, three participants reported that online collaboration gives them more confidence because the virtual environment offers more personal space and flexibility.

**Skills and Knowledge.** Collaboration will be smoother if their partners are experts in their area (P14, 16 & 18). Communication with experts is more easily while experts could understand the situation better. In some cases, participants complain about the ability of their partners, which may lead to inefficiency of the collaboration. Thus, good preparation could make discussions and meetings better and participants will focus more on content in remote collaboration. Since remote collaboration is communicated through a technology-mediated platform, the technology skills and literacy of participants are also influential, especially in virtual reality.

The ability of the facilitator also plays an essential role in collaboration, especially when facilitating online, since "It's almost impossible to use body language. It is more challenging for facilitators to perceive the group atmosphere, and encourage participants to join the discussion." (P13). A good facilitator could better grasp the audience's concentration and improve other participants' sense of immersion.

**Personality and Background.** The personality and cultural traits of partners will also influence the collaboration and the sense of social immersion, and it may change when moving the collaboration online. P19 observed that shy students prefer typing ideas to speaking them out in the online classroom. While P13 reported that online collaboration decreases the participants' enthusiasm. "people who love asking questions before asked fewer questions now. Besides, people who are more sensitive and empathetic may feel more uncomfortable in online collaboration due to the lack of social cues (P2).

# 5    Implications for Design

## 5.1   Design for Context

Different collaboration process requires corresponding media and platforms. Thus the platform design needs to take into account the type of tasks and communication process, such as decision-making scenarios or brainstorming. Some of the platforms have begun to differ between online learning and online meetings.

Ohl et al. [53] have summarized tele-collaboration into six typical communication graphs. Different communication graphs have different spatial and interaction modes, in which platform design should be considered. Besides, different channels of communication could be provided to support the flexible change of small group discussion, presentation, and team decision-making to meet the users' need for flexible interaction and fluent communication, and then enhance the sense of social immersion and social presence.

Furthermore, the traditional remote collaborative method, such as video conference, is not suitable for some exceptional work or tasks, such as remote collaboration in the field or remote instruction. To operate mobile phones or laptops would become a distraction for their work [54], and even in some situations, mobile phones could not be used for safety reasons (P4). Wearable devices, drones, or mixed-reality technology could be used to help communication and the transmission of field information.

Research has found that the systems cannot be designed to support all the users' individual goals [54]. However, from this research, we have found that the system could provide team personalization for the team task since the task is usually related to the occupation and the goal characteristics. The group could personalize the functions of the platform according to their collaborative goals, tasks, form, and other contexts so that the platform could provide more goal-oriented features and participants may get into a higher level of social immersion.

Social immersion requires a collaborative partner's mutual situation awareness, which is affected by the perception of the partners' environmental context. Participants reflected that the timing to speak is complex in the video and audio conferences since it lacks social cues to tell participants who are going to speak, especially as the number of participants increased. Research has found that spatial sound in VR could reduce this problem as the sound comes from the speakers' direction [55]. Sound art could also create a sense of collectivity and promote participating equality [56]. Designers for video and audio conference platforms could try to provide more sound cues by adding spatial sound, which could help participants feel closer during the interaction [55]. In the interview, participants reflected that noises, such as the sound of outside children or environmental noises, could reduce the sense of social immersion. To draw together the social sounds and adopt an effective approach to noises could be a method [56].

Besides, designers could take a page from the social game, such as Massive Multi-player Online Role-Playing Games (MMORPGs), where players could meet, interact, collaborate, and form relationships in the public space of the virtual environment, and at the same time, players could create personal space, form personal teams, and collaborate with teammates [57].

## 5.2  Design for Human Factors

The collaborative partners played a vital role in the collaboration and greatly influenced the participants' sense of immersion. However, in existing platforms, no matter audio and video conference systems, or virtual reality, the ways for users to perceive their partners are still limited. Participants reported their difficulty in perceiving their partners' situation, psychology, and physical status, which is one of the greatest barriers for them to get into social immersion.

Group mutual awareness could be supported through visualization of the group atmosphere according to the interaction frequency between participants, the physiological data of participants, or facial expressions and tones. Displaying and regulating group affective tones can be used as a sharing behavior to personalize workplace relationships, build mutual understanding and empathy, and provide feedback and interpersonal influence. It could also be used to support facilitators to better guide the collaboration. The group's physical status could be shown to the host or leader, to remind them that the team needs a break.

Tausch et al. [58] tried to present individual as well as group performance on the wall or table to support brainstorming sessions. However, this is designed for face-to-face collaboration and is unlikely to be applied in remote collaboration. Peng et al. [59] designed a "GremoBot" to visualize and regulate group emotion. However, this feature is designed based on text analysis, while the interview data reflected that fewer participants communicate through chat during synchronous remote collaboration such as video conferences. Thus there is still a lot of space for designers to extend the interaction form and promote mutual awareness between the users.

Interaction between group members will increase the level of involvement and participation equality, leading to better group performance, greater member satisfaction [60, 61], and deeper social immersion. Research has found that VR could offer closer interaction and promote gender equality, where women have a more positive experience in VR [55, 62]. Visualization could also be a method to foster interaction and participation equality [63]. Further research and design could examine how to promote equality through visualization, different design tools, or platforms, and explore whether the VR technique could reduce racial discrimination, and promote leader-member relationships.

# 6 Conclusion and Future Studies

This paper explored the factors that may influence the sense of immersion in the context of social collaborative work. The 13 factors are divided into three categories system, context, and human factors. Among the 13 factors, social motivation is considered the most important and basic promotion for the sense of social immersion. Personality and background, task content, and role in the collaboration could also greatly decide one's level of social immersion.

Potential design implications were derived to enhance social immersion according to the features and influencing factors of social immersion. However, this study adopts a qualitative research approach with a relatively small sample size. This may impact the generalizability of our findings to a broader population and careful understanding of the findings is needed. Future research should incorporate a larger sample size and use objective measurements. In addition, further research could be made on different user groups, such as vulnerable people who have difficulties using VR or video equipment, or the specific collaborative form, such as the differences between online and blended collaboration. Further studies are needed to validate the effectiveness of these factors.

# 7 Disclosure of Interests.

The authors have no competing interests to declare that are relevant to the content of this article.

# Appendix

See Table 1

**Table 1.** Interview protocol.

| Questions | |
| --- | --- |
| Demographic information | Age<br>Gender<br>Job<br>Education level<br>Work year |
| Collaboration scenario | Could you tell us one specific scenario when you were immersed in working with others remotely?<br>How many people participated in the collaboration?<br>How long it lasted?<br>What you did do, what did the others do in collaboration?<br>Where do you work remotely?<br>What kind of platform do you use to collaborate? And Why? |

(*continued*)

**Table 1.** (*continued*)

| Questions | |
|---|---|
| Demographic information | Age<br>Gender<br>Job<br>Education level<br>Work year |
| Collaboration feelings | Could you recall your feelings concerning the social aspects during that collaborative work? What are the influencing factors?<br>How do you interact with other people? What are the influencing factors?<br>Could you explain your status while collaborating with other people? What are the influencing factors?<br>How do you feel about your relationship with other people? What are the influencing factors?<br>What kinds of responses from others might interrupt your immersion, what kinds of responses helped you be immersed?<br>What would you do if the collaboration is interrupted?<br>How focused were you during the collaboration?<br>Could you imagine, what other factors may influence the collaboration? |
| | Please evaluate your collaboration, whether it is a comfortable collaboration or a bad collaboration. Why? |
| Platform user experience | What do you think about the platform you used to support remote collaboration?<br>Which function of the platform do you use in the collaboration and which part do you think could improve? |
| | What do you think about the platform which supports our interview today?<br>How does virtual reality/ video conferencing compare to the different media you use to communicate with others?<br>Do you have any suggestions or recommendations for improving the virtual reality/ video conferencing experience?<br>Is there anything else about the experience that you want to share? |

# References

1. Anders, A.: Team communication platforms and emergent social collaboration practices. Int. J. Bus. Commun. **53**, 224–261 (2016)
2. Kuruzovich, J., Paczkowski, W., Golden, T.D., Goodarzi, S., Venkatesh, V.: Telecommuting and job outcomes: a moderated mediation model of system use, software quality, and social exchange. Inf. Manag. **53**, 103431 (2021)
3. Randolph, R.V., Hu, H.-F., Silvernail, K.D.: Better the devil you know: inter-organizational information technology and network social capital in coopetition networks. Inf. Manage. **57**(6), 103344 (2020)
4. Skarzauskiene, A., Tamošiūnaitė, R., Žalėnienė, I.: Defining Social Technologies: evaluation of social collaboration tools and technologies. Electron. J. Inf. Syst. Eval. **16**, 232–241 (2013)
5. O'Brien, H., Toms, E.: The development and evaluation of a survey to measure user engagement. J. Am. Soc. Inform. Sci. Technol. **61**(1), 50–69 (2010)
6. Witmer, B., Singer, M.: Measuring presence in virtual environments: a presence questionnaire. Presence Tel. Virtual Enviro. **7**, 225–240 (1998)

7. Bleakley, A., Wade, V., Cowan, B.: Finally a Case for Collaborative VR? The Need to Design for Remote Multi-Party Conversations, pp. 1–3 (2020)
8. Daassi, M., Debbabi, S.: Intention to reuse AR-based apps: the combined role of the sense of immersion, product presence and perceived realism. Inf. Manag. **58**, 103453 (2021)
9. Miller, H., Bugnariu, N.: Level of immersion in virtual environments impacts the ability to assess and teach social skills in autism spectrum disorder. Cyberpsychol. Beh. Soc. Networking **19** (2016)
10. Agrawal, S., Simon, A., Bech, S., Brentsen, K., Forchhammer, S.: Defining immersion: literature review and implications for research on immersive audiovisual experiences. J. Audio Eng. Society (2019)
11. Slater, M.: A note on presence terminology. Presence Connect **3**(3), 1–5 (2003)
12. Slater, M., Wilbur, S.: A framework for immersive virtual environments (FIVE): speculations on the role of presence in virtual environments. Presence Teleop. Virt. **6**(6), 603–616 (1997)
13. Alanazi, A.A.: Online Learning Environments: Investigating the Factors Influencing Social Presence. University of Kansas (2019)
14. Newman, J., Cobley, P.: Videogames (Routledge Introductions to Media and Communications). Routledge (2004)
15. Oh, C.S., Bailenson, J.N., Welch, G.F.: A systematic review of social presence: definition, antecedents, and implications. Frontiers in Robotics & Ai 5 (2018)
16. Dengel, A., Mägdefrau, J.: Immersive learning explored: subjective and objective factors influencing learning outcomes in immersive educational virtual environments. In: Proceedings of the 2018 IEEE International Conference on Teaching, Assessment, and Learning for Engineering (TALE), pp. 608–615. IEEE (2018)
17. Lombard, M., Ditton, T.B., Weinstein, L.: Measuring presence: the temple presence inventory. In: Proceedings of the 12th Annual International Workshop on Presence, pp. 1–15 (2009)
18. Brown, E., Cairns, P.: A grounded investigation of game immersion. In: Proceedings of the CHI '04 Extended Abstracts on Human Factors in Computing Systems, pp. 1297–1300. Vienna, Austria (2004)
19. Riva, G., Wiederhold, B., Molinari, E.: An investigation into factors influencing immersion in interactive virtual reality environments. In: Virtual Environments in Clinical Psychology and Neuroscience, pp. 43–51. IOS (1998)
20. Georgiou, Y., Kyza, E.A.: Relations between student motivation, immersion and learning outcomes in location-based augmented reality settings. Comput. Hum. Behav. **89**, 173–181 (2018)
21. Yang, K.-C., Shih, P.-H.: Cognitive age in technology acceptance: At what age are people ready to adopt and continuously use fashionable products? Telematics Inform. **51**, 101400 (2020)
22. Seo, J.H., Corness, G. Aesthetics of immersion in interactive immersive installation: phenomenological case study. In: Proceedings of the Proceedings of International Symposium of Electronic Arts (ISEA), Vancouver, Canada (2015)
23. Bujic, M., Hamari, J.: Satisfaction and willingness to consume immersive journalism: experiment of differences between VR, 360 video, and article. In: Proceedings of the Proceedings of the 23rd International Conference on Academic Mindtrek, pp. 120–125. (2020)
24. Mütterlein, J., Hess, T.: Immersion, presence, interactivity: towards a joint understanding of factors influencing virtual reality acceptance and use (2017)
25. Mütterlein, J. The three pillars of virtual reality? Investigating the roles of immersion, presence, and interactivity. In: Proceedings of the 51st Hawaii International Conference on System Sciences (2018)
26. Mütterlein, J., Jelsch, S., Hess, T.: Specifics of collaboration in virtual reality: how immersion drives the intention to collaborate. In: Proceedings of the PACIS, p. 318 (2018)

27. Nah, F.F.-H., Schiller, S.Z., Mennecke, B.E., Siau, K., Eschenbrenner, B., Sattayanuwat, P.: Collaboration in virtual worlds: impact of task complexity on team trust and satisfaction. J. Database Manag. (JDM) **28**(4), 60–78 (2017)
28. Chamberlin, B., Trespalacios, J., Gallagher, R.: The learning games design model: immersion, collaboration, and outcomes-driven development. Int. J. Game-Based Learn. (IJGBL) **2**(3), 87–110 (2012)
29. Garcia, G., Jung, I.: Understanding immersion in 2D platform-based online collaborative learning environments. Australas. J. Educ. Technol. **37**(1), 57–67 (2021)
30. Mortensen, J., Vinayagamoorthy, V., Slater, M., Steed, A., Lok, B., Whitton, M.: Collaboration in tele-immersive environments. In: Proceedings of the EGVE, pp. 93–101 (2002)
31. Narayan, M., Waugh, L., Zhang, X., Bafna, P., Bowman, D.: Quantifying the benefits of immersion for collaboration in virtual environments. In: Proceedings of the Proceedings of the ACM Symposium on Virtual reality Software and Technology, pp. 78–81 (2005)
32. Oprean, D., Simpson, M., Klippel, A.: Collaborating remotely: an evaluation of immersive capabilities on spatial experiences and team membership. Int. J. Digit. **11**(4), 420–436 (2018)
33. Schouten, A.P., van den Hooff, B., Feldberg, F.: Virtual team work: group decision making in 3D virtual environments. Commun. Res. **43**(2), 180–210 (2016)
34. Wallace, S., Parsons, S., Westbury, A., White, K., White, K., Bailey, A.: Sense of presence and atypical social judgments in immersive virtual environments. Responses of adolescents with Autism Spectrum Disorders. Autism Int. J. Res. Pract. **14**(3), 199–213 (2010)
35. Jennett, C., Cox, A., Dhoparee, S., Epps, A., Tijs, T., Walton, A.: Measuring and defining the experience of the immersion in games. Int. J. Hum. Comput. Stud. **66**, 641–661 (2008)
36. Grinberg, A., Serrano-Careaga, J., Mehl, M., O'Connor, M.-F.: Social engagement and user immersion in a socially based virtual world. Comput. Hum. Behav. **36**, 479–486 (2014)
37. Cachia, M., Millward, L.: The telephone medium and semi-structured interviews: a complementary fit. Qual. Res. Organ. Manag. Int. J. **6**, 265–277 (2011)
38. O'Brien, H., Toms, E.: What is user engagement? A conceptual framework for defining user engagement with technology. J. Am. Soc. Inform. Sci. Technol. **59**(6), 938–955 (2008)
39. Gold, M., Mustafa, M.: 'Work always wins': client colonisation, time management and the anxieties of connected freelancers. N. Technol. Work. Employ. **28**(3), 197–211 (2013)
40. Braun, V., Clarke, V.: Thematic analysis (2012)
41. Braun, V., Clarke, V.: Using thematic analysis in psychology. Qual. Res. Psychol. **3**(2), 77–101 (2006)
42. Luthra, S., Govindan, K., Kannan, D., Mangla, S.K., Garg, C.P.: An integrated framework for sustainable supplier selection and evaluation in supply chains. J. Clean. Prod. **140**, 1686–1698 (2017)
43. Saaty, T.L.: Decision making with the analytic hierarchy process. Int. J. Serv. Sci. **1**(1), 83–98 (2008)
44. Darko, A., Chan, A.P.C., Ameyaw, E.E., Owusu, E.K., Pärn, E., Edwards, D.J.: Review of application of analytic hierarchy process (AHP) in construction. Int. J. Constr. Manag. **19**(5), 436–452 (2019)
45. Reiter, U., et al.: Factors influencing quality of experience. In: Möller, S., Raake, A. (eds.) Quality of experience. TSTS, pp. 55–72. Springer, Cham (2014). https://doi.org/10.1007/978-3-319-02681-7_4
46. Brunnström, K., et al.: Qualinet white paper on definitions of quality of experience (2013)
47. Datcu, D., Lukosch, S.G., Lukosch, H.K.: Handheld augmented reality for distributed collaborative crime scene investigation. In: Proceedings of the Proceedings of the 19th International Conference on Supporting Group Work, pp. 267–276 (2016)
48. Morrison, K.E., DeBrabander, K.M., Jones, D.R., Ackerman, R.A., Sasson, N.J.: Social cognition, social skill, and social motivation minimally predict social interaction outcomes for autistic and non-autistic adults. Front. Psychol. **11**, 3282 (2020)

49. Elfenbein, H.A., Polzer, J.T., Ambady, N.: Team emotion recognition accuracy and team performance. In: Functionality, Intentionality and Morality, Emerald Group Publishing Limited (2007)
50. George, J.M.: Personality, affect, and behavior in groups. J. Appl. Psychol. **75**(2), 107 (1990)
51. Kraut, R.E., Fussell, S.R., Brennan, S.E., Siegel, J.: Understanding effects of proximity on collaboration: implications for technologies to support remote collaborative work. Distributed Work 137–162 (2002)
52. Ohl, S.: Tele-immersion concepts. IEEE Trans. Visual Comput. Graphics **24**(10), 2827–2842 (2017)
53. Wigelius, H., Väätäjä, H., et al.: Dimensions of context affecting user experience in mobile work. In: Gross, T. (ed.) INTERACT 2009. LNCS, vol. 5727, pp. 604–617. Springer, Heidelberg (2009). https://doi.org/10.1007/978-3-642-03658-3_65
54. Campbell, A.G., Holz, T., Cosgrove, J., Harlick, M., O'Sullivan, T.: Uses of virtual reality for communication in financial services: a case study on comparing different telepresence interfaces: virtual reality compared to video conferencing. In: Arai, K., Bhatia, R. (eds.) FICC 2019. LNNS, vol. 69, pp. 463–481. Springer, Cham (2020). https://doi.org/10.1007/978-3-030-12388-8_33
55. Talianni, A.: Walking-with-sounds: creative agency, artistic collaboration and the sonic production of acoustic city spaces (2019)
56. Yee, N.: The psychology of massively multi-user online role-playing games: Motivations, emotional investment, relationships and problematic usage. In: Schroeder, R., Axelsson, A.S. (eds.) Avatars at Work and Play, pp. 187–207. Springer, Cham (2006). https://doi.org/10.1007/1-4020-3898-4_9
57. Tausch, S., Hausen, D., Kosan, I., Raltchev, A., Hussmann, H.: Groupgarden: supporting brainstorming through a metaphorical group mirror on table or wall. In: Proceedings of the Proceedings of the 8th Nordic Conference on Human-Computer Interaction: Fun, Fast, Foundational, pp. 541–550 (2014)
58. Peng, Z., Kim, T., Ma, X.: GremoBot: exploring emotion regulation in group chat. In: Proceedings of the Conference Companion Publication of the 2019 on Computer Supported Cooperative Work and Social Computing, pp. 335–340 (2019)
59. Zmud, R.W., Mejias, R.J., Reinig, B.A., Martinez-Martinez, I.M.: Participation equality: measurement within collaborative electronic environments-A three country study (2001)
60. Sauer, N.C., Kauffeld, S.: Meetings as networks: applying social network analysis to team interaction. Commun. Methods Meas. **7**(1), 26–47 (2013)
61. Kallioniemi, P., Keskinen, T., Hakulinen, J., Turunen, M., Karhu, J., Ronkainen, K.: Effect of gender on immersion in collaborative IODV applications. In: Proceedings of the Proceedings of the 16th International Conference on Mobile and Ubiquitous Multimedia, pp. 199–207 (2017)
62. Bresciani, S., Eppler, M.J.: Do visualizations foster experience sharing and retention in groups? Towards an experimental validation. In: Proceedings of the Proceedings of I-KNOW, Citeseer (2008)

# Sensory, Tangible and Embodied Interaction in VAMR

# Study of Perception and Cognition in Immersive Digital Twins for Robotic Assembly Processes

J. Cecil$^{(\boxtimes)}$, Vasavi Gannina, and Sriram Kumar Tentu

Center for Cyber-Physical Systems, Department of Computer Science, Oklahoma State
University, Stillwater, OK, USA
`{j.cecil,stentu}@okstate.edu`

**Abstract.** Today, various types of extended reality (XR) environments are becoming increasingly used in industrial engineering contexts for design, analysis as well as for training activities. User's perception plays a key role especially in such XR based learning and training contexts. Perception refers to the process by which individuals become aware and process the stimuli around them. Interdisciplinary researchers have studied the vital relationship between perception and cognition. In this groundbreaking study, the role of perception and its impact on cognition and learning in fully immersive Virtual Reality (VR) based digital twins is discussed. Schemas have been proposed to help lay the foundation to study the role of perception on cognition and learning. The primary outcomes of this research study underscored the relationships between perception and cognition while also emphasizing the impact of a participant's background in influencing their perception of the target robotics assembly environments.

**Keywords:** Virtual Reality (VR) · perception · cognition · Human-Computer Interaction (HCI) · schemas · learning environments

## 1 Introduction

The advent of the Fourth Industrial Revolution (sometimes referred to as Industry 4.0) has created a myriad of Information Technology (IT) based opportunities to impact the way we live, learn, work and play. With the introduction of low-cost Extended Reality (XR) platforms to consumers, the adoption of such XR based approaches in engineering, healthcare, space systems, transportation and other areas is becoming more widespread. XR based approaches and simulation environments are being widely adopted in these various domains in support of design, analysis, collaboration, and user training. The term 'Extended Reality' (XR) can encompass a range of immersive environments and technologies including Virtual Reality (VR), Mixed Reality (MR), Augmented Reality (AR) and Haptic Based Reality (HBR). There has been an increased interest in the role of such 3D immersive environments in various fields of engineering and medicine including advanced manufacturing and smart health [41–48]. Such XR environments also play a key role as a link between cyber and physical worlds [41, 45, 48]. As the adoption of such 3D cyber environments increases, the design of such 3D environments

J. Y. C. Chen and G. Fragomeni (Eds.): HCII 2024, LNCS 14707, pp. 147–158, 2024.
https://doi.org/10.1007/978-3-031-61044-8_11

assumes significance. Such 3D environments have to be user centric as well as enable users to accomplish their target engineering or medical tasks effectively and efficiently. Towards this goal, there is a critical need to study the role of Perception and Cognition in such 3D XR environments especially in the broader context of Human Computer Interaction (HCI) and Human Centered Computing (HCC) principles. This in turn will lay the foundation for understanding and recognizing the relationships between perception and cognition in such 3D information centric environments. In this paper, the role of perception on cognition is studied specifically involving the domain of robotic assembly. The 3D VR based simulation environments were created for robotic assembly processes involving robots in an automated shop floor environment. They were scaled down from advanced immersive simulation environments which were part of cyber modules functioning as 3D digital twins of targeted robotic assembly processes. These environments were created to allow users to interact with target activities using the fully immersive Vive VR platform; for some of the simulation environments, haptic based interactions were also supported as part of the research activities. The simulation models were created for two levels of abstraction and modeling detail: the first one was at the robotic assembly level and the second one was for a robotic factory level and context.

Human eXtended Reality Interaction (HXRI) can be defined as the application of current HCI-based principles and the formulation of novel principles for the creation of effective XR-based applications. Interest in investigating the various HCI criteria on the design and development of XR-based environments is continuing to increase [6, 16–19]. These XR environments can be viewed as Virtual Prototypes [49] or Digital Twins of target environments at various levels of abstraction. The notion of tactile affordance was introduced in [31, 33] in the context of how it impacts user interaction in such digital twins, which can be VR, AR or MR-based environments. Levels of modeling abstraction can lead to complex digital twins. These digital twins need to be designed taking into consideration HCI and HCC principles to ensure the human users are able to interact with them in an efficient and effective manner. The term 'affordance' was first coined in [20] by Gibson who defined it as what the environment offers to the individual. Others such as Norman [21] described it as action possibilities that are perceivable readily by an actor [21]. Affordance is closely related to perception potential. Researchers such as Gaver [22] studied the relationship between affordance and perceptual information. In [31, 32], affordance was classified into two main categories (Visual and Tactile Affordance). Tactile Affordance (TA) can be defined as the function of a scene's ability to support comprehension through the sense of touch.

Research in affordance related to XR-based environments has included conducting experiments to assess and measure perceptual fidelity in AR [23–27]. Learning affordance using various subjective and objective questionnaires has been the focus of other research efforts [28, 29]. There has been less research focusing on investigation of the measurement of tactile affordance during VR and MR based training. Further, while some researchers have investigated the relationship between perception and cognition, there has been no reported research in the literature on studying such relationships within XR environments and digital twins. In the broader context of digital twin created for collaborative manufacturing and robotic assembly, there have been no reports focusing on studying the relationship between perception and cognition. This paper seeks to address this void.

## 2  Perception, Cognition and Schemas

Perception refers to the process by which individuals become aware and process the stimuli around them. As perception involves an interpretation of stimuli, a subjective element comes into play during perception studies [35]. Several researchers have studied the relationships between perception and cognition. Cognition can be described as 'the mental action or process of acquiring knowledge and understanding through thought, experience, and the senses' [50]. Cognition helps in understanding information about the environment around a user or subject and helps them interact safely with that environment. It can be viewed as an ability to perceive and react, process and understand, make decisions and initiate responses [50].

In [34], Cahan and Tacca observe that perception is the informational and causal foundation for more advanced cognitive functions among humans; they note that perception influences our thinking, which in turn affects our actions or behavior in our surroundings and the world around us. A review of literature indicates there are some key challenges in the study of such relationships between perception and cognition. One of these challenges is related to how perception is defined and studied. It has been noted that this arises because some of the questions on these relationships cannot be empirically tested; rather, they depend on subjective methods, e.g. the participant responses are based on what they see and experience. In the general scientific research context, one of the core features of scientific research is the emphasis on findings based on empirical studies, which is research involving collection and assessment of data that is observable involving the 5 senses. Psychologists have explored various research methods to research these relationships between perception and cognition. These include experimental methods to study whether manipulating one variable (called the independent variable) will affect another (referred t as the dependent variable) while controlling external variables (extraneous/ confounding variables). Typically, such research involves an 'experimental group' and a 'controlled group' [35].

Such an experimental method can involve presenting a sensory stimulus to the participant and recording their perception response. Such stimuli include Visual effects, object recognition (or recall), detection of motion, among others. The challenge is that some of the related research questions cannot be empirically tested but depend on subjective methods. Haber and Levin [36] investigated size and distance perception. The study involved two experiments. The objects were grouped into (a) token variant objects (that is, the object is available in many sizes) or (b) token invariant objects (where the object typically is one standard size). The main findings were that there was little variability in responses when estimating the size of token variant objects. They concluded that size perception is based on our memory and past perception (instead of present visual perception). The other key finding was that participants were less accurate at estimating token variants and unfamiliar objects. The holistic conclusion was that participants estimated the size of token invariant objects better because they were relying on schemas, memories, and past experiences [36].

Schemas influence an individual's perception [37]. They can be described as categories of knowledge, or a type of mental template, which humans develop to understand and reason about the world in which we live in. A schema in psychology and other social sciences describes a mental concept [37]. Some researchers [37] view a schema as providing information to an individual about what to expect from diverse circumstances and providing a guide to one's cognitive processes and behavior. In HCI and psychology contexts, there can be different schemas such as event schemas, object schemas, person schemas, etc. Other ways to describe a schema is that it is a cognitive framework or concept that helps organize and interpret information [38]. The human brain uses such models to organize information about our surroundings. Other researchers view schemas as being built from memories of our unique experiences, which can be viewed as patterns of thinking and behavior that individuals use to interpret the world. This helps interpret large amounts of information through categorization and organization.

In [39], four main types of schemas are identified: person schemas, social schemas, self-schemas and event schemas. *Person schemas* deal with information about individuals. For example, a person's schema for other persons (humans) or individuals may include information about his/ her appearance, behavior, eating preferences, etc. The information in that person schema will vary and depend on each individual's background and experiences. *Social schemas* relate to general knowledge about human or people's behavior in certain social situations. *Self-schemas* deal with knowledge about yourself ('self'). This can include information about yourself (your height, weight, gender, likes/dislikes, strengths/weakness). *Event schemas* deal with patterns of behavior for different events. It can include information of how you should behave in a certain situation (for e.g.: an interview or social function), what you should do and say in a particular situation, among others.

## 3   Schemas of Interest

In this research, some schemas for supporting study of perception are proposed. This will enable devising ways to assess the relationship between and cognition. Learning and knowledge acquisition is a part of the cognitive process. For this research discussed in this paper, the domain of interest is robotics assembly and manufacturing when participants interacted with specially designed 3D VR environments using 3D headsets and controllers.

The following schemas are proposed: process schemas, worker schemas, hierarchy, and resource schemas. *Process* schemas are closely related to event schemas; they provide information about various manufacturing or robotic processes, what are the outcomes of a process as well as provide a relationship to the various resources needed to accomplish a process (which are described by resource schemas). *Worker* schemas can be viewed as a type of person schemas and may comprise of experience attributes, their educational background, skill levels, etc. *Resource* schemas may group information related to different types of machines: robots, drilling machines, conveyors, etc. *Hierarchy or Abstraction Schemas* describe the level of hierarchy that is of interest; for example, the process of interest can have a scope pertaining to a lower level of operation; for example, describing a robot cell which comprises of a robot, a machine tool, cameras, and sensors. At a higher level, a factory level can comprise several robot cells, conveyors to transport parts between work cells, and other resources. These schemas which in turn may have other hierarchical relationships at lower levels of abstraction.

## 4   Studying Perception and Learning in Robotics Assembly

In this research, the context is to study perception and cognition of users and participants during their interaction within immersive 3D Virtual Reality environments which simulated robotic assembly and automated shop floor activities. The participants interacted with these target environments using immersive 3D headsets and controllers as can be seen in Fig. 1. There were 2 objectives: (1) study the relationship of prior background/experience on human perception (2) the impact of audio cues on human perception (3) the impact of perception on cognition and learning.

**Fig. 1.** A Participant interacting with a digital twin environment using immersive 3D headset and controllers.

A view of these robotic assembly environments is shown in Fig. 2. The 3D simulation environments were created using Unity 3D engine and the HTC Vive immersive platform.

**Fig. 2.** (a, left) view of the robotic assembly factory. (b, right): close-up of a robotic work cell

## 4.1 Experiment 1

Four groups of 10 participants (students) interacted in the first experiment. Two groups (called C1-G1A and C1-G1B) were participants who had little or no background in robotics (they were undergraduate students, 5 women and 5 men, who were arts majors). A pre-test was conducted where their background in robotics was assessed; only students who scored less than 30 points out of 100 were selected; questions pertained to their ability to identify robots, conveyors, machines from images of these resources. The second group (called C2- G2A and C2-G2B) were students who had some background in robotics (undergraduate students, 5 women and 5 men, who were engineering or computer science majors). A pre-test was conducted to assess their background; students who scored more than 50 points were selected (same questions as group C1-G1).

Each of these groups interacted with specially designed immersive 3D environments. These environments were divided into 2 categories: The first category was a 3D environment simulating the assembly of objects with no audio cues or audio descriptions involving 2 work cells (work cell 1 on left, and work cell 2 on right). After work cell 1 completed an assembly, a robot R1 moved this object from work cell 1 to the conveyor, transported the part from work cell 1 to work cell 2. Once it reached work cell 2, another robot R2 picked up the object and placed in work cell 2 where another assembly was completed. The various objects were given text labels (Robot R1, conveyor, Robot R2, etc.). The participants were immersed in this environment using the Vive headset. They could walk around and observe the process from different positions and perspectives.

## 4.2 Experiment 2

The second category was the same 3D environment but with an avatar providing audio cues describing the assembly and other activities taking place. As before the participants could walk around the 3D environment using the 3D headset and navigate using the controllers (same as the participants as C1-G1). The result of the assessment is summarized in the subsequent paragraphs.

The students were given the following questions: describe the functionality of several devices (i) Identify two objects they recognize from the interactions with the target 3D environment (2 x 20 points). (ii) what does robot R1 do? (30 points) (iii) How are the parts transported between work cell 1 and work cell 2? (30 points).

**Perception and Cognition for Groups C1-G1A and C1-G1B.** For Groups C1-G1A (students with no or little background in robotics), in the first experiment without any audio, the students scored between 20 and 40 points. A different group of students (C1-G1B) repeated the same experiment with the audio enhanced simulation; the majority of the student participants showed an improvement of score by 30 to 40 points. A t-test was conducted to accept or reject the null hypothesis.

*The Null Hypothesis.* There is no significant difference in the response of participants (who had little background in robotics) between the two groups (C1-G1A (without audio, only labels) and (C1-G1B (with avatar-based audio).

**Table 1.** T-test summary for Groups C1-G1A and C1-G1B

| Statistic | Without Audio (CI GA) | With Audio (Cl GB) |
|---|---|---|
| Mean | 30 | 48 |
| Variance | 288.89 | 351.11 |
| Standard Deviation | 17 | 18.74 |
| Absolute T-statistic | 2.25 | |
| P-value | 0.0372 | |

|$T$-statistic|. 2.25 with a p-value of 0.0372 as can be seen in Table 1. Since the p-value is less than the significance level of 0.05, the null hypothesis. This indicates a statistically significant difference in the mean between the two conditions, suggesting that the presence of avatar-based audio significantly affects this group.

**Perception and Cognition for Group C2-G1A and C2-G1B.** For Group C1-G1A (students with a background in robotics), in the first experiment without any audio, the students scored ranged between 50 and 70 points. A different group of students (C1-G1B) repeated the same experiment with the avatar enhanced audio cues and overview.

**Table 2.** T-test summary for Group C2-G1A and C2-G1B

| Statistic | Without Audio (C2 GA) | With Audio (C2 GB) |
|---|---|---|
| Mean | 65 | 79 |
| Variance | 138.89 | 187.78 |
| Standard Deviation | 11.79 | 13.7 |
| Absolute T-statistic | 2.449 | |
| P-value | 0.0248 | |

The |t| statistic was 2.449 with a p-value of 0.0248 as can be seen in Table 2. As the p-value is less than 0.05, the null hypothesis is rejected, indicating a statistically significant difference between the groups. This indicates that the avatar-based audio plays a significant role in perception.

The results from both tests suggest rejecting the null hypothesis, indicating that the presence of audio significantly affects the response in both groups, regardless of their robotics background. However, the participants with a robotics and engineering background demonstrated a higher level of perception. This agrees with some of the previous research (Haber and Levin [36]) that prior background and experience may strongly influence perception of participants.

### 4.3   Experiment 3

The second group C2-G1B was given a series of questions to answer to measure their understanding of the target robotic assembly process they interacted with. They were asked to cluster objects in the 3D scenarios which had similar functionalities: in essence, form schemas of Objects of Interest (OOIs) in the target robotic scenarios. Subsequently, they were asked questions related to the relationships between *resource schemas* and *process schemas*. These included: (a) what was the process outcomes of work cell 1 (b) what is the relationship between two resources (such as a conveyor and a robot) (c) identify a task sequence linking two process (or event) schemas (such as the completion of an assembly of a part followed by transportation of that part from one work cell to another). Assessment of the performance of the group C2-G1 participants was based on the Pearson correlation test.

The Pearson correlation test indicated a R value of 0.7504 for the relationship between the Perception Score (X variable) and the Cognition Score (Y variable). This suggests a strong positive correlation between the two variables, indicating that individuals with higher Perception Scores also tend to have higher Cognition Scores, and vice versa. An increase in the Perception Score directly corresponds to an increase in the Cognition Score, indicating a direct relationship between the two measures.

The coefficient of determination, $R^2$, is calculated as 0.5631. Around 56.31% of the variability in Cognition Scores can be accounted for by the variability in Perception Scores. This emphasizes the influence perception has on cognition, indicating a close connection between these two aspects.

In addition, feedback on the interactions of the C2-G1B participants with the VR environment was obtained based on the modified NASA TLX. The NASA task load index (NASA TLX) [40] is a tool for measuring and conducting a subjective mental workload (MWL) assessment. It allows you to determine the MWL of a user while they are performing a task. In this research, it was used to throw light on the MWL of the user when interacting with the VR based VLEs. It rates performance across various factors listed below:

1. Mental demand: how much thinking, deciding, or calculating was required to perform the task.
2. Physical demand: the amount and intensity of physical activity required to complete the task.
3. Temporal demand: the amount of time pressure involved in completing the task.
4. Effort: how hard does the participant have to work to maintain their level of performance?
5. Performance: the level of success in completing the task.
6. Frustration level: how frustrated or content the participant felt during the interactions.

The TLX was adapted to suit this VR based learning context. In general, in the original TLX rating, users are asked to rate their score on an interval scale ranging from low (1) to high (20). In our adopted approach, we have modified the interval scale to range from 1 to 10. Table 3 provides the survey outcomes averaged for the 15 participants in Group C1-VLE.

**Table 3.** Outcomes of the NASA TLX for group C2-G1B

| Criteria (rating between 1 - 10) | Rating |
|---|---|
| 1. Clarity of the instructions in the AR platform | 8 |
| 2. The degree of usefulness of the 3D avatar-based interactions | 7.1 |
| 3. The degree of usefulness of the voice-based interactions | 8.3 |
| 4. The degree of usefulness of the text-based interactions | 8.6 |
| 5. The ease of completing tasks while wearing the headset | 8.9 |
| 6. The ease of navigating through the simulation environment | 7.6 |
| 7. The overall usefulness of the AR environment | 7.9 |
| 8. Effort: How hard did you have to focus in order to complete the tasks? (1:Low, 10:High) | 3.7 |
| 9. Frustration: How frustrated were you when trying to complete the tasks? (1:Low, 10:High) | 2 |
| 10. Mental Demand: How mentally demanding were the tasks? (1:Low, 10:High) | 2.9 |
| 11. Physical Demand: How physically demanding were the tasks? (1:Low, 10:High) | 2.7 |
| 12. Temporal Demand: How hurried or rushed were you during the tasks? (1:Low, 10:High) | 1.9 |

# 5  Discussion and Conclusion

With increasing adoption of 3D XR environments and Digital Twins in various engineering and medical applications, there is a critical need to study the role of Perception and Cognition in such contexts. These digital twins and XR environments need to be designed taking into consideration Human Computer Interaction (HCI) and Human Centered Computing (HCC) principles. Such 3D environments have to be user centric while enabling users to accomplish their target tasks effectively and efficiently. This paper addressed this important need by studying the relationship between perception and cognition and laying the foundation for understanding and recognizing the relationships between perception and cognition in such 3D information centric environments. The domain of interest was robotic assembly. The participants interacted with the Digital Twins using an immersive VR platform (wearing 3D headsets and interacting using controllers). The experiments conducted led to the following conclusions:

1. Prior background and experience influence the perception of information in 3D VR environments.
2. Audio enhanced simulations and audio clues play a significant role in perception of the target activities.
3. Improved perception leads to a higher level of cognition and knowledge acquisition.

**Acknowledgement.** Funding for this research was provided through grants from the National Science Foundation (NSF grant number 2106901 and 2050960).

# References

1. Panait, L., Akkary, E., Bell, R.L., Roberts, K.E., Dudrick, S.J., Duffy, A.J.: The role of haptic feedback in laparoscopic simulation training. J. Surg. Res. **156**(2), 312–316 (2009)
2. Huber, T., Paschold, M., Hansen, C., Wunderling, T., Lang, H., Kneist, W.: New dimensions in surgical training: immersive virtual reality laparoscopic simulation exhilarates surgical staff. Surg. Endosc. **31**(11), 4472–4477 (2017). https://doi.org/10.1007/s00464-017-5500-6
3. Echegaray, G., Herrera, I., Aguinaga, I., Buchart, C., Borro, D.: A brain surgery simulator. IEEE Comput. Graph. Appl. **34**(3), 12–18 (2014)
4. Choi, K.S., Soo, S., Chung, F.L.: A virtual training simulator for learning cataract surgery with phacoemulsification. Comput. Biol. Med. **39**(11), 1020–1031 (2009)
5. Pedersen, P., Palm, H., Ringsted, C., Konge, L.: Virtual-reality simulation to assess performance in hip fracture surgery. Acta Orthop. **85**(4), 403–407 (2014)
6. Ashtari, N., Bunt, A., McGrenere, J., Nebeling, M., Chilana, P.K.: Creating augmented and virtual reality applications: current practices, challenges, and opportunities. In: Proceedings of the 2020 CHI Conference on Human Factors in Computing Systems, pp. 1–13 (2020)
7. Tabrizi, L.B., Mahvash, M.: Augmented reality-guided neurosurgery: accuracy and intra-operative application of an image projection technique. J. Neurosurg. **123**, 206–211 (2015)
8. Botden, S.M., Buzink, S.N., Schijven, M.P., Jakimowicz, J.J.: ProMIS augmented reality training of laparoscopic procedures face validity. Simul. Healthc. **3**(2), 97–102 (2008)
9. Botden, S.M., de Hingh, I.H., Jakimowicz, J.J.: Suturing training in augmented reality: gaining proficiency in suturing skills faster. Surg. Endosc. **23**(9), 2131–2137 (2009)
10. Lu, S., Sanchez Perdomo, Y.P., Jiang, X., Zheng, B.: Integrating eye-tracking to augmented reality system for surgical training. J. Med. Syst. **44**(11), 1–7 (2020). https://doi.org/10.1007/s10916-020-01656-w
11. Ogawa, H., Hasegawa, S., Tsukada, S., Matsubara, M.: A pilot study of augmented reality technology applied to the acetabular cup placement during total hip arthroplasty. J. Arthroplasty **33**, 1833–1837 (2018)
12. Shen, F., Chen, B., Guo, Q., Qi, Y., Shen, Y.: Augmented reality patient-specific reconstruction plate design for pelvic and acetabular fracture surgery. Int. J. Comput. Assist. Radiol. Surg. **8**, 169–179 (2013)
13. Cho, H.S., Park, Y.K., Gupta, S., et al.: Augmented reality in bone tumour resection: an experimental study. Bone Joint Res. **6**, 137–143 (2017)
14. Elmi-Terander, A., Nachabe, R., Skulason, H., et al.: Feasibility and accuracy of thoracolumbar minimally invasive pedicle screw placement with augmented reality navigation technology. Spine (Phila pa 1976) **43**, 1018–1023 (2018)
15. Wang, H., Wang, F., Leong, A.P.Y., Xu, L., Chen, X., Wang, Q.: Precision insertion of percutaneous sacroiliac screws using a novel augmented reality-based navigation system: a pilot study. Int. Orthop. **40**(9), 1941–1947 (2015). https://doi.org/10.1007/s00264-015-3028-8
16. Sutcliffe, A.G., Poullis, C., Gregoriades, A., Katsouri, I., Tzanavari, A., Herakleous, K.: Reflecting on the design process for virtual reality applications. Int. J. Hum.-Comput. Interact. **35**(2), 168–179 (2019)
17. Moosavi, M.S., Williams, J., Guillet, C., Merienne, F., Cecil, J., Pickett, M.: Disassociation of visual-proprioception feedback to enhance endotracheal intubation. In: 2022 International Conference on Future Trends in Smart Communities (ICFTSC), pp. 233–236. IEEE (2022)
18. Moosavi, M.S., Raimbaud, P., Guillet, C., Plouzeau, J., Merienne, F.: Weight perception analysis using pseudo-haptic feedback based on physical work evaluation. Front. Virtual Reality **4**, 13 (2023)

19. Menekse Dalveren, G.G., Cagiltay, N.E., Ozcelik, E., Maras, H.: Insights from pupil size to mental workload of surgical residents: feasibility of an educational computer-based surgical simulation environment (ECE) considering the hand condition. Surg. Innov. **25**(6), 616–624 (2018)
20. Gibson, J.J.: "The concept of affordances." Perceiving, acting, and knowing 1 (1977)
21. Donald, N.: The Design of Everyday Things. ISBN: 0–465–06710–7. Originally published under the title The Psychology of Everyday Things (often abbreviated to POET)
22. Gaver, W.W.: Technology affordances. In: Proceedings of the SIGCHI Conference on Human Factors in Computing Systems, pp. 79–84 (1991)
23. Pointon, G., Thompson, C., Creem-Regehr, S., Stefanucci, J., Bodenheimer, B.: Affordances as a measure of perceptual fidelity in augmented reality. In: 2018 IEEE VR 2018 Workshop on Perceptual and Cognitive Issues in AR (PERCAR), pp. 1–6 (2018)
24. Wu, H., Adams, H., Pointon, G., Stefanucci, J., Creem-Regehr, S., Bodenheimer, B.: Danger from the deep: a gap affordance study in augmented reality. In: 2019 IEEE Conference on Virtual Reality and 3D User Interfaces (VR), pp. 1775–1779. IEEE (2019)
25. Regia-Corte, T., Marchal, M., Cirio, G., Lécuyer, A.: Perceiving affordances in virtual reality: influence of person and environmental properties in perception of standing on virtual grounds. Virtual Reality **17**(1), 17–28 (2013)
26. Van Vugt, H.C., Hoorn, J.F., Konijn, E.A., de Bie Dimitriadou, A.: Affective affordances: improving interface character engagement through interaction. Int. J. Hum. Comput. Stud. **64**(9), 874–888 (2006)
27. Gagnon, H.C., Rosales, C.S., Mileris, R., Stefanucci, J.K., Creem-Regehr, S.H., Bodenheimer, R.E.: Estimating distances in action space in augmented reality. ACM Trans. Appl. Percept. (TAP) **18**(2), 1–16 (2021)
28. Koutromanos, G., Mavromatidou, E., Tripoulas, C., Georgiadis, G.: Exploring the educational affordances of augmented reality for pupils with moderate learning difficulties. In: 9th International Conference on Software Development and Technologies for Enhancing Accessibility and Fighting Info-exclusion, pp. 203–207 (2020)
29. Thompson, C.J., Hite, R.: Exploring the affordances of computer-based assessment in measuring three-dimensional science learning. Int. J. Learn. Technol. **16**(1), 3–36 (2021)
30. Hart, S.G., Staveland, L.E.: Development of NASA-TLX (Task Load Index): results of empirical and theoretical research. Adv. Psychol. **52**, 139–183 (1998)
31. Gupta, A., Cecil, J., Pirela-Cruz, M., Shamsuddin, R., Kennison, S., Crick, C.: An Investigation on the role of affordance in the design of extended reality based environments for surgical training. In: 2022 IEEE International Systems Conference (SysCon), pp. 1–7. IEEE (2022)
32. Gupta, A., Cecil, J., Pirela-Cruz, M.: A cyber-human based integrated assessment approach for Orthopedic surgical training. In: 2020 IEEE 8th International Conference on Serious Games and Applications for Health (SeGAH), pp. 1–8. IEEE (2020)
33. Gupta, A., Cecil, J., Moosavi, M.S., Williams, J., Merienne, F.: Effect of tactile affordance during the design of extended reality-based training environments for healthcare contexts. In: Chen, J.Y.C., Fragomeni, G. (eds.) HCII 2023. LNCS, vol. 14027, pp. 441–452. Springer, Cham (2023). https://doi.org/10.1007/978-3-031-35634-6_31
34. https://www.frontiersin.org/journals/psychology/articles/10.3389/fpsyg.2013.00144/full
35. https://www.studysmarter.co.uk/explanations/psychology/cognition/perception-research/
36. Haber, R.N., Levin, C.A.: The independence of size perception and distance perception. Percept. Psychophys. **63**(7), 1140–1152 (2001). https://doi.org/10.3758/BF03194530
37. https://www.techtarget.com/searchdatamanagement/definition/schema
38. https://www.verywellmind.com/what-is-a-schema-2795873
39. https://www.verywellmind.com/what-is-a-schema-2795873#toc-types-of-schemas
40. NASA TLX. https://digital.ahrq.gov/health-it-tools-and-resources/evaluation-resources/workflow-assessment-health-it-toolkit/all-workflow-tools/nasa-task-load-index

41. Cecil, J., Albuhamood, S., Ramanathan, P., Gupta, A.: An Internet-of-Things (IoT) based cyber manufacturing framework for the assembly of micro devices, special issue on Smart Cyber Physical Systems. Int. J. Comput. Integr. Manuf. **32**, 430–440 (2019)
42. Gupta, A., Cecil, J., Pirela-Cruz, M., Ramanathan, P.: A virtual reality based cyber-human framework for orthopedic surgical training. IEEE Syst. J. **13**(3), 3501–3512 (2018)
43. Cecil, J.: A collaborative manufacturing approach supporting adoption of IoT principles in micro devices assembly. Procedia Manuf. J. **26**, 1265–1277 (2018)
44. Cecil, J., Gupta, A., Pirela-Cruz, M., Ramanathan, P.: An IoMT-based cyber training framework for orthopedic surgery using next generation internet technologies. Inform. Med. Unlocked **12**(2018), 128–137 (2018)
45. Cecil, J., Gupta, A., Pirela-Cruz, M.: Virtual reality based training environments for orthopedic surgery. Surg. Res. Rep. **1**(1), 1–6 (2018)
46. Cecil, J., Gupta, A., Pirela-Cruz, M.: An advanced simulator for orthopedic surgical training. Int. J. Comput. Assist. Radiol. Surg. **13**(2), 305–319 (2018)
47. Cecil, J., Albuhamood, S., Cecil-Xavier, A., Ramanathan, P.: An advanced cyber physical framework for micro devices assembly, special Issue on "Advanced CPS for Industry 4.0 - Enabling Technologies, Real-world Implementations, and Impact Assessments." IEEE Trans. Syst. Man Cybern. Syst. **49**(1), 92–106 (2017)
48. Cecil, J., Gupta, A., Pirela-Cruz, M., Ramanathan, P.: A network based virtual reality simulation training approach for orthopedic surgery. ACM Trans. Multimedia Comput. Commun. Appl. (TOMM) **14**(3), 1–21 (2018)
49. Cecil, J., Kanchanapiboon, A.: Virtual engineering approaches in product and process design. Int. J. Adv. Manuf. Technol. **31**(9–10), 846–850 (2007)
50. Cognition. https://cambridgecognition.com/what-is-cognition/

# A Literature Review and Proposal Towards the Further Integration of Haptics in Aviation

R. D. de Lange[✉]

NLR - Royal Netherlands Aerospace Centre,
Anthony Fokkerweg 2, 1059CM Amsterdam, The Netherlands
rudy.de.lange@nlr.nl
https://www.nlr.nl/

**Abstract.** Flight simulator training is essential for aircraft pilots to learn and maintain the ability to fly specific aircraft for both commercial and defence purposes. With recent advances in extended reality, the implementation thereof has made its way into proposed simulated flight training protocols. In conjunction to the advent of extended reality, research into the use of haptics or the sense of touch within VEs has accelerated. A few challenges persist within simulation training including training effectiveness, level of immersiveness, and the manageable exposure duration per training run. Extended reality experiences face similar challenges. The field of haptics might provide solutions for these challenges. Thus, this paper reviews the state-of-the-art of haptics, current challenges, and possible future applications within aviation simulation and training. It is found that research with respect to the integration of haptics in aviation training and simulation is not yet mature. A lot of potential exists for research into the improvement of training effectiveness, performance and immersiveness within extended reality based simulation for flight training and maintenance engineering purposes via haptics. Based thereupon future work is suggested to look into 1) decreasing simulator sickness by simulating and synchronizing expected real life perturbations within flight simulation via haptic wearables 2) simulating a sense of physical flight within a static simulator set-up by leveraging self-motion 3) enabling physical interaction of aircraft parts digital twins for improving extended reality based maintenance engineering performance by utilizing haptic wearables.

**Keywords:** Human-Machine Interaction · Tactile and haptic interaction · Multimodal interaction · Training education and tutoring · Simulator sickness

## 1 Introduction

Haptics refers to the sense of touch when manually interacting with the environment which is either real, virtual or a mixture thereof, via self or machine

J. Y. C. Chen and G. Fragomeni (Eds.): HCII 2024, LNCS 14707, pp. 159–178, 2024.
https://doi.org/10.1007/978-3-031-61044-8_12

[79]. Haptic technology spans a vast array of different modalities, applications, as well as possibilities [15].

Simulator training is essential for the education of pilots, as well as for maintaining their skills without having to make use of a physical aircraft, potentially endangering the crew and possible passengers, while cutting down costs and carbon emissions in the process [4,12,42]. A whole plethora of different flight simulators exist where their cost and fidelity (including realism), both often positively related to one another, ranges from low to high [41,50]. With the advent of Extended Reality (XR) a couple of decades ago, there has been a steady rise in different affordable commercial-off-the-shelf (COTS) devices the past few years. Alongside, came an increase in appeal for its usage within the academic field as a research tool [10]. This trend has also sparked interest in the development of lower-cost, immerisve flight simulators using XR devices [26,37].

XR is an umbrella term that encompasses virtual reality (VR), augmented reality (AR) and mixed reality (MR), which can be categorized even further based on hardware. VR makes use of a full Virtual Environment (VE), AR uses a mixture of real world and virtual content, whereas MR is a mixture of VR and AR [63]. Currently, most commercial XR devices focus mainly on providing visual and auditory experiences, and focus less on haptics. Haptics, or the sense of touch, have found their way into everyday commercial items, such as smartphones and video game consoles [53,91]. Other industries wherein implementations of haptics have been introduced include the medical field [28], automotive [94], nuclear [62], manufacturing [90], and maintenance [60].

XR implementations within flight simulators also exist. Some examples are seen in Fig. 1. Immersiveness plays a vital roll in effective pilot training within flight simulators. Since humans perceive the real world via multi-modal sensory input, it has been argued that adding haptics will elevate immersiveness in XR experiences [61]. I.e., it has been suggested that haptics have the potential to enhance presence in VEs [21]. Thus, the question arises as to how and to what extent haptics can be used within XR aviation training and simulation, and whether it leverages any potential benefit in improving immersiveness and training effectiveness. To answer the raised question, this paper reviews the state-of-the-art of different categories of haptics, current applications in aviation, discuss our findings and current open challenges thereof, future work based on identified research challenges, and our concluding remarks in Sects. 2, 3, 4, 5 and 6 respectively.

## 2    Categories of Haptics

Haptics can be categorized into two main groups: kinaesthetic and cutaneous. Kinaesthetic feedback, refers to the sensation of force. Cutaneous feedback mostly refers to the sense of touch, of which vibrotactility is an example [73]. As the field of haptics spans a broad spectrum, haptics are categorized per overarching research area within this section.

Section 2 discusses tele-haptics and haptic shared control, surface haptics, haptic wearables, multi-modal haptics, and mid-air haptics respectively. Within

**Fig. 1.** From left to right: NLR Virtual Cockpit, NLR VR Motion Simulator, NLR Helicopter Pilot Station

each category a further distinction is made whether task performance or immersiveness is improved.

### 2.1 Haptics in Teleoperation and Shared Control

Teleoperation refers to remote manual control of electronic devices. Remote control of an unmanned aerial vehicle (UAV) is an example. Such systems are costly, and mostly require high precision as there is a need for a sophisticated feedback system [23]. Traditionally teleoperation makes use of cameras to provide visual information to the human operator [75]. However, visual information alone proves insufficient for avoiding unwanted collisions [56]. Research into providing realistic haptic feedback for teleoperation to counteract said problem extends even to space applications. [58]. COTS haptic controllers such as the Omni Phantom 3D provide 6-DOF force feedback [76].

Over the past decade research into providing manual control guidance using haptics, or haptic shared control (HSC), has been conducted [2]. [9] found better performance at worse transparency for HSC in teleoperated robot manipulation tasks. [27] implemented a haptic feedback system for simulated teleoperated maintenance tasks for nuclear fusion reactors. HSC has some well documented research within the automotive industry [40,59,92]. [51] proposes a framework for collaborative steering as a means of communicating human intent of desired trajectory in a highly automated vehicle using HSC.

### 2.2 Surface Haptics

Over the past few years, researchers have successfully managed to implement the sensation of feeling different types of surfaces, including smooth and rough textures [38]. All different types of surface interactions and texture simulations are modulated by means of altering the vibration amplitude and frequency, per simulated surface texture, as done in [7].

Surface haptics is perhaps the most well known field of haptic research. Research into the use of localization of vibrotactile feedback e.g. by means of using piezo electronic in the periphery of either digital and/or clear glass displays is present [55]. Other techniques for localized haptic feedback include computational focussing methods such as elastic wave focussing [64].

Surface haptics can be used to render either sliding or mechanical clicking sensations on flat surfaces, mostly done via vibration feedback. [71] researched haptic representation of different types of mechanical buttons for implementation in digital touchscreens. These included latch buttons, toggle switches and push buttons were simulated in decreasing order of fidelity. It was concluded that the kinaesthetic tactile feedback associated with physical mechanical switches can not yet be haptically rendered in flat surfaces.

## 2.3  Haptic Wearables

Haptic wearables are haptic devices worn on the human body and have been researched extensively [87]. Most are intended for the hands, as these are the most subjective body part of the human to discern kinaesthetic and cutaneous feedback [15].

Commercial hand wearables are often bulky or obstructing some parts of the hand needed for real-world object manipulation. Examples are the SenseGlove Nova and the Manus Prime 3 [14,85]. [81] developed a light-weight haptic glove that does not obstruct the palmar side of the hand. By making use of electronic stimulation on the backside of the hand and wrist, tactile feedback on 11 distinct locations on the palmar side of the hand is rendered, allowing unobstructed physical interaction. This development proves to be hopeful in constructing smaller, unobtrusive, and lightweight commercial haptic gloves (Fig. 2).

[82] proposed a foldable finger wearable. Providing kinaesthetic feedback, the wearable can partly fold away, freeing the finger for physical interaction.

Full-body haptic suits also exist [43]. [78] attempted to link a flight simulator running X-Plane with the bHaptics TactSuit for future research purposes looking into full-body haptics and flight simulators, the concept suffered latency issues.

A rather unexplored field is the use of head-haptics. [89] proposed multimodal haptic feedback via vibration motors and thermal sources within a modified HTC Vive Head Mounted Display (HMD). Results indicated that multimodal feedback positively increased enjoyment and immersiveness within a VE.

**Fig. 2.** From left to right: Manus Prime 3, Senseglove Nova & Experimental Haptic Glove by [81]

## 2.4   Multi-modal Haptics

It is believed that to allow for full immersion within VE, more sensory modalities need to be provided. Mulsemedia focusses on multi-sensory media representation to enhance the immersiveness thereof including the addition of olfactory, thermoceptic and haptic feedback [80]. Other modalities such as wind have been researched [77]. [54] looked into the use of gaze-tracking vignette, a first person field of view with body part representation and wind and vibration feedback to study mitigation effects on cyber-sickness. No direct effects of wind were found, but lower heartrates were logged. [46] confirmed the ability to induce perception of non-thermal tactile cues via localized heating of a haptic display. [33] researched the simultaneity of thermal-tactile stimuli and found that distinction between either is perceived best when the thermal cue precedes the tactile one. These findings show the ability of enhancing tactile cues via localized heating by using synchronized vibrotactile cues.

## 2.5   Mid-air Haptics

Mid-air haptics (MaH) focusses on providing vibrotactile feedback without externally worn devices. MaH makes use of an array of ultrasonic transducers, which provides localized vibrotactile feedback by means of creating a focal point of ultrasonic soundwaves, which are perceived by the human as a sense of touch [30]. Although weak, it can be perceived notably and can therefore be used to render clicking, and sliding sensations. [6] proposed selective stimulation of human mechanoreceptors via air pressure for implementation in VR. MaH can be generated from heat conduction from porous silicone [74], or with an array of ultrasonic transducers to create a vocal point with air-pressure [29,30]. [49] proposed a concept for a floating virtual screen with MaH feedback. The mid-air projected images are created via the use of a transmissive mirror that display images in front of the mirror, where the vocal point of MaH coincides with the location of the projected images. A proposed concept of using MaH for full substitution of physical controls in flight simulators was made by [22].

## 3   Haptics in Aviation

Haptics are discussed further within the context of aviation. Section 3 discusses haptics for piloting tasks, haptic aiding implementations for aviation maintenance, and haptics for mitigating cyber- and simulator sickness.

### 3.1   Haptics for Piloting Tasks

**Haptic Feedback for Improving Task Performance.** [3] compared indirect haptic aid (IHA), direct haptic aid (DHA), and no haptic aid to one another on the basis of pilot performance in a tele-operated task controlling an UAV. IHA involves vibrotactile haptic cues to retrieve system information. Results indicate

DHA to be less natural and aiding compared to IHA. For maintaining level flight, having no haptic feedback had the highest performance. DHA was considered to be the most helpful aid, but only after familiarization.

[52] experimentally compared the effects of IHA, DHA and no haptic feedback on pilot performance in a manned flight tracking task. Simulation restults found pilots to be more compliant with DHA. However, both IHA and DHA increased tracking performance after adaptation. IHA outperformed DHA. In turn, DHA reduced pilot physical effort.

[45] proposed a haptic aiding system for UAV control. Tested for simulated longitudinal flight incorporating an ascending, descending, and altitude maintaining task, results indicate different levels of haptics to have significant task dependent effect on pilot performance. No feedback for altitude hold tasks, exaggerated force feedback for gaining altitude, and realistic force feedback for descending. Overall, haptic feedback improved immersion, deemed essential for the transition from simulated to real-life flight.

[93] proposed the use of haptic feedback for aiding an aircraft landing task to mitigate landing illusions associated with incorrect perception of visual cues. Pilots relied more on haptic compared to visual cues, implying that haptics can aid pilot performance during low visibility flight.

[26] conducted a study with 120 beginner level pilots. Comparing VR-, computer-based simulation, and no training. No difference in results were found between VR- and computer-based. Subjective results indicate participants judge individual performance to be better in VR . VR was regarded as readily available for home-use at reasonable cost, potentially helping flight-training preparations at home. A downside to VR was the inability to physically manipulate flight instruments.

[17] proposed a pilot intent estimator for inferring the most probable flight path trajectory, solely using pilot control input. [5] proposed a haptic aid system which adapts to the pilot input and performance. [16] combined [5,17] to make a 2 DOF HSC system to decrease helicopter pilot workload. Results from 1 expert and 13 general participants were positive and significant. Half of the participants performed flight trials better with haptics versus none. Haptic aid was more significant in longitudinal compared to lateral control, but significantly reduces overall pilot control effort.

**Haptic Feedback for Increasing Safety.** [8] proposed the use of haptic support in conjunction with a perspective flight-path display to minimize headsdown time of pilots associated with using said display. Results indicated that pilots were able to accurately follow a flight path with noticeably more headsup time when a minimal amount of haptic feedback was provided. The positive effect of haptic aid became stronger with increased task difficulty. Mental workload significantly decreases when the amount of haptic feedback increases. Haptic feedback thus allows for a longer heads-up time of pilots, increasing spatial awareness of the pilot during aircraft trajectory following tasks.

[84] proposed a haptic feedback system for flight envelope protection. Three different concepts for haptic aid in flight envelope protection were proposed and evaluated [83]. The first method utilizes guidance and discrete feedback as proposed in [83]. The second method used asymmetric vibrations via sawtooth waves. The third used HSC, as discussed prior in Sect. 2.1. Results for the first concept showed no significant statistical results with respect to an increase in pilot performance, safety or awareness. As opposed to this, subjective pilot interviews proved the contrary, thus insinuating that the stated benefits can potentially be attained with the use of haptic feedback and discrete feedback. The second concept showed that no effects were found for improving performance or safety, but indications were present that it did improve the learning rate of the participants. The third concept showed that haptic shared control increased safety when used from the beginning. However, it was observed that if haptic assistance disappeared afterwards, an over-reliance and instantaneous increase of workload presented itself as an after-effect.

[70] supplemented the work of [84] by adding visual indicators for the haptic feedback system on the aircraft's digital flight instruments for communicating flight envelope boundaries to the pilot. Although objective results were not conclusive, subjective results indicated that haptic feedback cues were interpreted more correctly with the visual aid of the updated display.

**Haptic Feedback for Increasing Immersiveness.** [69] looked into the learning effects of a full-body haptic controller for UAV control. The vest utilizes inflatable pockets of air indicating centripetal acceleration of the drone on the human body and cable-driven haptic guidance [68]. This research focusses on the realization of an intuitive haptic drone-controller using upper body input, to render the sensation of flight within VR.

From [88] it is found that motion within flight simulators seem important for some scenarios. Effects for helicopter, disturbance tasks and inexperienced pilots were stronger than those for fix-winged aircraft manoeuvring and expert pilots.

[18] referred to the sensation of motion purely via visual stimulus as induced motion. In other words; visually induced motion, or self-motion is the sensation of moving one's body while remaining stationary. Self-motion could be leveraged as a possible substitute for mechanical motion-based simulators. [13] proposed the use of a kinesthetic HMD within a VR flight simulator that induces self-motion via force feedback provided by a haption haptic device. Results indicated that the use of force-feedback within the HMD improved egocentric sensations of self-motion compared to a purely visual VR experience.

### 3.2   Haptics for Aircraft Maintenance Tasks

**Haptic Feedback and XR for Simulated Maintenance Training Within Aviation.** [1] utilized VR in combination with a table-top mounted force-feedback haptic controller for an aircraft maintenance simulation experiment. The results were encouraging, however more experimentation and possibly further advancements in haptic and XR technology were needed in order to test the perceived benefit of the combination of both, for simulation training.

[11] researched a haptic VR set-up for an aerospace grade carbon fiber reinforced polymer panel drilling task. Comparison between beginner and experts indicated that the VR system was usable for training beginners, cutting down costs as opposed to having to train on real panels.

It has to be noted that research into the use of XR and haptics within the scenario of aviation maintenance is not yet mature and more research is needed. However as aircraft maintenance engineering training procedure focuses on specific tool-based skill learning, a lot of research findings can be adopted from a larger body of literature work found in fields such as industrial assembly and medicine.

**Relevant Research from Other Fields.** [24] looked into several different set-ups for utilizing force-feedback haptics in simulated assembly tasks for educational purposes. They discussed the use of VR with haptic gloves for hand tracking and gesture recognition while using a real physical tool or model. Another method was the use of a physical model of a tool attached to a haptic manipulator. Lastly, as another alternative a robot's end effector was used to simulate the surface of a virtual object. [24] argued that the addition of tactile feedback was necessary for VEs to be deemed sufficiently useful for effective training of future operators. [31] conducted a research testing a haptic-based, mouse-based and traditional-based group of 24 participants in total for a digital assembly task. Results indicated that the use of a physics engine and haptics was not significantly different from the traditional training group with respect to training time. The mouse-based group was significantly slower and did not provide the same manner of familiarization as the haptics group, even though results with respect to learning the assembly sequence did not differ amongst the three tested groups. [25] made a systematic literature review of 86 papers in total, researching the use of XR in industrial maintenance. Therein, 8 papers where identified that utilized some sort of haptic feedback in combination with XR and maintenance engineering. The overall takeaway of [25] is that haptic feedback is deemed important for maintenance. Research indicates that the inclusion of haptics has a positive benefit with regards to situational awareness and operator performance.

Research within the medical field is overall positive towards the use of XR and/or haptics. However, a meta-analysis of 422 papers within said field involving XR and haptic interfaces concluded the available research evidence to be inadequate in supporting the perceived benefits thereof due to limited testing with surgeons, and overall poor experiment design [44].

### 3.3 Haptics for Mitigating Simulator Sickness

**What is Simulator Sickness?** SS is resemblant to motion sickness (MS), however the severity of the symptoms as well as the underlying causes differ. Due to comparable reasons to SS, cybersickness (CS) can occur while immersed in VEs. In short, SS or CS is a visually induced sensation of sickness and will be used interchangeably. This comes mostly due to visual-oculomotor and vestibular-oculomotor discrepancies. [39] details a large list of possible variables influencing the onset and experience of SS. A subjective method for studying SS is the Simulator Sickness Questionnaire (SSQ) [35].

[19] conducted a review of 39 articles that found evidence with respect to the progression of SS, possibility of adapting for SS in VR and persistence of symptoms after exposure to VR. The two most widely cited reasons for SS are the Sensory Conflict Theory (SCT) proposed by [65] and the Postural Instability Theory (PIT) proposed by [66]. The first theory attributes the onset of SS due to conflict of different modalities of sensory input, mostly being visual and vestibular in origin. In short; the SCT attributes SS to visuo-vestibular conflict. [66] argued against [65] on the grounds that sensory conflict is a common natural occurrence. [66] therefore proposed the PIT, which states that the human experiences symptoms of SS in the case that the body has not yet adapted to environments in which it can maintain adequate postural stability. This theory infers the possibility of adapting to VEs and eventually overcoming SS. To summarize, it has been stated that the temporal aspect of SS is two-fold, being that the onset of SS is positively correlated with the exposure duration of VEs during a single run and that repeated exposure to VEs can cause the onset of SS symptoms to decrease [36]. [19] goes more into depth with respect to these identified temporal aspects.

**How Can Simulator Sickness Be Mitigated?** [54] looked into mitigating SS in a first person view VR broomstick simulation by means of multi-modal feedback in the form of wind and vibrotactile feedback, self-representation of the human body and the addition of gaze-vignette. First person view and gaze-vignette increased SS. However, wind and vibrotactile feedback decreased heartrate, inducing a calming effect on the user.

[34] argued that, taken the SCT, if VR users experience minimal vibrotactile feedback at the feet in a simulated car driving experience, sensory mismatch between real-world expected stimuli should decrease and therefore the onset of SS symptoms should lessen. SSQs were taken mid-test using a Microsoft Surface Dial, as opposed to after the trials, which is standard within research [47]. The test were conducted using an off-road simulator in VR and participants were placed on a vibrating platform. Results based on galvanic skin response, pupil size, heart rate, self-rated levels of discomfort and an SSQ indicated that the 11 participants with haptic feedback from floor vibrations showed significantly reduced measures of SS as compared to 11 participants without said vibrations.

[57] conducted a 240-person study, wherein participants were exposed to a 9 min long walking video either with or without vibrotactile, visual and audio feedback. 8 different conditions were studied. Results indicated that vibrotactile feedback synchronized with an users' gait reduced SS and increased immersiveness.

[72] looked into synchronizing engine sounds and vibrations, coupled with the visual perception of speed in a motorcycle simulator. Results indicated that the addition of synchronized engine sound and vibration reduces SS.

[86] looked at the use of bone-conducted vibration at the mastoid processes, a bony projection on either side of the temporal bone, in order to mitigate SS. Bone-conducted vibration is a technique that evokes a similar oculomotor and myogenic response compared to that of the otholith organs as a response to linear accelerations. Results from an experiment conducted in a cave automatic VE and using a HMD indicated a small effect in reducing SS. Precise placement of bone-conducted vibration devices might prove that the technique will not have sufficient appeal for individual commercial use. However, future work is required to look into possible benefits for utilizing the technique in a simulator training scenario.

## 4   Discussion

The main categories, some noteworthy current applications of haptics, and current research with respect to haptics in the aviation industry have been discussed. In this section, interesting possibilities for the application of haptics within the aviation scenario and the current challenges thereof are discussed.

A larger focus on the implementation of each of the different categories of haptics within the context of aviation simulation and training applications is given. Reasoning for this is two-fold. Firstly, a lot of research exists towards the use of haptics for i.e. enhancing immersiveness in VEs. Secondly, there has been an increase of interest for utilizing XR in simulated training scenarios. The combination of both of these trends makes it a natural choice to look at the utility of haptics for training and simulation purposes within the aviation industry.

**Telehaptics and Haptic Shared Control in Aviation.** Some haptics implementations exist within aviation. Tele-haptics and HSC not much so [83].

An example of a teleoperation scenario within aviation that can utilize telehaptics or HSC is mid-air refuelling. Mid-air refuelling employs two techniques, one of which is the flying boom. A large fuel boom is manually controlled to refuel defence aircraft mid-flight.

As aircraft need to be flying in a certain envelope to engage with the flying boom, a variation of envelope protection using haptic feedback as proposed by [84] might prove as a beneficial addition for improving safety for both boom operator and aircraft pilot. Haptic shared control could be implemented to improve tracking performance. Vibrotactile feedback could also be used to convey the boom movement to increase immersiveness and transparancy. The same can be argued for a simulated training variant of the task above. As training for mid-air refueling tasks with a flying broom is costly if done in real life, a simulated training protocol using e.g. XR and a similar implementation of haptics discussed prior, might prove to be a cost-efficient alternative for effective pilot training. More research needs to be done in order to find out how exactly this type of haptic implementation should be realised technically. Such an implementation should be experimentally validated and the possible benefits and downsides thereof should be identified.

**Surface Haptics in Aviation.** As aircraft become more advanced, cockpits and their interfaces do so as well. Steadily coming to replace mechanical buttons within real and training cockpits, digital flight displays can be provided with high quality tactile feedback. A technological challenge lies in the fidelity or resolution of the vibrotactile feedback opposed to mechanical buttons, sliders, and switches. As identified in [71] operation of mechanical controls involves kinaesthetic-cutaneous feedback, whereas digital screens can only provide the former as of current. A challenge lies in the addition of kinaesthetic or force feedback of digitally simulated mechanical controls to improve the fidelity thereof.

**Haptic Wearables and Mid-air Haptics in Aviation.** With the adoption of MR technology within current aircraft cockpits such as the F-35, haptic wearables and mid-air haptics might prove beneficiary for providing tactile feedback when manipulating virtual content. Similarly so for XR simulation training.

Cutaneous and kinaesthetic feedback can also induce self-motion to increase immersiveness and alleviate CS symptoms while remaining physically static. Not mature enough to fully substitute physical motion, future research can possibly achieve substitution of motion-based simulators in due time.

Downsides to haptic wearables is their intrusiveness and size. Body parts are (partly) obstructed, hindering physical interaction with real-life objects. Additional weight increases discomfort during long exposure operations. If purely digital content is used, these downsides can be overlooked. In that case haptic wearables might prove beneficial for improving immersiveness in VE interaction. Advancement in wearables becoming more light-weight and unobstructive, demonstrated in [81], will improve potential for use in AR and MR applications.

MaH can only convey cutaneous feedback. Future research needs to be conducted to find whether MaH can provide kinaesthetic feedback as well, considering the sense of touch requires both. The addition thereof will improve haptic feedback fidelity. Communication devices can pick up interference from the used ultrasone transducers, rendering it as an obstruction. Currently MaH is not yet feasible for use in a real cockpit, unless interference issues are solved. Also argued by [22], MaH is more feasible for use in simulation and training. Also true for haptic wearables, MaH still has to be actively improved and researched before actual use can be justified.

**Multi-modal Haptics in Aviation.** Real-life interaction uses multi-modal sensory input. Immersiveness within VEs will arguably increase when more modalities are accounted for. Multi-modal haptics could be utilized in simulation training for e.g. piloting and maintenance tasks. Immersiveness increases while SS decreases with the addition of more sensory feedback from VEs. An example would be to provide thermal feedback when utilizing power tools that warm up due to friction. Another example would be to use wind to render a realistic sensation of aircraft velocity, combined with synchronized engine vibration as proposed by [72] to mitigate SS and improve flight simulation exposure time. More research on what combination of modalities provide what types of benefits as well as the how to successfully integrate these to work in conjunction with each other effectively requires more research.

## 5    Future Work

Research and application of haptics within aviation is limited. Multiple research opportunities exists. Focussing on the use of haptics for training and simulation applications within aviation, future work is suggested within this section.

### 5.1    Mitigating Simulator Sickness Using Haptics

SS persists to be a challenge hindering training in simulation. [34] found that minimal vibrotactile feedback at the feet during virtual driving reduces the onset of SS symptoms, as it reduces sensory mismatch to a certain extent. [57] found that the addition of synchronized haptic feedback within a VR HMD has significant effect on the reduction of SS and improves realism in virtual walking. [72] shows that synchronized auditory and vibrotactile cues simulating an engine reduce SS symptoms. Given these findings, vibrotactile feedback associated with expected real life perturbations within statically set-up VEs should alleviate the onset of SS symptoms to a certain degree.

To confirm this hypothesis the effect of the level of fidelity and synchronization of simulated expected vibrotactile cues within VEs on the reduction on the onset, propagation and decay of SS syptoms could be researched.

An example research set-up can include a haptic vest, or vibrotactile feedback in the pilot seat which mimicks aircraft vibrations in simulated flight. To look at the effect of different levels of fidelity and synchronization on SS, variations thereof can be researched by e.g. introducing phase, amplitude, intensity, or localization differences.

The goals is then to facilitate longer simulation exposure times per training run as an effect of alleviating or mitigating SS.

### 5.2    Leveraging Self-motion

Haptic feedback can induce a sense of self-motion in XR and alleviate SS [13,57]. From [67–69] it is found that humans can experience immersive flight using a VR HMD and a haptic suit. Given this research, the question arises as to how and to what extent one can approximate full physical flight in a static XR simulator set-up by using haptics to both induce self-motion and engine vibrations.

To answer this question, an example research set-up can include the use of a haptic vest to generate engine vibrations, similar to [72], and a XR HMD with kinaesthetic feedback to induce self-motion, as done by [13]. Using COTS flight controllers to control a simulated aircraft in conjunction therewith, this relatively low-cost flight simulator set-up can be used to research simultaneously increasing exposure time, immersiveness and alleviating SS within simulated flight training.

### 5.3   Haptic Aviation Maintenance

Maintenance engineering requires motorskills obtained via rigorous training. The necessary tools and to-be-maintained equipment are both costly. Simulations can be considered a cost-effective training alternative. Both kinaesthetic and cutaneous feedback are important when handling machinery and tools, which some haptic gloves can provide. Thus, it can be asked to what extent one can effectively utilize kinaesthetic-cutaneous feedback enabled haptic gloves for handling digital maintenance tools for fine motorskill training within virtual aircraft maintenance engineering training protocols.

A limited amount of research is currently available that validates said question. Some research utilize a combination of VEs with physical tools instead [24]. To answer the research question, an example set-up can consist of a COTS haptic glove within an XR environment to perform a similar experiment as [11] who used a haptic teleoperation controller for simulated aircraft panel drilling. This allows a comparison to be drawn between haptic wearables versus teleoperation controllers.

Digital twins could be used to train maintenance procedures on virtual versions of their exact real counterparts [32]. This could facilitate more specific training protocols with respect to the required maintenance intervention. With the recent introduction of Neural Radiance Fields [48], a method for creating 3D representations using a sparse input of images, interest for the use of quickly producable digital twins within aviation maintenance engineering has gained traction as a reference tool [20]. Given this trend the prior research question can be extended to look into the physical interaction with digital twins for aviation maintenance purposes, and to ask what perceived benefits of utilizing haptic wearable gloves for the interaction with digital twins intended for XR based aircraft maintenance solutions are. An example set-up could revolve around the comparison between maintenance training using a general digital model versus on a digital twin, either with or without haptics, and how this translates to task performance on the maintenance procedure with its exact real counterpart.

## 6   Conclusion

This work summarizes the current state-of-the-art of haptics within aviation. Haptics are interesting for researching improvement of performance in piloting and maintenance tasks, immersiveness, and exposure time within simulation training. Main current challenges of training and simulation utilizing XR includes the onset of simulator sickness, correlating short exposure times to VR and a need for a larger degree of immersivenes. Future work is suggested to look into 1) simulating and synchronizing expected real life perturbations via haptic wearables within flight simulation to decrease simulator sickness 2) leveraging self-motion for simulating a sense of physical flight using a static simulator set-up 3) utilizing haptic wearables for physical interaction of aircraft parts digital twins for improving extended reality based maintenance engineering performance.

**Disclosure Statement.** This paper has been conducted and funded entirely by the Royal Netherlands Aerospace Centre (NLR). The author is not aware of any third-party affiliations with respect to funding or potential interests that might affect the objectivity of this paper. Permission has been granted by the copyright holders of the images as used within this paper.

# References

1. Abate, A.F., Guida, M., Leoncini, P., Nappi, M., Ricciardi, S.: A haptic-based approach to virtual training for aerospace industry. J. Vis. Lang. Comput. **20**(5), 318–325 (2009). https://doi.org/10.1016/j.jvlc.2009.07.003
2. Abbink, D.A., Mulder, M., Boer, E.R.: Haptic shared control: smoothly shifting control authority? Cogn. Tech. Work **14**(1), 19–28 (2012). https://doi.org/10.1007/s10111-011-0192-5
3. Alaimo, S.M.C., Pollini, L., Bresciani, J.P., Bülthoff, H.H.: A comparison of direct and indirect haptic aiding for remotely piloted vehicles. In: 19th International Symposium in Robot and Human Interactive Communication, pp. 506–512. IEEE, September 2010. https://doi.org/10.1109/ROMAN.2010.5598647
4. Allerton, D.J.: The impact of flight simulation in aerospace. Aeronaut. J. **114**(1162), 747–756 (2010). https://doi.org/10.1017/S0001924000004231
5. Arenella, A., D'Intino, G., Bülthoff, H.H., Pollini, L.: An adaptive haptic aid system based on desired pilot dynamics. In: 2019 American Control Conference (ACC), pp. 4866–4871. IEEE, July 2019. https://doi.org/10.23919/ACC.2019.8814610
6. Asamura, N., Yokoyama, N., Shinoda, H.: Selectively stimulating skin receptors for tactile display. IEEE Comput. Graph. Appl. **18**(6), 32–37 (1998). https://doi.org/10.1109/38.734977
7. Basdogan, C., Giraud, F., Levesque, V., Choi, S.: A review of surface haptics: enabling tactile effects on touch surfaces. IEEE Trans. Haptics **13**(3), 450–470 (2020). https://doi.org/10.1109/TOH.2020.2990712
8. Beeftink, D.G., Borst, C., Van Baelen, D., van Paassen, M.M., Mulder, M.: Haptic support for aircraft approaches with a perspective flight-path display. In: 2018 IEEE International Conference on Systems, Man, and Cybernetics (SMC), pp. 3016–3021. IEEE, October 2018. https://doi.org/10.1109/SMC.2018.00512
9. Boessenkool, H., Abbink, D.A., Heemskerk, C.J.M., van der Helm, F.C.T.: Haptic shared control improves tele-operated task performance towards performance in direct control. In: 2011 IEEE World Haptics Conference, pp. 433–438. IEEE, June 2011. https://doi.org/10.1109/WHC.2011.5945525
10. Castelvecchi, D.: Low-cost headsets boost virtual reality's lab appeal. Nature **533**, 153–154 (2016). https://doi.org/10.1038/533153a

11. Chandra Sekaran, S., Yap, H.J., Liew, K.E., Kamaruzzaman, H., Tan, C.H., Rajab, R.S.: Haptic-based virtual reality system to enhance actual aerospace composite panel drilling training. In: Structural Health Monitoring of Biocomposites, Fibre-Reinforced Composites and Hybrid Composites, pp. 113–128. Woodhead Publishing, Buckingham, England, UK, January 2019. https://doi.org/10.1016/B978-0-08-102291-7.00007-1

12. Chen, X., Lelevé, A., McDaniel, T., Rossa, C.: Editorial: haptic training simulation, volume II. Front. Rob. AI **9**, 965113 (2022). https://doi.org/10.3389/frobt.2022.965113

13. Costes, A., Lécuyer, A.: Inducing self-motion sensations with haptic feedback: state-of-the-art and perspectives on "haptic motion". IEEE Trans. Haptics **16**(2), 171–181, May 2023. https://doi.org/10.1109/TOH.2023.3279267

14. Cox, C.M.J., Hicks, B., Gopsill, J., Snider, C.: From haptic interaction to design insight: an empirical comparison of commercial hand-tracking technology. Proc. Des. Soc. **3**, 1965–1974 (2023). https://doi.org/10.1017/pds.2023.197

15. Culbertson, H., Schorr, S.B., Okamura, A.M.: Haptics: the present and future of artificial touch sensation. Annu. Rev. Control Rob. Auton. Syst. **1**(1), 385–409 (2018). https://doi.org/10.1146/annurev-control-060117-105043

16. D'Intino, G., Olivari, M., Bülthoff, H.H., Pollini, L.: Haptic assistance for helicopter control based on pilot intent estimation. J. Aerosp. Inf. Syst. (2020). https://doi.org/10.2514/1.I010773

17. D'Intino, G., Olivari, M., Geluardi, S., Fabbroni, D., Pollini, L.: A pilot intent estimator for haptic support systems in helicopter maneuvering tasks. ResearchGate (2018). https://doi.org/10.2514/6.2018-0116

18. Duncker, K.: Induced motion. In: A Source Book of Gestalt Pscyhology, pp. 161–172 (1938). https://doi.org/10.1037/11496-012

19. Dużmańska, N., Strojny, P., Strojny, A.: Can simulator sickness be avoided? A review on temporal aspects of simulator sickness. Front. Psychol. **9**, 410742 (2018). https://doi.org/10.3389/fpsyg.2018.02132

20. Errandonea, I., Beltrán, S., Arrizabalaga, S.: Digital twin for maintenance: a literature review. Comput. Ind. **123**, 103316 (2020). https://doi.org/10.1016/j.compind.2020.103316

21. Gibbs, J.K., Gillies, M., Pan, X.: A comparison of the effects of haptic and visual feedback on presence in virtual reality. Int. J. Hum Comput Stud. **157**, 102717 (2022). https://doi.org/10.1016/j.ijhcs.2021.102717

22. Girdler, A., Georgiou, O.: Mid-air haptics in aviation – creating the sensation of touch where there is nothing but thin air. arXiv, January 2020. https://doi.org/10.48550/arXiv.2001.01445

23. Giri, G.S., Maddahi, Y., Zareinia, K.: An application-based review of haptics technology. Robotics **10**(1), 29 (2021). https://doi.org/10.3390/robotics10010029

24. Grajewski, D., Górski, F., Hamrol, A., Zawadzki, P.: Immersive and haptic educational simulations of assembly workplace conditions. Procedia Comput. Sci. **75**, 359–368 (2015). https://doi.org/10.1016/j.procs.2015.12.258

25. Guo, Z., Zhou, D., Zhou, Q., Zhang, X., Hao, A.: Applications of virtual reality in maintenance during the industrial product lifecycle: A systematic review. J. Manuf. Syst. **56**(3), 525–538 (2020). https://doi.org/10.1016/j.jmsy.2020.07.007

26. Guthridge, R., Clinton-Lisell, V.: Evaluating the efficacy of virtual reality (VR) training devices for pilot training. Purdue e-Pubs **12**(2), 1 (2023). https://doi.org/10.7771/2159-6670.1286

27. Heemskerk, C.J.M., de Baar, M.R., Boessenkool, H., Graafland, B., Visser, M.: Extending virtual reality simulation of ITER maintenance operations with dynamic effects. Fusion Eng. Des. **86**(9), 2082–2086 (2011). https://doi.org/10.1016/j.fusengdes.2011.04.066

28. Hooshiar, A., Najarian, S., Dargahi, J.: Haptic telerobotic cardiovascular intervention: a review of approaches, methods, and future perspectives. IEEE Rev. Biomed. Eng. **13**, 32–50 (2020). https://doi.org/10.1109/RBME.2019.2907458

29. Hoshi, T., Takahashi, M., Iwamoto, T., Shinoda, H.: Noncontact tactile display based on radiation pressure of airborne ultrasound. IEEE Trans. Haptics **3**(3), 155–165 (2010). https://doi.org/10.1109/TOH.2010.4

30. Iwamoto, T., Tatezono, M., Shinoda, H.: Non-contact method for producing tactile sensation using airborne ultrasound. In: Ferre, M. (ed.) EuroHaptics 2008. LNCS, vol. 5024, pp. 504–513. Springer, Heidelberg (2008). https://doi.org/10.1007/978-3-540-69057-3_64

31. Jiang, W., Zheng, J.J., Zhou, H.J., Zhang, B.K.: A new constraint-based virtual environment for haptic assembly training. Adv. Eng. Softw. **98**, 58–68 (2016). https://doi.org/10.1016/j.advengsoft.2016.03.004

32. Jiang, Y., Yin, S., Li, K., Luo, H., Kaynak, O.: Industrial applications of digital twins. Phil. Trans. R. Soc. A **379**(2207), 20200360 (2021)

33. Jodai, T., Terao, M., Jones, L.A., Ho, H.N.: Determination of the thermal-tactile simultaneity window for multisensory cutaneous displays. In: Proceedings of IEEE. World Haptics Conference 2023, July 2023

34. Jung, S., Li, R., McKee, R., Whitton, M.C., Lindeman, R.W.: Floor-vibration VR: mitigating cybersickness using whole-body tactile stimuli in highly realistic vehicle driving experiences. IEEE Trans. Visual Comput. Graph. **27**(5), 2669–2680 (2021). https://doi.org/10.1109/TVCG.2021.3067773

35. Kennedy, R.S., Lane, N.E., Berbaum, K.S., Lilienthal, M.G.: Simulator sickness questionnaire: an enhanced method for quantifying simulator sickness. Int. J. Aviat. Psychol. **3**(3), 203–220 (1993). https://doi.org/10.1207/s15327108ijap0303_3

36. Kennedy, R.S., Stanney, K.M., Dunlap, W.P.: Duration and exposure to virtual environments: sickness curves during and across sessions. Teleoper. Virtual Environ. **9**(5), 463–472 (2000). https://doi.org/10.1162/105474600566952

37. Khenak, N., Bach, C., Drouot, S., Buratto, F.: Evaluation of virtual reality training: effectiveness on pilots' learning, April 2023. https://hal.science/hal-04046414. Accessed 23 Aug 2023

38. Kodak, B.L., Vardar, Y.: FeelPen: a haptic stylus displaying multimodal texture feels on touchscreens. IEEE/ASME Trans. Mechatron. 1–11 (2023). https://doi.org/10.1109/TMECH.2023.3264787

39. Kolasinski, E.M., Va, A.R.I.F.T.B., Alexandria, S.S.: Simulator Sickness in Virtual Environments. DTIC, May 1995

40. Kondo, R., Wada, T., Sonoda, K.: Use of haptic shared control in highly automated driving systems. IFAC-PapersOnLine **52**(19), 43–48 (2019). https://doi.org/10.1016/j.ifacol.2019.12.084

41. Lee, A.T.: Flight Simulation: Virtual Environments in Aviation. Taylor & Francis, Andover, England, UK (2016). https://doi.org/10.4324/9781315255217

42. Lelevé, A., McDaniel, T., Rossa, C.: Haptic training simulation. Front. Virtual Real. **1**, 543795 (2020). https://doi.org/10.3389/frvir.2020.00003

43. Lindeman, R.W., Page, R., Yanagida, Y., Sibert, J.L.: Towards full-body haptic feedback: the design and deployment of a spatialized vibrotactile feedback system. In: VRST '04: Proceedings of the ACM symposium on Virtual reality software and technology, pp. 146–149. Association for Computing Machinery, New York, NY, USA, November 2004. https://doi.org/10.1145/1077534.1077562
44. Mackenzie, C.F., Harris, T.E., Shipper, A.G., Elster, E., Bowyer, M.W.: Virtual reality and haptic interfaces for civilian and military open trauma surgery training: a systematic review. Injury **53**(11), 3575–3585 (2022). https://doi.org/10.1016/j.injury.2022.08.003
45. Malik, H.A., Rasool, S., Maqsood, A., Riaz, R.: Effect of haptic feedback on pilot/operator performance during flight simulation. Appl. Sci. **10**(11), 3877 (2020). https://doi.org/10.3390/app10113877
46. Mayet, M., Le Carrou, J.L., Gueorguiev, D.: Perception of friction-related cues induced by temperature variation on a surface display. In: Proceedings of IEEE World Haptics Conference 2023, July 2023
47. McHugh, N., Jung, S., Hoermann, S., Lindeman, R.W.: investigating a physical dial as a measurement tool for cybersickness in virtual reality. In: VRST '19: Proceedings of the 25th ACM Symposium on Virtual Reality Software and Technology, pp. 1–5. Association for Computing Machinery, New York, NY, USA, November 2019. https://doi.org/10.1145/3359996.3364259
48. Mildenhall, B., Srinivasan, P.P., Tancik, M., Barron, J.T., Ramamoorthi, R., Ng, R.: NeRF: representing scenes as neural radiance fields for view synthesis. Commun. ACM **65**(1), 99–106 (2021). https://doi.org/10.1145/3503250
49. Monnai, Y., Hasegawa, K., Fujiwara, M., Yoshino, K., Inoue, S., Shinoda, H.: HaptoMime: mid-air haptic interaction with a floating virtual screen. In: UIST '14: Proceedings of the 27th Annual ACM Symposium on User Interface Software and Technology, pp. 663–667. Association for Computing Machinery, New York, NY, USA, October 2014. https://doi.org/10.1145/2642918.2647407
50. Myers III, P.L., Starr, A.W., Mullins, K.: Flight simulator fidelity, training transfer, and the role of instructors in optimizing learning. Scholarly Commons **5**(1), 6 (2018). https://doi.org/10.15394/ijaaa.2018.1203
51. Nakade, T., Fuchs, R., Bleuler, H., Schiffmann, J.: Haptics based multi-level collaborative steering control for automated driving. Commun. Eng. **2**(2), 1–13 (2023). https://doi.org/10.1038/s44172-022-00051-2
52. Olivari, M., Nieuwenhuizen, F.M., Bülthoff, H.H., Pollini, L.: Pilot adaptation to different classes of haptic aids in tracking tasks. J. Guidance Control Dyn. (2014). https://doi.org/10.2514/1.G000534
53. Orozco, M., Silva, J., El Saddik, A., Petriu, E.: The role of haptics in games. Haptics Render. Appl. 217–234 (2012)
54. Page, D., Lindeman, R.W., Lukosch, S.: Identifying strategies to mitigate cybersickness in virtual reality induced by flying with an interactive travel interface. Multimodal Technol. Interact. **7**(5), 47 (2023). https://doi.org/10.3390/mti7050047
55. Park, J., Han, J., Kyung, K.U.: Providing localized surface haptic on a thin- transparent vibrating panel. In: Proceedings of IEEE World Haptics Conference 2023 (2023)
56. Patel, R.V., Atashzar, S.F., Tavakoli, M.: Haptic feedback and force-based teleoperation in surgical robotics. Proc. IEEE **110**(7), 1012–1027 (2022). https://doi.org/10.1109/JPROC.2022.3180052

57. Peng, Y.H., et al.: WalkingVibe: reducing virtual reality sickness and improving realism while walking in VR using unobtrusive head-mounted vibrotactile feedback. In: CHI '20: Proceedings of the 2020 CHI Conference on Human Factors in Computing Systems, pp. 1–12. Association for Computing Machinery, New York, NY, USA, April 2020. https://doi.org/10.1145/3313831.3376847

58. Perret, J., Vercruysse, P.: Advanced force-feedback solutions and their application to space programs. In: Proceedings of the 9th ESA Workshop on Advanced Space Technologies for Robotics and Automation, November 2006

59. Petermeijer, S.M., Abbink, D.A., Mulder, M., de Winter, J.C.F.: The effect of haptic support systems on driver performance: a literature survey. IEEE Trans. Haptics **8**(4), 467–479 (2015). https://doi.org/10.1109/TOH.2015.2437871

60. Poyade, M.: Motor skill training using virtual reality and haptic interaction: a case study in industrial maintenance. Ph.D. dissertation, Universidad de Málaga (2013). https://investigacion.ujaen.es/documentos/6397d5e8b0ebee6c8799ca9f

61. Ramsamy, P., Haffegee, A., Jamieson, R., Alexandrov, V.: Using haptics to improve immersion in virtual environments. In: Alexandrov, V.N., van Albada, G.D., Sloot, P.M.A., Dongarra, J. (eds.) ICCS 2006. LNCS, vol. 3992, pp. 603–609. Springer, Heidelberg (2006). https://doi.org/10.1007/11758525_81

62. Rastogi, N., Srivastava, A.K.: Control system design for tokamak remote maintenance operations using assisted virtual reality and haptic feedback. Fusion Eng. Des. **139**, 47–54 (2019)

63. Rauschnabel, P.A., Felix, R., Hinsch, C., Shahab, H., Alt, F.: What is XR? Towards a framework for augmented and virtual reality. Comput. Hum. Behav. **133**, 107289 (2022). https://doi.org/10.1016/j.chb.2022.107289

64. Reardon, G., Goetz, D., Linnander, M., Visell, Y.: Rendering dynamic source motion in surface haptics via wave focusing. IEEE Trans. Haptics 1–7 (2023). https://doi.org/10.1109/TOH.2023.3274485

65. Reason, J.T., Brand, J.J.: Motion Sickness. Academic Press, London, England, UK (1975)

66. Riccio, G.E., Stoffregen, T.A.: What is XR? Towards a framework for augmented and virtual reality. Ecol. Psychol. **3**(3), 195–240 (1991). https://doi.org/10.1207/s15326969eco0303_2

67. Rognon, C., Koehler, M., Duriez, C., Floreano, D., Okamura, A.M.: Soft haptic device to render the sensation of flying like a drone. IEEE Rob. Autom. Lett. **4**(3), 2524–2531 (2019). https://doi.org/10.1109/LRA.2019.2907432

68. Rognon, C., Mintchev, S., Dell'Agnola, F., Cherpillod, A., Atienza, D., Floreano, D.: FlyJacket: an upper body soft exoskeleton for immersive drone control. IEEE Rob. Autom. Lett. **3**(3), 2362–2369 (2018). https://doi.org/10.1109/LRA.2018.2810955

69. Rognon, C., Ramachandran, V., Wu, A.R., Ijspeert, A.J., Floreano, D.: Haptic feedback perception and learning with cable-driven guidance in exosuit teleoperation of a simulated drone. IEEE Trans. Haptics **12**(3), 375–385 (2019). https://doi.org/10.1109/TOH.2019.2925612

70. de Rooij, G., Van Baelen, D., Borst, C., van Paassen, M.M., Mulder, M.: Supplementing haptic feedback in flight envelope protection through visual display indications. J. Aerosp. Inf. Syst. (2023). https://doi.org/10.2514/1.I011191

71. Sadia, B., Emgin, S.E., Sezgin, T.M., Basdogan, C.: Data-driven vibrotactile rendering of digital buttons on touchscreens. Int. J. Hum Comput Stud. **135**, 102363 (2020). https://doi.org/10.1016/j.ijhcs.2019.09.005

72. Sawada, Y., et al.: Effects of synchronised engine sound and vibration presentation on visually induced motion sickness. Sci. Rep. **10**(7553), 1–10 (2020). https://doi.org/10.1038/s41598-020-64302-y

73. See, A.R., Choco, J.A.G., Chandramohan, K.: Touch, texture and haptic feedback: a review on how we feel the world around us. Appl. Sci. **12**(9), 4686 (2022). https://doi.org/10.3390/app12094686

74. Shinoda, H., Nakajima, T., Ueno, K., Koshida, N.: Thermally induced ultrasonic emission from porous silicon. Nature **400**, 853–855 (1999). https://doi.org/10.1038/23664

75. Shiroma, N., Sato, N., Chiu, Y.H., Matsuno, F.: Study on effective camera images for mobile robot teleoperation (2004). https://doi.org/10.1109/ROMAN.2004.1374738

76. Silva, A.J., Ramirez, O.A.D., Vega, V.P., Oliver, J.P.O.: PHANToM OMNI haptic device: kinematic and manipulability. In: 2009 Electronics, Robotics and Automotive Mechanics Conference (CERMA), pp. 193–198. IEEE (2009). https://doi.org/10.1109/CERMA.2009.55

77. da Silveira, A.C., Rodrigues, E.C., Saleme, E.B., Covaci, A., Ghinea, G., Santos, C.A.S.: Thermal and wind devices for multisensory human-computer interaction: an overview. Multimed. Tools Appl. pp. 1–28 (2023). https://doi.org/10.1007/s11042-023-14672-y

78. Simonsson, C., Franzén, M.: A configurable interface between X-Plane and bHaptics TactSuit X40. Bachelor's thesis, Linköping University, Department of Computer and Information Science (2022). http://www.diva-portal.org/smash/record.jsf?pid=diva2%3A1673654&dswid=-5586

79. Srinivasan, M.A., Basdogan, C.: Haptics in virtual environments: taxonomy, research status, and challenges. Comput. Graph. **21**(4), 393–404 (1997). https://doi.org/10.1016/S0097-8493(97)00030-7

80. Sulema, Y.: Mulsemedia vs. multimedia: state of the art and future trends. In: 2016 International Conference on Systems, Signals and Image Processing (IWSSIP), pp. 23–25. IEEE (2016). https://doi.org/10.1109/IWSSIP.2016.7502696

81. Tanaka, Y., Shen, A., Kong, A., Lopes, P.: Full-hand electro-tactile feedback without obstructing palmar side of hand. In: CHI '23: Proceedings of the 2023 CHI Conference on Human Factors in Computing Systems, pp. 1–15. Association for Computing Machinery, New York, NY, USA (2023). https://doi.org/10.1145/3544548.3581382

82. Teng, S.Y., Li, P., Nith, R., Fonseca, J., Lopes, P.: Touch&Fold: a foldable haptic actuator for rendering touch in mixed reality. In: CHI '21: Proceedings of the 2021 CHI Conference on Human Factors in Computing Systems, pp. 1–14. Association for Computing Machinery, New York, NY, USA (2021). https://doi.org/10.1145/3411764.3445099

83. Van Baelen, D., Ellerbroek, J., van Paassen, M.M.R., Mulder, M.: Design of a haptic feedback system for flight envelope protection. J. Guidance Control Dyn. (2020). https://doi.org/10.2514/1.G004596

84. Van Baelen, D., van Paassen, M.M.R., Ellerbroek, J., Abbink, D.A., Mulder, M.: Flying by feeling: communicating flight envelope protection through haptic feedback. Int. J. Hum.-Comput. Interact. **37**(7), 655–665 (2021). https://doi.org/10.1080/10447318.2021.1890489

85. de Vries, J.: Redesigning a haptic glove for new features and improved assembly. Master's thesis, Delft University of Technology (2023). https://repository.tudelft.nl/islandora/object/uuid%3Ad0bf1147-f300-4412-9aa1-2fccc2240079

86. Weech, S., Moon, J., Troje, N.F.: Influence of bone-conducted vibration on simulator sickness in virtual reality. PLoS ONE **13**(3) (2018). https://doi.org/10.1371/journal.pone.0194137

87. van Wegen, M., et al.: An overview of wearable haptic technologies and their performance in virtual object exploration. Sensors **23**(3), 1563 (2023). https://doi.org/10.3390/s23031563

88. de Winter, J.C.F., Dodou, D., Mulder, M.: Training effectiveness of whole body flight simulator motion: a comprehensive meta-analysis. Int. J. Aviat. Psychol. **22**(2), 164–183 (2012). https://doi.org/10.1080/10508414.2012.663247

89. Wolf, D., Rietzler, M., Hnatek, L., Rukzio, E.: Face/on: multi-modal haptic feedback for head-mounted displays in virtual reality. IEEE Trans. Visual. Comput. Graph. **PP**(99), 1 (2019). https://doi.org/10.1109/TVCG.2019.2932215

90. Xia, P.: Haptics for product design and manufacturing simulation. IEEE Trans. Haptics **9**(3), 358–375 (2016). https://doi.org/10.1109/TOH.2016.2554551

91. Yoshida, K.T., et al.: Cognitive and physical activities impair perception of smartphone vibrations. IEEE Trans. Haptics **16**(4), 672–679 (2023). https://doi.org/10.1109/TOH.2023.3279201

92. Zhao, Y., Lv, C., Yang, L.: Chapter eleven - intelligent haptic interface design for human–machine interaction in automated vehicles. In: Human-Machine Interaction for Automated Vehicles, pp. 217–240. Academic Press, Cambridge, MA, USA (2023). https://doi.org/10.1016/B978-0-443-18997-5.00002-1

93. Ziat, M., Wagner, S., Frissen, I.: Haptic feedback to compensate for the absence of horizon cues during landing. In: Bello, F., Kajimoto, H., Visell, Y. (eds.) EuroHaptics 2016. LNCS, vol. 9775, pp. 47–54. Springer, Cham (2016). https://doi.org/10.1007/978-3-319-42324-1_5

94. Zwaan, H.M., Petermeijer, S.M., Abbink, D.A.: Haptic shared steering control with an adaptive level of authority based on time-to-line crossing. IFAC-PapersOnLine **52**(19), 49–54 (2019). https://doi.org/10.1016/j.ifacol.2019.12.085, 14th IFAC Symposium on Analysis, Design, and Evaluation of Human Machine Systems HMS 2019

# Investigation of the Impression Given by the Appearance and Gestures of a Virtual Reality Agent Describing a Display Product

Michiko Inoue[(⊠)], Shouta Hioki, Fuyuko Iwasaki, Shunsuke Yoneda, and Masashi Nishiyama[ID]

Graduate School of Engineering, Tottori University,
101 Minami 4-chome, Koyama-cho, Tottori 680-8550, Japan
mi.inoue@tottori-u.ac.jp

**Abstract.** In recent times, there has been a rise in virtual reality agents employed during virtual product exhibitions to describe a display product to users. Previous analytical studies investigated how the agent's appearance influences a user's impression in virtual product exhibitions. Here, we consider how the agent's gestures in addition to their appearance influences a user's impression. In this paper, we investigate the impression that the user perceives from the appearance and gestures of a virtual reality agent describing a display product to the user. Experimental results revealed that users' impressions were influenced by both the agent's appearance and gestures.

**Keywords:** VR Agent · Gestures · Appearance · Subjective Assessment · Impression

## 1 Introduction

Recently, the use of virtual reality (VR) agents in virtual product exhibitions has emerged. The VR agent introduces a product on display to a user in order to sell it. It is known that the VR agent's description influences a user's willingness to purchase a product [3]. However, when the VR agent is describing the product to the user, the user's impression of the VR agent is also important. For example, a user is more likely to purchase a product if the user has a good impression of the VR agent. Therefore, this paper discusses the impression of the VR agent that the user perceives when the VR agent describes a product to the user.

We aim to understand how the VR agent describes the product display influences the impression perceived by the users. There are many factors that affect this impression, such as the VR agent's appearance, gestures, conversation content, and voice quality. In this paper, we focus on the VR agent's appearance and gestures, as shown in Fig. 1, which strongly affect the impression of the VR agent through human visual perception. Existing analytical studies [2,4] reported that the VR agent's appearance affects the user's willingness to purchase when the

J. Y. C. Chen and G. Fragomeni (Eds.): HCII 2024, LNCS 14707, pp. 179–190, 2024.
https://doi.org/10.1007/978-3-031-61044-8_13

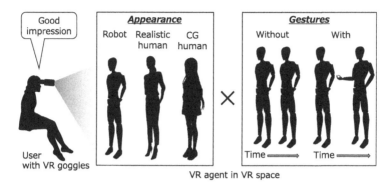

**Fig. 1.** Example of an agent bowing and pointing with their hand during a product description.

VR agent is describing a display product. However, these existing analytical studies did not consider how the combination of the VR agent's appearance and gestures affects the user's impression.

In this paper, we investigated the following hypotheses regarding the impression that the user perceives from the appearance and gestures of a VR agent describing a display product to the user.

$H_1$: The VR agent's appearance changes the strength of the good impression that the user perceives.

$H_2$: The VR agent's gestures change the strength of the good impression that the user perceives.

$H_3$: Combining the VR agent's appearance and gestures changes the strength of the good impression that the user perceives.

In the following, we explain the experimental design of the agent's appearance and gestures in VR space in Sect. 2, present the results of the subjective evaluation of the experimental subjects in Sect. 3, and summarize the study in Sect. 4.

## 2   Experimental Design

### 2.1   Overview

In this paper, we employ a two-factor analysis of variance to validate the three hypotheses: $H_1$, $H_2$, and $H_3$. In the analysis, if we observe the main effect of the agent's appearance, we support $H_1$; if we observe the main effect of the agent's gestures, we support $H_2$; and if we observe an interaction between the agent's appearance and the agent's gestures, we support $H_3$. We refer to users as "subjects" in the following. We also refer to an object described by the agent in virtual product exhibitions as a "display product."

We investigated three hypotheses concerning the description of a display product within a VR environment, exploring interactions between a VR agent and subjects. Specifically, we emulate interactions in which a human clerk agent describes a display product to subjects in the physical space. This study focuses on describing a display product in one-on-one interactions, which represent the minimum number of subjects. When describing a display product with two or more agents and subjects, it is essential to consider the impact of the relationships between the agents and subjects. Therefore, we initially experimented under conditions that minimize such influences.

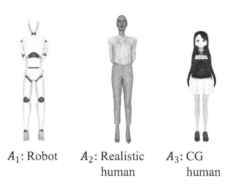

$A_1$: Robot    $A_2$: Realistic    $A_3$: CG
human    human

**Fig. 2.** Example of the three type of agents used for product description.

## 2.2   Agent Appearance

We consider the VR agent's appearance when investigating $H_1$, $H_2$, and $H_3$. A VR agent's appearance can exhibit considerable variation, ranging from humanoid to animal-like because of the extensive creative possibilities allowed within the VR environment. In this study, we opted for humanoid agents with a human skeletal structure to reproduce the gestures performed by human agents in the real world. While a diverse array of humanoid agents are used in virtual product exhibitions, we categorized them into three primary agent types.

$A_1$: Robot
$A_2$: Realistic human
$A_3$: Computer graphics (CG) human

The reasons for using the realistic human agent include the potential for subjects to feel as if they are receiving descriptions from a real human. The reasons for using the CG human agent include the lightweight nature of 3D data and the ease with which CG human model designers can convey their intentions to subjects; for example, by giving the VR agent a cute appearance. A robot agent is used because an agent possessing a human skeleton but lacking a face and clothing may yield effects distinct from typical human interactions. This study substantiates the hypotheses through the evaluation of these three agent types. Figure 2 presents examples of the three agents evaluated in this experiment.

### 2.3   Agent Gestures

We consider the gestures of the VR agent. Generally, the procedure an agent uses to explain a display product involves approaching the subject, greeting them, and then explaining the characteristics of a display product. In this study, we focused on display product descriptions in which the agent and the subjects are likely to engage in conversation rather than one in which the agent simply moves around. Therefore, we refer to the procedure of greeting the subjects and explaining a display product as "describing a display product." In the experiments, we incorporated gestures commonly used when describing a display product in the real world.

When describing a display product, an agent can perform gestures indicating the product, the subject, or the agent itself. Examples of an agent's gestures include bowing to express respect for the subject or identify the recipient of the display product description, pointing in the direction of the product, and making gestures suggesting happiness or success to convey the agent's feelings to the subjects. In this study, we considered gestures towards the products and the subjects, and excluded gestures aimed at the agent itself. During the validation of hypotheses $H_1$, $H_2$, and $H_3$, the agent describes the subjects using both a bowing gesture towards the subject and a pointing gesture towards the products. The agent's gesture conditions are as follows:

$G_{w/o}$: Without gestures
$G_{w/}$: With gestures

### 2.4   Stimuli

We designed six comparison conditions to validate the hypotheses by combining the agent's appearance, as described in Sect. 2.2, and the agent's gestures, as described in Sect. 2.3. These comparison conditions are as follows:

$M_1$: Robot without gestures $(A_1, G_{w/o})$
$M_2$: Robot with gestures $(A_1, G_{w/})$
$M_3$: Human without gestures $(A_2, G_{w/o})$
$M_4$: Human with gestures $(A_2, G_{w/})$
$M_5$: CG human without gestures $(A_3, G_{w/o})$
$M_6$: CG human with gestures $(A_3, G_{w/})$

We generated stimuli for all comparison conditions. Figure 3 shows examples of a stimulus for each condition. We controlled the timing and manner of the gestures across comparison conditions $M_2$, $M_4$, and $M_6$.

While describing a display product, the agent's gestures typically occur concurrently with the conversation. In this study, in addition to generating the agent's gestures, we incorporated verbal explanations. The agent's verbal content included the following phrases: "Welcome," "Today's recommendation is the two-seater sofa," and "Please consider buying it." The verbal content was presented in the above order. During the description of a display product, the

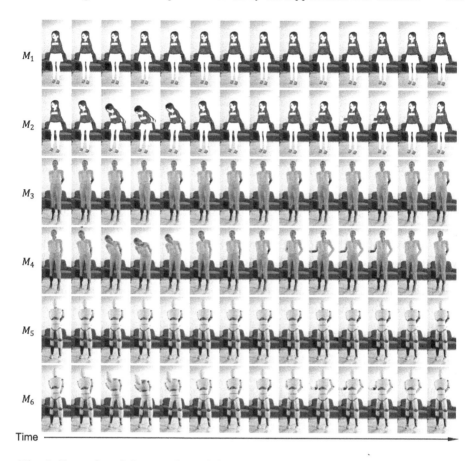

**Fig. 3.** Examples of the stimuli used during product description to test $H_1$ and $H_2$.

verbal content aligned with the intentions conveyed through the agent's gestures. For instance, the likelihood of the agent conveying "Welcome" and indicating a display product was exceedingly low. Incidentally, when the agent said "Please consider buying it," no gestures were performed.

### 2.5  Questions for the Subjects

We recruited 22 participants (18 males, four females) for the experiment, with an average age of 21.5 years. We conducted subjective evaluations to validate $H_1$, $H_2$, and $H_3$. The questionnaire item was as follows:

$Q_1$: Did you perceive a good impression of the agent?

To ensure that subjects remained unaware of the experiment's intention, we introduced the following dummy item:

$\hat{Q}_1$: Did you experience any discomfort with the appearance of the product?

**Fig. 4.** Example of the red sphere before product description. (Color figure online)

For each of the questions $Q_1$ and $\hat{Q}_1$, we formulated corresponding opposite items and presented a total of four questions to the subjects. The subjective evaluation values ranged from 1 ("Strongly Disagree") to 4 ("Strongly Agree"). The order of the questionnaire items presented to subjects was randomized across all subjects and comparison conditions. When presenting the questionnaire items, we did not disclose item names such as Q1 and $\hat{Q}_1$; only the text of the questions was provided. Opposite items were reverse-scored. The dummy items were not evaluated.

## 2.6  Procedure

The outline of the experimental procedures is as follows:

$P_1$: Subjects put on the VR headset.
$P_2$: We randomly choose one of the six comparison conditions.
$P_3$: We present the red sphere to subjects and subjects observe the sphere.
$P_4$: We present the selected stimulus to subjects.
$P_5$: We instruct subjects to orally respond to the subjective evaluation questionnaire.
$P_6$: We repeat steps $P_2$ to $P_5$ for each comparison condition.

The red sphere in $P_3$ is presented to ensure that at the beginning of the description, all subjects are looking at the same location for all comparison conditions. We displayed the red sphere to subjects at a position that intentionally does not overlap with the agent or the display product, as depicted in Fig. 4. To prevent surprising the subjects during the transition from $P_4$ to $P_5$, we issued the following verbal announcement: "We are now moving on to the questionnaire." During $P_5$, to ensure no impact on the results of the subjective evaluation questionnaire, we chose not to present the VR agent and display product to the subjects. Instead, we positioned the board with the questionnaire item written on it in front of the subject. They read the question and provided oral responses. If asked, the operator read the question aloud to the subject.

Before initiating the experiment, we explained the scenario to the subjects using three statements: "In this experiment, you work for a company," "You have come to purchase a two-seater sofa planned for installation in you company's virtual space while inspecting the virtual product exhibition," and "You

$S_1$                               $S_2$                               $S_3$

**Fig. 5.** Three agent types with a display product.

have the authority to make a purchase decision." These details were provided to immerse the subjects in a pseudo-situation in which they would receive information about a display product they are considering purchasing from the agent while simultaneously having the decision-making power for the purchase.

### 2.7 Other Conditions

We chose a two-seater sofa as the display product for the agent to describe. Our inspiration comes from scenarios in which subjects explore physical stores for real-world display product purchases. In such situations, subjects often browse catalogs on web browsers for display products they might consider buying. However, potential discrepancies in color due to the environment and the risk of misinterpreting actual product sizes highlight the necessity for subjects to physically visit stores to verify aspects such as color and size. Therefore, in this study, we selected furniture items, specifically two-seater sofas, as the display product. Subjects might visit a store to directly assess details such as size. Figure 5 shows examples of the agent describing the sofa[1] in the stimulus. Figure 6 shows the spatial relationships among the subject, product, and agent.

When viewing the front of the display product, the subject is situated 0.5 m to the right of the product's center, whereas the agent is positioned 1.5 m to the right of the product's center. Similarly, when observing the left side of the display product, the subject is placed 1.5 m to the right of the product's center, and the agent is positioned 0.1 m to the right of the product's center.

### 2.8 Experimental Setting

We used the VIVE Pro Eye (HTC Corp.) to display the VR space and mocopi (Sony Corp.) for motion capture. The mocopi motion capture system uses six sensors attached to the body, enabling 3D full-body tracking. In this study, our objective was to replicate gestures performed by a real-world clerk as they

---

[1] We sourced the 3D data for sofas ZT8303DS and WT5603AS, as well as the light bulb LSJ-3_NK from Karimoku FreeBANK. The various tables and other sofas are from Digital-Architex.

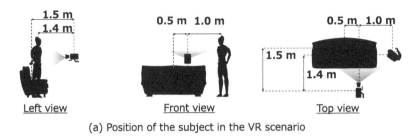

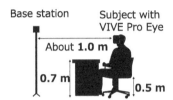

(a) Position of the subject in the VR scenario

Fig. 6. Position of the subject with respect to the agent.

Table 1. Results of an analysis of variance on subjective scores indicating a positive impression towards the agent. * $p < .05$

| Question | Variable factor | F-value | p-value |
|----------|-----------------|---------|---------|
| Q1 | Appearance($A_1$, $A_2$, $A_3$) | 4.03 | 0.02 * |
| | Gestures($G_1$, $G_2$) | 33.81 | 0.00 * |
| | Appearance($A_1$, $A_2$, $A_3$) × gestures($G_1$, $G_2$) | 0.21 | 0.81 |

describe a display product to the subject. To achieve this, we captured the gestures of actual humans using motion capture and applied the acquired data to the VR agent with a humanoid skeleton. When obtaining the bowing gestures, we instructed the real-world human agent to imagine a subject was in front of them. Additionally, when obtaining the pointing gestures, we instructed the real-world human agent to imagine a display product diagonally to their right, as depicted in Fig. 6. To create the audio data, we used the VOICEVOX: Haru-oto Ritsu voice synthesis software. We standardized the length of all stimuli to 10 s. The experimental setup, as shown in Fig. 5 (b), illustrates a subject sitting at the desk, adjusting themselves to a comfortable position for the experiment.

## 3    Subjective Assessment of Agent-Described Product Presentation with Gestures

### 3.1    Results of $H_1$ and $H_2$

We conducted subjective evaluations to verify $H_1$, $H_2$ and $H_3$, obtaining subjective scores assessed by the experimental subjects. The Shapiro-Wilk test was

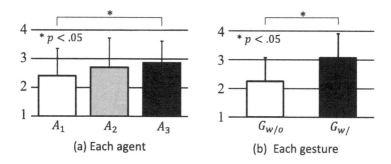

**Fig. 7.** Average subjective score for each agent or each gesture.

performed on the subjective scores rated by the subjects, and normality could not be assumed. Therefore, an aligned rank transform[1,5] was applied, and an analysis of variance was performed on the appearance and gesture conditions of the VR agent. The result is listed in Table 1. A main effect was found for the VR agent's appearance ($F = 4.03, p < .02$). A main effect was also found for the VR agent's gestures ($F = 33.81, p < .00$). There was no interaction ($F = 0.211, p < .81$). Because there was a main effect for the VR agent's appearance, we believe that impression given by the VR agent changed depending on its appearance. Therefore, $H_1$ clearly holds. Because there was also a main effect for the VR agent's gestures, the impression given by the VR agent changed depending on its gestures. Therefore, $H_2$ also holds. Moreover, because there was no interaction between the VR agent's appearance and the VR agent's gestures, $H_3$ did not hold.

The average subjective score for each VR agent is shown in Fig. 7(a). The VR agent with the highest subjective score was $A_3$, followed by $A_2$, and finally $A_1$. Next, a Wilcoxon signed rank test was performed as a multiple comparison, followed by Bonferroni's correction. The results showed a significant difference between $A_1$ and $A_3$ ($F = 0.334$, $p < .045$). These results indicate that the subjects had a better impression of the VR agent describing the product when it had a CG human-like appearance than when it had a robot-like appearance. The average subjective score for each gesture is shown in Fig. 7(b). The VR agent achieved higher average subjective scores of $3.07 \pm 0.84$ for the presence of gestures and $2.25 \pm 0.82$ for the absence of gestures. The order of higher average subjective scores was observed when actions were present compared with the findings when actions were absent. In conclusion, the agent achieved better outcomes when performing gestures while describing the display product.

## 3.2   Discussion

After analyzing the results of our hypothesis testing, we delve into the considerations arising from the subjective scores. This study focused on the influence of bowing and hand pointing gestures on the subjective scores of the agents.

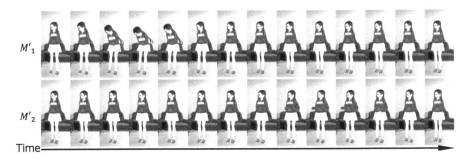

**Fig. 8.** Examples of stimuli during a display product description with either bowing or hand pointing

The evaluation of $H_1$ revealed that an active engagement of the agent in gestures during product description resulted in a better impression from subjects. However, our investigation at this juncture has not clarified whether an effect was present when the agent executed either a bow or hand gesture individually, or whether the combined execution of both gestures had a discernible impact. As explained in Sect. 2.3, a bowing gesture expresses respect for the subject, and a hand pointing gesture conveys the direction of the product. When two different gestures are combined, the strength of the good impression that the user perceives may vary dynamically. We hence introduce a new hypothesis using the CG agents, which gave the best impression to the subjects, as shown in Sect. 2.3.

$H_4$: The VR agent's bowing gesture changes the strength of the good impression that the user perceives.

$H_5$: The VR agent's hand pointing gesture changes the strength of the good impression that the user perceives.

$H_6$: Combining the VR agent's bowing gesture and hand pointing gesture changes the strength of the good impression that the user perceives.

### 3.3 Impact of Each Behavior on the Subjective Scores

We conducted experiments in which the agent exclusively engaged in either bowing or hand pointing gestures during product description, and we investigated how these gestures impact the subjects' perceptions of the agent by comparing them with the conditions outlined in Sect. 2.4, where gestures are either absent or present. The agent's bowing gesture conditions are as follows:

$B_1$: Without bowing
$B_2$: With bowing

The agent's pointing gesture conditions are as follows:

$P_1$: Without pointing
$P_2$: With pointing

**Table 2.** Results of an analysis of variance on the subjective scores representing positive impressions towards the CG agent. * $p < .05$

| Questuon | Variable factor | F-value | p-value |
|---|---|---|---|
| Q1 | Bowing($B_1$, $B_2$) | 6.286 | 0.0140 * |
| | Hand pointing($P_1$, $P_2$) | 4.010 | 0.0460 * |
| | Bowing($B_1$, $B_2$) $\times$ Hand pointing($P_1$, $P_2$) | 0.314 | 0.577 |

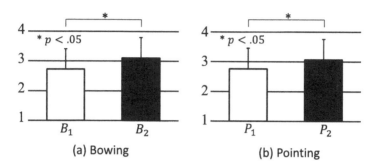

(a) Bowing     (b) Pointing

**Fig. 9.** Average subjective score for each bowing condition or pointing condition.

We introduced the following four comparison conditions by combining the agent's bowing gesture conditions and the agent's pointing gesture conditions:

$M_1'$: CG human without bowing and pointing
$M_2'$: CG human with bowing
$M_3'$: CG human with pointing
$M_4'$: CG human with gestures

We provide the examples of stimuli for the $M_2'$ and $M_3'$ conditions in Fig. 8. Those for the $M_1'$ and $M_4'$ conditions are shown in Fig. 3 $M_1$ and $M_2$. The remaining experimental conditions and procedures follow those detailed in Sect. 2.4.

We conducted subjective evaluations to verify $H_4$, $H_5$, and $H_6$, obtaining subjective scores assessed by the experimental subjects. The analysis of variance described in Sect. 3.1 was performed on the bowing and hand pointing gesture conditions of the VR agent. The result is listed in Table 2. A main effect was found for the VR agent's bowing gesture ($F = 6.286, p < .0140$). A main effect was also found for the VR agent's hand pointing gesture ($F = 4.010, p < .0460$). There was no interaction ($F = 0.211, p < .0460$). Because there was a main effect for the VR agent's bowing, we believe that impression given by the VR agent changed depending on its bowing gesture. Therefore, $H_4$ clearly holds. Because there was also a main effect for the VR agent's hand pointing gesture, the impression given by the VR agent changed depending on its hand pointing gesture. Therefore, $H_5$ also holds. Moreover, because there was no interaction between the VR agent's bowing gesture and the VR agent's hand pointing gesture, $H_6$ did not hold.

The average subjective score for each bowing gesture condition is shown in Fig. 9(a). The subjective score of bowing gesture condition $B_2$ was higher than that of $B_1$. This order of higher average subjective scores was observed when bowing gestures were present as opposed to when they were absent. The average subjective score for each pointing gesture condition is shown in Fig. 9(b). The subjective score of hand pointing gesture condition $P_2$ was higher than that of $P_1$. This order of higher average subjective scores was observed when hand pointing gestures were present compared with when they were absent. In conclusion, when the agent described the product, even if the agent performed only one gesture, either bowing or hand pointing, the subjects perceived a better impression than they did when no gestures were performed.

## 4   Conclusion

We investigated three hypotheses to confirm whether experimental subjects' impressions of an agent describing a VR display product would be affected by the agent's appearance and gestures. The agent's appearance included robot, realistic human, and CG human conditions during the product description, with bowing and hand pointing gestures categorized into "without gestures" or "with gestures" conditions. We evaluated the six stimuli, combining the three appearances and two gesture conditions in a VR environment. Experimental results showed that subjects' impressions changed based on both appearance and gestures. Additionally, subjects favored the CG human agent over the robot agent. In an additional experiment, we investigated the variation in impressions when the agent performed a single gesture, either bowing or hand pointing. The findings indicated a positive impression even with just one of these gestures. In future work, we intend to conduct further analysis of the agent's appearance and an in-depth investigation of its gestures.

## References

1. Elkin, L.A., Kay, M., Higgins, J.J., Wobbrock, J.O.: An aligned rank transform procedure for multifactor contrast tests. In: The 34th Annual ACM Symposium on User Interface Software and Technology, p. 754–768. Association for Computing Machinery (2021)
2. Hanus, M.D., Fox, J.: Persuasive avatars: The effects of customizing a virtual salesperson's appearance on brand liking and purchase intentions. Int. J. Hum Comput Stud. **84**, 33–40 (2015)
3. Moon, J.H., Kim, E., Choi, S.M., Sung, Y.: Keep the social in social media: the role of social interaction in avatar-based virtual shopping. J. Interact. Advert. **13**(1), 14–26 (2013)
4. Liew, T.W., Tan, S.M.: Exploring the effects of specialist versus generalist embodied virtual agents in a multi-product category online store. Telematics Inform. **35**(1), 122–135 (2018)
5. Wobbrock, J.O., Findlater, L., Gergle, D., Higgins, J.J.: The aligned rank transform for nonparametric factorial analyses using only ANOVA procedures. In: Proceedings of the SIGCHI Conference on Human Factors in Computing Systems, pp. 143–146. Association for Computing Machinery (2011)

# Assessing the Influence of Passive Haptics on User Perception of Physical Properties in Virtual Reality

Logan Kemper, Juan Lam, Matthew Levine, Aiden White Pifer, Seung Hyuk Jang, Markus Santoso, and Angelos Barmpoutis(✉)[iD]

University of Florida, Digital Worlds Institute, Gainesville, FL 32611, USA
{logankemper,juanlam,matthew.levine,awhitepifer}@ufl.edu,
{hyuk,markus,angelos}@digitalworlds.ufl.edu

**Abstract.** This paper presents a pilot study that explores the role of low-cost passive haptics on how users perceive physical properties such as the size and weight of objects within virtual reality environments. An A/B-type study was conducted as an air hockey simulation in which participants experienced two versions: one adhered to conventional VR settings, while the other incorporated a tangible surface, a real table. Statistical analysis of the data collected from post-study questionnaires indicated a shift in perception of size and weight when exposed to the haptic-enhanced simulation, with virtual objects perceived as larger or heavier. It was also noted that the observed shift of the user perception was stronger when the simulation with the tangible surface was experienced first. The paper presents details on the implementation of the air hockey simulation and the setup within the testing environment as well as the statistical analysis performed on the collected data, offering practical recommendations for future applications.

**Keywords:** Virtual Reality · Passive Haptics · User Perception

## 1 Introduction

Virtual reality (VR) has revolutionized the way we interact with digital environments, but achieving a truly immersive experience still poses challenges, particularly in replicating physical sensations. Various hardware solutions have been proposed such as electric muscle simulation [5] however the cost and setup implications of such interfaces are usually prohibitive for public use as mainstream hardware devices. Several studies have recently experimented the use of low-cost tangible objects within virtual environments [2,3], and it has been shown to influence the user experience in various ways [1,4,6–8,12]. Results from our previous studies indicated that the use of passive haptics contributes to an increase in the perceived level of enjoyment and realism [3].

This paper explores the impact of integrating low-cost passive haptic feedback into virtual environments on users' perception of size and weight. The focal point of this work is a pilot study conducted within the context of an air

© The Author(s), under exclusive license to Springer Nature Switzerland AG 2024
J. Y. C. Chen and G. Fragomeni (Eds.): HCII 2024, LNCS 14707, pp. 191–200, 2024.
https://doi.org/10.1007/978-3-031-61044-8_14

hockey simulation, utilizing a real-time tracked physical Table 3. The experimental design involved a randomized A-B testing sequence, wherein participants were exposed to two versions of the simulation. One version adhered to conventional VR settings, devoid of any passive haptic elements, while the other incorporated a tangible surface of interaction, i.e. a real table that served as the virtual air hockey table. Post-study questionnaires were administered to gather insights into participants' possible change of perception.

**Fig. 1.** Illustration of the experimental setup with a physical table. Components of the virtual environment are superimposed to show the alignment between the virtual and the real world.

The results yielded findings regarding the influence of passive haptic feedback on the perceived physical attributes of objects within the virtual environment. Participants consistently reported a notable shift in their perception of size and weight of the critical objects of interaction when exposed to the haptic-enhanced version of the simulation. Statistical analysis of the results that are presented in Sect. 4 indicate statistically significant differences between the two conditions. Participants consistently rated virtual objects within the haptic-enhanced simulation as larger or heavier compared to their counterparts in the conventional VR environment. More specifically, the virtual puck was perceived as heavier when the physical table was present. Furthermore, the 3D model of the air hockey table was perceived as smaller when the physical table was absent. These findings indicate that there is an impact of passive haptics on users' perceptual experiences, even with respect to the virtual (non-physical) objects within the simulation environment. This reaffirms and extends the observations from experiments presented recently in literature [9,11]. Our results also indicated that the order of experiencing A and B versions of the simulation had an additional influence on the user's perception. In particular, the effects of the passive haptics were more intense when the simulation with the tangible objects were experienced first.1

The paper is organized as follows: Sect. 2 presents details of the development of the VR air hockey simulation with passive haptic feedback. Section 3 describes the study protocol and the user's demographics. Section 4 presents the results and the corresponding statistical findings.

**Fig. 2.** Screen capture of the virtual reality environment that was developed for the needs of this study.

## 2 Methods

A VR application was developed to simulate the tabletop game known as air hockey (see Fig. 1). In this game, the center of interaction is a low-friction table, powered by air pressure, on top of which a circular puck slides when struck by the strikers held by the players. In front of the two opposing players, who stand on opposite sides of the table, there are two openings where players attempt to shoot the puck in order to score points. The sides around the table are slightly elevated to prevent the puck from falling off and can even be incorporated into the game by deliberately angling the puck off the side rail to change its trajectory and send it back towards the opponent's goal-a move known as a "bank shot".

A virtual air hockey simulation was created and deployed on Oculus Quest headsets using Unity 3D. The simulation featured a complete 3D surrounding environment themed as an unfinished basement, with a full-size air hockey table positioned in the center (see Fig. 2). At the beginning of the application, users had the option to calibrate the virtual air hockey table to a physical table using pass-through view. During this calibration step, users could intuitively set the position and orientation of the virtual table by placing the two Oculus Quest controllers upside down on the real table. The midpoint between the controllers determined the location of the virtual table, while the vector between them defined the table's orientation on the X-Z plane. This interaction constrained the user's degrees of freedom to ensure that the virtual table was properly leveled and parallel to the floor, with a fixed size of 55" in width, which is typical for an air hockey table.

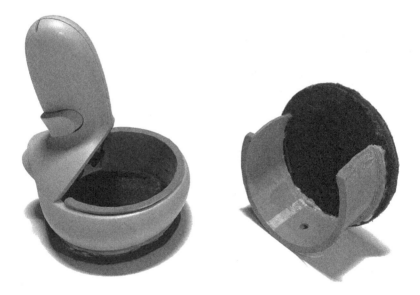

**Fig. 3.** Picture of the VR controllers with a 3D printed attachment and soft padding so that they can be used as air-hockey strikers on top of a physical table.

For the haptic version of this application, a physical table 55 in. wide or wider was required, such as a desktop, coffee table, workbench, or similar flat surface that was also clear of objects. In our testing environment, we used a classroom table that was 72 in. wide. The length of the table was generally not a concern, as the range of the user's motion is naturally restricted to the area in front of the user, covering the depth that the user can reach with stretched arms.

The alignment of the virtual table with the physical table produced natural passive haptic feedback when touching the virtual table and allowed for natural interaction with it, such as leaning on the table to reach the puck.

To further improve passive haptic feedback and create seamless user interaction, the two VR controllers were used as strikers by placing them upside down and sliding them on the surface of the table, mimicking real air hockey strikers. The VR controllers were enhanced with a 3D printed attachment that could fit inside the tracking band of each controller and had a soft adhesive circular pad attached to it to protect both the table and the controllers from wear and tear due to prolonged friction (see Fig. 3). The soft padding also facilitated smoother sliding of the controllers on the table, further enhancing the interaction. Overall, the combined use of the table and the controllers as strikers resulted in an enhanced virtual environment where the two major objects of interaction provided passive haptic feedback. In the absence of a real table, the interaction is reduced to conventional VR user interaction, where the table is purely virtual and the user moves the controllers in the air. This conventional setup of our environment was considered the control case in our experiments, while the haptic setup was the test case.

It is worth mentioning that the only other object involved, even indirectly, in user interaction is the puck, which in both environmental setups is virtual. In real-world air hockey, although users do not directly hold the puck during play, they feel its presence through the force it generates when struck by the strikers. In our VR application, while we could not generate forces of such magnitude, we triggered the vibratory motors of the VR controllers each time they collided with the puck. This active haptic feedback served as a cue that enhanced user interaction with the virtual puck in both forms of simulation.

The developed VR application included other features such as a table-top user interface (UI) with options that could be time-triggered by placing a VR controller on them, moving barriers in the middle of the table to add a video game flavor to the traditional air hockey game, a scoreboard, sound effects, animations, and a multiplayer networking setup that enabled two remote players to play together on opposite sides of a shared virtual table. A video demo of the VR air hockey environment is available at [10].

## 3   User Study

A pilot study was designed to investigate how the presence of passive haptics (in our case, the table) within the VR simulation affects the users' perception of the physical properties of the main objects of interaction in virtual reality.

The study was designed as a randomized controlled trial (RCT) with a crossover design. In this design, each participant experienced both the test condition (VR with passive haptics) and the control condition (conventional VR) in a randomized order. This form of study helps to minimize the influence of individual differences and other potential sources of bias, allowing for a more robust assessment of the intervention's effectiveness.

The study was approved by the University of Florida institutional review board (IRB protocol 17378, approval date: February 8, 2023). In the study we enrolled 13 individuals in the period between February 27, 2023 and April 12, 2023 from the university's community. The age of the subjects ranged from 18 to 34, with a specific breakdown of 18 to 24 ($N = 8$) and 25 to 34 ($N = 5$). The majority of the subjects reported having used VR a few times prior to this study ($N = 9$), while only a few reported using VR often ($N = 4$). The level of prior air hockey experience varied among the subjects, with some having no prior experience ($N = 4$), others having limited experience ($N = 5$), and some being more experienced players ($N = 5$).

The study began with participants responding to a series of demographic questions to collect information about their background and prior knowledge. Subsequently, participants underwent their first virtual reality experience, which involved playing a set of air hockey in single-player mode. The specific VR setup for this initial experience was randomly selected between the control and test conditions. Following this initial VR experience, participants answered a set of multiple-choice questions aimed at capturing their perceptions and impressions. The questions were in the form of statements such as "The puck was heavier than expected", "The puck was lighter than expected", etc. with the following possible responses: strongly agree, somewhat agree, neither agree or disagree, somewhat disagree, strongly disagree.

Next, participants engaged in the other VR experience, similar to the first, and subsequently provided feedback through the same set of questions. Finally, the study concluded with participants responding to a series of closing questions designed to gather additional feedback. These questions included a series of comparative multiple-choice questions with a 5-point scale and allowed participants to provide any other reflections they may have had after completing both VR experiences. Examples of questions included in the post-study questionnaire included: "In which experience did you feel that the puck was heavier?", "In which experience did you feel that the strikers were heavier?", etc. with the following possible answers: clearly the first, somewhat the first, about the same, somewhat the second, clearly the second. Because the first and second experiences were randomly chosen between the control and test conditions, the responses were normalized after the end of data collection. This was achieved by mapping the responses to the control and test cases accordingly, based on which experience was first and which one was second.

This sequential randomized controlled trial study protocol allowed for a structured examination of participants' experiences and perceptions across the two VR sessions.

# 4   Results

Due to the pilot nature of this study and the small number of participants, the results from the analysis of the collected data are not conclusive but their role is mostly indicative. The data were analyzed using Chi-squared test statistics or

Fisher's exact test when the assumptions of the former could not be met. The presence of five possible choices in each question led to small expected frequency counts in some cells of the corresponding contingency tables, violating one of the assumptions of the Chi-squared test. To address this issue, we grouped responses into broader categories, such as combining 'weak' and 'strong' acceptance.

**Table 1.** Results from post-condition questionnaires

| Metric | $\chi^2$ | $p$ | Direction |
|---|---|---|---|
| Strikers heavier than expected | 1.2 | NS | Test |
| Strikers lighter than expected | 3.84 | <0.05 | Control |
| Puck heavier than expected | 2.25 | NS | Test |
| Puck lighter than expected | 0.26 | NS | N/A |
| Table larger than expected | 0.65 | NS | N/A |
| Table smaller than expected | 3.47 | <0.10 | Control |
| Table lighter than expected | 3.91 | <0.05 | Control |
| Table heavier than expected | 0.68 | NS | N/A |
| User interaction smoother | 4.24 | <0.05 | Control |

Table 1 summarizes the results from the questionnaires completed immediately after each VR experience. For each question, we formulated a null hypothesis (H0), such as "there is no difference in the perceived weight of the strikers between the Control (traditional VR) and Test (VR with haptics) conditions", and an alternative hypothesis (H1), such as "there is a difference in the perceived weight of the strikers between the Control and Test conditions". When the $\chi^2$ value corresponds to a significance level with a small enough $p$-value, the observed difference between the two conditions is statistically significant, leading to the rejection of the null hypothesis. This suggests evidence of a significant difference in user perception between the Control and Test conditions.

According to the results in Table 1, users felt that the strikers were lighter in the traditional VR experience (control case). A possible explanation for this result is that in the passive haptic VR experience, there is friction between the table and the sliding strikers (VR controllers), which may result in the perception that the strikers are heavier compared to the traditional VR experience in which they feel much lighter. Similarly, the table was perceived smaller and lighter in the traditional VR case, which corresponded to the feeling that the user interaction was smoother. Finally, although not statistically significant enough, the puck was perceived heavier than expected when the haptic table was present. This can be explained by the fact that all other major objects of interaction are tangible and this unconsciously is transferred to the puck, which is also perceived tangible or at least heavier.

**Table 2.** Results from post-test comparative questionnaire

| Metric | Haptic VR |
| --- | --- |
| Felt like real air hockey | 96.16% |
| Felt like real strikers | 96.16% |
| Felt more immersive | 84.61% |
| The physical table helped puck interaction | 80.76% |
| Strikers felt heavier | 76.96% |
| Puck felt heavier | 69.23% |

Table 2 shows results from the comparative questionnaire administered at the end of the session. Based on these results, the VR experience with passive haptics felt more like real air hockey and with real strikers. Furthermore, the environment felt more immersive, and the presence of the table facilitated puck interaction. Finally, both the strikers and the puck felt heavier, which aligns with the observations from Table 1.

**Table 3.** Assessing the role of the order of experiences

| Metric | $\chi^2$ | $p$ |
| --- | --- | --- |
| First experience was more comfortable | 4.46 | <0.05 |
| Felt more sick in second experience | 3.00 | <0.10 |
| Puck feels heavier on table when test case is first | 7.00 | <0.05 |
| Table feels larger when test case is first | 3.80 | <0.10 |

Finally, we analyzed the data to assess if the order of experience has any effect on the results. Based on the data shown in Table 3, the first experience was more comfortable, while the second experience was more likely to make the subjects feel discomfort. This finding is not surprising because users naturally get tired after some time in VR, particularly when engaging in physically intense interactions. However, it is interesting to note that the puck is perceived as heavier and the table as larger (as seen previously in Table 1), and this difference in perception is more pronounced when the test case (VR with passive haptics) is experienced first.

## 5   Conclusions

In conclusion, the pilot study presented in this paper underscores the significant influence of low-cost passive haptics on users' perception of physical attributes within virtual reality. By integrating tangible surfaces into VR environments, in our case an air hockey simulation, participants demonstrated a notable shift in their perception of size and weight. The results also indicated that prior experiences within such hybrid simulations influence the user's perception in conventional VR simulations that will be experienced afterwards primarily due to a possible shift in their expectations. These findings highlight the potential of passive haptic feedback to enhance immersion and realism in VR experiences. Moving forward, further research is warranted to delve deeper into the mechanisms driving these perceptual shifts and to explore optimal integration strategies for passive haptic feedback in diverse VR applications.

**Acknowledgments.** The authors would like to thank the Digital Worlds Institute for providing the Reality Lab for the development and user study of this project. We would also like to thank the volunteers who participated in this study.

**Disclosure of Interests.** The authors have no competing interests to declare that are relevant to the content of this article.

# References

1. Azmandian, M., Hancock, M., Benko, H., Ofek, E., Wilson, A.D.: Haptic retargeting: dynamic repurposing of passive haptics for enhanced virtual reality experiences. In: Proceedings of the 2016 CHI Conference on Human Factors in Computing Systems, pp. 1968–1979 (2016)
2. Barmpoutis, A., Faris, R., Garcia, L., Gruber, L., Li, J., Peralta, F., Zhang, M.: Assessing the role of virtual reality with passive haptics in music conductor education: a pilot study. In: Chen, J.Y.C., Fragomeni, G. (eds.) Proceedings of the 2020 Human-Computer Interaction International Conference, vol. 12190, pp. 275–285 (2020)
3. Barmpoutis, A., et al.: Virtual kayaking: a study on the effect of low-cost passive haptics on the user experience while exercising. In: Stephanidis, C., Antona, M. (eds.) HCII 2020. CCIS, vol. 1225, pp. 147–155. Springer, Cham (2020). https://doi.org/10.1007/978-3-030-50729-9_20
4. Calandra, D., De Lorenzis, F., Cannavò, A., Lamberti, F.: Immersive virtual reality and passive haptic interfaces to improve procedural learning in a formal training course for first responders. Virtual Reality **27**(2), 985–1012 (2023)
5. Faltaous, S., et al.: Give weight to VR: manipulating users' perception of weight in virtual reality with electric muscle stimulation. In: Proceedings of Mensch und Computer 2022, pp. 533–538 (2022)
6. Franzluebbers, A., Johnsen, K.: Performance benefits of high-fidelity passive haptic feedback in virtual reality training. In: Proceedings of the 2018 ACM Symposium on Spatial User Interaction, pp. 16–24, October 2018
7. Fucentese, S.F., Rahm, S., Wieser, K., Spillmann, J., Harders, M., Koch, P.P.: Evaluation of a virtual-reality-based simulator using passive haptic feedback for knee arthroscopy. Knee Surg. Sports Traumatol. Arthrosc. **23**, 1077–1085 (2015)
8. Joyce, R.D., Robinson, S.: Passive haptics to enhance virtual reality simulations. In: AIAA Modeling and Simulation Technologies Conference, p. 1313 (2017)
9. Kim, D., Kim, Y., Jo, D.: Exploring the effect of virtual environments on passive haptic perception. Appl. Sci. **13**(1), 299 (2022)
10. Lam, J.: High noon air hockey. https://www.youtube.com/watch?v=cXw8-dAky9Y. Accessed 02 Feb 2024

11. Lee, S., Lee, M.: Can haptic feedback on one virtual object increase the presence of another virtual object? In: Proceedings of the 28th ACM Symposium on Virtual Reality Software and Technology, pp. 1–2, November 2022
12. Zenner, A., Krüger, A.: Shifty: a weight-shifting dynamic passive haptic proxy to enhance object perception in virtual reality. IEEE Trans. Visual Comput. Graph. **23**(4), 1285–1294 (2017)

# Collecting and Analyzing the Mid-Air Gestures Data in Augmented Reality and User Preferences in Closed Elicitation Study

Jieqiong Li[(⊠)], Adam S. Coler, Zahra Borhani, and Francisco R. Ortega

NUILab, Department of Computer Science, Colorado State University,
Fort Collins, CO 80521, USA
{ljq915,AdamWil,zahra.borhani,f.ortega}@colostate.edu

**Abstract.** For users of AR-HMDs (i.e., AR glasses), one option for interaction with the HMD is through midair gestures. This modality allows users to move their hands to grab objects, move objects, select menus, and interact with a multiple set of features provided by AR-HMDs. However, midair gestures are still difficult to recognize. For example, the Microsoft HoloLens 2 only provides a few gestures, and there are many false positives in the gesture recognition of the system. Further, it is not clear what gestures the users prefer. As a result, we performed a study with data collection on midair gestures for AR-HMDs with the aim of providing a gesture dataset that can be utilized in machine learning models. In addition, we analyzed the user gesture preferences for object manipulation. Our collected dataset includes the trajectory of hand gestures and eye gaze, which are captured by Articulated Hand Tracking (AHAT), inertial measurement unit (IMU) and other sensors. Our analysis showed that users have different gesture preferences for different categories of referents.

**Keywords:** Augmented Reality · Elicitation Study · Gesture Dataset · AR-HMD · Data Collection

## 1 Introduction

Elicitation studies started in 2009 with [1], followed by multiple studies (e.g., [2–4]) in the search for improved gesture interfaces. This has included elicitation studies in augmented reality (AR) head-mounted displays (HMDs), such as Williams et al. [5–7] and others [2,8,9]. The objective is to improve everyday use of HMDs in everyday life, work, and entertainment, aligning with the vision of Mark Weiser [10] to make the computer invisible. However, it is not known if there are preferences for different gesture sets (e.g., a gesture from set A and a gesture from set B), which are one of the products of elicitation studies. In

© The Author(s), under exclusive license to Springer Nature Switzerland AG 2024
J. Y. C. Chen and G. Fragomeni (Eds.): HCII 2024, LNCS 14707, pp. 201–215, 2024.
https://doi.org/10.1007/978-3-031-61044-8_15

this study, participants were asked to select their preferred gesture from different elicitation gesture sets while performing the gestures. In addition, we have collected all the videos and images, which can be found on the website[1].

The main contributions of this work are as follows: 1) preparing a well-curated mid-air gesture interaction dataset, aiming to improve the recognition of mid-air gestures in machine learning systems. 2) identifying users' preferences in gesture interaction for each referent by conducting a human-centric experiment.

## 2    Related Work

### 2.1    Mid-Air Gesture Data Collection

Li et al. (2019) pointed out that mid-air gestures can improve the overall user experience as compared to device-based remote control [11]. The collection of gesture data sets can greatly help the machine learning system learn and recognize mid-air gestures [11], thereby improving the user experience in the interactive environment, the system's flexibility, and the freedom of use. For example, Vogiatzidakis et al. (2020) improved the usability and user experience of smart furniture by adding mid-air gestures [4]. Williams et al. used an open elicitation study to develop a user-defined set of gesture interactions primarily for object manipulation to understand the user's gesture preferences in that direction [5]. Studying mid-air gestures by using elicitation studies has become one of the main research methods to understand user gesture types in different contexts.

The flexibility and feasibility of this research direction have gradually become an important topic in the field of HCI [12]. As a non-contact operation, mid-air interaction allows users to use mid-air gestures to remotely operate digital content displayed on the device [4,13]. This interaction method has the advantages of being intuitive, easy to execute, and memorable [14]. When wearing an AR-HMD (i.e., AR glasses), mid-air gestures are an option for interaction between the user and the HMD. Mid-air gestures allow users to move their hands to grab virtual objects, move objects, select menus, and interact with many of the features provided by AR-HMDs. The improvement and supplementation of the air gesture data set can increase the recognizability and diversity of AR-HMD's air gestures.

### 2.2    Closed Elicitation Study

An elicitation study is a classic method for researchers to study user action or interaction preferences [14]. This method was proposed by Vatavu et al. in 2009 [1]. Its main advantage is that the gestures are designed based on user preferences, thereby improving the user's interactive experience.

As a method suitable for gesture set design, elicitation studies can mainly help researchers understand user preferences for different devices [4], forms [3],

---

[1]  http://tinyurl.com/nuilabgs.

or application domains [1]. Wobbrock et al. compared three methods of designing gesture sets and came to the following conclusions [9]: The gesture sets designed by researchers and users are more suitably designed by users only or researchers only. This result demonstrates the importance of participatory design for researchers to understand user preferences and collect relevant action forms early in the experiment. The results of the research on gestures by using an elicitation study show that, under the same gesture, the user will change the size of the gesture according to the size of the interacting object [2]. For different numbers of target objects, the users prefer to use both hands to interact with two objects, and for a single object, users prefer to interact with one hand [8].

As compared with an open elicitation study, a closed elicitation study requires users to complete suggestions for gesture preferences based on the appropriate gestures provided as a reference [7]. Its main purpose is still to find the natural choice after participants understand the command. The preference study mentioned in this article, also called a closed induction study [7], requires users to select their favorite interaction after each reference (i.e., 3 gestures, a total of 3 recordings for each referent). This preference study not only has the primary purpose of obtaining a more diverse and richer dataset of ego-centric mid-air gestures, but also explores the relationship between gesture preferences, referents, and gesture types in comparison to previous studies.

**Fig. 1.** Screenshot of the initial interface of the experimental software (Left), and a researcher testing HoloLens 2 (right)

## 3   Methods

An elicitation study was conducted to investigate gesture interactions for manipulating rendered 3D objects in optical see-through AR environments. The input modality used was a unimodal gesture modality. A Wizard of Oz (WoZ) [4] experimental design was employed, where the experimenter emulated a live system. In a Wizard of Oz experiment, participants interact with a mock interface controlled by the experimenter. Participants were presented with a pre-recorded video demonstrating a specific gesture, and they were instructed to replicate the gesture in three consecutive trials. A total of 23 referents were tested in a within-subjects experiment design. The study incorporated canonical referents (translation, rotation, and scale) alongside abstract referents (copy, paste, cut, create, destroy, and select). Table 1 shows a list of gesture referents used in this study.

**Table 1.** Type of gestures and relative gesture referents. *C: Clockwise, CC: Counter Clockwise

| Manipulation | Gesture Referents | | |
|---|---|---|---|
| Translation | Move Up | Move Down | Move Left |
| | Move Right | Move Forward | Move Away |
| Rotation | Roll C | Roll CC | Yaw Left |
| | Yaw Right | Pitch Up | Pitch Down |
| Scale\ Selection | Enlarge one object | Shrink one object | Select one object |
| | Enlarge two objects | Shrink two objects | Select two objects |
| Abstract | Copy | Paste | Cut |
| | Create | Destroy | |

### 3.1    Apparatus

The AR environment was developed using Unity Game Engine 2019.2.18f1, Mixed Reality ToolKit (MRTK), and C# programming language. An Alienware Laptop with an Intel i7-8750h and NVIDIA Geforce RTX 2060 6 GB GPU was used for the development. The interface of the software is mainly composed of two 3D objects (cube and sphere) available for user manipulation, a text-based referent indicating the required manipulations, an animation illustrating the referents' actions, the name of the input modality (i.e., gesture only), and the trial number. Additionally, there are two hand-shaped icons serving as indicators of the user's hands within the device's field of view. If either of the user's hands is not detected on the screen, the corresponding hand icon disappears. Figure 1 (left) shows a screenshot of the participants' view during the experiment. Since there are task requirements for multi-object operation in this experiment, the yellow cube will be used as the main pseudo-interaction object for all of tasks, and the green sphere will be used as the auxiliary object for the multi-object task, as shown in Fig. 1 (left) and Fig. 2. In addition, the software collects the following data in the background: depth gesture images, finger joints, and eye gaze movement trajectories in the gesture data space.

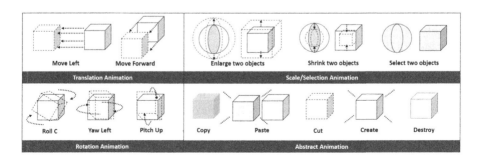

**Fig. 2.** Animation schematic diagram of some referents in the experiment application

This study was conducted using a Microsoft HoloLens 2 AR-HMD, which provides Articulated Hand Tracking (AHAT). The AHAT was used to collect the depth images of the participant's hand [15]. By using the AHAT depth camera, researchers captured the hand information from an ego-centric perspective. This information was then integrated with the Mixed Reality Toolkit (MRTK) in Unity to obtain depth gesture images, finger joint data, and the trajectory of eye gaze movement in a spatial position for each referent [15]. Furthermore, An inertial measurement unit (IMU) sensor was used to collect raw data from the accelerometer, gyroscope, and magnetometer during the experiment [15]. In addition to the depth camera, a GoPro Hero 7 mounted on an AR-HMD was employed to record color video.

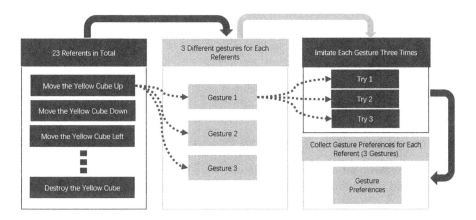

**Fig. 3.** Experiment Process

In order to improve the running performance of the software, depth gesture images were stored as RAW type images. After the experiment, the RAW type images were converted into PNG type gesture data images by using Unity scripts. In addition, the noise in data images was eliminated by using Python script. Its main methods involve eliminating noise in fixed areas, removing randomly appearing black spots, and deleting non-gesture data in error/experiment gaps. In addition to data processing, a Python script was utilized for image conversion video to generate a 4K video for each gesture. Each video contained three imitations of the gesture by the participant and used the name of referents to group and name the gesture depth videos. Except the processing of depth images, eye gaze spatial position data, position data of 19 joints of each hand, palm, and wrist, IMU data will be converted into CSV type files, and the color video will be cut and stored too.

## 3.2 Research Objective and Hypotheses

The aim of this research project was to explore the preferential differences between gesture types for various referents and different categories (e.g., translation, rotation, scale, etc.). This would also help us to summarize our findings and provide suggestions and ideas for future gesture designs. More specifically, we investigated the following research questions, which are inspired by similar previous work [5–7]:

- $R_1$: Does the type of referent in the translation category affect user preferences on how to perform a gesture (two fingers, one palm, or two palms)?
- $R_2$: Similarly, does the type of referent in the rotation category affect user preferences for associated gestures (two fingers, one palm, or two palms)?
- $R_3$: How do these preferences vary for referants in the translation and rotation categories?
- $R_4$: Do users strongly favor one of their options (pitch, grab x-axis, and graph y-axis) for the referents in the single-object scaling category?
- $R_5$: What about multi-object scaling; do users have a strong preference for any of their gesture options (palms two-hands, pitch two-hands, and grab two-hands)?
- $R_6$: How does the type of abstract referents (including copy, paste, and cut) affect user preference for the associated gestures (pitch three fingers, point two hands, and grab two hands)?

### 3.3    Procedure and Task

Before the experiment started, participants were asked to sign an informed consent form and were informed that the gesture data during the experiment would be recorded and used for research. An experimenter provided instructions on how to wear a Microsoft HoloLens 2 HMD and how to calibrate the eye gaze tracking. To ensure the accuracy of the depth image results and enhance the integrity of data collection, participants were asked to look straight ahead during the experiment (Fig. 4).

To minimize the impact of the order effect, the pre-recorded gesture videos for each referent were presented in a counter-balanced order using Latin squares. For each referent, the three different gestures were presented in random order. Participants were required to imitate the gestures shown in the pre-recorded videos and repeat them three times.Figure 3 shows this experiment process. After completing three gestures for one referent, the experimenter asked the participant about their gesture preference for that referent. Each experiment took around one hour. To reduce the experimental bias caused by fatigue, the researcher gave a break during the experiment based on agreement.

### 3.4    Participants

A total of 20 participants (10 Female, 10 Male) were recruited to participate in the experiment. All participants reported normal or corrected to normal vision. Two participants reported that they were left-handed. The participants included undergraduate and graduate students, faculty, or alumni of Colorado State University. Almost all participants were not familiar with AR and virtual

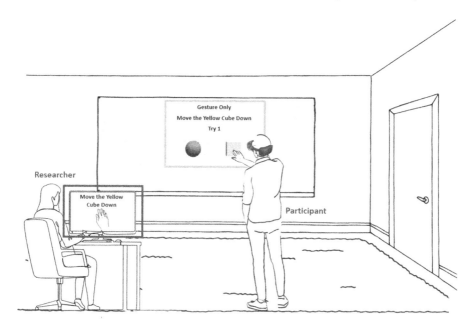

**Fig. 4.** Experimental simulation diagram, this figure includes a researcher (left), a participant (middle), and pre-recorded videos (left box), and the experimental animation demonstration which only can be seen when participants wearing HoloLens 2 (middle box).

reality (VR). Seventeen participants had never used an AR-HMD (e.g., Microsoft HoloLens 2 HMD) which can reduce the influence of participants' habits on the experimental results. Upon the completion of the experiment, participants could choose compensation in the form of 20$gift cards or in-class credit points. Or they could choose to participate in this experiment as volunteers.

## 4    Results

Our results consist of two main parts: 1) providing a mid-air gesture data set that can enhance the recognition of mid-air gestures. 2) assessing our hypothesis to explore users' preferences in gestures used for executing each referent.

### 4.1    Mid-Air Gesture Dataset

Our dataset includes three gestures per referent, each gesture was performed three times by users resulting in a total of nine gestures for each referent. Our study investigated a total of 23 referents across 20 participants, collecting information on 4,140 (23 ∗ 3 ∗ 3 ∗ 20) gesture trials. The AHAT depth camera on the Microsoft HoloLens 2 AR-HMD provided the ability to capture hand information from an egocentric perspective including depth gesture images, finger joints, and eye gaze trajectories in space. The recordings (depth images) were transformed, segmented, and denoised before being integrated with the data to produce independent depth videos for each gesture. Figure 5 shows some example images of these post-processed depth gesture videos. In addition, each of these 4k depth videos is accompanied by eye gaze spatial position data, and position data of 19 joints of each hand, palm, and wrist.

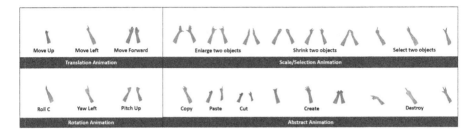

**Fig. 5.** Some results of gesture depth images

## 4.2   Gesture Preferences

The distribution of user preferences among three gesture types for canonical and abstract referents is presented in Table 2 and Table 3, respectively. Each table represents a distinct category, including its associated referents. For example, the translation category consists of six referents for translating an object in various directions: up, down, left, right, forward, and away. Users were presented with three different gesture options for each of these referents, as shown in the first column of each table. Figure 6 provides the image of these three gestures, in the same order as the rows of the tables, for each referent, along with the number of participants who chose that gesture among the three (out of 20).

## 4.3   Fisher–Freeman–Halton Exact Test

For each of the proposed research questions in Sect. 3.2, the statistical significance for gesture preferences is assessed using the Fisher–Freeman–Halton Exact test (FFH Exact test) [16], which is a statistical test used for analyzing contingency tables, particularly when the sample sizes are small (in our case, 20 participants) and the size of the contingency table is large (e.g., $3*6$ contingency table for the translation category). IBM SPSS Statistics (SPSS) was used for the analysis of the FFH Exact test [18]. Table 4 shows the p-value and value for the FFH Exact Test related to our six research questions.

$R_1$ explores how the type of referent in the translation category affects user preferences on how to perform a gesture. The translation category includes six referents (move up/down/left /right/forward/away), and three gesture types

**Table 2.** The percentage result of user preferences for first half of the referents. All gesture demonstrations and explanations can be found in Fig. 6. In each table, the last column labeled "All" displays the distribution of all referents within their corresponding categories. For each column, the largest value is presented in bold.

(a) The percentage result of user preferences for translation *F: forward, A: away,

| Translation | Gesture Referents | | | | | | All |
|---|---|---|---|---|---|---|---|
| Gestures | Move Up | Move Down | Move Left | Move Right | Move F* | Move A* | All |
| Two Fingers | 15% | 40% | 45% | **50%** | 15% | 20% | 32.5% |
| One Palm | **75%** | **60%** | **55%** | 45% | **50%** | **55%** | **56.7%** |
| Two Palms | 10% | 0 | 0 | 5% | 25% | 25% | 10.8% |

(b) The percentage result of user preferences for rotation *C: Clockwise, CC: Counter Clockwise

| Rotation | Gesture Referents | | | | | | All |
|---|---|---|---|---|---|---|---|
| Gestures | Roll C* | Roll CC* | Yaw Left | Yaw Right | Pitch Up | Pitch Down | All |
| Two Fingers | **60%** | **70%** | **60%** | **60%** | **55%** | 40% | **57.5%** |
| One Palm | 40% | 25% | 30% | 35% | 40% | **55%** | 37.5% |
| Two Palms | 0 | 5% | 10% | 5% | 5% | 5% | 5% |

(c) The percentage result of user preferences for scale one object

| Scale | Gesture Referents | | All |
|---|---|---|---|
| Gestures | Enlarge One Object | Shrink One Object | All |
| Pitch | **80%** | **75%** | **82.5%** |
| Grab X-axis | 20% | 15% | 17.5% |
| Grab Y-axis | 0 | 0 | 0 |

(d) The percentage result of user preferences for scale two objects

| Scale | Gesture Referents | | All |
|---|---|---|---|
| Gestures | Enlarge Two Objects | Shrink Two Objects | All |
| Palm Two Hands | 5% | 15% | 10% |
| Pitch Two Hands | **50%** | 35% | 42.5% |
| Grab Two Hands | 45% | **50%** | **47.5%** |

(two fingers, one palm, and two palms). The results from the FFH Exact test did not produce a statistically significant result ($p = 0.026$). This means that the differences in user preferences between the three gesture groups within the translation category were not large enough to be considered statistically significant. This indicates that there were no differences between participants' gesture choices for the referents in this category and the users' preferences were similar for these referents.

Similarly, $R_2$ examines whether there was any significant difference in user preferences when selecting among three gesture types for the referents in the rotation category (Roll C/CC, Yaw Left/Right, and Pitch Up/Down). The results from the FFH Exact test revealed no significant difference among the six rotation referents ($p = 0.745$), indicating that different rotation referents did not influence users' preferences in selecting gestures. As the values in Table 2 show, the participants' gesture choices were relatively uniform within this category, as well.

**Table 3.** The percentage result of user preferences for second half of the referents. All gesture demonstrations and explanations can be found in Fig. 6. In each table, the last column labeled "All" displays the distribution of all referents within their corresponding categories. For each column, the largest value is presented in bold.

(a) The percentage result of user preferences for select

| Select | Gesture Referents | Select | Gesture Referents |
|---|---|---|---|
| Gestures | Select One Object | Gestures | Select Two Objects |
| Point | **55%** | Point (2 Times) | **35%** |
| Pitch | 25% | Pitch (2 Times) | 30% |
| Grab | 20% | Grab (One Palm) | **35%** |

(b) The percentage result of user preferences for abstract

| Abstract | Gesture Referents | | | All |
|---|---|---|---|---|
| Gestures | Copy | Paste | Cut | All |
| Pitch Three Fingers | **90%** | 35% | **75%** | **66.7%** |
| Point Two Hands | 5% | **40%** | 25% | 23.3% |
| Grab Two Hands | 5% | 25% | 0 | 10% |

(c) The percentage result of user preferences for abstract *TS: Towards Self, SD: Swipe Diagonal, DX: Draw X

| Abstract | Gesture Referents | Abstract | Gesture Referents |
|---|---|---|---|
| Gestures | Create | Gestures | Destroy |
| Bloom Up | **90%** | Index Finger SD* | **65%** |
| Bloom Up TS* | 0 | Index Finger Dx* | 5% |
| Open Book | 10% | Grab and Throw | 30% |

$R_3$ investigated user gesture preferences across both rotation and translation categories. Although the results for $R_1$ and $R_2$ showed the types of referents within each of the translation and rotation categories did not have any effect on user preferences, the outcome from the FFH Exact test revealed significant differences for the preferences across these categories ($p < 0.001$). As shown in Table 4, the p-value is less than 0.005, indicating that users preferred different gesture types while performing the referents of these categories.

$R_4$ and $R_5$ explore whether the act of shrinking or enlarging an object can result in different gesture preferences, for single objects and multiple objects, respectively. The results obtained from the FFH Exact test indicate no significant difference for either single-object or multi-object analyses (P-value $= 0.407$ for single objects and p-value $= 0.44$ for multi-objects). This suggests that the act of shrinking or enlarging an object does not affect gesture preferences, whether applied to single-object scaling or multi-object scaling. The participants' choice among the three gestures was more uniform for the referents in the single-object scaling category.

Finally, our last research question, $R_6$, investigated the effect of copy, paste, and cut referents on the gestures that users preferred (Point, Pitch, and Grab). The outcome of the FFH Exact test produced statistically significant results

**Table 4.** FFH Exact test result, The value of exact sig. (s-tailed) are written in bold and marked by one star (**) for values less than 0.005. This emphasizes the statistically significant outcome of these research questions

| $R_1$ | Value | Exact sig. (2-tailed) | $R_2$ | Value | Exact sig. (2-tailed) |
|---|---|---|---|---|---|
| FFH Exact test | 18.804 | 0.026 | **FFH Exact test** | 6.820 | 0.745 |
| $R_3$ | Value | Exact sig. (2-tailed) | $R_4$ | Value | Exact sig. (2-tailed) |
| FFH Exact test | 16.603 | **0.00022 ** | FFH Exact test | – | 0.407 |
| $R_5$ | Value | Exact sig. (2-tailed) | $R_6$ | Value | Exact sig. (2-tailed) |
| FFH Exact test | 1.53 | 0.44 | **FFH Exact test** | 16.249 | **0.00087 ** |

($p < 0.001$). Participants had certain different gesture choices for these three referent types.

## 5    Discussion

By analyzing the gesture preference data collected in the experiment, we learned that participants showed a preference for the "one Palm" gesture followed by the "Two Fingers" gesture for translation gestures. However, in the case of rotation, the "Two Fingers" gesture emerged as the most popular choice. When it came to scaling a single object, the majority of participants favored the "Pitch" gesture. However, for scaling two objects, participants almost equally preferred both the "Pitch Two Hands" and "Grab Two Hands" gestures.

In addition, our findings showed that users preferred simple pantomimic mid-air gestures (i.e., a gesture of performance or imitate for a special task [19], such as the "bloom up" gesture in the create) over two-handed and complex gestures (i.e., "Open book" gesture in the create). This result aligns with the trends observed in prior elicitation studies [5,6].

Participants preferred to use pantomimic gestures for referents with more complex meanings (i.e., create object/ destroy object). These pantomimic gestures enabled users to convey a richer meaning compared to the simple directional gestures observed, where participants traced out a square with their fingertips to create an object.

Furthermore, some users seemed to have a consistent preference among the gesture types. For example, they are more likely to choose the palm gesture for a referent if they have already selected a palm gesture for the earlier referents. This tendency may have been caused by participants wanting to increase the memorability of their set of preferred interactions.

* ➝ : Solid arrow, gesture position and gesture shape, or only gesture position, change in the direction of the arrow

* ---▶ : Dashed arrow, only gesture shape, change in the direction of the arrow

* 2 times: Perform the same gesture twice

**Fig. 6.** Gestures schematic diagram for all of gestures with result of preferences. *C: Clockwise, CC: Counter

Our findings recommend following a certain level of uniformity for canonical gesture categories in the gesture design in future systems because users showed similar preferences among the three gesture types for the referents in each of these categories. However, this does not generalize to user gestures in different categories, so researchers need to consider the connection between user preferences and the corresponding category of the referent in future gesture designs.

Figure 6 shows that participants preferred to use the "Pitch Three Fingers" over "Point Two Hands" and "Grab Two Hands" gestures for both Copy and Cut referents. For the paste referent, they did not show any specific preferences among the three gestures. However, if we compare the one-hand gestures to two-hand gestures, our findings showed a preference for two-hand gestures over one-hand gestures (two-hand gestures: 65% and one-hand gestures: 35%). On the other hand, users favored one-hand gestures over two-hand gestures for Copy (one-hand gestures: 90%, two-hand gestures: 10%) and Cut (one-hand gestures: 75% and two-hand gestures: 25%) referents. A possible explanation for this preference may be attributed to the dynamic nature of the paste operation, involving transforming a single object into multiple objects. Participants generally agreed that this transition could be better conveyed using both hands.

# 6 Conclusion and Future Work

The user-centered mid-air gesture dataset presented here can be used to improve mid-air interactions in AR by improving training quality for real-time machine learning systems that enable gesture recognition. Deep gesture videos and photos contain more gesture information, and the data includes the spatial positions of finger joints, palms, etc., as well as the gaze position of the eyes. It can provide assistance and information supplements for future machine learning applications and analysis. In addition, due to issues such as gesture data sample size and referent classification, this article analyzes the independence between gesture types and referents. Furthermore, the insights from the analysis of participants' preferences can help better equip interaction designers when they seek to develop intuitive systems. One example of such a design guideline is that interactions for translation and rotation referents should be kept simple while abstract referents may benefit from pantomimic gestures. Last but not least, according to the data results, a unified type of gesture can be used for each operation type, providing more design ideas for subsequent gesture design and system development. For future work, we can increase the number of gesture options, increase the sample size, analyze the situation of closed elicitation study under object manipulation, and study more possibilities for users in gesture selection. In addition, we can utilize our existing gesture data information to train better gesture recognition systems.

**Acknowledge.** This work was supported by the National Science Foundation (NSF) awards NSF 1948254, NSF 2106590, NSF 2016714, NSF 2037417, and NSF 1948254. We would like to acknowledge Jo Carroll for the edits.

# References

1. Vatavu, R.-D., Wobbrock, J.O.: Formalizing agreement analysis for elicitation studies: new measures, significance test, and toolkit. In: Proceedings of the 33rd Annual ACM Conference on Human Factors in Computing Systems, CHI '15, pp. 1325–1334. Association for Computing Machinery, New York, NY, USA (2015)
2. Morris, M.R., Wobbrock, J.O., Wilson, A.D.: Understanding users' preferences for surface gestures. In: Proceedings of Graphics Interface 2010 (GI '10). Canadian Information Processing Society, CAN, pp. 261–268 (2010)
3. Vatavu, A.-D.: The dissimilarity-consensus approach to agreement analysis in gesture elicitation studies. In: Proceedings of the 2019 CHI Conference on Human Factors in Commputing Systems, CHI '19, pp. 1–13. Association for Computing Machinery, New York, NY, USA (2019)
4. Vogiatzidakis, P., Koutsabasis, P.: Mid-air gesture control of multiple home devices in spatial augmented reality prototype. Multimodal Technol. Interact. **4**, 61 (2020). https://doi.org/10.3390/mti4030061
5. Williams, A.S., Garcia, J., Ortega, F.: Understanding multimodal user gesture and speech behavior for object manipulation in augmented reality using elicitation. IEEE Trans Visual. Comput. Graph. **26**(12), 3479–3489 (2020). https://doi.org/10.1109/TVCG.2020.3023566
6. Williams, A.S., Ortega, F.R.: Understanding gesture and speech multimodal interactions for manipulation tasks in augmented reality using unconstrained elicitation. Proc. ACM Hum.-Comput. Interact. **4**, 21 p., 202 (2020). https://doi.org/10.1145/3427330
7. Williams, A.S., Ortega, F.R.: A concise guide to elicitation methodology. Proc. ACM Hum.-Comput. Interact (cs. HC). B. **4**, 62 p., A. 2, Journals CoRR (2021). arXiv:2105.12865, https://arxiv.org/abs/2105.12865
8. Chan, E., Seyed, T., Stuerzlinger, W., Yang, X.-D., Maurer, F.: User elicitation on single-hand microgestures. In: Proceedings of the 2016 CHI Conference on Human Factors in Computing Systems (CHI '16), pp. 3403–3414. Association for Computing Machinery, New York, NY, USA (2016). https://doi.org/10.1145/2858036.2858589
9. Wobbrock, J.O., Morris, M.R., Wilson, A.D.: User-defined gestures for surface computing. In: Proceedings of the SIGCHI Conference on Human Factors in Computing Systems (CHI '09), pp. 1083–1092. Association for Computing Machinery, New York, NY, USA (2009). https://doi.org/10.1145/1518701.1518866
10. Weiser, M.: The computer for the 21st century. SIGMOBILE Mob. Comput. Commun. Rev. **3**(3), 3–11 (1999). https://doi.org/10.1145/329124.329126
11. Li, X., Guan, D., Zhou, M., Zhang, J., Liu, X., Li, S.: Comparison on user experience of mid-air gesture interaction and traditional remotes control. In: Proceedings of the Seventh International Symposium of Chinese CHI (Chinese CHI '19), pp. 16–22. Association for Computing Machinery, New York, NY, USA (2019). https://doi.org/10.1145/3332169.3333570
12. Dewitz, B., Steinicke, F., Geiger, C.: Functional workspace for one-handed tap and swipe microgestures. In: Mensch und Computer 2019 - Workshopband, Bonn. Gesellschaft für Informatik e.V (2019)
13. Koutsabasis, P., Vogiatzidakis, P.: Empirical research in mid-air interaction: a systematic review. Int. J. Hum.–Comput. Interact. **35**, 1747–1768 (2019)
14. Morris, M.R., et al.: Reducing legacy bias in gesture elicitation studies. Interactions **21**(3), , 40–45 (2014). https://doi.org/10.1145/2591689

15. Ungureanu, D., Bogo, F., Microsoft etc.: HoloLens 2 Research Mode as a Tool for Computer Vision Research, Microsoft (2020). https://arxiv.org/abs/2008.11239
16. Freeman, G.H., Halton, J.H.: Note on an exact treatment of contingency, goodness of fit and other problems of significance. Biometrika **38**, 141–149 (1951)
17. Kim, H.Y.: Statistical notes for clinical researchers: chi-squared test and Fisher's exact test. Restor. Dent. Endod. **42**(2), 152–155 (2017). https://doi.org/10.5395/rde.2017.42.2.152. Epub 2017 Mar 30. PMID: 28503482; PMCID: PMC5426219
18. Mehta, C.R., Patel, N.R.: IBM SPSS Exact Tests. IBM Corporation, Armonk, NY (2011)
19. Aigner, R., et al.: Understanding Mid-Air Hand Gestures: A Study of Human Preferences in Usage of Gesture Types for HCI (2012)

# Research on the Multisensory Feedback Representation of the Menu Cards in VR Home Interface

Shangge Li[1], Jing Zhang[2], Xingcheng Di[2], and Chengqi Xue[1(✉)]

[1] Southeast University, NO. 2 Dongnandaxue Road, Jiangning District, Nanjing, China
ipd_xcq@seu.edu.cn
[2] Nanjing Forestry University, NO. 159 Longpan Road, Xuanwu District, Nanjing, China

**Abstract.** In the rapidly evolving field of virtual reality (VR), user experience issues in VR home interfaces are increasingly prominent as the user base expands. This study focuses on the VR home interface's tab menu, the initial point of user interaction with the VR system, pivotal in shaping first impressions and user motivation. The prevalent design approach extends traditional 2D interface methodologies, notably in menu card feedback representations, crucial for user navigation and understanding of VR environments. However, replicating 2D designs in VR often falls short of user expectations and the unique spatial nature of VR interfaces, highlighting the need for optimized design methods tailored to VR's interaction characteristics. This paper investigates user perceptions of different feedback representations in VR home interface menu cards. In a between-subjects experiment (N = 30), participants engaged with various feedback combinations in VR home interface menu cards and evaluated their experiences. Results indicate that while visual, auditory, and haptic feedback combination offers the highest immersion, the visual and auditory feedback mix scores best in user experience and usability, providing a balanced immersive experience. These findings suggest the visual-auditory combination as the optimal feedback representation for VR home interface menu selections, offering insights for future VR interface design.

**Keywords:** VR interaction · VR home interface · user experience · menu cards · selection feedback · usability

## 1 Introduction

Virtual Reality (VR) is an immersive interactive environment based on simulation technology, sensing technology, and multimedia computer technology [1]. It is generated by computers and acts on users through multiple sensory stimuli such as visual, auditory, tactile, and olfactory senses, providing users with an immersive experience [2]. However, as the number of users rapidly increases, issues related to user experience such as usability, affective ergonomics, and emotionalization in VR interfaces, which are closely related to users, have begun to emerge [3]. Apart from the technical bottlenecks, many issues causing poor user experience are rooted in the fact that the design of interface

© The Author(s), under exclusive license to Springer Nature Switzerland AG 2024
J. Y. C. Chen and G. Fragomeni (Eds.): HCII 2024, LNCS 14707, pp. 216–229, 2024.
https://doi.org/10.1007/978-3-031-61044-8_16

elements in many existing VR interactive interfaces is based on experience, directly applying traditional 2D interface designs. Rarely are they tailor-made and evaluated based on VR's unique characteristics of imaginativeness, interactivity, and immersion [4, 5]. Mismatched interface element designs lead to a user experience that is far from user expectations. Especially the VR home interface containing navigation menus, as the primary interface users encounter in the VR system, not only forms the first impression of the VR virtual world but is also crucial in quickly attracting user attention and stimulating the desire to explore further VR applications. Although the VR home interface menu continues the card-style menu of 2D interfaces [6], unlike traditional 2D interfaces with mouse or touch interactions, users browse the VR home interface's card menus by hovering, selecting, and clicking with a cursor controlled by the VR controller. During this process, the feedback rules and prompt information of these card menus play an important role in helping users perceive and understand the VR system, acting as the main elements for users to choose target applications or functions, directly affecting users' cognitive behavior and operational fluency. Therefore, in designing VR interfaces, designers should align with the depth of VR interaction, starting from VR interaction characteristics to tailor-make the most suitable home interface menu form for the VR virtual space, thereby enhancing the level of user experience in VR interactions from the moment users enter the VR world.

User experience extends beyond the realm of interaction technology; it represents a methodological approach that encompasses not only the structural and functional quality of products but also delves into users' emotional needs and experiential perspectives [7]. It encompasses all responses and outcomes related to the current or anticipated use of products, systems, or services [8], involving both the emotional experiences of the user and the functional experience of the usage entity [9]. Presently, numerous scholars have explored the relationship between VR interaction feedback modalities and user experience from various perspectives, such as feedback from gesture actions in VR games [10], high-fidelity passive haptic feedback [11], and precise touch input feedback [12]. However, these studies predominantly focus on the tactile feedback representations of VR gestures or controllers, emphasizing the gesture or tactile aspect at the user input end, and tend to overlook the multisensory feedback representations at the VR interface presentation end. For instance, Park (2017) [10] and other scholars explored the user experience differences in gesture trajectories and inputs under VR game gesture interactions with two different visual feedback types: line rendering and particle rendering. Franzluebbers (2018) [11], through an experiment with a VR simulated golf club, demonstrated that high-fidelity passive haptic feedback provides a better user experience than active feedback under tracking controllers. Matulic (2021) [12] found that semi-transparent thumb shadow overlays as a representation of visual feedback in VR environments can effectively enhance user experience. In the realm of application, current VR application development focuses primarily on the visual design and interaction mechanisms of VR applications or games [13–16], while the interaction experience in the VR home interface remains largely overlooked. The VR home interface, being the gateway to all VR applications or game programs, plays a crucial role. Prior to entering the main VR applications, a well-designed menu selection feedback mechanism can assist users in quickly and smoothly locating target objects. Conversely, poor design can lead to user confusion and disorientation, exacerbating the disorienting effects of VR interactions and negatively impacting user experience. Simply replicating traditional 2D home interface card menu feedback methods based on experience, without considering compatibility with the VR three-dimensional space, can directly diminish the user experience in VR interactions.

In this paper, we utilize subjective questionnaire scales to explore user experiences with different multimodal feedback methods for card menus in the VR home interface. We first categorize and organize the interaction feedback representations of card menus in the VR home interface. Then, we represent the different channel feedback representations in the experiment using the most common feedback representations for each of the three channels. Next, subjects will browse combinations of feedback representations across the three channels and complete subjective questionnaire scales afterwards. Finally, through the analysis of the scales, we discuss the reasons behind user preferences and offer suggestions for the design of feedback representations for design elements in the VR home interface.

## 2  Method

### 2.1  Participants

Given that college students are among the most interested and experienced users of VR technology, we recruited 30 students from Southeast University as participants for our study. As depicted in Table 1, the demographic characteristics of the participants consisted of 17 males (56.7%) and 13 females (43.3%). The age range of participants was between 21 to 27 years, with an average age of 24 years. Many of the participants (70%) expressed an interest in VR technology, while only 6.7% indicated a lack of interest. This trend was anticipated, considering that the younger generation has grown up in the digital age and is naturally inclined to be curious about and explore emerging technologies. Notably, 83.3% of the participants had previous experience with VR technology and had interacted with VR home interfaces, whereas only 10% had never engaged with VR technology and were unfamiliar with the interaction modalities of VR interfaces (see Table 1).

### 2.2  Apparatus and Stimuli

The experiment program was developed by Unity 3D and ran on Meta Quest 2. The screen resolution of the HMD was $1832 \times 1920$ pixels per eye, while the FOV was 97 and the refresh rate was 90 Hz. (see Fig. 1).

The experimental setup included eight VR home interface menu card sets, each with distinct multimodal feedback: 1) none; 2) vision; 3) auditory; 4) haptic; 5) vision-haptic; 6) auditory-haptic; 7) vision-auditory; 8) vision-auditory-haptic. Presented in a $2 \times 3$ matrix, each menu card measured $489 \times 276$ pixels. Aligning with Google's VR design guidelines (Daydream Stickersheet), all matrices were positioned centrally within the Field of View (FOV), ensuring a comfortable viewing angle of approximately 60°. To ensure unirepresentationity and reduce visual bias, each menu card set had identical

**Table 1.** Demographic characteristic of participants

| Characteristic | Group | Number of participants (%) |
| --- | --- | --- |
| Sex | Male | 17(56.7%) |
| | Female | 13(43.3%) |
| Age | <=24 | 20(66.7%) |
| | >=25 | 10(33.3%) |
| Interest | Uninterested | 21(70%) |
| | Normal | 7(23.3%) |
| | Interested | 2(6.7%) |
| Experience | Experienced | 25(83.3%) |
| | Inexperienced | 5(16.7%) |

**Fig. 1.** Visual Scope Design of the Interface

content and followed a standard design, featuring real VR application-derived content, screened and adapted for the experiment. The layout was a non-prioritized, palace-style format as per Google's guidelines [17]. The VR environment used a bright ambient background (#EEEEEE) against deep black card menus (#212121) to enhance contrast and prevent misjudgment.

## 2.3 Measurement

In this study, we conducted an experiment to investigate the impact of different multi-modal interaction feedback representations on user experience in the VR home interface menu cards. Multimodal sensory systems primarily involve three sensory channels:

visual, auditory, and haptic [18]. In the experiment, participants were instructed to freely browse through various sensory channel selection feedback representations on the VR home interface using the Oculus Quest 2 headset: 1) Visual channel feedback was represented by enlarging the hovered-over menu card to indicate selection; 2) Auditory channel feedback was conveyed through default sound effects to indicate selection; 3) Haptic channel feedback was indicated by a brief controller vibration. After browsing, participants filled out four sets of subjective questionnaire scales. Figure 1 illustrates the representation of feedback for these three channels.

**Visual Channel Feedback.** Visual channel feedback is the most common form of feedback in VR interactions. After surveying a wide range of VR selection feedback representations currently on the market, we decided to use an enlarged image to represent the visual channel feedback.

**Auditory Channel Feedback.** Auditory channel feedback in our study was delivered through the VR headset's speakers or headphones, using the default sound effects from the Oculus Quest 2's home interface as the material to represent the auditory channel feedback.

**Haptic Channel Feedback.** Haptic channel feedback is a unique and currently popular area of research in VR environments. Compared to various haptic gloves and other auxiliary equipment, the most widely used form of haptic feedback in VR technology remains controller vibration. In our study, we utilized the VR controller's vibration function to represent haptic channel feedback, with a vibration duration of 1 s and a median amplitude intensity of 0.5.

To comprehensively evaluate the user experience of different sensory channel selection feedback representations for the VR home interface card menus, our study, building upon previous research methodologies, proposed to assess user experience from two aspects: emotional and functional experiences in VR [19, 20]. Considering the importance of presence and immersion in the VR interaction experience, we used the UEQ (User Experience Questionnaire) and IPQ (Igroup Presence Questionnaire) scales [21, 22] to assess users' emotional and psychological experiences in VR. For evaluating the functional experience in VR, we used the SUS (System Usability Scale) and PSSUQ (Post-Study System Usability Questionnaire) scales [20]. Based on these four scales, our study explores the relationship between different sensory channel selection feedback representations in the VR home interface card menus and the level of user experience, aiming to provide effective references and suggestions for subsequent VR home interface design (see Fig. 2).

**Emotional Experience.** Emotional experience assessment comprises two parts, the UEQ and IPQ questionnaires. The UEQ (User Experience Questionnaire) is divided into seven levels, each involving a pair of antonymous word groups. The positive and negative words represent the extent of agreement or disagreement on a scale from 1 to 7. The IPQ (Igroup Presence Questionnaire) for immersion experience also has seven levels (0 to 6), where each level corresponds to a pair of antonymous words representing different degrees of sensation.

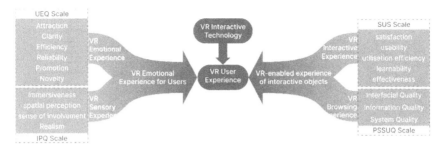

**Fig. 2.** User experience analysis of the main VR interface

**Functional Experience.** Functional experience assessment includes the SUS and PSSUQ scales. The SUS (System Usability Scale) is divided into five levels (1–5), each representing a different degree of agreement or disagreement, with 1 being strongly disagree and 5 being strongly agree. The PSSUQ (Post-Study System Usability Questionnaire) assesses overall system usability on a scale of seven levels (7 to 1), where 7 signifies strong disagreement and 1 signifies strong agreement.

In this case study, as described above, the multimodal feedback in the VR home interface menu cards provides users with three different channel representations: visual, auditory, and haptic. Although the different combinations of sensory channel feedback representations do not affect the content seen by participants, we hypothesize that users will have varying user experiences when interacting with different combinations of sensory channel feedback representations.

## 2.4  Procedure

In this study, participants, after entering their information, were assisted in donning the VR headset to begin the experiment. They initially read instructions and completed a practice task to familiarize themselves with the VR environment and controls. The main experiment involved freely browsing through eight different VR home interface card menu feedback representations (none; vision; auditory; haptic; vision-haptic; auditory-haptic; vision-auditory; vision-auditory-haptic), each for 10 s. Users interacted with the card menus using the VR controller, with each selection triggering corresponding feedback. Following each set, an interval screen appeared before proceeding to the next trial. Post-experiment, participants immediately completed four scales to assess their experience and minimize memory bias. A brief interview was also conducted for additional insights into their VR experiences. The experimental procedure and the recording of the scenarios and interfaces are depicted in Figs. 3 and 4, respectively.

## 2.5  Data Collection

The questionnaires were created and collected via the WJX website (www.wjx.cn), so all questionnaires were completed by participants using electronic devices. The ratings of the multimodal feedback representations of the different VR home interface menu cards came from the same subjects, suggesting a multifactorial within-subjects design

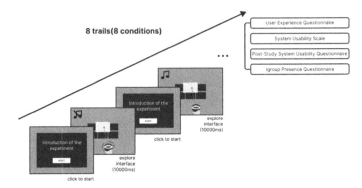

**Fig. 3.** Flowchart of the experiment

**Fig. 4.** Example of experimental scenarios and experimental interfaces

for the experiment. Data results for the four sets of scales were analysed by one-way ANOVA using R Studio software.

## 3    Result

### 3.1    UEQ Scores

The UEQ scale comprises six subscales: attractiveness, clarity, efficiency, reliability, facilitation, and novelty, with mean scores and standard errors detailed in Table 2. An 8 (feedback types: none/visual/auditory/tactile/visual + tactile/auditory + tactile/visual + auditory/visual + auditory + tactile) × 6 (UEQ subscales) repeated-measures ANOVA analyzed the scores. Significant differences emerged across the eight feedback representations in overall UEQ user experience ratings ($F = 37.76$, $p < 0.001$). The visual-auditory feedback ranked highest in user experience ($M = 1.82$, $SE = 0.13$), followed by visual ($M = 1.55$, $SE = 0.18$) and visual-auditory-tactile ($M = 1.47$, $SE = 0.14$). Additionally, significant variations were found in all six subscale scores: attractiveness ($F = 31.19$, $p < 0.001$), clarity ($F = 20.88$, $p < 0.001$), efficiency ($F = 23.63$, $p < 0.001$), reliability ($F = 33.8$, $p < 0.001$), facilitation ($F = 37.36$, $p < 0.001$), and novelty ($F = 20.41$, $p < 0.001$). Detailed data for total and subscale scores are presented in Fig. 5.

**Table 2.** Mean and standard error of UEQ user experience ratings

| Forms of feedback representation | Attraction (SE) | Clarity (SE) | Efficiency (SE) | Reliability (SE) | Promotion (SE) | Novelty (SE) |
|---|---|---|---|---|---|---|
| None | −1.78 (0.26) | −0.98 (0.25) | −1.37 (0.29) | −1.67 (0.28) | −1.77 (0.27) | −1.08 (0.28) |
| Vision | 1.79 (0.21) | 2.14 (0.19) | 1.78 (0.2) | 2.00 (0.2) | 1.56 (0.2) | 0.03 (0.23) |
| Auditory | 0.95 (0.21) | 1.12 (0.21) | 1.02 (0.17) | 1.07 (0.18) | 1.15 (0.17) | 0.26 (0.15) |
| Haptic | 0.76 (0.19) | 0.84 (0.15) | 0.86 (0.16) | 0.80 (0.17) | 1.12 (0.14) | 0.91 (0.14) |
| Vision-Haptic | 1.46 (0.17) | 1.24 (0.18) | 1.42 (0.17) | 1.59 (0.16) | 1.49 (0.17) | 1.25 (0.13) |
| Auditory-Haptic | 0.43 (0.17) | 0.41 (0.16) | 0.72 (0.17) | 0.75 (0.15) | 1.14 (0.16) | 1.09 (0.16) |
| Vision-Auditory | 2.02 (0.18) | 1.96 (0.18) | 1.92 (0.17) | 2.09 (0.13) | 1.96 (0.16) | 0.95 (0.15) |
| Vision-Auditory-Haptic | 1.36 (0.19) | 0.86 (0.25) | 1.27 (0.17) | 1.70 (0.19) | 1.84 (0.14) | 1.80 (0.16) |

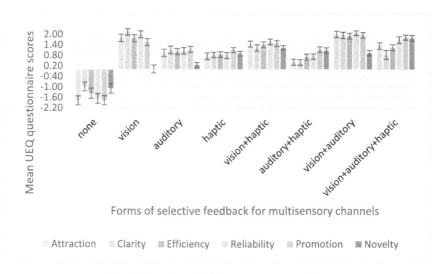

**Fig. 5.** Results of UEQ user experience ratings

## 3.2 IPQ Scores

The means and standard errors of the scores for the eight feedback representations are shown in Table 3. An ANOVA on the IPQ Immersion Scale revealed significant differences in immersion scores among the feedback representations, $F = 17.86$, $p <$ 0.001. The visual-auditory-haptic feedback representation emerged as the most immersive ($M = 0.97$, $SE = 0.16$), followed by the visual-auditory ($M = 0.92$, $SE = 0.15$) and visual-haptic forms ($M = 0.88$, $SE = 0.14$). The no-feedback representation scored the lowest for immersion ($M = -0.92$, $SE = 0.18$). Multichannel feedback consistently outperformed single-channel feedback in terms of immersion. Among single-channel feedback representations, visual feedback was rated highest in immersion ($M = 0.7$, $SE = 0.14$), with auditory ($M = 0.38$, $SE = 0.11$) and haptic feedback ($M = 0.33$, $SE = 0.1$) following. These findings are illustrated in Fig. 6.

**Table 3.** Mean and standard error of IPQ Immersive Experience ratings

| Forms of feedback representation | Means | SE |
|---|---|---|
| None | −0.92 | 0.19 |
| Vision | 0.7 | 0.14 |
| Auditory | 0.38 | 0.11 |
| Haptic | 0.33 | 0.1 |
| Vision-Haptic | 0.88 | 0.14 |
| Auditory-Haptic | 0.54 | 0.11 |
| Vision-Auditory | 0.92 | 0.15 |
| Vision-Auditory-Haptic | 0.97 | 0.16 |

### 3.3  SUS Score

Table 4 displays the mean scores and standard errors for the SUS System Usability Scale across eight feedback representations. The results indicated significant differences in usability scores among these forms, $F = 16.07$, $p < 0.001$. The visual-auditory feedback scored highest in usability ($M = 79.22$, $SE = 3.04$), followed by the visual-only feedback ($M = 78.02$, $SE = 3.43$) and visual-haptic feedback ($M = 68.19$, $SE = 2.45$). The no-feedback representation had the lowest usability score ($M = 39.05$, $SE = 3.1$). Among single-channel feedbacks, auditory feedback ranked second in usability ($M = 63.71$, $SE = 2.34$) after visual, with haptic feedback trailing ($M = 70.52$, $SE = 1.93$). For dual-channel feedbacks, visual-haptic feedback ($M = 68.19$, $SE = 2.45$) was second to visual-auditory, while auditory-haptic feedback scored the lowest ($M = 54.48$, $SE = 2.47$). These findings are represented in Fig. 7.

### 3.4  PSSUQ Scores

The PSSUQ usability scale, encompassing an overall score and three sub-dimensions (system quality, information quality, and UI quality), presents mean values and standard errors as shown in Table 4. In the PSSUQ, lower scores ($1 =$ strongly agree, $7 =$

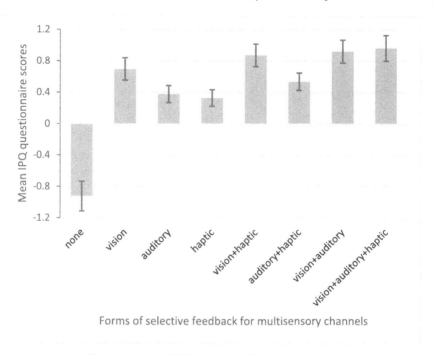

**Fig. 6.** Results of IPQ Immersive Experience ratings

**Table 4.** Mean and standard error of SUS System Usability ratings

| Forms of feedback representation | Means | SE |
|---|---|---|
| None | 39.05 | 3.09 |
| Vision | 78.01 | 3.43 |
| Auditory | 63.71 | 2.34 |
| Haptic | 60.52 | 1.93 |
| Vision-Haptic | 68.19 | 2.45 |
| Auditory-Haptic | 54.48 | 2.47 |
| Vision-Auditory | 79.22 | 3.04 |
| Vision-Auditory-Haptic | 59.66 | 3.51 |

strongly disagree) indicate higher usability. The results revealed significant differences in overall PSSUQ usability scores across the eight sensory channel feedback representations, $F = 28.37$, $p < 0.001$. The visual-auditory feedback representation achieved the highest usability (M = 1.79, SE = 0.17), followed by visual (M = 2.21, SE = 0.20) and visual-haptic feedback (M = 2.38, SE = 0.14). Similarly, significant variations were observed across the three sub-dimensions: system quality ($F = 21.22$, $p < 0.001$), information quality ($F = 30.29$, $p < 0.001$), and interface quality ($F = 24.44$, p

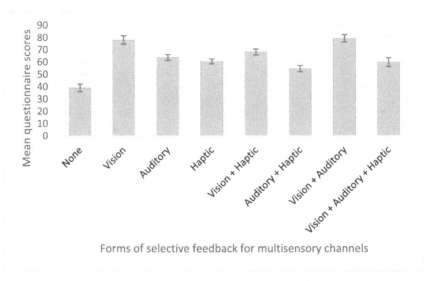

**Fig. 7.** Results of SUS System Usability ratings

< 0.001). The visual-auditory feedback scored the lowest across these sub-dimensions, indicating superior usability. Conversely, the no-feedback representation scored highest in all sub-dimensions, denoting the lowest usability. These results are illustrated in Fig. 8 (Table 5).

**Table 5.** Mean and standard error of PSSUQ Usability ratings

| Forms Of Feedback Representation | System Quality | Information Quality | Interface Quality | Total Quality |
|---|---|---|---|---|
| None | 5.16 | 5.48 | 5.30 | 5.72 |
| Vision | 2.14 | 2.17 | 2.32 | 2.21 |
| Auditory | 2.93 | 3.16 | 3.14 | 3.10 |
| Haptic | 3.03 | 3.10 | 3.24 | 3.28 |
| Vision-Haptic | 2.39 | 2.27 | 2.43 | 2.38 |
| Auditory-Haptic | 3.33 | 3.17 | 3.24 | 3.45 |
| Vision-Auditory | 1.89 | 1.91 | 1.92 | 1.79 |
| Vision-Auditory-Haptic | 2.72 | 2.35 | 2.48 | 2.69 |

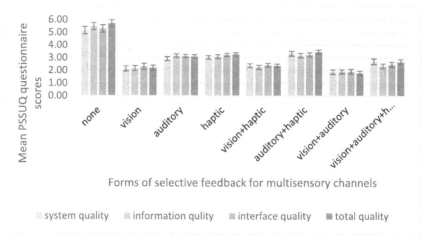

Fig. 8. Results of PSSUQ Usability ratings

## 4   Discussion

The menu card layout of the home interface of VR, as the home interface that users come into contact with in a VR system, not only constitutes their first impression of the VR virtual world, but is also crucial for users to perceive and orientate themselves to the VR application. Therefore, it is a major challenge to design effective selection feedback for menu card menus to attract users' attention in virtual space and enhance their experience. This study evaluated the user experience of 30 participants using eight forms of multisensory feedback in a VR environment. It was found that visual-auditory feedback outperformed the other seven forms of sensory feedback in terms of usability and user experience. Additionally, the no-feedback representation at scored the lowest in terms of user experience, usability, and immersion, while visual-auditory-haptic feedback provided the most immersion.

### 4.1   Emotional Experiences

According to the IPQ immersion questionnaire results, participants perceived the visual-auditory-haptic feedback as the most immersive, likely due to the increased sensory engagement during interaction. However, this contrasts with Martinez-Hernandez et al. (2017), who found that visual-haptic interaction offered stronger immersion than auditory feedback [23], possibly due to experimental noise levels or auditory feedback design differences. Based on UEQ results, participants favored the visual-auditory feedback, diverging from Chen et al. (2017), who highlighted the popularity of auditory-haptic feedback [24]. This discrepancy may be attributed to differences in interaction objects and heart rate feedback methods in our study.

### 4.2 Function Experiences

Usability of representations without feedback was ranked lowest in the SUS and PSSUQ usability ratings, which is in line with Dey et al. (2018), who argued that the experimental group with feedback was more usable than the experimental group without feedback [25]. Visual-auditory feedback had the highest usability score, which is in line with Santangelo et al. (2008), who argued that multisensory representations with visual feedback are more likely to attract users' attention [26].

## 5  Conclusion

This study investigated the relationship between eight multisensory channel feedback representations in VR home interface menu cards and multidimensional user experience ratings. The experiment assessed emotional and functional experiences in VR, following participants' free browsing of the eight feedback representations, using four scales: UEQ (User Experience), IPQ (Immersion), SUS (System Usability), and PSSUQ (Overall Usability). Results revealed that the visual-auditory feedback representation yielded better user experiences compared to single and triple sensory channel feedbacks, indicating that simultaneous visual and auditory feedback in VR home interface selection enhances user perception and understanding of the VR system. This research offers new insights and guidance for future design approaches in VR home interface feedback representations.

**Acknowledgments.** This paper is supported by the National Nature Science Foundation of China Grant No. 72201128, the China Postdoctoral Science Foundation No. 2023M730483 and the Collaborative Education Program of the Chinese Education Ministry No. 202102298009.

**Disclosure of Interests.** The authors have no competing interests relevant to the content of this article.

## References

1. Bao, A., Wei, Q., Sun, Y.: Overview of research on the application of virtual reality to spatial cognitive ability. In: SHS Web of Conferences, vol. 145, p. 01018. EDP Sciences (2022)
2. Jianwu, Z., Hongju, K.: Application of virtual reality technology in practical training teaching. e-Educ. Res. (4), 109–112 (2010)
3. Hongbo, G.: Development status, issues and trends of China's virtual reality industry. Mod. Commun. (J. Commun. Univ. China) **39**(02), 8–12 (2017)
4. Yiyu, H.: A review of research on virtual reality applications in education. Chin. J. ICT Educ. **01**, 11–16 (2018)
5. Burdea, G., Coiffet, P.: Virtual Reality Technology, 2nd edn., pp. 3–4. Wiley, New York (2003)
6. Manjoo, F.: How Google Taught Itself Good Design? International New York Times, NA-NA (2013)
7. Sagnier, C., Loup-Escande, E., Valléry, G.: Effects of gender and prior experience in immersive user experience with virtual reality. In: Ahram, T., Falcão, C. (eds.) Advances in Usability and User Experience. AISC, vol. 972, pp. 305–314. Springer, Cham (2020). https://doi.org/10.1007/978-3-030-19135-1_30

8. Tong, Y., Liang, Y., Liu, Y., et al.: Integrating hedonic quality for user experience modelling. In: International Design Engineering Technical Conferences and Computers and Information in Engineering Conference, 85376: V002T02A052. American Society of Mechanical Engineers (2021)
9. Yi, D., Fu, G., Mingcai, H.: A review of domestic and international research on user experience. Ind. Eng. Manag. **19**(04), 92–97+114 (2014)
10. Park, H., Jeong, S., Kim, T., et al.: Visual representation of gesture interaction feedback in virtual reality games. In: 2017 International Symposium on Ubiquitous Virtual Reality (ISUVR), pp. 20–23. IEEE (2017)
11. Franzluebbers, A., Johnsen, K.: Performance benefits of high-fidelity passive haptic feedback in virtual reality training. In: Proceedings of the 2018 ACM Symposium on Spatial User Interaction, pp. 16–24 (2018)
12. Matulic, F., Ganeshan, A., Fujiwara, H., et al.: Phonetroller: visual representations of fingers for precise touch input with mobile phones in VR. In: Proceedings of the 2021 CHI Conference on Human Factors in Computing Systems, pp. 1–13 (2021)
13. Dirin, A.: User experience of mobile virtual reality: experiment on changes in students' attitudes. Turk. Online J. Educ. Technol.-TOJET **19**(3), 80–93 (2020)
14. Hao, F., Chuqi, Z., Weixi, L.: A study on the design of a virtual reality intervention game for children with ADHD. Chin. J. Ergon. **29**(02), 1–7 (2023)
15. Chenglong, D., Ming, Z., Shu-Guang, K.: The effect of body tilt on the head-gaze interaction in virtual reality. Chin. J. Ergon. **28**(04), 24–30+67 (2022)
16. Xiu, M., Wenjun, H., Yanan, X.: Digital innovation of intangible cultural heritage based on virtual reality technology. Packag. Eng. **43**(16), 303–310+409 (2022)
17. Houran, Z.: Research on VR interface design based on emotional imagery. Nanjing Forestry University (2022)
18. Jiang, B., Zhao, Y.: Cognitive-psychology-based study on interactive design of preschool children's picture books. In: Stephanidis, C. (ed.) HCI International 2018 – Posters' Extended Abstracts. CCIS, vol. 852, pp. 59–64. Springer, Cham (2018). https://doi.org/10.1007/978-3-319-92285-0_9
19. Somrak, A., Pogačnik, M., Guna, J.: Suitability and comparison of questionnaires assessing virtual reality-induced symptoms and effects and user experience in virtual environments. Sensors **21**(4), 1185 (2021)
20. Saidon, Z.L., Safian, A.R., Nasrifan, M.N.: Usability evaluation of a virtual reality interactive music appreciation module (E-Marz) for secondary school (2021)
21. Jiahui, L., Xiaoxiao, K., Yamin, W.: The reliability and validity of Chinese version of lgroup presence questionnaire. Chin. J. Ergon. **27**(02), 39–44+80 (2021)
22. Sophie, G., Vincent, B.: Video games in adolescence and emotional functioning: emotion regulation, emotion intensity, emotion expression, and alexithymia. Comput. Hum. Behav. **61**(5), 344–349 (2016)
23. Martinez-Hernandez, U., Boorman, L.W., Prescott, T.J.: Multisensory wearable interface for immersion and telepresence in robotics. IEEE Sens. J. **17**(8), 2534–2541 (2017)
24. Chen, H., Dey, A., Billinghurst, M., Lindeman, R.W.: Exploring the design space for multi-sensory heart rate feedback in immersive virtual reality. In: Proceedings of the 29th Australian Conference on Computer-Human Interaction, OZCHI 2017, pp. 108–116. ACM, New York, NY, USA (2017)
25. Dey, A., Chen, H., Zhuang, C., Billinghurst, M., Lindeman, R.W.: Effects of sharing real-time multi-sensory heart rate feedback in different immersive collaborative virtual environments. In: 2018 IEEE International Symposium on Mixed and Augmented Reality (ISMAR), pp. 165–173. IEEE, October 2018
26. Santangelo, V., Ho, C., Spence, C.: Capturing spatial attention with multisensory cues. Psychon. Bull. Rev. **15**, 398–403 (2008)

# Augmented Reality Compensatory Aid for Improved Weapon Splash-Zone Awareness

Domenick M. Mifsud[1], Chris D. Wickens[1], Richard Rodriguez[1]($\boxtimes$), Francisco R. Ortega[1], and Mike Maulbeck[2]

[1] Colorado State University, Fort Collins, CO, USA
{dmifsud,richir,fortega}@colostate.edu, pandawickens94@aol.com
[2] VRR, Inc., Orlando, FL, USA
mmaulbeck@virtualrealityrehab.com

**Abstract.** One of the most important roles of the joint terminal attack controller (JTAC) in combat scenarios is accurately and efficiently communicating scene information with attack aircraft pilots. In this experiment we tested how the use of a north-up instant situational awareness display (ISA) impacts the performance of a task similar to the ones performed by JTACs, in terms of accuracy and response time. This experiment was a follow-up to verify the results of a previous experiment performed in virtual reality. The task involved determining the location of boxes relative to other boxes in an environment viewed from different simulated directions. An augmented reality head mounted display (AR-HMD) was used to project the ISA above the task as well as present the answers to the subject. Results showed an improvement in response time when subjects used the ISA after the control condition, and little change when the ISA was presented first. Participants who scored the lowest in accuracy appeared to benefit the most from the ISA. As expected, both the error rate and response time were lower in the north and south orientations versus the east and west directions.

**Keywords:** Head-mounted display · Augmented reality · Situation awareness · Mental rotation

## 1 Introduction

The joint terminal attack controller (JTAC) is in charge of integrating information about enemy attack units, nearby friendly forces, and using this information to safely coordinate and route fighter aircraft pilots to neutralize the enemy [7]. Part of this safe coordination is to describe the surrounding area verbally to the pilot, this effort is currently supported by a variety of nonintegrated, often head down information sources with little automation, such as binoculars, laser range finders, charts, notepads, radios, and even Android-based tablets. However, the current hardware is often bulky and not ideal for scenarios in which

J. Y. C. Chen and G. Fragomeni (Eds.): HCII 2024, LNCS 14707, pp. 230–240, 2024.
https://doi.org/10.1007/978-3-031-61044-8_17

the JTAC must remain mobile and aware of his surroundings. Because of this, we explored using principles of head-mounted display (HMDs) design typical of aviation rotorcraft operations [2,8] to help the JTAC operator make spatial judgements. These spatial judgments are integral to the attack sequence because the JTAC operator must ensure that what they are visually describing is understood and easily seen by the pilots, to prevent attack on friendly units or civilians. These spatial judgements also must be made under intense time pressure, as the pilot they are in communication with is rapidly approaching the target area.

The objective of this experiment was to validate results produced in a previous virtual reality (VR) experiment [9] that examined the use of a north-up instant situational awareness display (ISA) to aid in making spatial judgements. In this previous experiment, subjects made spatial judgements at different viewing angles with the same virtual targets. Using the ISA resulted in either the elimination or a reduction in the time required to mentally rotate the environment, which is of high importance to aircraft pilot en-route to a target. We seek to validate the results by conducting a similar experiment as that performed in VR, but now in a real-world environment. The objects that participants make spatial judgments about are no longer virtual but physical, colored boxes placed on the ground surface. The ISA visualization used in the VR study was produced in an augmented reality head mounted display (AR-HMD), the HoloLens 2. The subjects still make allocentric or world referenced judgments, using terms like "north" or "west" to refer to relative positions (in contrast to the egocentric terms like "left of," "beyond," or "right of" because these terms are relative to the JTAC's perspective). The direction of north was changed on every trial by rotating a virtual compass to try and keep the subject from developing a world referenced frame of the area. Because mental rotation from a given scene into a world reference frame is costly and error prone [1,3–6,10], providing the JTAC operator with an allocentric display (the ISA) should increase accuracy and speed of coordinating attacks.

## 2 Methodology

### 2.1 Participants

The participants are twenty-five students, primarily undergraduates, from a local university. Eight of whom were in the first two years the Army Reserve Officer Training Candidate (ROTC) program, none had previous JTAC training. Participants received a gift card in exchange for participation.

### 2.2 Task

The participants viewed a total of 20 scenarios, each of which presented a mix of physical objects as well as the ISA visualization in augmented reality (AR). The task involved choosing the correct statement about the distance and direction of the given arrangement of four physical objects, relative to each other, from a list of 4 options presented in AR. To make this task more difficult, the relative direction from an object was classified with cardinal directions (N, S, E, W) and the position of north was changed between each trial with a virtual compass. We examined the impact of ISA by presenting the same scenario both with (ISA condition) and without (control condition) and analyzing the differences in response time as well as accuracy.

**Fig. 1.** The experimental setup. Pictured is the blue tarp with the blue and red boxes on top of it as well as the participant wearing the Hololens 2 with our AC cooling tubing attached. The non-participant standing next to the blue tarp has been covered with a silhouette to preserve anonymity. (Color figure online)

### 2.3  Materials

For the target objects we chose from a set of five colored (2 red, 2 blue, and 1 yellow) cardboard boxes. Two of the boxes were rectangular (2.0-feet by 2.0-feet by 4.0-feet) and three were cubic (2.0-feet by 2.0-feet by 2.0-feet). The rectangular boxes are referred to as "wide red box" or "wide blue box" while the other boxes were referred to as their color ("red box", "blue box" "yellow box"). Only four of the five objects were placed on the tarp at a time (outside of the practice trials). To keep the indicated the positions of the boxes static, a 30.0-feet by 30.0-feet blue tarp was used with 9 different designated object positions on it, the middle of this tarp was placed 37.5-feet from the subject. This distance emulated a look down angle of 8.34° for a subject who was 5-feet 5-in. A HoloLens 2 was used as the AR-HMD to overlay the visualizations. To input the responses indicated by the participant, the experimenter used the four-letter buttons ($A$, $B$, $X$, $Y$) on an Xbox-one controller connected to the HoloLens. A laptop was used to display what the subject was seeing to the experimenter through a streamed video. This experiment was performed outdoors, so to keep everything from getting too hot, as well as to prevent the sun from interfering with sensors, a tent was placed over the subject and laptop. To ensure that the HoloLens stayed cool enough to use outside without shutting down we attached an air conditioning (AC) unit to the back of the device via tubing. The experimental setup can be seen in Fig. 1.

**Fig. 2.** An artificially augmented scene that shows the visualizations used in the ISA condition. Note the virtual compass at the top of the image shows south (in green), while the ISA always displays the North up view of the scene. The choices available to the participant are shown on the right-hand side, which correspond the buttons on the Xbox-one controller. The non-participants to the right of the blue tarp have been covered with a silhouette to preserve anonymity. (Color figure online)

## 2.4    Software

A shown in Fig. 2, the overlaid visualizations had 4 main components: (1) A 27-feet red circle with the middle aligning to our blue tarp called the "splashzone", along with a white -unit bar (for assessing distance) attached to either or both of the bottom of the splashzone or the ISA. (2) A virtual compass, displayed above the participant's forward line of sight at about 45° upwards. (3) The four possible answer choices along with their corresponding letters ($A$, $B$, $X$, $Y$) appears to the right above the tarp. (4) when not in the control condition, then the ISA map would also be displayed above the middle of the splashzone. Figure 2 depicts the image representing what a participant would see in the ISA condition. Twenty scenes were created that had the boxes positioned in different locations, these scenes contain one correct description for that specific arrangement of boxes as well as, in the ISA condition, their positions displayed from an overhead view. The answers were formatted such that three would contain incorrect descriptions with only 1 correct one. The descriptions, such as "the blue box is 2 north of the red box", involved relative positions of the boxes to each other (based off the white unit bar presented). The software would change the virtual direction the subject was facing via the virtual compass after every completed scenario. (This was done to avoid having to have the subject walk around the 75-feet circle between each trial to attain a different viewing orientation).

## 2.5    Procedure

The participants first completed a consent form, demographics survey and read the instructions indoors before heading outside to begin the experiment. They completed two practice trials before starting either the control or ISA conditions, each of which contained eight trials. The trial procedure was as follows: first the participant verbally indicated that they were ready to begin the trail, then they read the four virtual answers presented to them and selected which they thought was correct by speaking the corresponding letter. Once they read out their answer, the experimenter marked it with the controller. Then the experiment helper would move the real-world boxes to the positions for the next scene and indicate to the experimenter that the next trial was ready to begin. Once all twenty trials were completed, the subject completed a final survey before receiving their compensation.

## 2.6    Design

There were two within-participant variables: facing direction (the cardinal direction indicated by the virtual compass when looking forwards), and whether or not the ISA was presented (Control vs ISA). There were 3 between-participant variables:

1. the counterbalancing order (Control → ISA and ISA → Control),
2. the cohort group (ROTC vs non-ROTC), and

3. the specific order of facing directions of each trial.

Four trials were presented for each facing direction (N & W were shown in the practice trials so they were seen six time each). To counterbalance the ordering of the facing direction, both the first and second conditions were grouped based on facing direction (North and South, East and West), within those two groups the direction alternated between the two directions (e.g.: NS implies the sequence to be followed as N → S → N → S). This led to two possible trials direction orderings for both the first and second conditions: NS → EW and EW → NS. This left us with four possible orderings that are independent of whether ISA or control was the first condition; these were then indexed via a Latin square.

## 3   Results

Normality was checked with both the Shapiro test as well as QQ plots, this required us to $\log_{10}$ transform the response time variable as well as arcsine transform the accuracy variable to meet normality assumptions. A repeated measures ANOVA was used to determine statistical significance with a repeated-measures t-test post-hoc.

### 3.1   Response Time (RT)

There was a small (2.9 s), non-significant, benefit of the ISA display on response time ($F_{1,17} = 2.58, p > .1, \eta_p^2 = .13$). There was a highly significant effect of facing direction on response time as shown in Fig. 3 ($F_{3,51} = 19, p < .0001, \eta_p^2 = .13$).

The data reveals that responses made in the north oriented direction were 5.4 s faster than those made in the south direction, 8.2 s faster than the west direction, and 11.2 s faster than in the east direction. The differences in response time were significant ($p < .05$) between all directions except between east and west as well as between south and west. The presence of ISA did not significantly interact with facing direction ($F_{3,51} = .57, p > .5, \eta_p^2 = .03$) indicating that the small, non-significant benefit of the ISA was equal across all directions.

There was a marginally significant interaction between display and counterbalancing group ($F_{1,17} = 3.3, p < .1, \eta_p^2 = .16$), as shown in Fig. 4, which revealed that the [Control → ISA] group significantly ($p < .005$) benefited from the second-seen ISA display: RT shortening from 31.94 s to 25.43 s. While this effect could be attributed to practice effects, a corresponding benefit was not seen for the [ISA → Control] group.

### 3.2   Response Time Comparisons Based on Participant Performance

There was as wide range of accuracy across performers. Based on the assumption that best performers might show a different pattern of effects from those performing at a lower level, we performed a median split of the sample with the

**Fig. 3.** Mean response time per facing direction (a lower response time is better). The bars indicate standard error. The North up direction had the fastest response time, while the East up direction had the slowest response time.

top half ($n = 9$) all performing perfectly (100%) and the bottom half ($n = 16$) showing a mean accuracy of 80%.

The best performers responded somewhat faster (mean of 24.2 s) than the worst performers (mean of 31.7 s) ($F_{1,17} = 2.8, p > .1, \eta_p^2 = .14$) and both groups showed the same non-significant 3 s benefit of ISA. As shown in Fig. 5, both groups showed the same pattern of RT effects of facing direction, reflecting the pattern of the two groups together in Fig. 3.

### 3.3 Accuracy Analyses

The analyses of accuracy revealed only one statistical effect, other than the obvious one that best performers were more accurate than the poorer performers since this was the criterion for the median split. This single effect of facing direction is shown in Fig. 6. Note that the best performers group scored 100% on all directions so the differences in this chart reflect the worst performers.

The ANOVA reveals a marginally significant main effect of facing direction ($F_{3,51} = 2.35, p = .08, \eta_p^2 = .12$), reflecting a pattern similar to that shown for RT in that North facing showed highest accuracy. As noted above, there were no interactions with other variables, nor was the main effect of modality significant (only a 2% benefit for ISA).

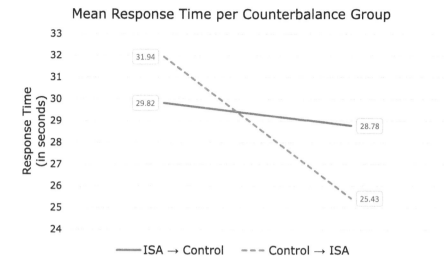

**Fig. 4.** Mean response time per counterbalancing group order. The response time in the ISA → Control group exhibited a small gain in RT when switching from the ISA condition to the Control condition (29.82 → 28.78). In contrast, the Control → ISA group a larger gain in RT when switching from the Control condition to the ISA condition (31.94 → 25.43). The latter gain is 6x faster than the former.

## 4    Discussion

This study examined the benefits of the ISA display on spatial judgements in a real-world outdoor environment. These spatial judgements are similar to those made by a JTAC observer when describing a target spatially to a pilot using contextual landmarks that are easily observable from the air. The trends that we observed in terms of response time benefit from the ISA were not statistically significant, but with such a low sample size even the marginal effects that emerged suggested that there was a difference. However, we showed that for both the high performing and low performing groups the same non-significant 3 s decrease in response time. This is good news for the JTAC operator because this implies that even with when already making extremely accurate spatial judgements, such as those from experienced JTAC operators, the use of the ISA still provides a 3 s decrease in response time which could be crucial if in a warfare situation. We also believe that while this study did not result in the same levels of significance as the previous experiment [9], which had considerably higher statistical power, the same trends emerged that show the ISA provides a benefit to both speed and accuracy when making spatial judgements.

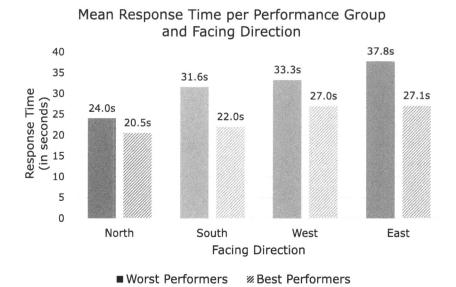

**Fig. 5.** A comparison of response time from the best or worst performers per facing direction. The bars indicate the standard error. Within each performance group, the North up view performed better than the rest of the views. The mean for the best performers was 24.2 s, while the mean for the worst performers was 31.7 s.

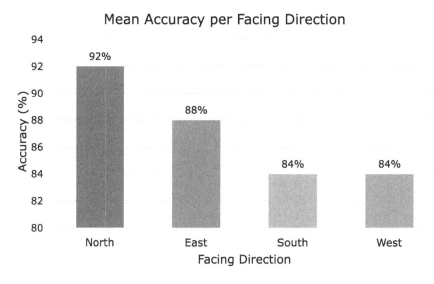

**Fig. 6.** Mean accuracy per facing direction (higher is better). The bars denote the standard error. The North up direction had the highest accuracy, while the South and West directions had the lowest accuracy.

# 5    Limitations and Future Work

We expected to see a large improvement in both accuracy and speed when using the ISA display, however, only minor effects emerged for the response timing and no accuracy effects were recorded. We feel that this is in part due to the ease of the task as well as a low sample size, a constraint that was imposed upon us because of the limited time-availability of the outside venue shown in Fig. 1. Because of the group of 9 participants that scored 100% accuracy on both conditions we felt as though we did not fully capture the benefit that the ISA display provides in terms of improving accuracy. And the low sample size was due to COVID restrictions as well as scheduling conflicts with the location. With an increased sample size, the marginal effects shown here should only grow in significance, so we feel as though the 3 s decrease in response time shows the ISA display does provide benefits. Future work could examine a more difficult task, such as identifying real buildings, to obtain a better estimate of the accuracy improvements that the ISA display may provide.

**Acknowledgements.** We acknowledge the funding support from ONR N00014-19-C-2026, ONR N00014-21-1-2580, and VRR 19-C-2026-CSU-PHII, N00014-21-1-2949 and N00014-21-1-2580. We would like to express thanks to Dutch Alessi from Virtual Reality Rehab, Inc. Dr. Peter Squire was the scientific/technical monitor with the Office of Naval Research.

**Declarations.** Distribution A - Approved for Public Release by the Office of Naval Research (ONR). Document Control Number (DCN): 43-4872-22.

# References

1. Aretz, A.J., Wickens, C.D.: The mental rotation of map displays. Hum. Perform. **5**(4), 303–328 (1992). https://doi.org/10.1207/s15327043hup0504_3
2. Dey, A., Billinghurst, M., Lindeman, R.W., Swan, J.E.: A systematic review of 10 years of augmented reality usability studies: 2005 to 2014. Front. Rob. AI **5** (2018). https://doi.org/10.3389/frobt.2018.00037
3. Hickox, J.C., Wickens, C.D.: Effects of elevation angle disparity, complexity, and feature type on relating out-of-cockpit field of view to an electronic cartographic map. J. Exp. Psychol. Appl. **5**(3), 284 (1999). https://doi.org/10.1037/1076-898X. 5.3.284
4. Macedo, J.A., Kaber, D.B., Endsley, M.R., Powanusorn, P., Myung, S.: The effect of automated compensation for incongruent axes on teleoperator performance. Hum. Factors **40**(4), 541–553 (1998). https://doi.org/10.1518/ 001872098779649256
5. Oscar Olmos, C.C.L., Wickens, C.D.: Electronic map evaluation in simulated visual meteorological conditions. Int. J. Aviat. Psychol. **7**(1), 37–66 (1997). https://doi. org/10.1207/s15327108ijap0701_3
6. Schreiber, B.T., Wickens, C.D., Renner, G.J., Alton, J.D., Hickox, J.C.: Navigational checking using 3D maps: the influence of elevation angle, azimuth, and foreshortening. Hum. Factors **40**(2), 209–223 (1998). https://doi.org/10.1518/ 001872098779480497

7. United States Marine Corps: Marine aviation weapons and tactics squadron one (2023). https://www.29palms.marines.mil/Units/MAWTS1/
8. Wickens, C.D., Ververs, P., Fadden, S.: Head-Up Displays, pp. 103–140. Ashgate (2004). https://doi.org/10.4324/9781315253039
9. Wickens, C.D., Mifsud, D., Rodriguez, R., Ortega, F.R.: Mitigating the costs of spatial transformations with a situation awareness augmented reality display: assistance for the joint terminal attack controller 3–17. Hum. Factors **65**(4), 651–662 (2023). https://doi.org/10.1177/00187208211022468
10. Wickens, C.D., Vincow, M., Yeh, M.: Design applications of visual spatial thinking: the importance of frame of reference. In: Cambridge Handbooks in Psychology, pp. 383–425. Cambridge University Press (2005). https://doi.org/10.1017/CBO9780511610448.011

# Augmented Virtuality–A Simplified, Scalable, and Modular Open-Source Unity Development System for Tangible VR with the Meta Quest 2

Bjarke Kristian Maigaard Kjær Pedersen$^{(\boxtimes)}$ ⓘ, Patricia Bianca Lyk ⓘ, and Daniel Alexander Auerbach ⓘ

Maersk Mc-Kinney Moller Institute, Game Development and Learning Technologies, University of Southern Denmark, Campusvej 55, 5230 Odense M, Denmark
bkp@mmmi.sdu.dk

**Abstract.** With this article, we present the first – to our knowledge – development system for developing Augmented Virtuality (AV) applications with dynamic and tangible interfaces. In addition, we also propose a new taxonomy for differentiating between various types of AV applications.

*The System*: The system presented in this article, is developed for the Meta Quest 2 VR headset, and automatically handles the synchronization between virtual objects and their physical counterparts using the controller's position. To ensure persistent real time alignment and synchronization during physical manipulations, it uses sensor feedback wirelessly transmitted from microcontrollers through UDP. In addition, the implemented user-interface for Unity enables users to use the system without the need for writing code. Furthermore, we have released the system as an open-source Unity assets package and invite others to use it for AV research-, educational-, industry-, or gaming purposes: https://github.com/BP-GITT/Tangible-VR/releases/tag/v1.0.0.

*Taxonomy*: The article also provides an overview of identified types, approaches, and methods for achieving Augmented Virtuality and propose a new practical orientated taxonomy for how to differentiate between them. The overview and taxonomy are a great place for AV application developers and new researchers to begin and includes the following six dimensions: 1) Type of AV, 2) approach to alignment, 3) synchronization method and sub-method, 4) number of synchronizable objects 5) the flexibility of their positioning and 6) their state.

**Keywords:** Augmented Virtuality · Tangible VR · Virtual Reality · VR · Oculus Quest · Meta Quest · Unity · 3D printing · Arduino · Raspberry · Taxonomy · IoT · Human-Computer Interaction

## 1 Introduction

In this article, we will present our new open-source system, for developing Augmented Virtuality applications for Meta Quest 2 VR headsets in Unity, featuring scalable, modular, dynamic and tangible interfaces.

© The Author(s), under exclusive license to Springer Nature Switzerland AG 2024
J. Y. C. Chen and G. Fragomeni (Eds.): HCII 2024, LNCS 14707, pp. 241–262, 2024.
https://doi.org/10.1007/978-3-031-61044-8_18

The article will first introduce the background for Virtual Reality (VR) research and how Augmented Virtuality (AV) positions itself on the reality-virtuality continuum and in relation to the more well-known Augmented Reality (AR), in addition we will be proposing a new taxonomy for differentiating between various types of, approaches to, and methods for achieving AV. In the Method section, the tools and methods used to develop our system will be presented. The result and discussion sections will focus on the development process and implementation of our system, its functionalities, strengths, and limitations, in addition to future work. Lastly, the article will conclude on the efficiency of the developed system, in relation to our research question.

### 1.1 Augmented Virtuality–What It is and Why

**Introduction to VR.** Virtual Reality (VR) is a transformative technology that immerses users in artificially created environments [1, 2], blurring the lines between the physical and virtual worlds. It offers an interactive and simulated experience, where users can engage with three-dimensional environments in ways that feel remarkably authentic [1].

At the core of understanding VR lies Milgram and Kishino's Reality-virtuality continuum, a conceptual framework that categorizes realities along a spectrum from completely real (the "real world") to completely virtual (the "virtual world") [1] (see. Fig. 1). The continuum becomes particularly relevant when exploring the relationship between VR, Augmented Reality (AR) and Augmented Virtuality (AV).

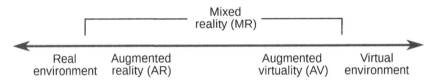

**Fig. 1.** Milgram and Kishino's reality-virtuality continuum [1].

AR, in contrast to VR, overlays digital elements onto the real world, enhancing our perception of the physical environment, positioning it closer to the real-world end of the continuum. AV goes a step further towards the virtual world, describing environments where physical elements are seamlessly integrated into a predominantly virtual setting. This hybrid experience combines the advantages of tangible, real-world components with the immersive possibilities of virtual environments. For example, in AV, physical objects can coexist and interact within the digital realm, blurring the boundaries between what is real and what is virtual.

Building upon Milgram's Reality-Virtuality Continuum Pine and Korn introduce the Multiverse, which adds the extra dimension "Matter" thus arriving at 8 forms of mixed realities, compared with Milgram and Kishino's 4 [3] (see Fig. 2). It introduces three pairs of variables—Space/No-Space, Time/No-Time, and Matter/No-Matter, each with two opposite physical/digital dimensions.

The first realm, Reality, encompasses Time, Space, and Matter (Actual/Real/Atoms). It represents the physical experiences of the real world, grounding our understanding in

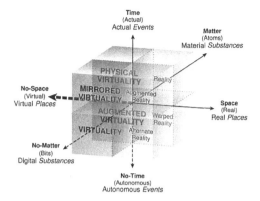

**Fig. 2.** The Multiverse [3].

familiar, tangible encounters. Opposite to Reality is Virtuality, existing in No-Time, No-Space, and No-Matter (Autonomous/Virtual/Bits). Virtuality, along with Reality, forms the anchors of the Multiverse. Augmented Reality (AR), characterized by Time, Space, and No-Matter, utilizes digital technology to enhance our physical world experiences. Augmented Virtuality (AV), on the other hand, operates in No-Time, No-Space, and Matter, seamlessly integrating physical elements into predominantly virtual settings, as seen in applications like digital twins.

Alternate Reality, distinct from AR, plays with the dimension of Time in addition to digital substance and physical place (No-Time/Space/No-Matter). It constructs a digital experience and overlays it onto a real place, creating an alternate view of physical reality. Physical Virtuality, the opposite, designs real-world objects virtually (Time/No-Space/Matter), blurring the lines between the actual and the virtual through processes like 3D printing.

Warped Reality, existing in No-Time, Space, and Matter, shifts a firmly grounded reality by manipulating time. This realm involves experiences simulating another time, whether in the past or future. Lastly, Mirrored Virtuality, characterized by Time, No-Space, and No-Matter, ties Virtuality to Real Time. It provides a real-time view, mirroring what is happening in the world.

**Presence and Immersion.** The concepts immersion and presence play important roles in the realm of Virtual Reality (VR), as extensively discussed by Slater [4], and Waterworth and Riva [5].

Presence is described as the subjective feeling of "being there" in a virtual world [5–8]. It emerges when technology's role blurs or is erased, allowing users to feel present in the virtual environment, transcending their physical location. The degree of presence experienced is subjective and can vary among users in the same virtual world.

In contrast, immersion, as defined by Slater and Wilbur [7], is an objective measure of the extent to which a system's physical framework offers users a sense of presence. One system is considered more immersive than another if it for example provides better resolution and tracking capabilities. Immersion therefore forms the framework in which presence can arise, and a higher level of immersion increases the likelihood of a heightened sense of presence. Slater [4] further dissects presence into two fragments: Place Illusion (PI) and Plausibility Illusion (Psi). PI represents the feeling of being present in the virtual world, aligning with the common understanding of presence. Psi, on the other hand, signifies the illusion that the shown scenario is genuinely taking place. When both PI and Psi coexist, users tend to react realistically to experiences in the virtual world.

Studies suggest a connection between presence, immersion, and enhanced learning outcomes [9, 10]. Rupp et al. [10], for instance, compared devices with varying degrees of immersion and found that increased immersion was associated with better learning of declarative knowledge, stronger interest in the subject, and reduced cybersickness.

It's worth noting that the term "immersion" is sometimes used interchangeably with the individual feeling of being present, described above as "presence" [2, 11]. In this context, immersion will be employed to characterize the objective qualities of the virtual system that enhance the subjective sense of "being there," namely presence.

**Tangible User Interfaces.** Tangible User Interfaces (TUIs) were introduced by Ishii and Ullmer over two decades ago, defining them as interfaces that give physical form to digital information, utilizing physical artifacts as both representations and controls for computational media [12, 13]. In the context of VR, TUIs have significant potential, providing a distinctive opportunity to enhance user experiences.

In VR, the incorporation of tangible interactions becomes crucial due to the rich haptic cues provided by physical objects, addressing the often-missing tactile dimension in traditional VR interfaces. Unlike generic controllers, TUIs in VR allow users to manipulate virtual objects with clear physical counterparts, providing a more authentic sensory experience, including a sense of weight, temperature, and texture [14].

The integration of tangible interactions in VR markedly enhances the objective features of the VR system, elevating its immersive attributes. As mentioned above, Slater notes that optimizing factors such as resolution and frame rate contributes to a more immersive system [4]. Similarly, the integration of tangible interactions aims to boost these objective qualities, seeking to create a more realistic experience and potentially cultivating a heightened sense of presence [15, 16].

This not only makes the VR experience more enjoyable but also holds significant potential in educational contexts. TUIs align with constructivist learning principles, providing users with a hands-on approach to interact with digital information. This hands-on engagement facilitates the acquisition of tacit knowledge, promoting a deeper understanding of concepts through embodied experiences [13, 17].

In educational settings, the ability to manipulate virtual objects with tangible interactions also caters to diverse learning styles. The tactile feedback provided by TUIs contributes to a richer and more immersive learning environment [18]. This multisensory approach has the potential to enhance memory retention and engagement, creating a dynamic and effective learning experience. Moreover, TUIs can unlock the potential for experiential learning. Students can engage in hands-on activities within the VR environment, fostering problem-solving, and creativity [16]. The integration of TUIs in VR aligns with the idea of embodied cognition, emphasizing the importance of bodily experiences in the learning process [17].

TUI-enhanced VR environments have demonstrated potential in training scenarios across different fields.

For instance, in medical training, a mixed reality (MR) approach combined physical manikins with virtual avatars [19]. This allowed first responders to practice procedures using real tools within an immersive VR setting. Users could engage in a realistic situation, such as assessing a car accident scene and using actual medical equipment. The approach resulted in high physical- and self-presence and increased stress levels.

In another case tangible VR was used for job training in a steam car wash training program [20]. This approach allowed job trainees to utilize real tools within a virtual environment, aligning a virtual vehicle model with the real vehicle body for a tangible and immersive experience. This method ensured a safe and repeatable training but also minimized expert intervention.

Likewise, VR has been used for Workplace Design. Here physical prototyping was combined with VR, using 3D CAD geometry to create an immersive experience that bridges the virtual and physical worlds. A demonstration in a human-robot interaction work cell showed an enhancement in the overall workplace design process [21].

Moreover, TUIs in VR cater to the needs for customized and interactive training simulations. For instance, in emergency response training, individuals can simulate crisis situations with tangible controls, fostering quick decision-making and coordination skills. This adaptability of TUIs allows for scenario-based training, providing a dynamic learning environment that adapts to the evolving needs of the trainee.

While AV has high promises for application usage, its implementation varies widely. In the following sub-section, we will go through diverse approaches to achieving AV and introduce a taxonomy for or differentiating between these methods.

## 1.2 Ways of Achieving Augmented Virtuality and a New AV Taxonomy

This sub-section will present an overview of different types, approaches, and methods used for achieving Augmented Virtuality (AV) and propose a new practical oriented 6-dimensional taxonomy for how to differentiate between these models (see Table 1).

The taxonomy is developed based on our analysis of state-of-the-art AV applications, which show that the type of AV aimed at achieving could be divided into two categories: actual AV, or emulated AV. The approach to synchronization likewise fell within two categories: Aligning the virtual space with the physical, aligning the physical space with the virtual.

Furthermore, the method used for synchronizing the alignment was divided into the following four methods: Physical tracking, visual tracking, manual alignment, physical impact.

In addition, our analysis also showed that objects can either be limited or unlimited in number, while their level of synchronization could be divided into two components (position, state), each of which can be described as dynamic, partly dynamic, or static: Position (fully dynamic) – the object can be moved around freely after synchronization without limitations. Position (partly dynamic) – the object can be moved around, with limitations. Position (static) – the objects position is static after synchronization. State (fully dynamic) – the object's state can be freely altered without limitations. State (partly dynamic) – the objects' state can be altered, with limitations. State (static) – the objects' state is static and cannot be altered.

**Table 1.** 6-dimensional Taxonomy for Augmented Virtuality applications.

| Type of AV: | Approach to alignment: | Synchronization method and sub-method: | Number of objects | Synchronized object position: | Synchronized object state: |
|---|---|---|---|---|---|
| Actual, emulated | Virtual, physical | Physical tracking: Controller, tracker Visual tracking: Fiducial markers, object recognition Manual alignment: Augmented objects, unmodified objects Physical impact: Haptic feedback, changes to environment | Unlimited, limited | Fully dynamic, partly dynamic, static | Fully dynamic, partly dynamic, static |

In the following sub-sections, we will use state-of-the-art examples to exemplify how different AV applications and systems fit within the taxonomy.

However, it is important to note that the methods list is expected to be expanded upon in the future when new methods are identified. Likewise, it should be noted that an application can make use of more than one method concurrently.

**Actual AV with Virtual Alignment - Synchronization Using Physical Tracking.** This approach aims at achieving actual AV by letting users touch the real object, while viewing a visual representation. The synchronization is performed by aligning an objects virtual position, with that of the tracker, thus ensuring same space occupancy between physical and virtual objects. While these trackers technically are tracked using emitted infrared light, they are set apart from visual tracking due to their physical casings and presence. Although relatively similar in technique, the usage of physical trackers can be further divided into two sub-methods.

*Native Controllers*

- Limited objects - partly dynamic position, static state:

An example of this includes attaching 3D printed objects to Meta Quest 2 controllers and using the controller's position to synchronize the position of the object's virtual counterpart. The objects position is partly dynamic since it can be moved around although dependent on the tracker, while its state remains static and as is [22].

- Unlimited objects - static position, static state:

The approach is similar to the one above, however, in this case the objects position remains static after the synchronization, allowing the controller to be moved away and used to synchronize additional objects [21].

*Additional Trackers*

- Unlimited objects - partly dynamic position, static state:

This approach is similar to that of native controllers, although it deviates from it by using additional trackers attached to physical objects, thus increasing the number of synchronized objects with partly dynamic positions [23, 24].

**Actual AV with Virtual Alignment – Synchronization Using Visual Tracking.** This approach aims at achieving actual AV by letting users touch the real object, while viewing a visual representation. The synchronization is performed using visual tracking of a physical objects position and aligning a virtual object with it. The method can be divided into two sub-methods depending on whether the visual tracking relies on fiducial markers or computer vision used to recognize and identify physical objects.

*Fiducial Markers*

- Unlimited objects - partly dynamic position, partly dynamic state:

An example of this is to place fiducial markers[1] on physical objects. This allows the objects to be moved around although still dependent on the visibility of the markers [19, 20, 25]. In addition, it allows the state to be partly dynamic, since different components of an object can be equipped with individual markers, allowing the application to detect changes in the objects' state [25].

*Object Recognition*

- Unlimited objects - Dynamic position, static state:

An example of this is to use computer vision to recognize the outline of objects and thereby track their position and orientation. This allows for independent and dynamic positioning of the object, although its state has to remain static [26, 27].

**Actual  AV  with  Virtual  Alignment–Synchronization  Using  Manual Alignment.** This approach aims at achieving actual AV by letting users touch the real object, while viewing a visual representation. However, it is also the least flexible of the methods, since it requires that the developer manually synchronize the virtual and physical object. The approach can be divided into two sub-methods, depending on whether the physical objects are augmented or remain unmodified.

*Augmented Object*

- Unlimited objects - partly dynamic position, static state:

---

[1] https://en.wikipedia.org/wiki/fiducial_marker.

An example of this is to augment an object with an IMU sensor to track its orientation, allowing the user to rotate the object without tracking its position or alter its state [28].

*Unmodified Object*

- Unlimited objects - static position, static state:

An example of this is to 3D scan a room and then manually position the model in relation to the physical room, thereby providing a static position and state of the scanned objects [29].

**Emulated AV with Physical Alignment–Synchronization Through Physical Impact.** This approach aims at letting users feel the emulating touch of virtual objects, by adapting the physical world to the virtual. Either by providing haptic feedback or by altering the physical environment itself.

*Haptic Feedback*

- Unlimited objects - dynamic position, dynamic state (in theory):

An example of this is haptic gloves [30] or gloves using shoulder mounted strings to restrict the user movement [31]. While there is no physical object to be touched, the user can freely move around virtual objects and alter their state, limited only by the software.

*Changes to Environment*

Limited objects - partly dynamic position, partly dynamic state:

An example of this is to divide a floor into a grid of inflatable cubes that can rise from the floor to emulate virtual objects [32]. The physical representation thus roughly emulates the space occupancy of the virtual objects, while their position and state are restricted to that of the grid and the cubes level of inflation.

### 1.3 Research Questions

Despite the promising applications of Tangible User Interfaces (TUIs) in VR and a broad support for developing VR applications using engines like Unity[2] and Unreal[3], a noticeable gap exists in the availability of user-friendly modular systems for creating dynamic tangible VR experiences. Of the two we have found, one is the official support for HTC Vive Trackers[4] to track a physical objects position and rotation, while the second is support for using an IMU sensor to track a physical objects rotation [28]. Unfortunately, none of them has support for altering the state of synchronized objects.

This situation led us to formulate the following research questions, in the hope that it can help push the research of Augmented Virtuality forward, by making the development of AV applications featuring dynamic and interactive Tangible User-Interfaces, more accessible:

- RQ1: Can we develop a system for developing AV applications, featuring dynamic and tangible user objects as interfaces?

---

[2] https://unity.com/.
[3] https://www.unrealengine.com/en-US.
[4] https://www.vive.com/eu/accessory/tracker3/.

- RQ2: What will its limitations be?
- RQ3: Can we develop it within a user-centric setting, enabling non-programmers to use it?
- RQ4: Can we make it cheap?

## 2 Method

In this section we will present the model our developed system uses to achieve Augmented Virtuality, how it positions itself inside our proposed taxonomy, and the technologies it relies on.

### 2.1 Augmented Virtuality Model

We aimed for a system that enables users to interact with and physically touch real physical objects, while immersed in virtual space.

While visual tracking using fiducial markers seemingly provide the most dynamic level of synchronized objects and smart phones being a stable household inventory, we wanted to support a precision and graphical level which lays outside the realm of this technology. Unfortunately, the Varjo XR-3[5], despite providing direct access to the camera feedback, had to be excluded due to its high cost. Consequently, we faced challenges in finding a widely adopted and cost-effective Head Mounted Display (HMD). To ensure broader accessibility, we consequently opted for physical tracking.

In addition, while the HTC Vive's support for additional trackers can increase the number of synchronized objects, both the trackers and the HTC Vive HDM are relatively expensive compared with the (Oculus) Meta Quest 2[6] [33]. In addition, the latter has been adopted by a largely wider audience [33]. Taking this into account, we deemed that the Quest 2 has the potential to attract the largest number of users.

To enable user interaction with synchronized objects, we developed a composite object model incorporating microcontrollers and sensors, allowing our objects to have partly dynamic states.

**The Selected Model.** The final model for our AV system positions itself within our proposed taxonomy as: *Actual Augmented Virtuality* achieved by aligning the *virtual* with the physical space, using *physical tracking* of *native controllers* to support an *unlimited number of objects*, with *static positions* and *partly dynamic states*.

### 2.2 Technology

**Head Mounted Display.** We selected the (Oculus) Meta Quest 2 HMD due to its comparatively low price, widespread adoption, and ability to run applications without the need for any additional setup.

**Development Engine.** We opted for Unity due to its relatively low entry level.

---

[5] https://varjo.com/products/varjo-xr-3/.

[6] https://www.meta.com/dk/en/quest/products/quest-2/.

**Microcontrollers.** We selected the Arduino Uno WiFi Rev 2[7] and ESP32[8] to cover a wide range of adopted, low-cost, and WiFi enabled microcontrollers. The system draws from the strength of IoT (Internet of Things) and wirelessly transmit sensor feedback using UDP (User Datagram Protocol).

**Sensors.** We used potentiometers for tracking joint and disc rotations, and switches/pushbuttons for click/push interactions.

**3D Printing.** A simple solution for creating physical counterparts to virtual objects.

# 3   Result

The system presented in this article, automatically handles the synchronization between virtual objects and their physical counterparts, using sensor feedback wirelessly transmitted from microcontrollers to ensure persistent real time alignment and synchronization during physical manipulations. In addition, the implemented user-interface for Unity, enables users to use the system without the need for writing code.

Sub-section "*3.1 Overview of the System*" will provide a brief overview of the system, while sub-sections "*3.2 Virtual and Physical Objects*" and "*3.3 The Synchronization Process*", will describe the composition of the virtual- and physical objects and the synchronization process.

Sub-section "*3.4 Developing Augmented Virtuality Applications using the Systems Integrated Unity User Interface*" will describe how to use the systems Unity user-interface to develop Augmented Virtuality applications, including how to: auto-generate the necessary microcontroller code, adding synchronizable objects to the application, registering objects as synchronizable, setting up objects to receive sensor data through UDP, and how to interact with developed applications.

The last sub-section "*3.5 Dependencies, and Supported Platforms and Hardware*" will list the systems dependencies, and currently supported platforms and hardware.

## 3.1   Overview of the System

**User Interaction.** In brief, the system works by tracking the right Quest 2 controller's (see Fig. 3) position in the physical world (see Fig. 4-A). When the user places the controller on a physical object's anchor base and activates the synchronization process by pressing the A-button, a virtual counterpart is positioned at the same position (see Fig. 4-B). This process can be repeated for any number of objects (the object selection can be browsed using the analog stick). Afterwards the user can then set aside the controller to activate hand-tracking and begin interacting with the physical object. The state of the virtual object is then continuously updated using sensor feedback from the physical object (see Fig. 4-C). Since objects are updated using sensor feedback, it also removes the requirement for these to be within camera view, while enabling others to likewise interact with these.

---

[7] https://docs.arduino.cc/hardware/uno-wifi-rev2/.

[8] https://ardustore.dk/produkt/nodemcu-wemos-esp32-d1-mini-cp2104-udviklingsboard.

**Developer Interaction.** To enable others to develop Augmented Virtuality applications using the system, we have implemented a user-interface for Unity. The interface is designed for non-programmers, and it does therefore not require coding to use it. Developers simply create objects by combining multiple components using drag and drop. Drag and drop features are likewise implemented for registering objects as synchronizable and for enabling sensor feedback through UDP. The necessary microcontroller code required for reading the involved sensors and transmitting the feedback, is likewise auto generated by the system.

**Video Demonstration.** A video demonstration of the system can be seen at the following link: https://github.com/BP-GITT/Tangible-VR/releases/tag/v1.0.0.

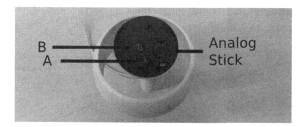

**Fig. 3.** (Oculus) Meta Quest 2 - right controller.

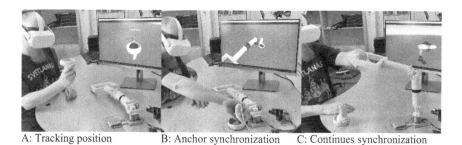

A: Tracking position        B: Anchor synchronization        C: Continues synchronization

**Fig. 4.** User Interaction with the System – Synchronizing a mechanical arm.

## 3.2  Virtual-and Physical Objects

To ensure flexibility and reconfigurability, objects are composites assembled using three different component types selected from an extendable catalog – it should be noted that any object of which the user poses a virtual and physical representation, can be used as a component:

- **Anchor base** (see Fig. 5-A): Functions as the anchor point between the virtual and physical object. The Anchor base is shaped after the negative space found within the tracking ring of a Quest 2 controller. In addition, the anchor base features an area for attaching dynamic and static objects.
- **Dynamic components** (see Fig. 5-B): Components facilitating physical interaction via embedded sensors, such as angular joints and rotation dials (potentiometers) and push/clickable parts (switches). The sensors are wired to a microcontroller transmitting the feedback to the application through UDP.
- **Static components** (see Fig. 5-C): Static components, such as handles, are attached to or connecting dynamic components.

Objects must contain only a single anchor base but can otherwise consist of multiple dynamic and static components. An example is the mechanical (arm see Fig. 4) which consists of an Anchor Base, 3x dynamic components (1x dial, 2x joints), 3x static components (2x tubes, 1x handle).

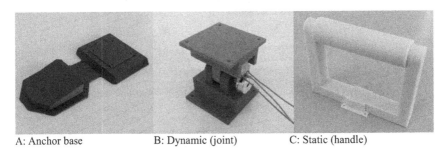

A: Anchor base          B: Dynamic (joint)          C: Static (handle)

**Fig. 5.** Object component types.

### 3.3 The Synchronization Process

The synchronization process consists of two steps: The initial synchronization and continues synchronization.

**Initial Synchronization-Anchoring the Physical Object Within Virtual Space.** The system uses the right Quest 2 controller's position and rotation data to generate an anchor point between virtual- and real-world space. This anchor point ensures that the virtual object's anchor base is located and rotated identically to the physical object's base anchor base.

The process is initiated by placing the controller on the anchor base. With the anchor base being shaped after the controller, this ensures that the controller can only be rotated in one specific way, once placed upon it, enabling a very high precision in the process.

Once the controller is placed on the anchor base, the user can press the A-button, to synchronize the virtual anchor base component of a desired object, to the established anchor point between the virtual- and real-world (see Fig. 6).

The controller can then be removed and used to synchronize additional objects or set aside after which the user can switch to hand-tracking and interact with the object(s).

**Continuous Synchronization - Updating the Virtual Object to Match Manipulations Performed on the Physical Object.** The system relies on sensor feedback from the sensors attached to the dynamic components of an object. The sensor feedback is sent wirelessly from the attached microcontroller(s) to the VR application, using the UDP protocol. Each transmission is sent using the following protocol: "BoardID|SensorID|SensorValue".

- The received sensor feedback value is then mapped to the respective dynamic components rotation (potentiometer) or position (switch), in order to maintain the synchronization between the virtual- and physical object.
- In contrast to the initial synchronization, this step is a continuous process which runs every time a physical object is manipulated by the user (see Fig. 7). The internal update cycle on the microcontroller is run every 10 ms and if a physical change in a components state is detected, the new value is sent to the application which updates the components virtual state.

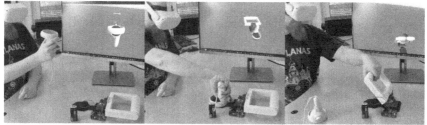

A: Tracking position        B: Anchor synchronization        C: Switch to hand-tracking

**Fig. 6.** The initial synchronization – synchronizing a handle object.

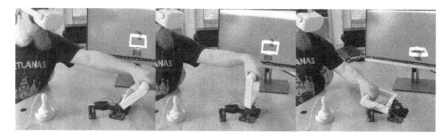

**Fig. 7.** The continues synchronization – the state of the handle object is updated in real time.

### 3.4 Developing Augmented Virtuality Applications Using the Systems Integrated Unity User Interface

In this section, we will describe how to use the Unity integrated user interface to develop an AV application for a tangible handle (see Fig. 5, 12), how to auto-generate the necessary code for the microcontroller, navigating the developed Unity AV scene hierarchy, constructing new synchronizable objects, registering objects as synchronizable, and setting up the automatic and continuous synchronization of synchronizable objects.

**Auto-generating the Necessary Microcontroller Code.** When the system has been loaded, a new menu will appear in the main navigation bar. Here the user can click on the "Tangible VR" tab and select "Microcontroller Code Generator" (see Fig. 8).

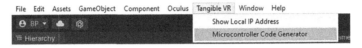

**Fig. 8.** The "Tangible VR" menu.

Users can then add new microcontrollers to their project and select "Generate Code" (see Fig. 9):

**BOARD:**
*Board ID*: User defined.
*BoardType*: Select board type.

**WiFi settings:**
*SSID*: Network name.
*Password*: Network password.

**UDP settings:**
*IP Address*: Application IP[9]
*UDP Port*: User defined[10]

**Attached Sensors:**
*Sensor type*: Select sensor type.
*Sensor ID*: User defined.
*I/O Pin*: The used pin.
*Sensitivity Threshold*:
The needed deviation from the last read sensor value, for the microcontroller to register a change in the components state.

**Fig. 9.** The Code Generator sub-menu.

Upon completion, the user can select "Generate Code" to auto-generate the necessary microcontroller code and upload it using their preferred IDE (see Fig. 10).

**Fig. 10.** The auto-generated code output.

**The Unity Development Scene.** The system provides a Unity scene that is setup and prepared for AV development. The scene is found in the "Scenes" folder and includes the following objects in its hierarchy (see Fug. 11) Directional Light:

– Default Unity light source.

  • Oculus Interaction Sample Rig:

– Enables VR and controller/hand-tracking, included in the Unity Oculus Integration SDK (version 57.0.1)[9].

  • Tangible VR Manager:

– Object Synchronizer:

  • Handles the initial synchronization process between physical and virtual objects, ensuring same space occupancy.

– UDP Listener:

  • Handles continuous synchronization process, keeping virtual objects persistently synchronized with their physical counterparts during user interaction.

– Object Container:

  • Synchronizable objects can be stored anywhere in the scene hierarchy, however, for a better overview the system provides a container for storing these (Fig. 11).

**Adding Objects.** There are three ways for adding objects:

• Adding a pre-assembled object from the collection
• Constructing a new object an anchor base and dynamic and static components from the collection
• Constructing a new object using an anchor base and user created 3D models.

---

[9] https://assetstore.unity.com/packages/tools/integration/oculus-integration deprecated-82022.

**Fig. 11.** The object hierarchy of the AV Unity development scene.

*Adding a Pre-assembled Object.* Select the object from the prefab folder and drag it to the Unity scene hierarchy (see Fig. 12).

*Constructing a New Object From Collection Components.* Select the "Synchronizable Object" from the prefab folder and drag it to the Unity scene hierarchy. Select the additional dynamic and static components from the folder that the object should consist of and drag these onto the Anchor Base (see Fig. 12). Depending on the type of dynamic component used, select either the "AngleUpdater" or "PushUpdater" script component, and fill in the information (see Fig. 13 and Fig. 14). The "Min"/" Max Rotation Degree" are the physical constraints of a dynamic component, while "Min"/"Max Input Value" are the sensor values read in this position, the values are used to map physical to virtual movement. Note that forward kinematic is used to update an objects state. In case of the "Left Handle" object, the "Joint" component should follow the position/orientation of the "Anchor Base" and is therefore a child of this. Likewise, the "Handle" should follow the "Joint – Top" part of the "Joint" component, why it is a child of this.

*Constructing a New Object From Collection Components.* Select the Anchor Base from the prefab folder and drag it to the Unity scene hierarchy. Select the additional user created dynamic and static components the object should consist of and drag these onto the Anchor Base. Attach either the "AngleUpdater" or "PushUpdater" script from the script folder. Fill in the required information, similar to when using dynamic and static components from the prefab collection (see above).

A: The virtual "Left Handle"      B: The virtual "Left Handle"      C: The physical "Left Handle"
  object in scene hierarchy.         object in scene view.            object when assembled.

**Fig. 12.** The "Left Handle" object in its virtual and physical form.

**Fig. 13.** Angle Updater script component – note that the joint use for the handle has a min/maximum rotation of 90 degrees in each direction. However, while the ADC on the used Arduino is in range 0–1023, the sensor values for each position are in this case: min input value (148), maximum input value (921).

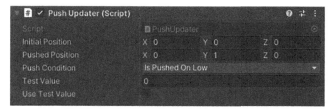

**Fig. 14.** Push Updater script component – note that when "Test Value" is checked, the debugging and testing different values, can be performed by typing these into the "Test Value" field.

**Registering Objects as Synchronizable.** Select the "Object Synchronizer" from the hierarchy and add a new element to the "Synchronizable Objects" list. Provide a user-defined "Object Name" and drag the objects "Anchor Base" component from the scene hierarchy to the "Object To Synchronize" field. The object is then registered in the system as synchronizable (see Fig. 15).

For static objects e.g. a table, the development process can stop at this step. For dynamic objects that should track the user's physical manipulation, the object still needs to be setup to receive sensor data through UDP – see the next step.

**Setting up an Object to Receive UDP Data.** Select the "UDP Listener" and type in the UDP port that the application should use to listen for sensor feedback.

Then add a new element to the "Boards" list, fill in the Board ID and Sensor ID fields, and drag the moveable part of dynamic component to the "Target Object" field (Fig. 16). This activates the automatic synchronization of the dynamic component of the object. Note that an object can consist of multiple dynamic and static components. To synchronize additional dynamic components, simply repeat this process.

**Use the Application.** Once a physical object has been assembled and its virtual counterpart has been added to the scene hierarchy, registered as synchronizable, and setup to receive sensor data through UDP, the user is ready to engage with the application.

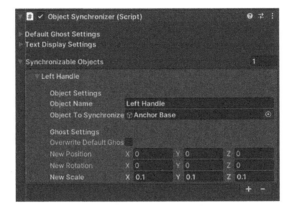

**Fig. 15.** The Object Synchronizer

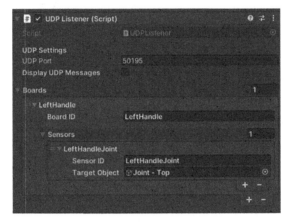

**Fig. 16.** The UDP Listener

When the application is running, the user can select between the registered objects using the analog-stick (left/right) on the right-controller (see Fig. 3), then place the controller on the physical anchor base component of a selected object and press the A-button to synchronize (see Fig. 4-A).

The user is now free to set down the controllers to enable hand-tracking and engage with their application and its tangible interface (see Fig. 4-B and Fig. 4-C). Should the user wish to remove the virtual object again, this can be done by pressing the B-button.

For development purposes, the user can also flick the analog-stick (up/down) to select between the object shifter and the debugging tool. The debugging tool displays the local IP-address of the application, which is especially useful when an application has been installed and is running locally on the (Oculus) Meta Quest 2 headset.

### 3.5  Supported Platforms and Hardware, and System Dependencies

**Supported Platforms**

- VR Headsets: (Oculus) Meta Quest 2 (OS vSQ3A.220605.009.A1).
- Development engines: Unity (v2021.3.13f1).

**Supported Hardware**

- Microcontrollers: Arduino Uno WiFi Rev 2, ESP32.
- Sensors: Potentiometers, switches/pushbuttons.

**System Dependencies.** The system comes pre-packed and is dependent on the Unity Oculus Integration SDK (v57.0.1). In addition, the Arduino Uno WiFi Rev 2 and ESP32 microcontrollers are dependent on the WiFiNINA library (v1.8.12)[10].

## 4  Discussion

In this section, we will discuss the developed system in relation to state-of-the-art, our proposed taxonomy and research questions, in addition we will comment on its future usage and distribution, as well as future work.

**RQ1 and RQ2.** In relation to our research question RQ1 and RQ2 we have with the developed system demonstrated that it supports the synchronization objects with partly dynamic states. This is also what sets it apart from other systems we have found aiming at actual Augmented Virtuality using physical tracking [21–24].

In relation to our proposed taxonomy, the only other model we have found for achieving actual AV while providing this feature, is through visual tracking with fiducial markers [25]. This model, due to its simultaneous partly dynamic feature of the object's positions, achieves a higher level of synchronization. Unfortunately, we have not been able to find a provider outside of smart phones or custom hardware, which enable the necessary functionality required for this (direct access to the camera feed). However, partly dynamic positioning can still be achieved with the current system, if the users continuously update the position synchronization, although this will effectively limit the number of objects to two, one for each controller. In addition, while the UDP transmitted sensor feedback enables the interaction with out-of-view objects, we are currently planning to likewise use it to enable actuator equipped objects with force-feedback functionalities, to strengthen the immersion further.

Furthermore, outside of emulating AV through haptic feedback [30, 31], we have not been able to find a system that supports objects with fully dynamic positioning and fully dynamic states (in theory). If we will see actual AV systems featuring this in the near future, is anyone's guess. However, as we can only imagine the immense resources this would take to implement, our guess would be no.

---

[10] https://www.arduino.cc/reference/en/libraries/wifinina/.

**RQ2 and RQ3.** In relation to our research question RQ3 and RQ4, we have demonstrated how the system can be used to developed AV application by non-programmers without the necessity of writing any code. In addition, we will argue that the usage of the Unity engine and the (Oculus) Meta Quest 2 headset, and low-cost microcontrollers, we have succeeded in making it relatively cheap to develop with and in turn also widely accessible. However, only the future can tell if this holds true.

**Usage cases and Distribution.** It is our hope that the implemented user-interface and relative low-cost involved in developing AV applications with our system, can help in lowering the entry level and making AV research more accessible to a wider audience.

We likewise hope that these factors can also help in pushing AV forward within educational settings and provide students with a solid place to begin developing their own prototypes without the need for advanced calibrations or expensive hardware.

In addition, we hope that it can provide industry small-to-medium enterprises within VR training with a framework, allowing for more rapid prototyping of offered solutions to lower the cost involved herein and help grow the AV safety training community.

For the (indie) gaming community and industry, we hope that the prospect of being able to distribute a set of 3D-files and assembly guides to enable users to print their own AV gaming peripherals, will prove all kinds of amazing. Just imaging souring through the skies in a steampunk airship with a navigation interface that you can physically touch and steer with. Or, set out to navigating the uncharted ocean depths in your alien submarine, the limitations are simply a 3D model away.

To achieve this, we hereby with this article release the developed system as an open-source Unity asset package, free of charge for everyone to use and modify[11]: https://git hub.com/BP-GITT/Tangible-VR/releases/tag/v1.0.0.

## 5  Conclusion

With this article we have presented and demonstrated our new system for developing Augmented Virtuality applications, with interactive and tangible interfaces. In addition, we have presented an overview of different types, approaches, and methods for achieving AV and proposed a new taxonomy for how to differentiate between AV applications. Lastly, we have released the developed system as open-source Unity asset package and invited everyone to use it and contribute to its development: https://github.com/BP-GITT/Tangible-VR/releases/tag/v1.0.0

**Disclosure of Interests.** The authors have no competing interests to declare that are relevant to the content of this article.

## References

1. Milgram, P., et al.: Augmented reality: a class of displays on the reality-virtuality continuum. In: Telemanipulator and Telepresence Technologies. SPIE (1995)

---

[11] Military applications and purposes are exempt from this.

2. Murray, J.H.: Hamlet on the Holodeck. Updated edition: The Future of Narrative in Cyberspace. MIT Press (2017)

3. Pine, B.J., Korn, K.C.: Infinite Possibility: Creating Customer Value on the Digital Frontier. Berrett-Koehler Publishers (2011)

4. Slater, M.: Place illusion and plausibility can lead to realistic behaviour in immersive virtual environments. Philos. Trans. Roy. Soc. B Biol. Sci. **364**(1535), 3549–3557 (2009)

5. Waterworth, J., Riva, G.: Feeling Present in the Physical World and in Computer-Mediated Environments. Springer, London (2014). https://doi.org/10.1057/9781137431677

6. Lombard, M., Ditton, T.: At the heart of it all: the concept of presence. J. Comput.-Mediated Commun. **3**(2), JCMC321 (1997)

7. Slater, M., Wilbur, S.: A framework for immersive virtual environments (FIVE): speculations on the role of presence in virtual environments. Presence Teleoperators Virtual Environ. **6**(6), 603–616 (1997)

8. Witmer, B.G., Singer, M.J.: Measuring presence in virtual environments: a presence questionnaire. Presence **7**(3), 225–240 (1998)

9. Schrader, C.: The relation between virtual presence and learning outcomes in serious games-the mediating effect of motivation. IxD&A **19**, 38–46 (2013)

10. Rupp, M.A., et al.: Investigating learning outcomes and subjective experiences in 360-degree videos. Comput. Educ. **128**, 256–268 (2019)

11. Elmezeny, A., Edenhofer, N., Wimmer, J.: Immersive storytelling in 360-degree videos: an analysis of interplay between narrative and technical immersion. J. Virtual Worlds Res. **11**(1) (2018)

12. Ishii, H., Ullmer, B.: Tangible bits: towards seamless interfaces between people, bits and atoms. In: Proceedings of the ACM SIGCHI Conference on Human Factors in Computing Systems (1997)

13. Ullmer, B., Ishii, H.: Emerging frameworks for tangible user interfaces. IBM Syst. J. **39**(3.4), 915–931 (2000)

14. Hinckley, K., et al.: Passive real-world interface props for neurosurgical visualization. In: Proceedings of the SIGCHI Conference on Human Factors in Computing Systems (1994)

15. Insko, B.E.: Passive haptics significantly enhances virtual environments. The University of North Carolina at Chapel Hill (2001)

16. Araujo, B., et al.: Snake charmer: physically enabling virtual objects. In: Proceedings of the TEI 2016: Tenth International Conference on Tangible, Embedded, and Embodied Interaction (2016)

17. Dourish, P.: Where the Action Is: the Foundations of Embodied Interaction. MIT Press (2001)

18. Johnson, M.P., et al.: Sympathetic interfaces: using a plush toy to direct synthetic characters. In: Proceedings of the SIGCHI Conference on Human Factors in Computing Systems (1999)

19. Uhl, J.C., et al.: Tangible immersive trauma simulation: is mixed reality the next level of medical skills training? In: Proceedings of the 2023 CHI Conference on Human Factors in Computing Systems (2023)

20. Baek, S., Gil, Y.-H., Kim, Y.: VR-based job training system using tangible interactions. Sensors **21**(20), 6794 (2021)

21. Van Campenhout, L., Van Camp, M., Vancoppenolle, W.: Exploring tangible VR as a tool for workplace design. In: Companion Proceedings of the 2020 Conference on Interactive Surfaces and Spaces (2020)

22. Palma, G., Perry, S., Cignoni, P.: Augmented virtuality using touch-sensitive 3D-printed objects. Remote Sens. **13**(11), 2186 (2021)

23. Mercado, V.R., et al.: Alfred: the haptic butler on-demand tangibles for object manipulation in virtual reality using an ETHD. In: 2021 IEEE World Haptics Conference (WHC). IEEE (2021)

24. Matviienko, A., et al.: VRtangibles: assisting children in creating virtual scenes using tangible objects and touch input. In: Extended Abstracts of the 2021 CHI Conference on Human Factors in Computing Systems (2021)

25. Cardoso, J.C., Ribeiro, J.M.: Tangible VR book: exploring the design space of marker-based tangible interfaces for virtual reality. Appl. Sci. **11**(4), 1367 (2021)

26. Morikubo, Y., et al.: Tangible projection mapping: Dynamic appearance augmenting of objects in hands. In: SIGGRAPH Asia 2018 Emerging Technologies, pp. 1–2 (2018)

27. Nomoto, T., Koishihara, R., Watanabe, Y.: Realistic dynamic projection mapping using real-time ray tracing. In: ACM SIGGRAPH 2020 Emerging Technologies, pp. 1–2 (2020)

28. Harley, D., et al.: Tangible VR: diegetic tangible objects for virtual reality narratives. In: Proceedings of the 2017 Conference on Designing Interactive Systems (2017)

29. Valentini, I., et al.: Improving obstacle awareness to enhance interaction in virtual reality. In: 2020 IEEE Conference on Virtual Reality and 3D User Interfaces (VR). IEEE (2020)

30. Lou, W.J., Teh, A.S., Phang, S.K.: Low cost haptic and motion based mixed reality peripheral interface. In: AIP Conference Proceedings. AIP Publishing (2019)

31. Fang, C., et al.: Wireality: enabling complex tangible geometries in virtual reality with worn multi-string haptics. In: Proceedings of the 2020 CHI Conference on Human Factors in Computing Systems (2020)

32. Teng, S.-Y., et al.: TilePoP: tile-type pop-up prop for virtual reality. In: Proceedings of the 32nd Annual ACM Symposium on User Interface Software and Technology (2019)

33. VR.Space: Which Popular VR Headsets Have Generated the Most Revenue? (2023). https://vr.space/news/equipment/which-popular-vr-headsets-have-generated-the-most-revenue/

# An Analysis of the Sense of Presence and Cybersickness in Virtual Reality: The Influence of Content Type, Exposure Time, and Gender

Pedro Reisinho$^{(\boxtimes)}$ 🆔, Cátia Silva🆔, Maria Ferreira🆔, Rui Raposo🆔, Mário Vairinhos🆔, and Nelson Zagalo🆔

DigiMedia, Department of Communication and Art, University of Aveiro, 3810-193 Aveiro, Portugal
pedro.reisinho@ua.pt

**Abstract.** As the adoption of XR progressively grows across diverse domains, it is paramount to delve into the factors that can affect the user experience while using XR technology. The purpose of this research was to understand the influence of content type, exposure time, and gender on presence and cybersickness within the context of virtual reality experiences. The evaluation was conducted with a sample of 20 participants who were randomly exposed to four content types: a digital game, a simulator, a synthetic cultural environment, and a 360-degree video. No significant changes regarding global presence were observed. However, upon analysing its subdimensions, the values indicate a correlation between content type and both spatial presence and experienced realism. Gender disparities were detected, with male participants considering the digital game less realistic compared to other content types, while female participants scored it on par with the others. Moreover, the total exposure time positively correlated with higher global presence for female participants, with a difference also being observed in terms of experienced realism. Regarding cybersickness, the correlation between gender and total exposure time indicated that female participants reported less cybersickness as exposure time increased. The research conducted, currently entering a second phase in which the same type of content will be tested across different head-mounted displays, has provided relevant results that are already being applied to other studies focused on virtual reality experiences, such as the therapeutic use of the technology by users diagnosed with phobias or neurocognitive disorders.

**Keywords:** User Experience · Interaction Design · XR · Virtual Reality · Presence · Cybersickness

## 1 Introduction

Technological progress has progressively made virtual reality accessible to the masses, thanks to the improvements made in portable, cost-effective, and technologically advanced head-mounted displays capable of delivering satisfactory immersive experiences[1]. The proliferation of virtual reality technology has simultaneously unveiled new

J. Y. C. Chen and G. Fragomeni (Eds.): HCII 2024, LNCS 14707, pp. 263–282, 2024.
https://doi.org/10.1007/978-3-031-61044-8_19

possibilities for research and academic opportunities across a wide spectrum of scientific areas. By offering immersive experiential worlds, the potential of virtual reality lies in its adaptability to various contexts, from providing a safe and controlled environment for students and professionals to simulate practice scenarios and complex procedures, allowing them to enhance their skills and knowledge without exposure to real-world risks [2, 3] to enabling entirely personalized experiences in therapeutic contexts [4].

With the gradual adoption of virtual reality across multiple domains, it becomes increasingly important to perceive the factors that are able to affect the user experience in virtual reality worlds. In this study, we considered the content type, exposure time and gender. While the last two are self-explanatory, content type can be more complex and refers to the nature of the virtual world, encompassing aspects like world fidelity, engagement elements, the quantity of stimuli delivered, and other related attributes. This research is driven by the desire to optimize virtual reality experiences by providing guidelines to tailor content and exposure duration to heighten the presence and decrease the manifestation of cybersickness symptoms. This study is influenced by the research conducted by Narciso et al. [5] and Melo et al. [6], who explored the utilization of different video and sound formats [5], content types, exposure times [6] and gender [5, 6]. Nonetheless, our study differs in certain respects. While Narciso et al. [5] assessed video and sound formats and Melo et al. [6] primarily focused on realistic or synthetic content with users limited to three degrees of freedom, our study introduces additional layers regarding the content type variable, as explained in the methodology section. Furthermore, our team considers that the time required for each user to adapt to the content may vary in terms of exposure time. Instead of imposing a homogenous exposure time for all content types, as seen in Melo et al. [6], where the time intervals varied between 1, 3, 5, or 7 min, we decided to assign different time limits to each content type. Our approach was supported on the rationale that content with higher engagement elements should be granted more time – as it may have a steeper learning curve due to the variety of mechanics –, whereas content with lower engagement elements, whether due to monotony or limited interactivity (e.g., degrees of freedom), should be experienced for a shorter duration to avoid compromising the user experience. In this sense, the purpose of our research is to evaluate whether variables such as content type (i.e., digital game, simulator, synthetic cultural environment, and 360° video), exposure time, or gender can exert any influence on the sense of presence within immersive virtual reality worlds. Additionally, considering the potential long exposure time during the evaluation sessions, it is sought to understand whether exposure time or gender impact the manifestation of symptoms of cybersickness. The following research questions were formulated and guided the study:

- Can content type, exposure time, or gender exert an influence on the sense of presence in virtual reality experiences?
- Can exposure time or gender influence the development of cybersickness symptoms?

In the following sections we begin by establishing the theoretical foundation of our study and explaining the chosen approach for conducting the experimental study. Subsequently, a detailed presentation of our findings is provided, followed by a thorough analysis of the results within the context of existing literature. We conclude by summarizing our key findings, presenting technical principles and guidelines for improving the cinematic virtual reality user experience, and discussing potential future research directions.

## 2 Background

The interest in XR has been progressively growing, driven by hardware and software advancements in recent years, making XR technologies increasingly capable of providing users with a diverse array of engaging experiences. To gain a comprehensive understanding of the XR landscape, it is essential to start by examining the taxonomy that many consider foundational in this field, the Reality–Virtuality Continuum [7]. This taxonomy outlines a spectrum that ranges from the real environment, representing the physical world, to the virtual environment, which is a fully synthetic world that immerses users sensorially [7–9], commonly known as virtual reality. Between these two extremes are mixed realities, which involve the visual combination of real and digital elements [7], encompassing augmented reality and augmented virtuality. Augmented reality involves the superimposition of digital information onto the physical world [9] and, consequently, it can be found more closely aligned with the real environment on the Reality-Virtuality Continuum. In contrast, augmented virtuality, less utilized, leans closer to the virtual environment, as it involves the digitization of real-world objects into the virtual domain [7]. Nearly three decades later, a contemporary framework aligned with current technological panorama is proposed by Rauschnabel et al. [10], known as the xReality Framework, where the variable X in XR can represent any form of reality, primarily distinguished by whether the physical environment is visible or hidden [10].

In line with this conceptual framework, as proposed by Reisinho et al. [4], virtual reality, as a subset of XR, can be defined as "a sensory simulation that induces in the user the perception existing both physically and mentally within a virtual world". Given this interpretation, the author argues that three key principles compose the bedrock of virtual reality: immersion, presence, and the virtual world. In line with these fundamental principles, this study seeks to contribute to the advancement of scientific research in the field of the sense of presence, often described as a sensorimotor illusion arising from the inability to recognize that the experience is being mediated [11], giving the user the sensation of existing in the virtual world. This is a key feature for enhancing the overall enjoyment and effectiveness of a virtual reality experience, as users who feel a higher sense of presence are more engaged in the virtual world and exhibit behaviours akin to those observed in the physical world [12]. This conceptualization of presence aligns with the theory of optimal experience, as described by Csikszentmihalyi [13], in which deep involvement in a task induces a state wherein an individual's attention becomes fully absorbed in the current activity. This results in a psychological sensation of existing within an alternative reality, a phenomenon often colloquially referred to as *the flow* [14]. However, virtual reality also introduces a negative side effect known as cybersickness, that has been attracting growing scientific interest [1]. Cybersickness stands as one of the paramount impediments to virtual reality widespread adoption, inducing users with a variety of symptoms akin to motion sickness [1, 15, 16]. It is crucial to recognize, however, that the occurrence of adverse effects is not certain after exposure to virtual reality and can vary among individuals. Several factors contribute to this variability, including an individual's adaptation to repeated use, the specific hardware utilized, and the nature of the content experienced during a virtual reality session [1]. Consequently, the severity of cybersickness can also vary, causing anything from mild discomfort in some users to significantly disrupting the overall virtual reality experience in others. As the manifestation of symptoms can divert users' attention away from the virtual world [1], it is believed to be negatively correlated with the sense of presence [15].

# 3   Methodology

## 3.1   Sample

The sample of our study was selected though non-probabilistic convenience sampling and involved 20 participants, 12 males and 8 females, with ages between 17 and 43 years (M = 21.02, SD = 4.604). Participants reported low levels of experience in virtual reality (M = 2.30, SD = 1.08), assessed on a scale of 1 to 5, where 1 indicated no experience and 5 indicated a high level of experience.

## 3.2   Variables, Materials, and Instruments

**Variables and Correlations.** In this study, our aim was to explore the potential influence of several independent variables, namely content type, exposure time, and gender, on a range of dependent variables. Our first objective was measuring global presence, encompassing three distinct dimensions – spatial presence, involvement, and experienced realism. Additionally, given that participants would experience extended periods of interaction with virtual reality during our evaluation sessions, we sought to assess the potential occurrence and impact of cybersickness and its possible correlation with prolonged exposure time and gender differences. Table 1 summarizes the variables and how we correlated them.

**Materials.** Starting with the content, in contrast to the study by Melo et al. [6], we selected four types that exhibits variations in several dimensions: Digital Game (DG): – synthetic, closer to abstraction, six degrees of freedom, auditory and visual stimuli, a high requirement for bodily movement, and an outcome. Beat Saber engages players in a rhythm-based gaming experience where the primary goal is to slice musical beats that appear on the screen in sync with the music and advance towards the player [17]; Simulator (S): Mission: ISS – synthetic, closer to realism, six degrees of freedom, visual stimuli, a moderate requirement for bodily movement, and no specific outcome. Mission: ISS offers users the unique opportunity to explore the International Space Station while navigating through a zero-gravity environment [18]; Synthetic Cultural Environment (CE): Talasnal House VR – synthetic, closer to realism, six degrees of freedom, visual and auditory stimuli, a low requirement for bodily movement, and no specific outcome. Talasnal House VR invites users to visit a typical 20th-century house nestled in Serra da Lousã, Portugal [19]; 360° Video (V): Festivities of S. Gonçalinho – captured, realistic, three degrees of freedom, visual stimuli, no requirement for bodily movement, and no specific outcome. The 360° video was recorded during the celebrations of São Gonçalinho, a religious festival that takes place in Aveiro, known for devotees fulfilling their

**Table 1.** Dependent and independent variables correlations.

| Dependent Variable | Independent Variables Correlations |
|---|---|
| Presence: Global Presence = Spatial Presence + Involvement + Experienced Realism | All Content Types<br>All Content Types × Total Exposure Time<br>All Content Types × Gender<br>All Content Types × Total Exposure Time × Gender<br>Digital Game × Exposure Time<br>Simulator × Exposure Time<br>Cultural Environment × Exposure Time<br>360° Video × Exposure Time<br>Digital Game × Gender<br>Simulator × Gender<br>Cultural Environment × Gender<br>360° Video × Gender<br>Digital Game × Exposure Time × Gender<br>Simulator × Exposure Time × Gender<br>Cultural Environment × Exposure Time × Gender<br>360° Video × Exposure Time × Gender |
| Cybersickness | Total Exposure Time<br>Gender<br>Total Exposure Time × Gender |

vows by tossing *cavacas* (a conventual sweet) from the top of São Gonçalinho chapel down to the crowd below, who attempt to catch them [20]. Table 2 presents the variables introduced to differentiate each content type.

**Table 2.** Differences between each content type.

| Content | Virtual World | Abstraction – Realism Continuum | Degrees of Freedom | Stimuli | Body Movement | Outcome |
|---|---|---|---|---|---|---|
| DG | Synthetic | Closer to Abstraction | 6 | Auditory Visual | High | Yes |
| S | Synthetic | Closer to Realism | 6 | Visual | Moderate | No |
| CE | Synthetic | Closer to Realism | 6 | Auditory Visual | Low | No |
| V | Captured | Realistic | 3 | Visual | No | No |

Regarding the hardware, we selected the Meta Quest 2 [21] head-mounted display due to its wireless functionality, affordability, and performance. This decision aligns with the functional requirements demanded by our research, providing participants with freedom of movement while delivering a seamless virtual reality experience without technological disruptions.

**Igroup Presence Questionnaire.** The users' sense of presence within the virtual world was measured using the Igroup Presence Questionnaire [22]. This decision was based on the questionnaire's validation for the Portuguese population [23] and its alignment with our theoretical framework concerning immersion and presence. The questionnaire consists of 14 questions, using a 5-point Likert scale (Strongly Disagree [1] to Strongly Agree [5]), encompassing one global dimension – global presence (the general "sense of being there") – and three subdimensions: spatial presence (the sense of physical presence in the virtual world), involvement (attention to and engagement with the virtual world), and experienced realism (subjective realism in the virtual world) [24].

**Simulator Sickness Questionnaire.** The degree of cybersickness was assessed with a Portuguese version of the Simulator Sickness Questionnaire [25], obtained through a rigorous translation process conducted by our research team and a linguist, incorporating retrotranslation methods (see Appendix 1). The questionnaire comprises 16 symptoms distributed across three components. To quantify the degree of cybersickness, specific weights are assigned to each symptom within each of the three components. Subsequently, the score for each component is calculated by multiplying the user's classification values for each symptom (none (0), slight (1), moderate (2), or severe (3)) by their respective weights and then summing them. The final cybersickness score is then determined by aggregating the total scores from each component and multiplying the result by an overall weight [25].

### 3.3   Evaluation Protocol

Each evaluation session was structured with an approximate duration of 60 min. Participants were exposed to a digital game, simulator, cultural environment and 360° video in a randomized sequence to eliminate potential bias. Interactions were time-limited, with a maximum of 15 min allocated for the digital game, 10 min for both the simulator and the cultural environment, and 5 min for the 360° video. The rationale behind assigning different time limits for each content type was based on their levels of engagement. We propose that content with higher interactivity and more engagement elements, like the digital game, should be given more time to account for its learning curve and variety of mechanics. Conversely, content with reduced interactivity or low engagement elements, such as the 360° video, should be assigned shorter durations to avoid hindering the user experience. Following each exposure to a content type, participants completed the Igroup Presence Questionnaire. The Simulator Sickness Questionnaire was administered exclusively at the conclusion of the entire session. Throughout the session, the research team documented pertinent observations and the duration of user interaction with each content, utilizing an observation grid to register the study's findings. Both questionnaires were implemented using a secure online survey tool, with servers hosted at the university, ensuring the privacy and confidentiality of participants' data throughout the research process.

# 4 Results

The research aimed to understand which factors can influence the users' sense of presence and the occurrence of cybersickness in the virtual reality context. Specifically, we explored the impact of content type, exposure time, and gender on users' sense of presence and examined whether the total exposure time or gender influenced the development of cybersickness among a sample of 20 participants. Due to non-normal data distribution, non-parametric tests were used for assessing presence and cybersickness scores. Subsequent post hoc tests were conducted to understand specific statistically significant differences within the analysed data.

## 4.1 Presence

**All Content Types.** *Global Presence:* A Friedman Test was conducted to assess the global presence across all content types, revealing no statistically significant differences ($X^2 = 1.736, p = 0.629$). The median (IQR) global presence scores for the digital game, simulator, cultural environment, and 360° video were 3.43 (3.09 to 3.73) with a mean of 3.45 ($SD = 0.52$), 3.56 (3.38 to 3.95) with a mean of 3.64 ($SD = 0.44$), 3.66 (2.99 to 3.81) with a mean of 3.47 ($SD = 0.59$), and 3.64 (2.81 to 3.99) with a mean of 3.46 ($SD = 0.69$), respectively. *Spatial Presence:* A Friedman Test was conducted to assess the spatial presence across all content types, revealing a statistically significant difference ($X^2 = 11.078, p = 0.011$). The median (IQR) spatial presence scores for the digital game, simulator, cultural environment, and 360° video were 3.83 (3.54 to 4.33) with a mean of 3.91 ($SD = 0.51$), 3.83 (3.54 to 4.00) with a mean of 3.73 ($SD = 0.44$), 3.59 (3.04 to 4.00) with a mean of 3.51 ($SD = 0.52$) and 3.50 (3.04 to 3.83) with a mean of 3.38 ($SD = 0.76$), respectively. A post hoc analysis using Wilcoxon signed-rank tests was performed, with a Bonferroni correction applied, setting the significance level at $p < 0.008$. No statistically significant differences were detected between various pairs of conditions, specifically between the digital game and simulator ($Z = -0.827, p = 0.408$), digital game and cultural environment ($Z = -2.291, p = 0.022$), simulator and cultural environment ($Z = -1.686, p = 0.092$), simulator and 360° video ($Z = -2.218, p = 0.027$) and cultural environment and 360° video ($Z = -0.580, p = 0.562$). However, a statistically significant reduction in spatial presence was evident when comparing the digital game and the 360° video ($Z = -3.154, p = 0.002$). *Involvement:* A Friedman Test was conducted to assess the involvement across all content types, revealing no statistically significant differences ($X^2 = 1.754, p = 0.625$). The median (IQR) involvement scores for the digital game, simulator, cultural environment, and 360° video were 3.75 (2.75 to 4.19) with a mean of 3.59 ($SD = 0.85$), 3.63 (3.06 to 4.50) with a mean of 3.71 ($SD = 0.84$), 3.25 (2.63 to 3.94) with a mean of 3.35 ($SD = 0.91$), and 3.63 (2.75 to 4.00) with a mean of 3.41 ($SD = 0.86$), respectively. *Experienced Realism:* A Friedman Test was conducted to assess the experienced realism across all content types, revealing a statistically significant difference ($X^2 = 8.741, p = 0.033$). The median (IQR) experienced realism scores for the digital game, simulator, cultural environment, and 360° video were 2.75 (1.75 to 3.50) with a mean of 2.85 ($SD = 1.17$), 3.25 (3.00 to 4.19) with a mean of 3.49 ($SD = 0.77$), 3.63 (3.00 to 4.25) with a mean of 3.55 ($SD = 0.76$) and 3.50 (3.00 to 4.63) with a mean of 3.58 ($SD = 1.03$), respectively. A post hoc analysis using Wilcoxon signed-rank tests was performed, with a Bonferroni correction applied, setting the significance level at $p < 0.008$. No statistically significant differences were detected between various pairs of conditions, specifically between the digital game and simulator ($Z = -2.423$, $p = 0.015$), digital game and 360° video ($Z = -2.471$, $p = 0.013$), simulator and cultural environment ($Z = -0.398$, $p = 0.691$), simulator and 360° video ($Z = -0.233$, $p = 0.815$) and cultural environment and 360° video ($Z = -0.066$, $p = 0.947$). However, a statistically significant reduction in experienced realism was evident when comparing the digital game and the cultural environment ($Z = -2.816$, $p = 0.005$).

**All Content Types × Total Exposure Time.** A Spearman's Rank-Order Correlation was conducted to examine potential differences between the mean presence and the total exposure time. The analysis did not reveal a statistically significant correlation between the total exposure time and mean global presence ($rs = 0.439$, $p = 0.053$), total exposure time and mean spatial presence ($rs = 0.076$, $p = 0.750$), total exposure time and mean involvement ($rs = 0.298$, $p = 0.201$) or total exposure time and mean experienced realism ($rs = 0.352$, $p = 0.128$).

**All Content Types × Gender.** *Global Presence:* A Friedman Test was conducted to examine potential differences in the global presence between both genders across all content types, revealing no statistically significant differences in female participants ($X^2 = 4.747$, $p = 0.191$) and male participants ($X^2 = 2.975$, $p = 0.396$). The median (IQR) global presence scores for the digital game, simulator, cultural environment, and 360° video were 3.75 (3.00 to 4.15) with a mean of 3.68 ($SD = 0.67$) for female participants and 3.38 (3.09 to 3.56) with a mean of 3.29 ($SD = 0.34$) for male participants, 3.60 (3.43 to 4.05) with a mean of 3.75 ($SD = 0.45$) for female participants and 3.56 (3.23 to 3.84) with a mean of 3.57 ($SD = 0.43$) for male participants, 3.57 (2.87 to 3.81) with a mean of 3.44 ($SD = 0.72$) for female participants and 3.70 (3.12 to 3.86) with a mean of 3.49 ($SD = 0.52$) for male participants, 3.79 (3.12 to 4.14) with a mean of 3.70 ($SD = 0.61$) for female participants and 3.54 (2.59 to 3.93) with a mean of 3.29 ($SD = 0.71$) for male participants, respectively. *Spatial Presence:* A Friedman Test was conducted to examine potential differences in the spatial presence between both genders across all content types, revealing no statistically significant differences in female participants ($X^2 = 7.356$, $p = 0.061$) and male participants ($X^2 = 6.057$, $p = 0.109$). The median (IQR) spatial presence scores for the digital game, simulator, cultural environment, and 360° video were 3.92 (3.42 to 4.33) with a mean of 3.92 ($SD = 0.45$) for female participants and 3.75 (3.54 to 4.29) with a mean of 3.90 ($SD = 0.57$) for male participants, 3.83 (3.50 to 4.13) with a mean of 3.77 ($SD = 0.43$) for female participants and 3.75 (3.67 to 3.96) with a mean of 3.70 ($SD = 0.46$) for male participants, 3.17 (3.00 to 4.05) with a mean of 3.36 ($SD = 0.60$) for female participants and 3.67 (3.37 to 4.00) with a mean of 3.61 ($SD = 0.46$) for male participants, 3.59 (3.08 to 4.13) with a mean of 3.46 ($SD = 0.85$) for female participants and 3.42 (3.04 to 3.79) with a mean of 3.33 ($SD = 0.74$) for male participants, respectively. *Involvement:* A Friedman Test was conducted to examine potential differences in the involvement between both genders across all content types, revealing no statistically significant differences in female participants ($X^2 = 2.956$, $p = 0.398$) and male participants ($X^2 = 1.893$, $p = 0.595$). The median (IQR) involvement scores for the digital game, simulator, cultural environment, and 360° video were 2.88 (2.56 to 4.00) with a mean of 3.31 ($SD = 0.91$) for female participants and 3.86 (2.94 to 4.25) with a mean of 3.77 ($SD = 0.79$) for male participants, 3.75 (3.13 to 4.44) with a mean of 3.72 ($SD = 0.93$) for female participants and 3.25 (3.06 to 4.69) with a mean of 3.71 ($SD = 0.82$) for male participants, 3.25 (2.50 to 3.75) with a mean of 3.19 ($SD = 0.60$) for female participants and 3.25 (3.06 to 4.00) with a mean of 3.46 ($SD = 0.82$) for male participants, 3.75 (2.56 to 4.19) with a mean of 3.56 ($SD = 0.90$) for female participants and 3.38 (2.75 to 4.00) with a mean of 3.31 ($SD = 0.85$) for male participants, respectively. *Experienced Realism:* A Friedman Test was conducted to examine potential differences in the experienced realism between both genders across all content types, revealing no statistically significant differences in female participants ($X^2 = 0.243$, p $= 0.970$) and a statistically significant difference in male participants ($X^2 = 16.243$, p $= 0.001$). The median (IQR) experienced realism scores for the digital game, simulator, cultural environment, and 360° video were 3.88 (2.94 to 4.81) with a mean of 3.81 ($SD = 0.99$) for female participants and 2.13 (1.75 to 2.75) with a mean of 2.21 ($SD = 0.77$) for male participants, 3.63 (3.06 to 4.44) with a mean of 3.75 ($SD = 0.71$) for female participants and 3.12 (2.56 to 3.94) with a mean of 3.31 ($SD = 0.78$) for male participants, 3.88 (3.06 to 4.25) with a mean of 3.78 ($SD = 0.67$) for female participants and 3.50 (2.56 to 4.19) with a mean of 3.40 ($SD = 0.81$) for male participants, 4.25 (3.50 to 4.94) with a mean of 4.09 ($SD = 0.88$) for female participants and 3.13 (2.81 to 4.06) with a mean of 3.23 ($SD = 1.01$) for male participants, respectively. A post hoc analysis using Wilcoxon signed-rank tests was performed considering the male participants, with a Bonferroni correction applied, setting the significance level at $p < 0.008$. No statistically significant differences were detected between three pairs of conditions, specifically between the simulator and cultural environment ($Z = -0.588$, $p = 0.556$), simulator and 360° video ($Z = -0.460$, $p = 0.645$) and cultural environment and 360° video ($Z = -0.723$, $p = 0.469$). However, a statistically significant reduction in experienced realism was evident in male participants when comparing the digital game and the simulator ($Z = -2.861$, $p = 0.004$), the digital game and the cultural environment ($Z = -3.064$, $p = 0.002$) and the digital game and 360° video ($Z = -2.705$, $p = 0.007$).

**All Content Types × Gender × Total Exposure Time.** A Spearman's Rank-Order

Correlation was conducted to examine potential differences between the mean presence and total exposure time across both genders. The analysis did not reveal a statistically significant correlation between the total exposure time and mean spatial presence (*rs* $= 0.180$, $p = 0.670$) or total exposure time and mean involvement (*rs* $= 0.500$, $p = 0.207$) for female participants, nor between the total exposure time and mean global presence (*rs* $= 0.309$, $p = 0.329$), total exposure time and mean spatial presence (*rs* $= -0.007$, $p = 0.983$), total exposure time and mean involvement (*rs* $= 0.235$, $p = 0.463$) or total exposure time and mean experienced realism (*rs* $= 0.291$, $p = 0.358$) for male participants. However, a statistically significant strong positive correlation was found between the total exposure time and mean global presence (*rs* $= 0.762$, $p = 0.028$) and total exposure time and mean experienced realism (*rs* $= 0.778$, $p = 0.023$) for female participants.

**Digital Game × Exposure Time.** A Spearman's Rank-Order Correlation was con-

ducted to examine potential differences between the presence and the exposure time to the digital game. The analysis did not reveal a statistically significant correlation between exposure time and global presence ($rs = 0.352, p = 0.128$), exposure time and spatial presence ($rs = 0.021, p = 0.930$), exposure time and involvement ($rs = 0.220, p = 0.352$) or exposure time and experienced realism ($rs = 0.362, p = 0.117$).

**Digital Game × Gender.** A Mann-Whitney U Test was conducted to examine potential differences in the presence in the digital game between both genders, revealing no statistically significant differences in the global presence ($U = 30.00, Z = -1.389, p = 0.181$), spatial presence ($U = 45.50, Z = -0.194, p = 0.851$) and involvement ($U = 62.50, Z = 1.130, p = 0.270$). However, a statistically significant difference was found in the experienced realism ($U = 10.50, Z = -2.922, p = 0.002$).

**Digital Game × Exposure Time × Gender.** A Spearman's Rank-Order Correlation

was conducted to examine potential differences between the presence and the exposure time to the digital game across both genders. The analysis did not reveal a statistically significant correlation between exposure time and global presence ($rs = 0.082, p = 0.846$), exposure time and spatial presence ($rs = 0.584, p = 0.128$), exposure time and involvement ($rs = 0.084, p = 0.843$) or exposure time and experienced realism ($rs = 0.168, p = 0.691$) for female participants, nor between exposure time and global presence ($rs = 0.563, p = 0.057$), exposure time and spatial presence ($rs = 0.193, p = 0.548$), exposure time and involvement ($rs = 0.478, p = 0.116$) or exposure time and experienced realism ($rs = 0.294, p = 0.353$) for male participants.

**Simulator × Exposure Time.** A Spearman's Rank-Order Correlation was conducted

to examine potential differences between the presence and the exposure time to the simulator. The analysis did not reveal a statistically significant correlation between exposure time and spatial presence ($rs = 0.048, p = 0.840$) or exposure time and experienced realism ($rs = 0.339, p = 0.144$). However, a statistically significant moderate positive correlation was found between the exposure time and global presence ($rs = 0.537, p = 0.015$) and exposure time and involvement ($rs = 0.584, p = 0.007$).

**Simulator × Gender.** A Mann-Whitney U Test was conducted to examine potential

differences in the presence in the simulator between both genders, revealing no statistically significant differences in the global presence ($U = 39.50, Z = -0.657, p = 0.521$), spatial presence ($U = 44.00, Z = -0.313, p = 0.792$), involvement ($U = 44.50, Z = -0.272, p = 0.792$) or experienced realism ($U = 30.50, Z = -1.360, p = 0.181$).

**Simulator × Exposure Time × Gender.** A Spearman's Rank-Order Correlation was

conducted to examine potential differences between the presence and the exposure time to the simulator across both genders. The analysis did not reveal a statistically significant correlation between exposure time and spatial presence ($rs = 0.303, p = 0.466$), exposure time and involvement ($rs = 0.578, p = 0.133$) or exposure time and experienced realism ($rs = 0.570, p = 0.140$) for female participants, nor between exposure time and global presence ($rs = 0.526, p = 0.079$), exposure time and spatial presence ($rs = -0.086, p = 0.792$) or exposure time and experienced realism ($rs = 0.372, p = 0.234$) for male participants. However, a statistically significant strong positive correlation was found between the exposure time and global presence ($rs = 0.731, p = 0.040$) for female participants and between exposure time and involvement ($rs = 0.674, p = 0.016$) for male participants.

**Cultural Environment × Exposure Time.** *Exposure Time:* A Spearman's Rank-Order Correlation was conducted to examine potential differences between the presence and the exposure time to the cultural environment. The analysis did not reveal a statistically significant correlation between exposure time and global presence ($rs = 0.251, p = 0.287$), exposure time and spatial presence ($rs = 0.187, p = 0.430$), exposure time and involvement ($rs = 0.309, p = 0.185$) or exposure time and experienced realism ($rs = 0.301, p = 0.197$).

**Cultural Environment × Gender.** A Mann-Whitney U Test was conducted to examine potential differences in the presence in the cultural environment between both genders, revealing no statistically significant differences in the global presence ($U = 52.00, Z = 0.309, p = 0.792$), spatial presence ($U = 59.50, Z = 0.894, p = 0.384$), involvement ($U = 55.50, Z = 0.583, p = 0.571$) or experienced realism ($U = 35.00, Z = -1.013, p = 0.343$).

**Cultural Environment × Exposure Time × Gender.** A Spearman's Rank-Order Correlation was conducted to examine potential differences between the presence and the exposure time to the cultural environment across both genders. The analysis did not reveal a statistically significant correlation between exposure time and global presence ($rs = 0.299, p = 0.471$), exposure time and spatial presence ($rs = -0.158, p = 0.709$), exposure time and involvement ($rs = 0.566, p = 0.143$) or exposure time and experienced realism ($rs = 0.442, p = 0.273$) for female participants, nor between exposure time and global presence ($rs = 0.014, p = 0.966$), exposure time and spatial presence ($rs = 0.356, p = 0.256$), exposure time and involvement ($rs = -0.021, p = 0.947$) or exposure time and experienced realism ($rs = 0.165, p = 0.607$) for male participants.

**360° Video × Exposure Time.** A Spearman's Rank-Order Correlation was conducted to examine potential differences between the presence and the exposure time to the 360° video. The analysis did not reveal a statistically significant correlation between exposure time and global presence ($rs = -0.018, p = 0.939$), exposure time and spatial presence ($rs = 0.210, p = 0.373$), exposure time and involvement ($rs = -0.171, p = 0.470$) or exposure time and experienced realism ($rs = 0.064, p = 0.790$).

**360° Video × Gender.** A Mann-Whitney U Test was conducted to examine potential differences in the presence in the 360° video between both genders, revealing no statistically significant differences in the global presence ($U = 32.00, Z = -1.235, p = 0.238$), spatial presence ($U = 40.50, Z = -0.581, p = 0.571$), involvement ($U = 41.50, Z = -0.505, p = 0.624$) or experienced realism ($U = 23.00, Z = -1.942, p = 0.057$).

**360° Video × Exposure Time × Gender.** A Spearman's Rank-Order Correlation was conducted to examine potential differences between the presence and the exposure time to the cultural environment across both genders. The analysis did not reveal a statistically significant correlation between exposure time and global presence ($rs = 0.299$, $p = 0.471$), exposure time and spatial presence ($rs = -0.158$, $p = 0.709$), exposure time and involvement ($rs = 0.566$, $p = 0.143$) or exposure time and experienced realism ($rs = 0.442$, $p = 0.273$) for female participants, nor between exposure time and global presence ($rs = 0.014$, $p = 0.966$), exposure time and spatial presence ($rs = 0.356$, $p = 0.256$), exposure time and involvement ($rs = -0.021$, $p = 0.947$) or exposure time and experienced realism ($rs = 0.165$, $p = 0.607$) for male participants.

Table 3 presents the correlation where statistically significant differences were found. GP = Global Presence, SP = Spatial Presence, I = Involvement, ER = Experienced Realism.

**Table 3.** Statistically significant correlations pertaining to presence indicators.

| Independent Variables | Presence | | | |
|---|---|---|---|---|
| | GP | SP | I | ER |
| All Content Types | - | X | - | X |
| All Content Types × Total Exposure Time | - | - | - | - |
| All Content Types × Gender | - | - | - | X |
| All Content Types × Total Exposure Time x Gender | X | - | - | X |
| Digital Game × Exposure Time | - | - | - | - |
| Simulator × Exposure Time | X | - | X | - |
| Cultural Environment × Exposure Time | - | - | - | - |
| 360° Video × Exposure Time | - | - | - | - |
| Digital Game × Gender | - | - | - | X |
| Simulator × Gender | - | - | - | - |
| Cultural Environment × Gender | - | - | - | - |
| 360° Video × Gender | - | - | - | - |
| Digital Game x Exposure Time × Gender | - | - | - | - |
| Simulator x Exposure Time × Gender | X | - | X | - |
| Cultural Environment × Exposure Time × Gender | - | - | - | - |
| 360° Video × Exposure Time × Gender | - | - | - | - |

## 4.2  Cybersickness

The median (IQR) cybersickness scores were 20.55 (3.70 to 71.05) with a mean of 34.59 (SD = 37.49).

**Total Exposure Time.** A Spearman's Rank-Order Correlation was conducted to examine potential differences between the cybersickness and the total exposure time, revealing no statistically significant correlation between both variables ($rs = -0.314$, $p = 0.178$).

**Gender.** A Mann-Whitney U Test was conducted to examine potential differences in the cybersickness between both genders, revealing no statistically significant differences ($U = 28.00, Z = -1.549, p = 0.135$). The median (IQR) cybersickness scores were 37.40 (10.30 to 73.83) with a mean of 47.21 ($SD = 42.34$) for female participants and 9.35 (0.93 to 63.58) with a mean of 26.17 ($SD = 33.07$) for male participants, respectively.

**Total Exposure Time × Gender.** A Spearman's Rank-Order Correlation was conducted to examine potential differences between the cybersickness and the total exposure time across both genders. The analysis did not reveal a statistically significant correlation between cybersickness and exposure time for male participants ($rs = -0.050, p = 0.878$). However, a statistically significant very strong negative correlation was found between the cybersickness and total exposure time for female participants ($rs = -0.898$, $p = 0.002$). Table 4 presents the correlation where statistically significant differences were found.

**Table 4.** Statistically significant correlations pertaining to cybersickness indicators.

| Independent Variables | Cybersickness |
| --- | --- |
| Total Exposure Time | - |
| Gender | - |
| Total Exposure Time x Gender | X |

## 5  Discussion

***Research Question.*** Can content type, exposure time, or gender exert an influence on the sense of presence in virtual reality experiences?

The results suggest that content type does not significantly impact the global presence. However, an examination of the latter subdimensions revealed statistically significant variations in the spatial presence and experienced realism. Participants reported a significant difference in spatial presence between the digital game and the 360° video, with the former yielding a higher spatial presence score. The digital game being the one eliciting the higher spatial presence could be better explained by Huizinga's [27] concept of the 'magic circle'. According to this concept, when playing a game, players experience a psychological sensation of being transported to a "magic circle" – a safe space with defined rules, isolated from the real world, also related to the concept of flow [14] and akin to the concept of presence. Another possible explanation for this disparity is the interactivity allowed by the 360° video, where users' movement was limited to three degrees of freedom. The concept of embodiment [26] may have also contributed to this result, as Beat Saber detects users' arm movements through controllers and represents them in the virtual world with lightsabres, while a 360° video cannot replicate the user's body, at least in real time. The content type also affected experienced realism, with a notable difference between the digital game and the cultural environment. This outcome could be attributed to the digital game's proximity to abstraction, while the cultural environment leans towards realism, as it recreates a typical house in Serra da Lousã. However, as the 360° video represents a captured, fully realistic content, it should theoretically elicit a higher level of experienced realism. Hence, it is essential to understand the reasons behind being surpassed by the cultural environment in this dimension. By analysing the data that we registered in our observation grid, one participant referred to the cultural environment as seeming more realistic than the 360° video because the latter had low quality (pixelization artefacts), which may be the reason that hindered the reported experienced realism.

When examining gender-specific distinctions, it became evident that content type did not exert an influence on global presence, spatial presence, or involvement. However, a difference was observed in terms of experienced realism. An analysis of the specific content type highlighted that male participants rated the digital game as having low experienced realism, scoring it lower than the other three content types. These findings corroborate those reported by Melo et al. [6], where female participants attributed higher experienced realism scores to synthetic content, mirroring our study's results when comparing the experienced realism scores of both genders in relation to the digital game. Melo et al. suggest that these differences may stem from variations in spatial cognition between genders, hypothesizing that women perceive synthetic content as more natural, while men consider realistic content as more natural [6].

By introducing the total exposure time variable in the gender-specific comparison, the results demonstrated that female participants who spent more time immersed scored higher in global presence and in the subdimension experienced realism. The correlation between these variables indicates that extended exposure translated in a more engaging experience for female participants. Finally, when analysing each content individually, no significant differences were observed in the digital game, cultural environment, and 360° video. In the simulator, however, participants who spent more time exposed tended to report higher values of global presence (female participants) and involvement (male participants).

***Research Question.*** Can the exposure time or gender influence the development of cybersickness symptoms?

The analysis conducted on cybersickness revealed no statistically significant differences between symptom manifestation and either total exposure time or participants' gender, with the latter being inconsistent with the claim of women being more likely to develop cybersickness symptoms [27]. However, when correlating both independent variables with the cybersickness scores, we observed a negative trend in total exposure time among female participants. Upon examining the data regarding the evolution of presence scores over total exposure time between genders, it was observed that female participants reported higher levels of global presence and experienced realism the longer they remained immersed. Comparing this with the cybersickness negative correlation, we can theorize that the presence results could be attributed to the manifestation of cybersickness over time. That is, female participants who experienced moderate to severe symptoms earlier in the session stopped viewing the content that triggered cybersickness and scored lower global presence and experienced realism. In contrast, those who experienced none to light symptoms spent more time viewing each content type and scored higher presence values in the aforementioned dimensions. These findings support the statement that cybersickness can negatively influence the sense of presence, particularly in the case of female users, leading them to disengage from the virtual world earlier due to symptoms.

While the influence of content type on cybersickness was not within the scope of our study, during the evaluation sessions we registered some information in our observation grid. We observed that nine out of the 20 participants, accounting for 45% of our sample, reported cybersickness while experiencing the 360° video, with symptoms mainly related to blurred vision, dizziness, nausea, and vertigo. The reason behind this significant number of cybersickness reports may stem from technical aspects of the content. Upon analysing the 360° video along with the participants who reported cybersickness, we identified a set of factors that may explain the high number of symptoms developed and the impairment in experienced realism, in which we were expecting the content to score highly, considering that it is a realistic representation of the real world: 1) Level of Interactivity: the participant was limited to three degrees of freedom; 2): Brightness Variations: the video began in a staircase with low lighting, in a dimly lit path with small windows allowing little light to enter; after reaching the end of the staircase, the participant encountered a brightly lit balcony with sunlight; 3) Visual and Vestibular Misalignment: the image was trembling throughout the video, but most incisively during the staircase ascent; unnatural and fast camera movements; camera held in the air over a balcony.

## 6  Conclusion

As the adoption of XR gradually grows across diverse domains, it becomes increasingly necessary to understand the indicators that can affect the user experience while using XR technologies. Within the academic field, there has been a noticeable focus on multiple aspects [15, 16, 28, 29], aiming to contribute to a more incisive view of what may be established as guidelines for optimizing XR experiences. The work our team develops at DigiMedia's XRLab is focused on improving the user experience across a diverse range of interdisciplinary applications of XR, spanning from augmented reality in cultural tourism [30] and nutrition education [31], to virtual reality in psychology [32] and neurosciences [33]. The work presented in this paper represents an additional contribution to this search for theoretical and practical evidence that may help ground useful guidelines for designing XR experiences, particularly focusing on virtual reality. In this paper we aimed to assess whether the type of the exhibited content, the exposure duration or the gender of the participant are factors that can shape the sense of presence. Additionally, we also sought to understand if the prolonged use of virtual reality and gender had any influence on the manifestation of cybersickness symptoms.

### 6.1  Study Contributions

The data suggests that the content type did not significantly influence global presence. However, it did affect spatial presence and experienced realism. Participants considered the digital game to have the highest spatial presence but the lowest experienced realism. When comparing genders, male participants tended to perceive the digital game as less realistic than other content types, while female participants considered it similarly to other content types, thereby supporting Melo et al. [6]'s hypothesis that women perceive synthetic content as more natural, while men consider realistic content as more natural. The results also demonstrated that exposure time influenced the sense of presence reports. Female participants who remained immersed for longer periods reported increased global presence and experienced realism. The same trend was observed with the simulator, where increased exposure time resulted in higher global presence for female participants and higher involvement for male participants.

When analysing the manifestation of cybersickness symptoms, no statistically significant differences were found in total exposure time or gender. However, when crossing both independent variables, we noted that female participants who experienced cybersickness symptoms tended to abandon the virtual world earlier and report lower values on presence, sustaining the claim that the cybersickness has a negative impact on the sense of presence indicators.

**Cinematographic Virtual Reality Technical Principles and Guidelines.** During the evaluation sessions we noted that the 360° video was the one eliciting higher manifestation of symptoms, reported by 45% of the participants. After analysing the content, our team a set of principles and guidelines aimed at enhancing the user experience in cinematic virtual reality. These principles and guidelines are outlined in Table 5.

**Table 5.** Cinematographic Virtual Reality Technical Principles and Guidelines

| Principle | Guideline |
|---|---|
| Camera Movement | Ensure that camera movements are smooth. Alternatively, refrain from moving the camera while recording. |
| Camera Stability | Maintain camera stability to avoid trembling or "floating." |
| Brightness | Prevent abrupt brightness changes, such as transitioning from a dark scene to a bright one. |
| Monoscopic vs Stereoscopic | Prioritize stereoscopic videos as they can create a sense of depth, unlike monoscopic videos, which give the impression of a flat image. |
| Image and Sound | Guarantee good image and sound quality with correct synchronization. |

## 6.2 Study Limitations and Future Work

A limitation of this study is our sole reliance on measurement scales, may not have been the most suitable approach, as the responses obtained might offer only a partial glimpse of what participants believe they felt during the experience, potentially not accurately representing their genuine state. To address this limitation, a potential solution could involve the incorporation of a portable electroencephalography device or presence counters [34]. We believe that the combined use of these instruments, along with subsequent parallel analysis, would yield more reliable and pertinent data. Another limitation was the 60-min duration of the evaluation sessions. While this duration was chosen to ensure comprehensive data collection, it may have been excessively long, potentially impacting the results. Firstly, the prolonged duration might have led to increased participant fatigue or discomfort, which could, in turn, affect their perception of presence and susceptibility to cybersickness. Secondly, this extended duration may have inadvertently discouraged some potential participants from taking part in the study, contributing to a reduced sample size.

Future research could benefit from the inclusion of additional data collection instruments and the exploration of shorter test sessions to mitigate these limitations. Furthermore, forthcoming studies should evaluate 360° videos according to the guidelines we propose to avoid hindering the user experience in this domain. Finally, replicating the same experiment with equal time limits would be interesting to validate or refute our theory regarding the time allocation to each content.

**Acknowledgements.** This work was financially supported by national funds through FCT – Foundation for Science and Technology, I.P., under the Grant Agreements No. 2021.06634.BD, 2021.07253.BD, and 2022.10675.BD and Project UIDB/05460/2020.

**Disclosure of Interests.** The authors have no competing interests to declare that are relevant to the content of this article.

# Appendix

| Simulator Sickness Questionnaire |
| :---: |
| (Versão Original: Kennedy et al., 1993) |
| (Versão Traduzida: Reisinho et al., 2024) |

**Para cada um dos seguintes sintomas, assinale a intensidade que está a sentir neste momento.**

| | | | | |
| :--- | :---: | :---: | :---: | :---: |
| **Desconforto Geral** | Ausente | Leve | Moderado | Grave |
| **Fadiga** | Ausente | Leve | Moderado | Grave |
| **Dor de Cabeça** | Ausente | Leve | Moderado | Grave |
| **Cansaço Visual** | Ausente | Leve | Moderado | Grave |
| **Dificuldade em Manter a Atenção / o Foco** | Ausente | Leve | Moderado | Grave |
| **Aumento da Salivação** | Ausente | Leve | Moderado | Grave |
| **Suores** | Ausente | Leve | Moderado | Grave |
| **Náuseas** | Ausente | Leve | Moderado | Grave |
| **Problemas de Concentração** | Ausente | Leve | Moderado | Grave |
| **Sensação de Cabeça Pesada** | Ausente | Leve | Moderado | Grave |
| **Visão Turva ou Embaçada** | Ausente | Leve | Moderado | Grave |
| **Tontura (com os olhos abertos)** | Ausente | Leve | Moderado | Grave |
| **Tontura (com os olhos fechados)** | Ausente | Leve | Moderado | Grave |
| **Vertigens** | Ausente | Leve | Moderado | Grave |
| **Desconforto Abdominal** | Ausente | Leve | Moderado | Grave |
| **Arrotos Frequentes** | Ausente | Leve | Moderado | Grave |

# References

1. LaValle, S.M.: Virtual Reality. Cambridge University Press (2019)
2. Frederiksen, J.G., et al.: Cognitive load and performance in immersive virtual reality versus conventional virtual reality simulation training of laparoscopic surgery: a randomized trial. Surg. Endosc. **34**, 1244–1252 (2020). https://doi.org/10.1007/s00464-019-06887-8
3. Harrington, C.M., et al.: 360° operative videos: a randomised cross-over study evaluating attentiveness and information retention. J. Surg. Educ. **75**, 993–1000 (2018). https://doi.org/10.1016/j.jsurg.2017.10.010
4. Reisinho, P., Raposo, R., Zagalo, N., Ribeiro, O.: Interactive Narrative in virtual Reminiscence Therapy to Stimulate Memory and communication in People with Dementia (2024)
5. Narciso, D., Bessa, M., Melo, M., Coelho, A., Vasconcelos-Raposo, J.: Immersive 360° video user experience: impact of different variables in the sense of presence and cybersickness. Univers. Access Inf. Soc. **18**, 77–87 (2017). https://doi.org/10.1007/s10209-017-0581-5
6. Melo, M., Vasconcelos-Raposo, J., Bessa, M.: Presence and cybersickness in immersive content: effects of content type. Expo. Time Gender. Comput. Graph. **71**, 159–165 (2018). https://doi.org/10.1016/j.cag.2017.11.007
7. Milgram, P., Kishino, F.: Taxonomy of mixed reality visual displays. IEICE Trans. Inf. Syst. **12**, 1321–1329 (1994)
8. Jerald, J.: The VR book: human-centered design for virtual reality. Assoc. Comput. Mach. (2016). https://doi.org/10.1145/2792790.2792814
9. Azuma, R.T.: A survey of augmented reality. Virtual Augment. Real. **6**, 355–385 (1997). https://doi.org/10.1162/pres.1997.6.4.355
10. Rauschnabel, P.A., Felix, R., Hinsch, C., Shahab, H., Alt, F.: What is XR? Towards a framework for augmented and virtual reality. Comput. Hum. Behav. **133**, 107289 (2022). https://doi.org/10.1016/j.chb.2022.107289
11. Coelho, C., Tichon, J., Hine, T.J., Wallis, G., Riva, G.: Media presence and inner presence: the sense of presence in virtual reality technologies. IOS Press (2006)
12. Slater, M., Wilbur, S.: A framework for immersive virtual environments (FIVE): speculations on the role of presence in virtual environments. Presence Teleoperators Virtual Environ. **6**, 603–616 (1997). https://doi.org/10.1162/pres.1997.6.6.603
13. Csikszentmihalyi, M.: Flow: The Psychology of Optimal Experience. Harper & Row (1990)
14. Murray, J.H.: Hamlet on the Holodeck: The Future of Narrative in Cyberspace. The Free Press (1997)
15. Weech, S., Kenny, S., Barnett-Cowan, M.: Presence and cybersickness in virtual reality are negatively related: a review. Front. Psychol. **10** (2019). https://doi.org/10.3389/fpsyg.2019.00158
16. Caserman, P., Garcia-Agundez, A., Gámez Zerban, A., Göbel, S.: Cybersickness in current-generation virtual reality head-mounted displays: systematic review and outlook. Virtual Real. **25**, 1153–1170 (2021). https://doi.org/10.1007/s10055-021-00513-6
17. Beat Games: Beat Saber. https://www.oculus.com/experiences/quest/2448060205267927/
18. Oculus: Mission: ISS. https://www.oculus.com/experiences/quest/2094303753986147/
19. FSDesign: Talasnal House VR. https://www.meta.com/experiences/5315654131846251/
20. Reis, F.: S. Gonçalinho VR Experience. https://www.youtube.com/watch?v=TQhS5M EXkwE
21. Meta: Quest 2. https://store.facebook.com/quest/products/quest-2/
22. Schubert, T., Friedmann, F., Regenbrecht, H.: The experience of presence: factor analytic insights. Presence Teleoperators Virtual Environ. **10**, 266–281 (2001). https://doi.org/10.1162/105474601300343603

23. Vasconcelos-Raposo, J., et al.: Adaptation and validation of the Igroup presence questionnaire (IPQ) in a Portuguese sample. Presence Teleoperators Virtual Environ. **25**, 191–203 (2016). https://doi.org/10.1162/PRES_a_00261

24. Schubert, T., Friedmann, F., Regenbrecht, H.: Igroup Presence Questionnaire (2016)

25. Kennedy, R.S., Lane, N.E., Berbaum, K.S., Lilienthal, M.G.: Simulator sickness questionnaire: an enhanced method for quantifying simulator sickness. Int. J. Aviat. Psychol. **3**, 203–220 (1993). https://doi.org/10.1207/s15327108ijap0303_3

26. Kilteni, K., Groten, R., Slater, M.: The sense of embodiment in virtual reality. Presence Teleoperators Virtual Environ. **21**, 373–387 (2012). https://doi.org/10.1162/PRES_a_00124

27. Kelly, J.W., Gilbert, S.B., Dorneich, M.C., Costabile, K.A.: Gender differences in cybersickness: clarifying confusion and identifying paths forward. In: Proceedings - 2023 IEEE Conference on Virtual Reality and 3D User Interfaces Abstracts and Workshops, pp. 283–288 (2023). https://doi.org/10.1109/VRW58643.2023.00067

28. Dudley, J., Yin, L., Garaj, V., Kristensson, P.O.: Inclusive immersion: a review of efforts to improve accessibility in virtual reality, augmented reality and the metaverse. Virtual Real. **27**, 2989–3020 (2023). https://doi.org/10.1007/s10055-023-00850-8

29. Baker, L., Ventura, J., Langlotz, T., Gul, S., Mills, S., Zollmann, S.: Localization and tracking of stationary users for augmented reality. Vis. Comput. **40**, 227–244 (2024). https://doi.org/10.1007/s00371-023-02777-2

30. Silva, C., Zagalo, N., Vairinhos, M.: Towards participatory activities with augmented reality for cultural heritage: a literature review. Comput. Educ. X Real. **3**, 100044 (2023). https://doi.org/10.1016/j.cexr.2023.100044

31. Reisinho, P., Silva, C., Vairinhos, M., Oliveira, A.P., Zagalo, N.: Tangible interfaces and augmented reality in a nutrition serious game for kids. In: 2021 IEEE 9th International Conference on Serious Games and Applications for Health (SeGAH), pp. 1–8 (2021). https://doi.org/10.1109/SEGAH52098.2021.9551852

32. Martins, S., Vairinhos, M.: Ludic and narrative immersion in virtual reality exposure therapy to animal phobias: a systematic literature review. Virtual Worlds **2**, 303–325 (2023). https://doi.org/10.3390/virtualworlds2040018

33. Reisinho, P., Raposo, R., Zagalo, N.: A systematic literature review of virtual reality-based reminiscence therapy for people with cognitive impairment or dementia. In: 2022 International Conference on Interactive Media, Smart Systems and Emerging Technologies (IMET), pp. 1–8 (2022). https://doi.org/10.1109/IMET54801.2022.9930000

34. Grassini, S., Laumann, K.: Questionnaire measures and physiological correlates of presence: a systematic review. Front. Psychol. **11** (2020). https://doi.org/10.3389/fpsyg.2020.00349

# Proof-of-Concept MARG-Based Glove for Intuitive 3D Human-Computer Interaction

Pontakorn Sonchan[✉], Neeranut Ratchatanantakit, Nonnarit O-larnnithipong, Malek Adjouadi, and Armando Barreto

Department of Electrical and Computer Engineering, Florida International University, Miami, FL, USA
{psonc001,nratc001,nolarnni,adjouadi,barretoa}@fiu.edu

**Abstract.** Numerous applications of Virtual Reality (VR) and Augmented Reality (AR) continue to emerge. However, many of the current mechanisms to provide input in those environments still require the user to perform actions (e.g., press a number of buttons, tilt a stick) that are not natural or intuitive. It would be desirable to enable users of 3D virtual environments to use natural hand gestures to interact with the environments. The implementation of a glove capable of tracking the movement and configuration of a user's hand has been pursued by multiple groups in the past. One of the most recent approaches consists of tracking the motion of the hand and fingers using miniature sensor modules with magnetic and inertial sensors. Unfortunately, the limited quality of the signals from those sensors and the frequent deviation from the assumptions made in the design of their operations have prevented the implementation of a tracking glove able to achieve high performance and large-scale acceptance. This paper describes our development of a proof-of-concept glove that incorporates motion sensors and a signal processing algorithm designed to maintain high tracking performance even in locations that are challenging to these sensors, (e.g., where the geomagnetic field is distorted by nearby ferromagnetic objects). We describe the integration of the required components, the rationale and outline of the tracking algorithms and the virtual reality environment in which the tracking results drive the movements of the model of a hand. We also describe the protocol that will be used to evaluate the performance of the glove.

**Keywords:** MARG module · Orientation Estimation · Magnetic Disturbance · Hand Tracking Glove

## 1 Motivation

### 1.1 Limitations of Traditional Hardware Input Devices

Applications of Virtual Reality (VR) and Augmented Reality (AR) continue to rapidly emerge in multiple industries. For example, important applications of VR and AR have been found in the education, sports, and military arenas [3, 13, 16]. This hardware and software technology allows humans to execute tasks in virtual spaces through their

© The Author(s), under exclusive license to Springer Nature Switzerland AG 2024
J. Y. C. Chen and G. Fragomeni (Eds.): HCII 2024, LNCS 14707, pp. 283–297, 2024.
https://doi.org/10.1007/978-3-031-61044-8_20

actions in physical space, for entertainment or training purposes. However, the potential for convincing user immersion in VR and AR environments is degraded by the kind of input devices used, which could be mere adaptations of legacy 2-D controllers. Controllers, such as the mouse, allow a user to control the computer in a 2D virtual space. However, those traditional controllers are not fully adequate to maximize the potential of working with a 3D virtual environment. Even though there have been new hardware developments for modern 3D simulation such as the Wii Mote or a variety of VR remote controllers (such as HTC's Vive, Oculus Quest hand controller, etc.), they do not provide the user with a full hand control experience. Even in some of the newest VR systems, such as the Meta Quest 3 and the PlayStation VR2 the input devices are non-anthropomorphic hand-held devices. These devices require the user to provide input to the system by pressing a few buttons in the device.

In this context, several groups have pursued the development of a glove that could track the position and configuration of the user hand [5, 11], allowing for the use of more natural and intuitive hand gestures and micro gestures to provide input to the VR and AR systems. Several attempts to the development of such glove have used Magnetic, Angular-Rate and Gravity (MARG) sensor modules as their main sensing devices. However, the limited accuracy of this Micro Electro-Mechanical System (MEMS) sensors has challenged the successful implementation of the glove, with particular vulnerabilities in environments where the magnetic field is not uniform (possibly due to the pervasive presence of ferromagnetic objects) [4, 18]. In this paper we present the development of a proof-of concept implementation of a proposed human-computer interaction glove which employs our custom processing algorithm to obtain the orientations of the MARG modules embedded in the glove.

## 2 System Design and Hardware Components

The human-computer interaction glove we seek must have the ability to track the position and configuration (orientation of articulated segments) of the user's hand in real time. Our glove pursues that goal on the basis of the hardware components described in Sects. 2.1 and 2.2, the virtual reality interpretation of the glove signals described in Sect. 2.3, and the custom orientation estimation algorithm outlined in Sect. 3.

### 2.1 A MARG-Based Glove

There are now in the market multiple miniature Magnetic, Angular-Rate, Gravity (MARG) sensor modules, which are small, lightweight and low-power. These characteristics of MARG modules have inspired multiple groups to attach them to diverse articulated segments of the body, such as the fingers, to track their orientation. Each of these MARG modules comprises:

- *Tri-axial gyroscopes* which track the angular change rate ($\omega$) of the module.
- *Tri-axial accelerometers* which, if the MARG is static, sense only the gravity vector. If there is linear acceleration applied to the module, the accelerometer responds to the superposition of those 2 vectors.

- *Tri-axial magnetometers* meant to measure the geomagnetic vector, which points to the magnetic north.

If the MARG is properly attached to an articulated segment of the body (e.g., a phalanx in the hand), the signals provided by the MARG are processed by a controller to estimate the MARG orientation (and, by extension, the orientation of the articulated segment), in real time. An initial estimate of the orientation can be obtained by integration of the angular velocities reported by the gyroscope in the MARG to the controller. However, this initial estimation of the orientation of a MARG must frequently be corrected, since even small offsets commonly included in the outputs of consumer-grade MEMS gyroscopes [1] will produce increasing orientation errors ("drift") when they are integrated [2, 6, 21]. This significantly challenges the use of MEMS MARG modules for hand tracking, in the context of human-computer interaction, with several of the devices previously developed confined to mainly clinical applications, in restricted use environments.

We propose the development of a glove instrumented with one MARG in the dorsal surface of the hand and two of them in each finger (proximal and middle phalanges), except for the thumb, which is tracked with three modules. We utilize the Yost Labs 3-Space Nano MARG modules [23] in their carrier printed circuit boards (16 × 17 × 1.7 mm, 0.9 g). Signals from all the MARG modules are collected by a controller, also placed in the dorsal region of the hand, and are then transmitted wirelessly to the computer system. The proposed placement of the MARG modules is shown in Fig. 1.

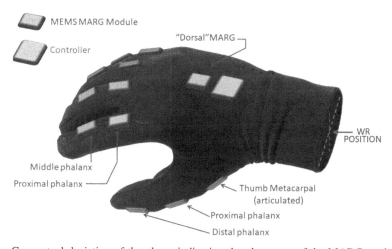

**Fig. 1.** Conceptual depiction of the glove, indicating the placement of the MARG modules. In the first proof-of-concept implementation two MARG modules are used to instrument the middle finger, two for the index finger and three for the thumb, in addition to the module placed on the dorsal surface of the glove.

For a first proof-of-concept prototype we have placed a total eight sensors attached to the outside of the glove to track the orientation of the dorsal surface of the metacarpal mass, the thumb and the index and middle fingers (exclusively). The proposed placement of the sensors in the prototype is shown in Fig. 2.

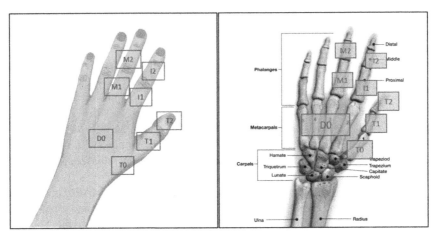

**Fig. 2.** Correspondence between the bone structure of the hand and the proposed placement of MARG modules for the prototype glove (Right pane is modified from an iStock image, www.ist ockphoto.com, used with permission).

The D0 sensor is placed on the dorsal surface of the glove to track the orientation of the metacarpal mass, i.e., the volume occupied by the $2^{nd}$, $3^{rd}$, $4^{th}$ and $5^{th}$ metacarpals, which we are considering as a single rigid body. Therefore, the signals from D0 are used to track what would normally be described as the "orientation of the palm", or less precisely "the orientation of the hand" (which disregards the orientations of the fingers).

To track movement of the middle finger, there are two modules on the glove. Sensor M1 is attached on the proximal phalanx of the middle finger. The second segment of the middle finger is its middle phalanx, and sensor M2 is placed at this location. Similarly, tracking the orientation of the segments of the index finger is accomplished by using two modules, I1 and I2, attached to the index finger's proximal phalanx and middle phalanx, respectively.

On the thumb, which is different from those two fingers, the glove needs three sensors to be able to track all the possible movements. Because the thumb metacarpal is articulated, sensor T0 is dedicated to tracking this segment. Sensor T1 tracks the proximal phalanx. Since the thumb does not have the middle phalanx, sensor T2 is tracking the distal phalanx.

We have not attempted to attach MARG sensors on the distal phalanges of the index and middle fingers because the joint between the middle and distal phalanges of these fingers has only one degree of freedom (like a door hinge), so that the distal phalanx can only turn in the plane in which the middle phalanx lies. Furthermore, the angle by which the distal phalanx turns (with respect to the middle phalanx), $\theta_{Distal}$, is proportional to the angle by which the middle phalanx turns (with respect to the proximal phalanx),

$\theta_{Middle}$, according to Eq. 1, reproduced from [9].

$$\theta_{Distal} = \frac{2}{3}\theta_{Middle} \tag{1}$$

Table 1 summarizes how the orientation of the segments tracked is measured or calculated.

**Table 1.** Measurement/calculation of the orientation of hand segments

| Finger | Phalanges* | Sensor ID | Tracker |
|---|---|---|---|
| Dorsal | Dorsal | D0 | MARG Module |
| Middle Finger | Proximal | M1 | MARG Module |
| | Middle | M2 | MARG Module |
| | Distal | - | Calculation |
| Index Finger | Proximal | I1 | MARG Module |
| | Middle | I2 | MARG Module |
| | Distal | - | Calculation |
| Thumb | *Metacarpal | T0 | MARG Module |
| | Proximal | T1 | MARG Module |
| | Distal | T2 | MARG Module |

## 2.2  RGB-D Camera and Nuitrack Software Development Kit (Nuitrack SDK)

The second hardware component of our system is the RGB-D camera used to obtain the spatial position of the hand in real time. We model each finger as a kinematic chain that includes the metacarpal mass and the phalanges of that finger, whose lengths can be measured in advance. Accordingly, instantaneous knowledge of the 3D position of just the wrist end of the metacarpal mass and the orientation of all the segments of the chain allows the determination of the 3D positions of all the joints in the chain. We have used the commercially available Intel® RealSense™ Depth Camera D455 [8] in conjunction with the Nuitrack SDK [17] to track the 3D coordinates of the wrist. This is a low-cost camera of compact size ($124 \times 29 \times 26$ mm) which is, therefore, suitable for operating in a general working space, for example, a desk with a personal computer. The D455 camera can be connected to the system by using a USB 3 cable. The recommended distance range for the D455 camera is from 60 cm to 600 cm, which should be appropriate for a variety of prospective VR or AR use cases.

The Nuitrack SDK uses machine learning techniques to perform skeleton tracking, aiming at the identification of the shape of a human in the frame and yielding estimates of the X, Y, Z positions of the major joints of the body, including both wrists. Because the system seeks the tracking of the complete skeleton, it is less susceptible to disruptions in the wrist location recognition due to partial occlusion of the arm of the user, making this approach to position tracking a robust one (Fig. 3).

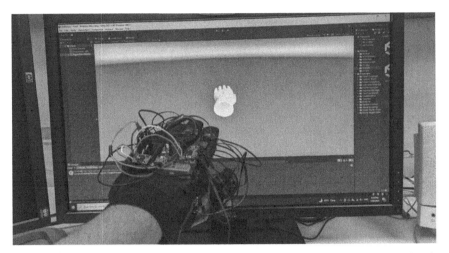

**Fig. 3.** Proof-of-concept prototype glove (The discrete circuit boards placed on the dorsal surface of the glove could eventually be consolidated in a single chip).

## 2.3   Virtual Environment Simulation

The third element in our development of the glove interface is the virtual hand representation that moves in response to the movements performed in the physical world by the user who wears the glove. The virtual hand is represented in a virtual working space developed within Unity®, the game engine that provides 3D development tools, including the creation and manipulation of basic 3D components (cube, sphere, plane, etc.) in the development environment. The components in Unity® can be animated by using the C# programming language (scripting with the MonoBehavior API). For our project, a virtual hand model was defined and the position of the hand in the virtual environment is determined by the 3D wrist coordinates obtained from the Nuitrack SDK. Simultaneously, the articulated segments of the virtual hand are oriented according to the orientation estimates defined from the signals of each corresponding MARG module.

One of the key objectives of the procedure designed to evaluate the prototype (detailed in Sect. 4) is the study of its robustness with respect to the potential magnetic field distortions present in the physical operating environment of the glove due to the presence of ferromagnetic objects within it. Accordingly, virtual 3D targets (cubes) were placed in regions of the virtual environment that correspond to physical regions with and without magnetic distortions.

Figure 4 shows the 3D simulation of the experiment where the user will perform an evaluation task. The user will visualize the virtual scenario including the virtual hand controlled by the glove and a number of cubic targets. The user will then be asked to reach to and "acquire" the targets by simultaneously touching the top and bottom surfaces of the virtual cubes.

The three green cubes shown on the left section of Fig. 4 have virtual placements that match locations in the physical world where the geomagnetic filed is not distorted. In contrast, the three orange cubes shown on the right section of Fig. 4 have virtual placements that match physical world locations where the geomagnetic field will be

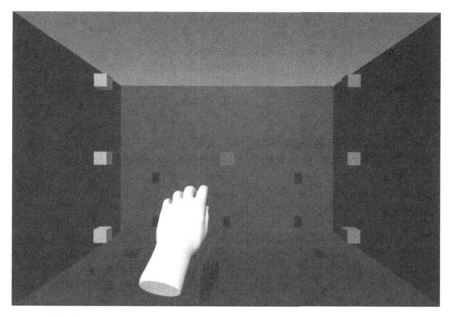

**Fig. 4.** The 3D simulation for a user to perform the evaluation experiment.

distorted by the placement of ferromagnetic bars of high magnetic permeability (M35 HSS high speed steel). This setup will allow the comparison of system performance under both types of condition: with and without magnetic distortions, which is one of the important objectives of the evaluation.

When the users move their hand in the physical space, the D455 camera and Nuitrack SDK will report the sequence of X, Y, and Z coordinates traveled by the subject's wrist. In response, the position of the virtual hand will be updated accordingly in the simulation.

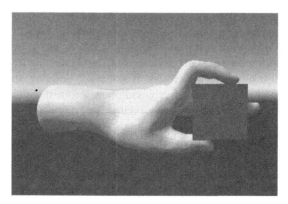

**Fig. 5.** A user must touch the top and the bottom of the virtual target with the index finger and thumb for target acquisition

The user can move the 3D hand model freely as long as the hand in the physical world is still within in the camera's view.

Figure 5 exemplifies the hand actions required for the completion of a successful cube "acquisition" in the system. The index finger of the 3D model must touch the top surface of a cube while, simultaneously, the thumb must touch the bottom surface of the cube.

# 3   MARG Orientation Estimation Algorithm, the Gravity and North Vector-Double SLERP with $\mu_k$ (GMVD$\mu$k)

The efficacy of the system described in the preceding sections depends critically on the correctness of the orientation estimates obtained for each articulated hand segment from the gyroscope, accelerometer and magnetometer signals output by the corresponding MARG modules. While there have been numerous algorithms proposed for this type of MARG orientation estimation [14, 15], we use our Gravity and North Vector – Double SLERP with $\mu_k$ (GMVD$\mu$k) algorithm [19]. The algorithm seeks to judiciously combine all available readings from the MARG module, to obtain a final orientation estimate. This approach systematically selects the level of involvement of each sensor type after assessing their trustworthiness parameters. These trustworthiness parameters reflect the instantaneous characteristics of the sensor's environment. If the instantaneous MARG conditions diverge significantly from the assumptions made pertaining the use of accelerometer or magnetometer data to enrich the orientation estimate, then the corresponding sensor information will not be involved strongly in the definition of the final orientation estimate. That is, GMVD$\mu$k implements a form of conditional involvement of the available information sources. The following sections outline how this goal is achieved. For a more detailed description of the algorithm, the reader is referred to [19].

## 3.1   Information Flow in the GMVD$\mu$k Algorithm

At the beginning of each iteration of the algorithm, the latest raw data of gyroscope readings, $\omega$, accelerometer readings, $a_0$, and magnetometer readings, $m_0$, will be read. (In this algorithm description vector quantities are represented by bold symbols.) The readings from the gyroscope, $\omega$, will be "de-biased" by subtracting from them dynamic estimates of the most recent levels of bias. It is known, however, that processes like this have only limited effectiveness in removing bias levels, therefore, the rest of the processing steps described here become necessary. The "de-biased" gyroscope signals, denoted $\omega_B$, are used for the rest of the iteration.

GMVD$\mu$k represents orientations as quaternions [7, 12, 20] (which will also be represented by bold symbols). An initial orientation estimation is represented in quaternion form as $q_G$. In each iteration, $q_G$ can be established by recursive integration of the gyroscope's readings, as indicated in Eqs. 2 and 3. In these equations $\dot{q}$ is "quaternion rate of change" that is computed from $\omega_B$ and $q_0$, which is the quaternion representing the orientation resulting from the previous iteration. In Eq. 2 the symbol $\otimes$ represents quaternion multiplication. In Eq. 3, the rate of change is integrated (accumulated) to represent a first estimation of the current orientation quaternion, $q_G$, where $\Delta t$ is the sampling interval and $q_0^*$ is the quaternion conjugate of $q_0$.

$$\dot{q} = \frac{1}{2} q_0 \otimes \omega_B \tag{2}$$

$$q_G = e^{((\Delta t)\dot{q} \otimes q_0^*)} \otimes q_0 \tag{3}$$

Now the algorithm has an initial quaternion representing the orientation of the MARG. However, unavoidable offset remnants in the gyroscope signals, $\omega_B$, will gradually introduce "drift" in the $q_G$ estimate obtained from rotational speed integration alone. Thus, a correction of this initial estimate, leveraging the information contained in the accelerometer and magnetometer signals, is implemented next. In fact, our approach implements two parallel processes to correct $q_G$ using accelerometer information and magnetometer information, but restraining their relative correction weights when the corresponding assumptions are not fully met. For the sake of brevity only the process that yields the accelerometer-corrected version of $q_G$, designated by $q_{SA}$, will be outlined here, noting that the generation of the magnetometer-corrected version, $q_{SM}$, is analogous and is further detailed in [19].

When the MARG is static (or nearly static) the accelerometer's real-time readings, $a_0$, point in the direction of the gravitational vector (perpendicular to the floor, pointing downwards). On the other hand, Eq. 4 shows how an initial measurement of the gravitational vector, $A_{INIT}$, acquired during the system startup (while the MARG was at its reference orientation), is mapped to the current orientation of the MARG body frame. The resulting $a(q_G)$ is a "computed" version of the current accelerometer readings.

$$a(q_G) = q_G^* \otimes A_{INIT} \otimes q_G \tag{4}$$

If the initial estimate $q_G$ were not affected by drift these body frame-referenced directions should match. In practice, however, we assume there might be a distortion already present in $q_G$, which produces a "quaternion difference" between the calculated version and the measured version of the instantaneous accelerometer readings. We express this orientation difference as a quaternion, $\Delta q_A$, (the A-subscript stands for Accelerometer) by calculating its vector part (Eq. 5) and its scalar part (Eq. 6), and then fusing them into the difference quaternion (Eq. 7), with the "H operator".

$$q_{Av} = a_0 \times a(q_G) \tag{5}$$

$$q_{Aw} = \|a_0\| \|a(q_G)\| + a_0 \cdot a(q_G) \tag{6}$$

$$\Delta q_A = H(q_{Av}, q_{Aw}) \tag{7}$$

This $\Delta q_A$ is, in fact, the supplementary rotation that would be needed to make the computed $a(q_G)$ match with the measured $a_0$. Equivalently, the two vectors would also match if $\Delta q_A$ were to be "compounded" with the original $q_G$, to yield a fully-accelerometer-corrected quaternion $q_{GA}$ as indicated in Eq. 8.

$$q_{GA} = q_G \otimes \Delta q_A \tag{8}$$

In a parallel track of processing, a fully-magnetometer-corrected orientation estimate, $q_{GM}$, is obtained by implementation of equations similar to Eqs. 4–8, which operate with the magnetic counterparts to the accelerometer concepts cited above ($M_{INIT}$, $m_0$, $m(q_G)$, etc.).

Since the appropriateness of the accelerometer- and magnetometer-based corrections are predicated on the fulfillment of specific assumptions (e.g., that the local geomagnetic field is undistorted), our algorithm uses Spherical Linear Interpolation (SLERP), to defined partially-corrected quaternions where the strength of the corresponding correction has been restricted in proportion to the values of accelerometer and magnetometer trustworthiness parameters ($0 \leq \alpha \leq 1$ and $0 \leq \mu \leq 1$), assessed by the algorithm for every iteration. The partially accelerometer- and magnetometer-corrected orientation estimates, $q_{SA}$ and $q_{SM}$, respectively, are therefore computed as indicated in Eq. 9 and Eq. 10.

$$q_{SA} = SLERP(q_G, q_{GA}, \alpha) \tag{9}$$

$$q_{SM} = SLERP(q_G, q_{GM}, \mu) \tag{10}$$

Each one of these equations represents the use of SLERP to interpolate a quaternion from $q_G$ to a second quaternion ($q_{GA}$ or $q_{GM}$) under control of the third parameter. So, for example, if alpha is close to zero, $q_{SA}$ will be close to $q_G$ (minimal correction from accelerometer information), whereas if alpha is close to one, $q_{SA}$ will be close to $q_{GA}$ (close to full correction based of accelerometer information). Finally, $q_{SA}$ and $q_{SM}$ are fused through a second tier of SLERP interpolation, controlled by alpha, at the end of each iteration to obtain the final orientation estimate quaternion $q_{OUT}$, as indicated in Eq. 11. This $q_{OUT}$ is the effective result of each orientation estimation iteration, to be utilized by external orientation tracking applications.

$$q_{OUT} = SLERP(q_{SM}, q_{SA}, \alpha) \tag{11}$$

Additionally, this $q_{OUT}$ is the "previous orientation" considered at the beginning of the next iteration of the correction process, as mentioned in Eqs. 2 and 3. Equation 12 shows the relation between $q_0$ and $q_{OUT}$.

$$q_0 = \begin{cases} [0001], & iteration = 1 \\ q_{OUT}, & iteration > 1 \end{cases} \tag{12}$$

## 4   Evaluation Environment

We have designed an experimental process to evaluate the effectiveness of interaction in a virtual environment afforded by the glove. The evaluation focuses on a 3D target acquisition task where the total time required to complete a fixed number of target acquisitions will be measured to assess the efficiency of the interaction. The robustness of the MARG orientation estimation method to magnetic distortions will be studied by involving targets whose acquisition require moving the glove in physical regions with and without known magnetic distortions.

To have available a basis for comparison, the subjects recruited for experimentation will be asked to complete the protocol with the virtual hand movements driven by two orientation algorithms (OA). One of them will be the well-known Kalman Filter [10, 22] (KF) method (OA = KF), which is available in an internal implementation within each MARG sensor. In other cases, the orientation estimates will be calculated with the GMVDμk method, described in Sect. 3 (OA = GMVDμk).

We will also seek to determine if the distance from the subject to the RGB-D camera has an impact on the efficiency of the interaction. To study this, each experimental subject will complete the protocol with the camera placed at D = D1 = 1 m and with the camera placed at D = D2 = 2 m, from the physical vertical plane that corresponds to the virtual plane in which the cubic virtual targets are placed. These variations of the setup are illustrated in Fig. 6.

### 4.1 Environment Setup

It is important that no large ferromagnetic materials be initially present in the space where the glove will be operated during the evaluation. This is necessary to avoid unknown distortions of the geomagnetic field. On the other hand, bars of M35 HSS high speed steel will be purposely placed near the right edge of the experimental area, to introduce a known magnetic distortion in the right edge of the experimental space. (These magnetic disrupters will be supported by a wooden pole in the neighborhood of the space where the magnetic distortion is desired, as described below.).

A large screen display will be provided for the visualization of the virtual scenario by the subject. This screen will be connected to the host computer to display the Unity® simulation to the subject. In this screen the subject will see the movement of the virtual hand in response to his/her physical hand movements.

A first wooden pole will be placed at the left side of the experiment area to provide the subjects with an initial physical landmark reference. The subjects will be told that it is expected that hand movements they will need to execute will take place to the right of this reference wooden pole.

A second wooden pole will be placed at the right side of the experiment area, symmetrically with respect to the left pole. In this case, subjects will be told that it is expected that hand movements they will need to execute will take place to the left of this reference wooden pole. In addition to serving as a physical reference, this right wooden pole will be used to support bars of M35 HSS high speed steel at the heights that will approximately match the virtual location of the cubes simulated in a column to the right of the virtual environment. This is for the purpose of introducing a known magnetic distortion that will affect the glove when the user attempts to acquire those targets ("4", "5" and "6" in Fig. 6).

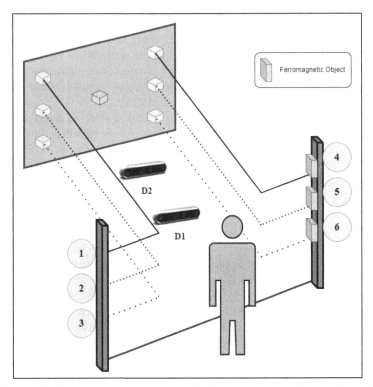

**Fig. 6.** Sketch showing the evaluation setup, including the location of the subject, the ferromagnetic materials, and the visualization screen, along with the 2 optional RGB-D camera locations.

### 4.2 Experiment Procedure

Each experimental subject will complete the evaluation protocol 4 times, with the orientation algorithm assigned at random to minimize ordering effects:

1. Two times with the RGB-D camera at 1 m (OA = KF followed by OA = GMVDμk, or OA = GMVDμk followed by OA = KF, assigned at random)
2. Two times with the RGB-D camera at 2 m (OA = KF followed by OA = GMVDμk, or OA = GMVDμk followed by OA = KF, assigned at random)

The subject will not be informed of the fact that there are two orientation algorithms being considered. The subject will not be told which algorithm is driving the simulation at any time. After providing informed consent, the subject will be asked to wear the glove and to adjust it comfortably in his/her hand.

The protocol requires the subject to acquire three (green) cubic targets located on the left side of the virtual scene (which will not require the glove to be operated in the magnetically distorted area). Then the user must acquire three (orange) cubic targets located on the right side of the virtual scene (which will require the glove to be operated in the magnetically distorted area).

Specifically, the protocol will start by presenting the (red) home cube in the center of the scene. When the red cube is acquired by the subject, timer TIMER1 will start at 0, the red cube will disappear, and a first green cube ("1" in Fig. 6) will be presented in the virtual environment, to be acquired by the subject. When the first green cube is successfully acquired by the subject it will disappear, the time in TIMER1 will be recorded as T11, and the second green cube ("2" in Fig. 6, about 15 cm below "1", in the physical world) will be presented, for the subject to acquire it. When the second green cube is successfully acquired the time in TIMER1 will be recorded as T12, the second green cube will disappear and the third green cube ("3" in Fig. 6, about 15 cm below "2", in the physical world) will be shown, for the subject to acquire it. When the third green cube is successfully acquired the time in TIMER1 will be recorded as T13 and the third green cube will disappear.

When the subject has acquired all three of the green cubes, the home (red) cube will re-appear in the center of the scene, and the same process of sequential acquisition of three targets will be repeated for the orange cubes "4", "5" and "6" in Fig. 6, positioned on the right side of the virtual scene, symmetrically with respect to cubes "1", "2" and "3". A different timer TIMER2 will be used to record the times (T21, T22 and T23) at which the orange cubic targets are sequentially acquired.

The values of the recorded times (T11, T12, T13, T21, T22 and T23) will be the results from the experiment. Smaller values for these resulting times will indicate a lower difficulty in successfully acquiring the 3-D targets with the glove, allowing the comparison of performance with and without magnetic disturbances, and with respect to the camera distances (D1 or D2) and the orientation algorithms used (KF or GMVD$\mu$k).

## 5  Concluding Remarks

In this paper we have provided an outline of the development of our real-time hand tracking system based on a glove instrumented with MARG modules to estimate the orientation of the articulated segments of the hand.

Our approach relies on the real-time position tracking of just the wrist of the user, as provided by an RGB-D camera (Intel® RealSense™ D455) through the Nuitrack Software Development Kit. The 3-D positions of the joints in each of the fingers of the hand are determined from that root wrist position by considering each of the fingers as a kinematic chain with segments of known lengths, and by using MARG sensor modules to obtain real-time orientation estimates of all the components in that kinematic chain: The metacarpal mass (modeled as a single rigid body), the proximal phalanx, and the middle phalanx. The orientation of the distal phalanx is not measured with a MARG module, and it is instead approximated by the relationship between the angle in the joint between the distal and the middle phalanges and the angle in the joint between the middle and the proximal phalanges [9].

Tracking the movements of the thumb requires the involvement of three MARG modules, since its metacarpal is articulated with respect to the metacarpal mass which includes the remaining four metacarpals. Therefore, MARG sensors were attached to all three of the articulated thumb segments: metacarpal, proximal phalanx and distal phalanx.

The fidelity with which the configuration of the physical gloved hand can be replicated in a corresponding virtual hand will be critically affected by the correctness of the orientation estimates generated by the algorithms that are used to process the output signals from the gyroscopes, accelerometers, and magnetometers in the MARG modules. For our prototype we use our GMVDμk algorithm [19] which was developed with the aim of achieving resilient performance, even in areas where the geomagnetic field might be distorted by the presence of ferromagnetic objects. Section 3 of this paper provided an outline of the GMVDμk method.

For the implementation of an initial proof-of-concept prototype we have created a glove in which only the thumb, the index finger and the middle finger are instrumented, which is sufficient to program the acquisition of virtual cubic targets.

In this paper we have also described the evaluation mechanism that we have designed for our interaction glove. It has been organized in such a way that it should allow us to study the impact of the distance between the glove user and the RGB-D camera. It has also been structured to explore the increased robustness of the GMVDμk orientation estimation with respect to the well-known Kalman Filter estimation method.

**Acknowledgements.** This work was supported by the US National Science Foundation grant CNS-1920182. Mr. Pontakorn Sonchan was supported by FIU's DYF fellowship.

**Disclosure of Interests.** The authors have no competing interests to declare that are relevant to the content of this article.

# References

1. Advanced Navigation: Inertial Measurement Unit (IMU) – An Introduction. Tech Articles 8 January 2024. https://www.advancednavigation.com/tech-articles/inertial-measurement-unit-imu-an-introduction/. 10 Jan 2024
2. Aggarwal, P., Syed, Z., Noureldin, A., El-Sheimy, N.: MEMS-Based Integrated Navigation. Artech House GNSS Technology and Applications Series, vol. xiii, 197 p. Artech House, Boston, Mass.; London (2010)
3. Chen, Y., Wang, Q., Chen, H., Song, X., Tang, H., Tian, M.: An overview of augmented reality technology. J. Phys. Conf. Ser. **1237**(2), 022082 (2019)
4. de Vries, W.H.K., Veeger, H.E.J., Baten, C.T.M., van der Helm, F.C.T.: Magnetic distortion in motion labs, implications for validating inertial magnetic sensors. Gait Posture **29**(4), 535–541 (2009)
5. Dipietro, L., Sabatini, A.M., Dario, P.: A survey of glove-based systems and their applications. IEEE Trans. Syst. Man Cybern. Part C (Appl. Rev.) **38**(4), 461–482 (2008)
6. Foxlin, E.: Motion tracking requirements and technologies. In: Stanney, K.M. (ed.) Handbook of Virtual Environments, Design, Implementation, and Applications. Lawrence Earlbaum Associates (2002)
7. Hanson, A.: Visualizing quaternions. Morgan Kaufmann Series in Interactive 3D Technology, vol. xxxi, 498 p. Morgan Kaufmann, San Francisco, Amsterdam, Boston. Elsevier Science distributor (2006)
8. Intel: Intel® RealSenseTM Product Family D400 Series Datasheet 2023 p. https://www.intelrealsense.com/download/21345/?tmstv=1697035582

9. Ip, H.H.S., Chan, C.S.: Dynamic simulation of human hand motion using an anatomically correct hierarchical approach. In: 1997 IEEE International Conference on Systems, Man, and Cybernetics. Computational Cybernetics and Simulation, vol. 1302, pp. 1307–1312. IEEE (1997)

10. Kalman, R.E.: A new approach to linear filtering and prediction problems. J. Basic Eng. **82**(1), 35–45 (1960)

11. Kortier, H.G., Sluiter, V.I., Roetenberg, D., Veltink, P.H.: Assessment of hand kinematics using inertial and magnetic sensors. J. Neuroeng. Rehabil. **11**, 70 (2014)

12. Kuipers, J.B.: Quaternions and rotation sequences: a primer with applications to orbits, aerospace, and virtual reality, vol. xxii, 371 p. Princeton University Press, Princeton, N.J. (1999)

13. López-Belmonte, J., Moreno-Guerrero, A.-J., López-Núñez, J.-A., Hinojo-Lucena, F.-J.: Augmented reality in education. A scientific mapping in web of science. Interact. Learn. Environ. **31**(4), 1860–1874 (2023)

14. Madgwick, S.: An efficient orientation filter for inertial and inertial/magnetic sensor arrays. Report x-io Univ. Bristol (UK) **25**, 113–118 (2010)

15. Mahony, R., Hamel, T., Pflimlin, J.M.: Complementary filter design on the special orthogonal group SO (3). In: 44th IEEE Conference on Decision and Control, pp. 1477–1484. IEEE (2005)

16. Manuri, F., Sanna, A.: A survey on applications of augmented reality. ACSIJ Adv. Comput. Sci. Int. J. **5**(1), 18–27 (2016)

17. Nuitrack: NUITRACK SDK, 10 January 2024. https://nuitrack.com/#api

18. Ratchatanantakit, N., O-larnnithipong, N., Barreto, A., Tangnimitchok, S.: Consistency study of 3D magnetic vectors in an office environment for IMU-based hand tracking input development. In: Kurosu, M. (ed.) Human-Computer Interaction. Recognition and Interaction Technologies. LNCS, vol. 11567, pp. 377–387. Springer, Cham (2019). https://doi.org/10.1007/978-3-030-22643-5_29

19. Sonchan, P., Ratchatanantakit, N., O-larnnithipong, N., Adjouadi, M., Barreto, A.: A self-contained approach to MEMS MARG orientation estimation for hand gesture tracking in magnetically distorted environments. In: Kurosu, M., Hashizume, A. (eds.) HCII 2023. LNCS, vol. 14011, pp. 585–602. Springer, Cham (2023). https://doi.org/10.1007/978-3-031-35596-7_38

20. Vince, J.: Quaternions for Computer Graphics, p. xiv, 140 p. Springer, London; New York (2011). https://doi.org/10.1007/978-0-85729-760-0

21. Woodman, O.J.: An introduction to inertial navigation. University of Cambridge (2007)

22. Xiaoping, Y., Aparicio, C., Bachmann, E.R., McGhee, R.B.: Implementation and experimental results of a quaternion-based Kalman filter for human body motion tracking. In: Proceedings of the 2005 IEEE International Conference on Robotics and Automation (2005)

23. YostLabs: 3-Space Nano IC - Product Description Page. Product Description for the 3-Space Nano IC MARG. https://yostlabs.com/product/3-space-nano/. Cited 5 Feb 2023

# An Effective Design on Locomotion and View Management for an Immersive Analytics Platform in Everyday Use

Bo Sun[✉] and Benjamin Daniel Weidner

Department of Computer Science, Rowan University, Glassboro, NJ 08028, USA
sunb@rowan.edu

**Abstract.** Immersive Analytics brings 3D data visualization to virtual reality, immersing users directly into the data. The technology focuses on bringing humans and computers closer together to develop human intuition via human computer interaction. In order to effectively utilize this technique to benefit data analytics, principles must be established to see what kind of 3D user interfaces are the best fit for an everyday immersive analytics platform. In an immersive environment embedded with natural hand interaction, we found that users who perform in a static state, where no physical or virtual navigation of the environment is present, are more beneficial to the interpretation of the data. Prior VR experience and spatial ability also affect the completion time of given task, while reported human factors in gender and age do not seem to play a major role.

**Keywords:** Immersive Analytics · 3DUI Design · Visual Analytics

## 1 Introduction

Immersive Analytics (IA) is an emerging field in data science. It refers to technologies utilizing 3D data visualization within an immersive environment for visual analytics. A good example of an immersive environment would be one inside of a Head Mounted Display (HMD). These technologies support data analytics in a 3D immersive space around users. Utilizing HMD for IA can be a pathway to support multiple users in each environment at a cheaper cost [1].

IA can bring innovation and opportunity to data analytics. Creating immersive environments for people to interact with is the first step to creating natural interactions between the user and the data [2]. Additionally, bringing data into 3D virtual spaces can produce more varied designs and flexibility to design choices. Giving users and designers more freedom in exploring and creating data visualizations is vital for a natural, immersive experience [3]. Along with this, the qualitative experience of users has been seen to improve when using IA platforms. Higher usability, user preferences, low simulation sickness, detection of clustered data, and lower measured mental workload can be achieved through this technology [4, 5]. IA can be engaging, interactive, and collaborative between users. Connecting virtual reality with immersive and integrated worlds can bring new perspectives and opportunities to data analytics technology [6].

J. Y. C. Chen and G. Fragomeni (Eds.): HCII 2024, LNCS 14707, pp. 298–312, 2024.
https://doi.org/10.1007/978-3-031-61044-8_21

IA has a positive impact on data analysis as a whole. Giving a visual representation and meaningful ways to interact and transform data is essential for researchers and analysts, allowing them to observe and tell the data's story. However, as a new field, IA lacks of many guidelines, particularly on the design choices of locomotion, 3DUI and view point. So, this paper aims to develop some guided principles in these aspects based on informational datasets.

Locomotion, points of view toward data, and interactivity are three major areas that one has to design for an effective IA platform. Since we focused on everyday use of the IA platform, natural hand interactivity (NHI) presents a great advantage [7], particularly for users with little to no VR experience. Therefore, this research aims to investigate an ideal combination design of locomotion and point of view (L&PoV) while adopting NHI as interactivity approach. Our study operated on a typical informational dataset consisting of temporal and spatial attributes, referred to as abstract dataset that does not consist of 3D data structures as seen in scientific data. We conducted an evaluation study with 58 subjects. Our study compared two different views, a bird's eye view, and a grounded view, with three different modes of locomotion in sitting/stillness, walking, and teleporting under each view, respectively. Additionally, we tested and collected participants' spatial ability, age, gender, and prior VR experiences, then analyzed these human factors related to the design.

The rest of the paper is organized as follows: Sect. 2 shows the related work in the area; Sect. 3 details our method; Sect. 4 presents our results using statistical analysis; Sect. 5 discusses the result, and Sect. 6 concludes the study.

## 2 Related Work

As a new interdisciplinary field, IA has recently drawn the attention of researchers in Computer Graphics, Visualization, VR/AR, and Human-Computer Interaction. In 2018, Marriott and 38 experts [7] in the related areas explored the definition of IA and provided a sensible continuity of the concept for future research investigations through a book. Furthermore, Ens and 23 other international experts [8] established 17 key research challenges for IA in Spatially Situated Data Visualization, Collaborative Analytics, Interacting with IA Systems, and User Scenarios & Evaluation at ACM CHI 2020. Since then, related work in IA applications and design studies has been developing rapidly.

### 2.1 IA Applications

Visualization of spatial attributes for abstract data is often difficult in 2D space because a 2D map chart can only present a limited amount of information at a time, particularly when involving temporal attributes simultaneously. Many recent IA applications focused on spatial data display and analysis.

Yang et al. [9] presented Tilt Map, an IA platform that can transition between 2D and 3D map charts. Tilt Map took advantage of accurate analysis in 3D maps and fast observation from 2D maps and produced an effective analytical platform in VR. In 2017, Cordeil et al. [10] developed an HMD immersive analytics tool called ImAxes.

ImAxe can visualize multidimensional datasets based on the manipulations of data axe in VR space. Later, Cordeil et al. [11] investigated IATK, an IA API. The software allows users to create visualization design, interaction, and experience IA with their own data. Batch et al. [12] adopted ImAxes in 2020 for economic data analysis and found a majority of participants feel more engaged in IA than in the traditional environment. Additionally, Cordeil et al. [13] proposed Embodied Axes, a hardware-controlled device that can project 3D datasets through AR. The Embodied Axes offers tangible and actuated interactions for 3D AR data space. Zhang et al. [14] developed UbanVR, an IA system for urban design. This tool included parallel coordinates plots, natural interface interaction, and viewpoint optimization to assist context awareness. To help with immersive map design, Newbury et al. [15] recently proposed four embodied gesture interactions. These interactions permit users to manipulate immersive maps and explore data in new ways. Additionally, Proxemic Maps, a most recent virtual map for IA proposed by Ghaemi et al. [16], can adjust its view based on the spatial location of viewers. The technique includes interactions to alter the map's content and type and a transformation that changes the map's geometry.

### 2.2 L&PoV Designs for IA

To guild the rapid growth of IA applications, fundamental principles related to L&PoV design for data analytics tasks are essential for researchers.

Yang et al. [17] investigated the navigations in IA related to abstract data without spatial attributes. The study shows that a zoom interface without locomotion provides more effective user analysis than an interface including standard locomotion. Satriadi et al. [18] presented a study regarding 2D virtual maps in 3D multiview layouts around users in IA. The study shows that users would likely arrange multiview maps in a spherical cap layout around them, then rearrange them during the analytical task. Liu et al. [19] developed a study for interactive data visualizations of small multiples in IA. The research shows that users prefer a flat layout when facing a few multiples, even though walking is involved. However, when the number of multiples is increased, a semicircular layout is preferred over a fully surrounding layout or a flat layout, where locomotion plays a major role. Ens et al. [20] developed Uplift, a tangible and immersive tabletop system for IA collaboration. The evaluation study shows that the tangible tabletop view successfully supports analytical tasks in casual collaboration. Lages and Bowman [21] found that locomotion design in IA depends on a user's game experiences and spatial ability when analyzing complex 3D structure data where spatial attributes are not present. Nevertheless, to our best knowledge, combining VR views with locomotion to effectively analyze abstract data consisting of spatial and temporal attributes is under investigated in the IA field.

## 3 Method

### 3.1 Dataset and Representation

Our dataset is modeled after the 2018 VAST Challenge, but the exact measurements were not used since the study focuses on the L&PoV design principles. Figure 1 (a) displays an example how data was populated on the map. Each location on the map is represented by a column of multi-colored segments. Each segment represents a different chemical tested in that given location. Each stacked column of segments represents the number of chemicals collected in that location in a given year. Chemical testing was performed over the course of 19 years, and the data ranges from 1998 to 2016. There are a total of ten locations and ten different chemicals tested. The location name is printed at the bottom of the column; the first letter of each location is capitalized and extends out to the right of each column and will follow the sight of the user so that users can always read the location easily. When the participants focus their gaze on a specific color of a segment, the value that pertains to it along the type of chemical appears in the text in front of the segment, as shown in Fig. 1 (b).

In some design settings, the map is presented on a table so that users can walk around. In others, the map itself is projected directly on the ground so that users can walk on. Major landmarks are placed in the background of the simulated environment to reduce disorientation. In each cardinal direction, we depicted a different, clearly identifiable landmark: a house, a tree, a mountain, or a lake, as seen in Fig. 1 (b). A blue sky with clouds and sun is presented above, and solid green landscape is at ground level. This clearly defined environment ensures participants do not become disoriented when performing actions such as turning, teleporting, or manipulating the map.

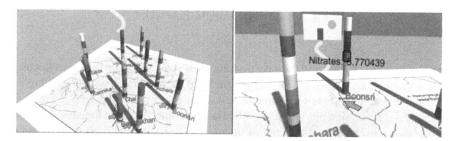

**Fig. 1.** (a) Map Chart (b) Chemical Reading and Landmarks

## 3.2 Data Navigation Using Natural Hand Gestures

Natural user interface (NUI) using human gestures to interact with computers has been widely adopted by computing technology lately, particularly in VR and AR. In the past few years, NUI was often seen in information visualization [22], and it clearly serves as ideal interactivity for IA [7].

We developed five hand gestures in our interactivity design to navigate the data space and manipulate the dataset. These five gestures are:

**Control Panel and Time Slider (CP).** The Control Panel, as seen in Fig. 2(a), is a workbench showing up when users face their left palm towards their face. The control panel consists of a time slider on the top and a legend of the chemicals at the bottom. Users can press the button embedded in the slider and drag it to change the year. It is set to 2008 by default and ranges from 1998 to 2016. The users were advised to use an open palm with their index or middle finger to operate the time slider. The legend of the chemicals is color coded, and the color corresponds to the type of chemical as shown in the data columns. At the bottom of the control panel, there is a pink cube within a pink-colored wireframe box, which acts as the panel's anchor. If a user grabs the pink cube at the bottom, or the panel itself, the user can bring the control panel away from the left hand and place it anywhere in the virtual space. The control panel will always stay in place facing the user, as seen in Fig. 2(b). Since navigation is a large part of the study, this control panel can be closed. To place it back into the left hand, the user must grab the pink cube on the control panel with their right hand and place it within the wireframe cube attached to the left hand.

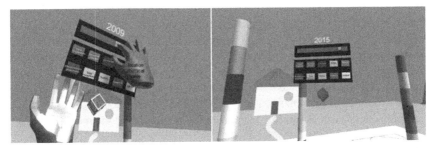

**Fig. 2.** (a) Control Panel (b) Time Slider

**Save Gesture (S).** To perform the save gesture, users must first have their gaze focused on the chemical segment of interest. Then use the right hand in view by extending the index and middle finger while keeping the rest of the fingers down, as seen in Fig. 3(a). It resembles a peace sign or a cub scout salute with the fingers placed together. The save gesture allows users to save the data of interest in the right hand with year, location, chemical, and reading.

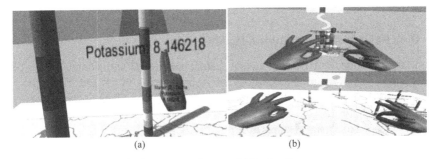

**Fig. 3.** (a) Save Gesture (b) Resize Gesture

**Resize Gesture (R).** To resize the map, both hands must be in view of the user's gaze. To initiate the size change, the user must touch their index finger and thumb together on each hand as if to perform a pinch. Figure 3 (b) shows this motion. The Resize Gesture will continuously change the map size if the gesture is held. If the user takes their hands and brings them further from each other while performing the pinch, the map will start to grow. It is the same case for shrinking the map; bringing the hands closer together while pinching will cause the map to shrink. Figure 3 (b) shows an example of an enlarged map vs. a shrunken one.

**Rotate Gesture (Ro).** The Rotate Gesture rotates the map either clockwise or counter-clockwise. The participants would rely on the gesture to change the view of the data in a sitting or still mode. To initiate this gesture, a user must extend the right hand into view and ball the hand into a fist. Once it is done, if the user extends their thumb out, the map will begin to rotate, as seen in Fig. 4 (a). If the user flips their wrist to point their thumb in the opposite direction, then the map will rotate in the opposite direction.

**Teleporting Gesture (T).** The Teleport Gesture will cast an aiming beam on the traversable ground and teleport users to the location specified on the blue marker at the end of the beam. To initiate this gesture, users must extend their left hand out as if they were pushing a door and their index and middle fingers (just as it is on the right hand with the Save Gesture), as seen in Fig. 4 (b). A pink beam will be cast over a blue marker on any ground that can be teleported to.

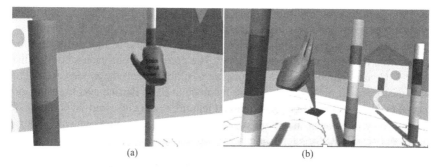

(a)                                   (b)

**Fig. 4.**  (a) Rotate Gesture (b) Teleporting Gesture

### 3.3  Viewpoint and Locomotion Designs

We introduce two views between the subject and the data in concurrence with three different modes of locomotion to navigate the virtual environment.

In order to fully understand what designs are most effective in immersive analytics, different viewpoints and modes of locomotion must be considered. In a virtual environment, we can enhance the user experience through the level of immersion which comes with two different viewpoints: a Godly view by allowing users to manipulate and view data points from above or an immersive view by plunging users into the data forest itself. These two viewpoints are the Bird's Eye View (BEV), looking from above in an aerial view, and the Grounded View (GV), walking among the data points as if it were the natural environment like a data forest around them. Figure 5 shows the comparison of the two views, where the camera represents a subject's eye position/viewpoint.

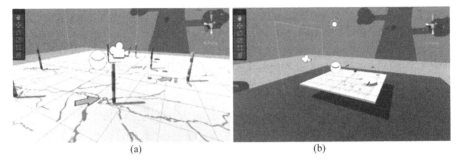

(a)                                    (b)

**Fig. 5.** (a) Grounded View (b) Bird's Eye View

Besides the two views, locomotion, the way users move around in the virtual environment, is important since it could directly impact the effectiveness of IA. Combined with the views, the different modes of locomotion tested in the virtual environment are sitting/stillness, walking, and teleportation. Six different design settings are created to test this: three bird's eye view simulations and three grounded view simulations in sitting, walking, and teleporting, respectively. Each set of simulations is of a different view but dictates three different ways the user physically or naturally moves in the virtual space. In each mode of locomotion, participants are questioned through visual confirmation. They are either given hand gestures or the ability to walk or teleport the space to manipulate the data. Participants would complete the three simulations that differ the modes of locomotion based on their assigned view. The comparison of each setting is listed in Table 1. Control panel and save gesture are available for all the modes. Resize, and rotation gestures are only available for sitting mode in BEV. Participants in sitting mode under the GV view rely on body rotation and leaning to get close and far from the data point since they are placed inside the data with a clear, surrounding view. Teleporting gesture is only available for teleporting mode under both views. Under BEV, participants can only walk or teleport around the map chart to remain in the top view of the data.

**Table 1.** Experiment Setting

| Views | Locomotion | Answer Confirmation | Data Navigation |
|---|---|---|---|
| Bird's Eye View | Sitting/Stillness | Visual | Hand Gesture-CP, S, R, Ro, Arm & Body Rotation |
| | Walking | Visual | Hand Gesture-CP, S, Walking & Body Rotation |
| | Teleporting | Visual | Hand Gesture-CP, S, T, Arm & Body Rotation |
| Grounded View | Sitting/Stillness | Visual | Hand Gesture-CP, S, Arm & Body Rotation |
| | Walking | Visual | Hand Gesture-CP, S, Walking & Body Rotation |
| | Teleporting | Visual | Hand Gesture-CP, S, T, Arm & Body Rotation |

In contrast, participants in GV can only walk or teleport inside the map to stay with an immersive view of the data columns. Arm and body rotation are permitted throughout the study in all modes and views.

### 3.4 Experimental Design

**Participants and Tutorials.** Testing different age and gender groups help us tell if certain demographics play any specific role in the effectiveness of an immersive analytics platform. The age factor comprises two groups: individuals under the age of 30 and individuals over the age of 30. Under each age group, we recruited a comparable number of male and female participants. We had 56 subjects in total for the experiment, including 9 males and 10 females in the age group over 30, and 21 males and 16 females in the age group under 30. The VR experience of each subject was collected before the experiment. The majority of our subjects did not have prior VR experience, and very few of them had the experience. So, we assigned a comparable portion of subjects with some vs. none prior VR experience under each view respectively. The distribution of participants for the experiment is detailed in Table 2.

**Table 2.** Participant Distribution

| Views/Demo-graphics | Males >30 | Females >30 | Males <30 | Females <30 | Some VR Experience | None VR Experience | Total |
|---|---|---|---|---|---|---|---|
| Bird's Eye View | 4 | 5 | 12 | 10 | 5 | 26 | 31 |
| Grounded View | 5 | 5 | 9 | 6 | 3 | 21 | 25 |

First, the participants are brought into a components scene where no observations would be held. Here, the participants would go over the functions and tools of the environment before conducting the test. Each participant was sent a video demonstration via email before the study. A short walkthrough between the user and investigator was also conducted to show the participant how to perform in the platform. If the participant had questions on how to use a tool or what gesture to perform, they were reminded during the study as they were not required to memorize every gesture provided in the immersive workspace.

The first thing each participant completed was the entry survey. It was a series of questions to gather information about the participant, including age, gender, and experiences with virtual reality. Then participant number was assigned to keep our collected data confidential.

Besides the human factors, we also collected participants' spatial ability using the spatial ability test from Ekstrom [27]. It is a cognitive test that measures the spatial awareness of an individual, referred to as the cube score test. Considering this factor can help determine whether this spatial awareness benefits a user. Each participant took the spatial ability test on a laptop and was given the option to use the touchscreen, trackpad, or attached mouse to complete the test on Google Forms. The participants are told the instructions of the spatial ability test and given example explanations before moving on to the test. Once the test starts, the participants have one minute to answer the shown six questions at a time. Once participants completed the six questions, they would move on to the next set of six, and the timer would restart. Participants are given warnings on each set of questions at ten and thirty seconds. They are scored out of 42, the total number of questions, on how keen their sense of spatial ability was.

After the study was complete, the participant was asked to fill out an exit survey asking for any comments or concerns about the experiment.

**Tasks.** Each participant was asked to test three different locomotion modes in sitting, walking, and teleporting under one assigned view. Each mode consists of three questions. The total time each subject spent on each question is collected by our scripts. The complexity of each question and an example of the questions for sitting mode are as follows:

- *Search task (Q1):* observe all data points in one year. For example, which location had the highest level of Nitrates in 2012? A: Kannika
- *Comparisional task (Q2):* compare two data points in one year. For example, of the two, Decha and Kannika, which had a higher Ammonium level in 2008? A: Decha
- *Analytical task: (Q3):* compare two data points in two years. For example, which location and time have the higher value of Calcium? Sakda in 1999 or Chai in 2001? A: Sakda 1999

These questions were asked in the same order from 1 to 3 for each locomotion mode; however, the mode of locomotion order is switched per participant for randomization under the assigned view.

## 4　Results

In this section, we analyzed the collected measurements among different settings in views and locomotion along with the demographics of the participants.

### 4.1　Effective Design on Locomotion and Point of View

Figure 6 shows the time spent on each question in seconds for each locomotion mode and view. Participants in BEV have much better average performance (cross sign in Fig. 1) than GV in search task (Q1, low intensity among all three colors). We believe this is because the overview in BEV eases the search task compared with the immersive view in GV. However, this advantage is no longer valid in comparsional and analytical tasks, as seen in the performance of Q2 and Q3 (middle and high intensities of all three colors), where the immersive view in GV provides more intuitions than other settings. Surprisingly, we observed that the search task, although designed as a simple task, costs more time to accomplish in all modes under both views except walking mode in BEV. It could be because it is always performed in the first place among all three tasks, where the subjects may need time to adjust to the new locomotion.

In general, sitting mode (green color) is much more effective locomotion than walking and teleporting in all three tasks, as seen in Fig. 6. Teleporting received a pretty quick turnout in comparsional task (Q2, middle intensity in blue) in both BEV and GV. We believe it benefits from the quick navigation of teleporting. However, the navigation speed does not contribute to the search and analytical task, particularly when subjects are in the GV with the immersive data view, as seen in Fig. 6. Because the search task relies on observations and the analytical task requires hand gestures to change the time panel.

In BEV, the average total time for all three questions is 172.48, 207.72, and 203.24 s in the sitting, walking, and teleporting modes, respectively. One-way ANOVA found no significant difference (p = 0.189) among these performances. In contrast, in GV, the average total time for all three tasks is 163.53, 220.98, and 276.49 s in the sitting, walking, and teleporting modes, respectively. One-way ANOVA found a significant difference (p = 0.006) among the three locomotion, where sitting mode is the most effective.

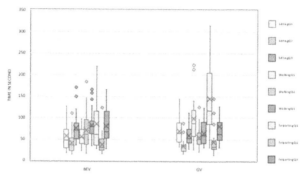

**Fig. 6.** Time Spent on Each Question in All Three Locomotion and Two Views. The boxplot shows median values (line inside box), mean (cross), 2$^{nd}$ and 3rd quartiles (top and bottom of the boxes), and lowest and highest of duration of each task (whiskers).

## 4.2 Age Factor

In BEV, age is not a significant factor that impacts performance. As seen in Fig. 7(a), the age group below 30 has slightly better performance than the group over 30 in all three locomotion. However, the t-test shows that the overall performance in total time spent on all tasks between the two-age group has no significant differences with p scores of 0.25 (t = −0.71), 0.19(t = −0.90), and 0.35(t = −0.40) in the sitting, walking and teleporting modes, respectively. On the other hand, age is significant factor in GV for both walking (p = 0.03, t = −2.08) and teleporting (p = 0.04, t = −1.93) modes that would impact the performance time. As seen in Fig. 7 (b), the age group younger than 30 performs much better than those older than 30. However, no significant difference is found in sitting mode, where the p score is 0.14 (t = −1.11) in the t-test. The immersive view in GV could be overwhelming when subjects have to operate in either walking or teleporting navigation meanwhile. It is particularly true for older subjects whose ages are above 30.

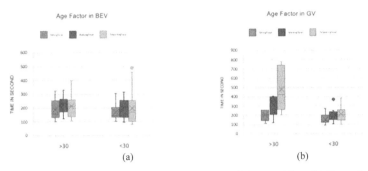

**Fig. 7.** Performance in Different Age Group under (a) Bird's Eye View (b) Grounded View

### 4.3 Gender Factor

In BEV, gender is not a significant factor impacting performance. The t-test shows that the p score between male and female subjects is 0.33 (t = −0.45), 0.36(t = −0.36), and 0.19(t = −0.91) in the sitting, walking, and teleporting modes, respectively. As seen in Fig. 8 (a), the average performance time has no major difference between male and female subjects. In GV, gender is neither a significant factor with the p scores of 0.25 (t = 0.69), 0.09 (t = 1.37), and 0.18(t = 0.94) for the sitting, walking and teleporting, respectively. As seen in Fig. 8 (b), the male subjects performed slightly better than the female subjects in all three locomotion.

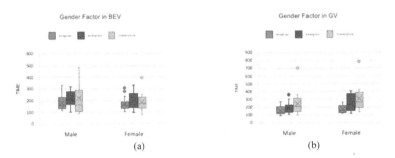

**Fig. 8.** Performance in Different Gender Group under (a) Bird's Eye View (b) Grounded View

### 4.4 Prior VR Experience Factor

In BEV, VR experience is a significant factor impacting performance. The t-test found a significant difference in all three locomotion between the subjects with some VR experience and no experience. The p score is 0.0005 (t = 3.73), 0.0023 (t = 3.53), and 0.001 (t = 3.43) in the sitting, walking and teleporting modes, respectively. As seen in Fig. 9 (a), the average performance time is much better for the subject group with some prior VR experience.

In GV, VR experience is a significant factor only in sitting mode, where the p score is 0.027 (t = 2.10). However, in walking (p = 0.18, t = 1.09) and teleporting (p =

**Fig. 9.** Performance in Different VR Experience Group under (a) Bird's Eye View (b) Grounded View

0.29, t = 0.63) modes, VR experience is not significant factor impacting the performance. Although, as seen in Fig. 9 (b), subjects with some experience had better average performance than subjects who never had VR experience.

### 4.5 Spatial Ability Factor via Cube Score

The cube score indicates the spatial ability of individuals. As seen in Fig. 10, in BEV, the performances in walking and teleporting modes are somewhat associated with most subjects' spatial ability. Generally, the higher the score (high spatial ability), the better performance (shorter time) it shows. However, this trend is not observed in sitting mode, where subjects are not required to navigate in 3D space using spatial ability.

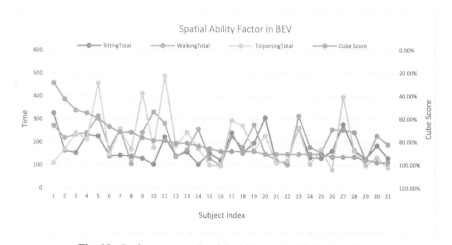

**Fig. 10.** Performance vs Spatial Ability under Bird's Eye View

In GV, the same pattern is observed in all three locomotion for most subjects, where the high spatial ability likely produces better performance, as seen in Fig. 11. We believe this is because the immersive view in GV places a subject in a data forest that requires spatial ability, where one would need to rotate the body quite often to perform the data analysis tasks.

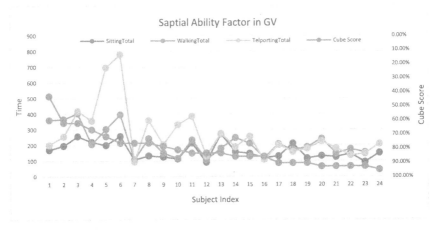

**Fig. 11.** Performance vs Spatial Ability under Grounded View

## 5   Discussion

### 5.1   Effective Design in IA

According to our analysis, the sitting mode in GV is the most effective design compared with other settings. The sitting mode, regardless of the point of view, is the best locomotion choice for abstract data analysis. Although several studies [23–25] claimed that increased physical navigations in VR could increase subjects' spatial memory in data searching, this principle may not apply to IA operated on HMD. In contrast, the sitting mode is a feasible design for everyday VR, which can be easily adopted by the general public, who has little to no space for traditional VR platform that requires psychical spaces to operate. On the other hand, Both GV and BEV have their own advantages in different locomotion. According to our results, GV is the ideal view for sitting mode, while BEV outperformed GV in walking and teleporting modes.

Mulders et al. [26] suggested that unneeded and irrelevant interactions designed for VR learning environments should be avoided. In this IA study, we believe the navigation choices in walking and teleporting are not necessary. Therefore, they should be avoided when the setting mode is available. However, if walking and teleporting modes are selected, BEV would be the best point of view.

### 5.2   Human Factors

We collected several human factors in age, gender, prior VR experience, and spatial ability. According to our results, gender is not a significant factor impacting design performance. Age is not a significant factor in most designs except in walking and teleporting modes under GV, where the surrounding view and physical navigation could be intimating for older subjects over 30. VR experience is a significant factor in most of the designs except in walking and teleporting modes in GV, although in which the subjects who had prior VR experiences received better average performance than those who never had experience. After all, the immersive view (GV) combined with physical locomotion (like walking/teleporting) not only produces the least effective performance among other designs presented in our study but also lead to very different results according to the demographics of users in age and VR experience.

Furthermore, spatial ability is a key factor that could impact the performance of IA where either physical locomotion is required or a surrounding view is presented. Sitting/still mode in BEV is not directly related to spatial ability. Nevertheless, we recommend sitting mode in GV for abstract data analysis in IA, although prior VR experience would help enhance the performance.

### 5.3 Limitations

Our study adopted spatial-temporal data with an immersive map design. The results presented in the paper are limited to this type of design study. When targeted data have their natural 3D attributes, such as 3D MRI data or dynamic particles, our results may not apply. The presented results neither apply to abstract data that may have a different visual representation in IA, for example, data are presented in a unique 3D design or a cluster.

## 6    Conclusion

This paper presents a comparative study on locomotion and point-of-view design in IA. Our targeted data are abstract data that consist of spatial and temporal attributes. The data are presented in a 3D map chart in VR with designed hand gestures. We compared the top view in BEV and the surrounding view in GV. Under each view, we adopted three locomotion: sitting/still, walking, and teleporting. Demographics of human subjects in age, gender, prior VR experience, and spatial ability are also analyzed. Our results show that sitting/still mode in GV is the most effective design among other combinations, where prior VR experience could enhance users' performance. GV with walking and teleporting modes are the least effective design, where users could produce very different performance depending on their age, VR experience, and spatial ability.

**Acknowledgments.** We would like to thank the US Dept. of Education for the GAANN fellowship award to support this research work.

## References

1. Marai, G.E., Leigh, J., Johnson, A.: Immersive analytics lessons from the electronic visualization laboratory: a 25-year perspective. IEEE Comput. Graph. Appl. **39**(3), 54–66 (2019)
2. Lu, A., Huang, J., Zhang, S., Wang, C., Wang, W.: Towards mobile immersive analysis: a study of applications. IEEE (2016)
3. Polys, N., et al.: Immersive analytics: crossing the gulfs with high-performance visualization. IEEE (2016)

4. Wagner Filho, J.A., Stuerzlinger, W., Nedel, L.: Evaluating an immersive space-time cube geo-visualization for intuitive trajectory data exploration. IEEE Trans. Visual Comput. Graphics **26**(1), 514–524 (2019)

5. Kraus, M., Weiler, N., Oelke, D., Kehrer, J., Keim, D.A., Fuchs, J.: The impact of immersion on cluster identification tasks. IEEE Trans. Visual Comput. Graphics **26**(1), 525–535 (2019)

6. Hackathorn, R., Margolis, T.: Immersive analytics: building virtual data worlds for collaborative decision support. IEEE (2016)

7. Marriott, K., et al.: Immersive Analytics. Springer, Cham (2018). https://doi.org/10.1007/978-3-030-01388-2

8. Ens, B., et al.: Grand Challenges in Immersive Analytics (2021)

9. Yang, Y., Dwyer, T., Marriott, K., Jenny, B., Goodwin, S.: Tilt map: interactive transitions between choropleth map, prism map and bar chart in immersive environments. IEEE Trans. Visual Comput. Graphics **27**(12), 4507–4519 (2020)

10. Cordeil, M., Cunningham, A., Dwyer, T., Thomas, B.H., Marriott, K.: ImAxes: immersive axes as embodied affordances for interactive multivariate data visualisation (2017)

11. Cordeil, M., et al.: IATK: an immersive analytics toolkit (2019)

12. Batch, A., et al.: There is no spoon: evaluating performance, space use, and presence with expert domain users in immersive analytics. IEEE Trans. Visual Comput. Graphics **26**(1), 536–546 (2019)

13. Cordeil, M., et al.: Embodied axes: tangible, actuated interaction for 3D augmented reality data spaces (2020)

14. Zhang, C., Zeng, W., Liu, L.: UrbanVR: an immersive analytics system for context-aware urban design. Comput. Graph. **99**, 128–138 (2021)

15. Newbury, R., et al.: Embodied gesture interaction for immersive maps. Cartogr. Geogr. Inf. Sci. **48**(5), 417–431 (2021)

16. Ghaemi, Z., Engelke, U., Ens, B., Jenny, B.: Proxemic maps for immersive visualization. Cartogr. Geogr. Inf. Sci. **49**(3), 205–219 (2022)

17. Yang, Y., Cordeil, M., Beyer, J., Dwyer, T., Marriott, K., Pfister, H.: Embodied navigation in immersive abstract data visualization: is overview + detail or zooming better for 3D scatterplots? IEEE Trans. Visual Comput. Graphics **27**(2), 1214–1224 (2020)

18. Satriadi, K.A., Ens, B., Cordeil, M., Czauderna, T., Jenny, B.: Maps around me: 3D multiview layouts in immersive spaces. Proc. ACM Hum.-Comput. Interact. **4**(ISS), 1–20 (2020)

19. Liu, J., Prouzeau, A., Ens, B., Dwyer, T.: Design and evaluation of interactive small multiples data visualisation in immersive spaces. IEEE (2020)

20. Ens, B., et al.: Uplift: a tangible and immersive tabletop system for casual collaborative visual analytics. IEEE Trans. Visual Comput. Graphics **27**(2), 1193–1203 (2020)

21. Lages, W.S., Bowman, D.A.: Move the object or move myself? Walking vs. manipulation for the examination of 3D scientific data. Front. ICT **5**, 15 (2018)

22. Lee, B., Isenberg, P., Riche, N.H., Carpendale, S.: Beyond mouse and keyboard: expanding design considerations for information visualization interactions. IEEE Trans. Visual Comput. Graphics **18**(12), 2689–2698 (2012)

23. Marriott, K., et al.: Immersive analytics: time to reconsider the value of 3D for information visualisation. In: Marriott, K., et al. (eds.) Immersive Analytics. LNCS, vol. 11190. Springer, Cham (2018)https://doi.org/10.1007/978-3-030-01388-2_2

24. Ball, R., North, C., Bowman, D.A.: Move to improve: promoting physical navigation to increase user performance with large displays (2007)

25. Dourish, P.: The Foundations of Embodied Interaction. MIT (2001)

26. Mulders, M., Buchner, J., Kerres, M.: A framework for the use of immersive virtual reality in learning environments. Int. J. Emerg. Technol. Learn. (iJET) **15**(24), 208–224 (2020)

# Author Index

**A**

Abboud, Osama   I-290, II-105
Adjouadi, Malek   II-283
Albayrak, Armagan   II-41
Alexander Auerbach, Daniel   II-241
Alghofaili, Rawan   III-304
Al-Sada, Mohammed   III-84
Amaral, Ângelo   I-182
Amorim, Paula   III-142
Ando, Masayuki   I-60
Ascione, Mariarca   I-13

**B**

Bai, Long   I-224
Balakrishnan, Prabhakaran   I-145
Barmpoutis, Angelos   II-191
Barreto, Armando   II-283
Bedard, Andrew   I-166
Bedard, Kevin   I-166
Beese, Nils Ove   III-154
Bharti, Priyanka   II-3
Bhide, Sanika   II-3
Bonacin, Rodrigo   I-182
Borhani, Zahra   II-201
Bothwell, Samantha   I-200
Brewer, Ralph W.   II-86
Byun, Boyoung   III-304

**C**

Caruso, Federica   II-41
Ceccon, Lorenzo   II-41
Cecil, J.   II-147, III-191
Chan, Antoni B.   I-224
Chan, HsinChiao   II-16
Chandra Dronavalli, Sri   III-286
Chellatore, Maruthi Prasanna   III-286
Chen, Guangdai   III-204
Chen, Ruiyang   I-301
Chen, Yuetong   III-3
Chen, Zhimin   III-204
Cheng, Wanning   I-200

Ching, Carrie   III-19
Chu, Junjie   I-128
Chung, Yoosun   III-304
Coler, Adam S.   II-201
Cui, Wei   III-64

**D**

de Lange, R. D.   II-159
Di, Xingcheng   II-216
Dias, Paulo   III-142, III-224
Dixit, Manish K.   II-74
Dorneich, Michael C.   I-277

**E**

Easley, Madeline   I-3
Ebert, Achim   I-44
Eichhorn, Christian   III-123
Ertl, Lukas   III-235

**F**

Farkhatdinov, Ildar   I-244
Feng, Huining   III-304
Ferreira, Maria   II-263
Ferrer-Garcia, Marta   I-13
Flaig, David   III-235
França, Milton   I-182
Friesen, Stefan   II-60
Fu, Rongrong   I-106
Fujimura, Shigeru   II-116

**G**

Gaetani, Flora   II-41
Gannina, Vasavi   II-147
Gao, Jie   II-128
Ge, Chenchen   III-214
Genaro Motti, Vivian   III-304
Gilbert, Stephen B.   I-277
Gisa, Kevin   III-154
Gokhale, Shreekant   I-200
Guo, Hung-Jui   I-145

J. Y. C. Chen and G. Fragomeni (Eds.): HCII 2024, LNCS 14707, pp. 313–316, 2024.
https://doi.org/10.1007/978-3-031-61044-8

Gupta, Avinash   I-200
Gutierrez-Maldonado, Jose   I-13

**H**
Hart, Chris   I-259
Hartman, Chris   III-44
He, Hanfu   III-64
He, Zhuoning   I-22
Hedlund, Martin   III-235
Hioki, Shouta   II-179
Hiramoto, Yuichiro   III-84
Hu, Xin   III-103
Hua, Min   III-3
Huang, Haikun   III-325
Huang, Yinghsiu   II-16

**I**
Inoue, Michiko   II-179
Iwasaki, Fuyuko   II-179
Izumi, Tomoko   I-60

**J**
Jadram, Narumon   I-213
Jang, Seung Hyuk   II-191
Javadpour, Nikoo   I-277
Jedel, Izabella   I-259
Jiang, Bingnan   III-170

**K**
Kapadia, Nimit   I-200
Kaschub, Lina   I-73
Kelly, Jonathan W.   I-277
Kemper, Logan   II-191
Keser, Thore   I-73
Kessens, Chad C.   II-86
Kim, Inki   III-44
Kim, Jung Hyup   I-3
Klinker, Gudrun   III-123
Kobayashi, Takato   I-213
Ködel, Laura   III-235
Kojić, Tanja   I-290, II-105

**L**
Lachmann, Thomas   III-154
Lam, Juan   II-191
LC, RAY   I-224
Lee, Jamie W.   II-29
Lee, Kwang   II-29
Levine, Matthew   II-191

Li, Dan   III-112
Li, Jieqiong   II-201
Li, Jixing   I-224
Li, Meng   II-41
Li, Shangge   II-216
Li, Yang   I-22
Li, Yanheng   I-224
Liao, Wenjie   II-116
Ling, Jie   III-112
Liu, Ruisi   I-128
Liu, Shujie   III-170
Löber, Jannik   I-44
Lyk, Patricia Bianca   II-241

**M**
Maio, Rafael   III-224
Mao, Yaxuan   I-224
Marques, Bernardo   III-142, III-224
Mathews, Maureen   I-200
Mauer, Sven-Tizian   III-235
Maulbeck, Mike   II-230
Meier, Jannis   III-268
Meixner, Gerrit   III-235
Memmesheimer, Vera M.   I-44
Mendoza-Medialdea, Maria-Teresa   I-13
Meschberger-Annweiler, Franck-Alexandre
        I-13
Mifsud, Domenick M.   II-230
Milde, Jan-Torsten   II-60
Milde, Sven   II-60
Moersler, Lukas   III-123
Mohanty, Siddarth   I-3
Möller, Sebastian   I-290, II-105
Mori, Kairyu   I-60
Mostowfi, Sara   I-3

**N**
Nakajima, Tatsuo   III-84
Nepomuceno, Anthony   I-200
Nikolaenko, Mikhail   III-252
Nishiyama, Masashi   II-179

**O**
O'Neal, Tiffany   III-304
O-larnnithipong, Nonnarit   II-283
Oliveira, Sérgio   III-142
Oprean, Danielle   I-3
Ortega, Francisco R.   II-201, II-230
Otaran, Ata   I-244

Otsu, Kouyou    I-60
Ou Yang, Li    III-112

**P**

Palmquist, Adam    I-259
Pariafsai, Fatemeh    II-74
Pedersen, Bjarke Kristian Maigaard Kjær    II-241
Peiffer, Johannes-Hubert    II-60
Peng, Xuening    I-224
Perez Colado, Victor Manuel    I-259
Peters, Nina Christine    III-154
Plecher, David A.    III-123
Porras-Garcia, Bruno    I-13
Pulipati, Varun    I-3

**R**

Rampalli, Swati    III-304
Raposo, Rui    II-263
Ratchatanantakit, Neeranut    II-283
Reddy Pesaladinne, Rishitha    III-286
Reisinho, Pedro    II-263
Reke, Michael    III-268
Rodeck, Rebecca    I-73
Rodriguez, Richard    II-230
Rosa, Ferrucio de Franco    I-182
Rueda-Pina, Alejandra    I-13
Runzheimer, Tabea    II-60
Ryu, Jeeheon    III-44

**S**

Sabouni, Hila    I-277
Salehi, Faezeh    II-74
Sanaei, Mohammadamin    I-277
Santoso, Markus    II-191
Savaliya, Chirag    II-3
Scalise, Rosario    II-86
Schaefer, Kristin E.    II-86
Schmied-Kowarzik, Rahel    I-73
Scholl, Daniel    III-268
Schultz, Celeste    I-200
Seo, Kangwon    I-3
Shallat, John S.    I-200
Sharma, Sharad    III-286
Shen, Shuhan    III-3
Silva, Cátia    II-263
Sinlapanuntakul, Pitch    I-93
Soellaart, Aedan    I-259
Sonchan, Pontakorn    II-283

Sousa Santos, Beatriz    III-142, III-224
Spilski, Jan    III-154
Steffny, Laura    III-154
Su, Simon    III-325
Su, Weilin    III-112
Sugaya, Midori    I-213
Sun, Bo    II-298
Sun, Xu    II-128

**T**

Tan, Ruiguang    III-170
Tang, Ming    III-252
Tentu, Sriram Kumar    II-147, III-191
Tetnowski, John A.    III-191
Tong, Xin    I-224

**V**

Vairinhos, Mário    II-263
van Eijk, Daan    II-41
Vergari, Maurizio    I-290, II-105
Voigt-Antons, Jan-Niklas    I-290, II-105

**W**

Wang, Chaoguang    III-204
Wang, Fang    I-3
Wang, Yu    III-64
Warsinke, Maximilian    I-290, II-105
Weidner, Benjamin Daniel    II-298
Wende, Gerko    I-73
Werth, Dirk    III-154
White Pifer, Aiden    II-191
Wickens, Chris D.    II-230
Wickwire, Joshua    II-86
Wu, Like    II-116

**X**

Xiao, Xun    I-290, II-105
Xie, Xintong    III-204
Xu, Shihui    II-116
Xue, Chengqi    II-216

**Y**

Yan, Chuan    III-325
Yang, Canjun    II-128
Yang, Yi    I-22
Yang, Yifan    II-128
Yoneda, Shunsuke    II-179
Yu, Ching-Yun    I-3
Yu, Lap-Fai    III-304, III-325

Yu, Liuchuan   III-304
Yu, Xiaowen   I-106

**Z**
Zachry, Mark   I-93
Zagalo, Nelson   II-263
Zhang, Jie   III-170
Zhang, Jing   II-216

Zhang, Qiping   I-166
Zhang, Sheng   II-128
Zhang, Yongqi   III-325
Zhang, Yu   II-41
Zhang, Zehao   I-224
Zhao, Zehui   I-128
Zhou, Junyu   I-301
Zhou, Ziqi   II-128